The Babylonian Esther Midrash

Program in Judaic Studies
Brown University
BROWN JUDAIC STUDIES

Edited by
Ernest S. Frerichs
Shaye J. D. Cohen, Calvin Goldscheider

Number 291

The Babylonian Esther Midrash

A Critical Commentary

(Volume 1: To the End of Esther Chapter 1)

by
Eliezer Segal

The Babylonian Esther Midrash

A Critical Commentary
(Volume 1: To the End of Esther Chapter 1)

by
Eliezer Segal

Scholars Press
Atlanta, Georgia

The Babylonian Esther Midrash

A Critical Commentary
(Volume 1: To the End of Esther Chapter 1)

by
Eliezer Segal

Library of Congress Cataloging-in-Publication Data
Segal, Eliezer.
The Babylonian Esther midrash : a critical commentary / by Eliezer Segal.
p. cm. — (Brown Judaic studies ; no. 291-293)
"The present volume and its successors consist of a translation and critical commentary to folios 10b-17a of the Babylonian Talmud Tractate Megillah"—Introd., v. 1.
Includes bibliographical references and indexes.
Contents: v. 1. To the end of Esther chapter 1 — v. 2. To the beginning of Esther chapter 5 — v. 3. Esther chapter 5 to end.
ISBN 1-55540-996-2 (v. 1). — ISBN 1-55540-997-0 (v. 2). — ISBN 1-55540-998-9 (v. 3)
1. Bible. O.T. Esther—Commentaries. 2. Talmud. Megillah I, 10b-17a—Criticism, Redaction. 3. Midrash—History and criticism. I. Talmud. Megillah I, 10b-17a. English. II. Title. III. Title: Esther Midrash. IV. Series.
BS1375.3.S44 1994
296.1'25—dc20 94-25966
CIP

Printed in the United States of America
on acid-free paper

This volume is dedicated to

Ellie and Reuven Gellman

and their family

Table of Contents

Acknowledgments

My friends have often observed with a touch of humor—though hardly with exaggeration—how I can respond to virtually any question by citing a passage from the Tractate *Megillah*. My specialized involvement in this delightful tractate began some fifteen years ago when my late revered teacher at the Hebrew University of Jerusalem, Prof. Eliezer Shimshon Rosenthal of blessed memory, inspired by his own fascination with the Yemenite manuscripts of the Babylonian Talmud, urged me to study its textual traditions as a doctoral dissertation. As Prof. Rosenthal knew well, when one commits oneself to a talmudic text everything else becomes a commentary upon that text, whether one is studying some other passage in the rabbinic corpus, examining archaeological realia, or discussing literary theory. I hope that some traces of my late teacher's thoroughness and enthusiasm for the subject are discernible in the present commentary.

The research that was invested in this study was facilitated by the generosity of several individuals and institutions. Preliminary stages of the work were encouraged by grants from the Saul Lieberman Institute for Talmudic Research of the Jewish Theological Seminary of America. As the project began to take distinct form a grant from the University of Calgary Research Services allowed me to travel to Jerusalem to consult the indispensable Hebraica resources of the Jewish National and University Library. Most recently, the graciousness and hospitality of the Calgary Institute for the Humanities and its director Prof. Harold Coward have enabled me to free myself for one year from the responsibilities of teaching and academic administration and to devote my undivided energies to the present work. I hope that this volume justifies their confidence in me and my project.

Eliezer Lorne Segal,
Department of Religious Studies,
University of Calgary

Note: This volume was completed in Spring of 1992 and has not been rewritten since. Scholarly literature which appeared or became available to me subsequent to that date has not been incorporated into this section of the study.

Introductory Remarks

The Babylonian Esther Midrash

The Midrash of the Synagogue and the Midrash of the *Yeshivah*

The present volume and its successors consist of a translation and critical commentary to folios 10b–17a of the Babylonian Talmud Tractate *Megillah*. The material contained therein comprises the only full midrashic exposition of an entire biblical book to have been incorporated into the Babylonian Talmud, making it the only complete midrashic work that has come down to us from that prominent Jewish community and its rabbinic teachers. While approximately one third of the "Bavli" is said to be devoted to various forms of Aggadah,[1] much of it in the form of midrashic comments on scriptural passages, there is nothing else that compares with the scope of the present work, which comments on the whole Book of Esther and is preceded by a series of "proems" after the manner of the well known Palestinian midrashic collections.

Although no justification is necessary for the publication of any midrashic or Talmudic text, there are several features which single out the present work as uniquely interesting. Of course the mere fact of its Babylonian provenance, so rare an occurence in aggadic midrash, lends to the Esther-Midrash a special importance as a document which should assist us in obtaining a clearer picture of the people who produced it. It

---

[1] The statistic is taken from I. H. Weiss, *Dor dor vedoreshav* [*Zur Geschichte der jüdischen Tradition*] (Vienna-Pressburg: 1891-1871) 3:19; see also W. Bacher, "Talmud," in *The Jewish Encyclopedia*, ed. I. Singer *et al.*, 1-27, 12 (New York and London: Funk and Wagnalls), 1907, 22.

was this geographical uniqueness that attracted the attentions of modern rabbinic scholarship, whose primary interests lay in the identification of its literary sources[2] and distinctive world–views.[3] As we shall be noting in the course of our commentary, it turned out that the most impressive new conclusions to be unearthed in the present study relate not so much to the midrash's "Babylonian-ness" as to the fact that it has been preserved in the Talmud.

In order to elucidate this last–mentioned claim we shall have to venture into some fundamental questions concerning the origins and purposes of aggadic midrash and to take a stand on some controversial issues. For this purpose it is useful to review some well–known characteristics of the classical midrashic *oeuvre*.

A widely held view in rabbinic scholarship has it that the typical venue of aggadic midrash was usually the synagogue, and more particularly the Palestinian synagogues of the 3rd to 6th centuries. This position, which I consider to be a very persuasive one, provides simple explanations for some of the peculiarities of the genre. Thus, the formal structures of the classical aggadic collections make little sense unless we view them in connection with the Sabbath and festival services, and especially the public readings of the assigned biblical lections.[4]

---

[2] This was the principal concern of Abraham Weiss' examination of the Esther-Midrash in *Studies in the Literature of the Amoraim* (New York, 1962), 277–92 [an English summary of his conclusions may be found in: Meyer S. Feldblum, "Prof. Abraham Weiss: His Approach and Contribution to Talmudic Scholarship," in *The Abraham Weiss Jubilee Volume*, ed. S. Belkin *et al.*, 7-80 (New York: Shulsinger Bros., 1964), 50-1; reprinted in: J. Neusner, ed., *Origins of Judaism*, Vol. 13 (New York and London: Garland, 1990), 76-7].

[3] Joseph Heinemann, *Aggadah and Its Development*, Sifriyyat Keter: 4: Hagut Vehalakhah, ed. J. Dan (Jerusalem: Keter, 1974), 163–79.

[4] In light of the fact that this claim has been challenged or ignored by some recent scholarship, I will reiterate here some of the more obvious structural features that attest to the synagogue provenance of the classical aggadic anthologies:

•The selection of the biblical books to which midrashic collections would be compiled—primarily the Pentateuch and the "Five Scrolls" of the Hagiographa—closely dovetails with the list of books that were read formally in the synagogue service.

Continued on next page...

...Continued from previous page

•The fact that the chapter divisions of the midrashic anthologies correspond with the lectionary divisions in use in the synagogues testifies to their close connections with the public scriptural readings, a conclusion which is given further confirmation by the necessity for the genre of "*pesiqta*" designed to bring within the scope of aggadic literature material that does not connect directly to the sequential readings of the Pentateuch.

•The pivotal role played by the otherwise incomprehensible classical *petiḥta*, which is structured so as to culminate in the quotation of the verse to be expounded, makes little sense unless we see it as an introduction to the public reading from the Bible [as argued convincingly by Joseph Heinemann, "The Proem in the Aggadic Midrashim: A Form-Critical Study," *Scripta Hierosolymitana* 22 (1971), 100-22].

Taken together, all these factors testify that, as a *genre*, aggadic midrash is first and foremost the creation of the synagogue and that the classical Palestinian collections drew primarily from a body of oral sermons. As far as I have been able to discern, this feature has been virtually ignored in the many studies of Palestinian aggadah by Jacob Neusner, who treats all rabbinic compendia as consistent, distinct and individual "documents" expressing the [theological] positions of their respective authors [In the more extreme statements of his position, Neusner makes little allowance for any meaningful redaction of earlier units, whether from the synagogues or elsewhere]. In general I have been unsuccessful in my attempts to trace any meaningful basis for his claims which, in the absence of detailed literary or philological analysis of primary texts, appear to rest on nothing more than a dogmatic faith in their validity. [Neusner's work is almost completely devoid of conventional scholarly annotation or consideration of previous scholarship; he claims to be interested only in the broader external structures of the pericopes, having little to say about the specific details on which the generalizations should normally be based.] Among the dozens of works in which he outlines his theory, see e.g. his *Making the Classics in Judaism: The Three Stages of Literary Formation*, Brown Judaic Studies, ed. J. Neusner *et al.* (Atlanta: Scholars Press, 1990). The theories have been refuted by most students of midrash; see, e.g., J. Heinemann, *Aggadah and Its Development*, 44-7; Peter Schäfer, "Research into Rabbinic Literature: An Attempt to Define the Status Quaestionis," *JJS* 37 (1986), 146-52; Steven D. Fraade, "Interpreting Midrash 1: Midrash and the History of Judaism," *Prooftexts* 7 (1987), 179-94; Gerald L. Bruns, "The Hermeneutics of Midrash," in *The Book and the Text: The Bible and Literary Theory*, ed. Regina M. Schwartz, 189–213 (Oxford: Basil Blackwell, 1990), 210, n. 5, and 212, n. 22 [cf. *Idem.*, "Midrash and Allegory: The Beginnings of Scriptural Interpretation," in *The Literary Guide to the Bible*, ed. Robert Alter and Frank Kermode, 625-46 (Cambridge, Mass.: The Belknap Press of Harvard University Press, 1987), 629 and 645, n. 9]; E. P. Sanders, *Jewish Law from Jesus to the Mishnah: Five Studies* (London and Philadelphia: SCM Press and Trinity Press International, 1990), 309 ff. [with reference to the Mishnah; Neusner does not relate to this issue in his "Mr. Sanders' Pharisees and Mine: A Response to E. P. Sanders,

Continued on next page...

This is not to say that all the material contained in the aggadic collections originated in synagogue sermons. The fact is that surprisingly few examples have been preserved of complete rabbinic sermons as they might have been preached in their original state. Classical midrashic collections are typified by their fragmentary and disconnected character, as they string together dissociated comments attributed to sages from assorted generations and locales. This quality presumably derives not from their original sermonic contexts, but rather from the nature of the editorial activities of the later redactors who dismembered coherently structured literary homilies and redistributed the pieces into new composite "commentaries." In spite of the efforts and achievements of several generations of midrashic scholars we still know very little about this redactional process, including such fundamental questions as: whether this change occurred as part of the transformation of the aggadic traditions from oral to written form or while aggadah was still an exclusively oral enterprise; if it was the original preachers who sprinkled their homilies with quotations from their predecessors, or is the widespread distribution of attributed dicta an outgrowth of the anthologizing process?[5] There are many other basic lacunae in our knowledge of the channels through which aggadah was transmitted to the midrashic compendia in which

...Continued from previous page
Jewish Law from Jesus to the Mishnah," *Scottish Journal of Theology* 44 (1991), 73-95]. See also Marc Bregman, "Early Sources and Traditions in the Tanḥuma–Yelammedenu Midrashim," *Tarbiẓ* 60 (1991), 269-74, and n. 1 [Bregman seems to imply that Sarason's and Neusner's methodologies are the same, which is somewhat misleading; in actuality, the former proposes to combine the study of "documentary contexts" with other considerations, whereas for the latter there is no apparent need to study anything other than the complete document]. For an attempt (unpersuasive, to my mind) to refute the scholarly consensus regarding the synagogal origins of the proem, and to argue that it is a purely exegetical form, see Martin S. Jaffee, "The 'Midrashic' Proem: Towards the Description of Rabbinic Exegesis," in *Approaches to Ancient Judaism*, ed. William Scott Green, 95–112, 4: Studies in Liturgy, Exegesis, and Talmudic Narrative (Chico: Scholars Press, 1983).

[5] Cf. R. S. Sarason, "Toward a New Agendum for the Study of Rabbinic Midrashic Literature," in *Studies in Aggadah, Targum and Jewish Liturgy in Memory of Joseph Heinemann*, ed. J. Petuchowski and E. Fleischer, 55-73 (Jerusalem and Cincinnati: The Magnes Press and Hebrew Union College Press, 1981), 65-6 and n. 27.

they have been preserved, but none of these obscurities is serious enough to refute the basic and overwhelming impression that classical Palestinian aggadic midrash reflects principally the preaching that took place in the synagogues on Sabbaths and festivals.[6]

The second major corpus of rabbinic literature, that which is associated principally with the Palestinian and Babylonian Talmuds, was not the product of the synagogues, but of the houses of study, the *yeshivot* or *batei midrash*.[7] The stamp of the halakhic curriculum is as clearly imprinted upon the literature of the Talmuds as the life of the synagogues is on the aggadic midrash. These were of course very dif-

---

6 See Joseph Heinemann, *Derashot beṣibbur bitequfat ha-talmud*, Dorot (Jerusalem: Mosad Bialik, 1971); *Idem.*, *Literature of the Synagogue*, Library of Jewish Studies, ed. Neal Kozodoy (New York: Behrman House, 1975), 107-97. We should note here that the midrashic texts attest that the preachers were assuming an extraordinary level of erudition on the part of their congregations, even after we have made allowances for the likelihood that the versions that have come down to us, having gone through processes of transmission and redaction, are considerably more cryptic and allusive than they were in their original oral delivery. This holds true as well with respect to the congregations to whom the *payyeṭanim* Yannai and the Kalir were addressing their erudite liturgical poems. Cf. Lewis M. Barth, "Literary Imagination and the Rabbinic Sermon: Some Observations," in *Seventh World Congress of Jewish Studies in Jerusalem*, edited by D. Krone (World Union of Jewish Studies, 1981), 30. Jonah Fraenkel, *Darkhei ha-'aggadah veha-midrash*, Yad Ha-Talmud, ed. E. E. Urbach (Givatayim: Massadah, 1991) argues that the literary sophistication of the aggadah attests to an audience of extraodinary scholarly erudition and aesthetic appreciation; i.e., of rabbis. His claim is based largely on his own interpretations of a large corpus of specific texts, and I question whether all the textual interpretations upon which he bases his evaluation can reasonably be ascribed to the intentions of the original authors. It should also be noted that Fraenkel's conclusions seem to be based more on Babylonian narrative aggadah than on the Palestinian midrashic aggadah with which I am dealing here.

7 The existence of formal academies, in the sense that they are known from the Ge'onic period, has been challenged by David Goodblatt in his *Rabbinic Instruction in Sasanian Babylonia*, Studies in Judaism in Late Antiquity, ed. Jacob Neusner (Leiden: Brill, 1975). Goodblatt posits a more flexible model of master-student relationships as the norm during the talmudic era. Though I am not persuaded by his argument, I should note that the matter has no material bearing on my argument here. For a well-argued attempt to refute Goodblatt see Isaiah M. Gafni, *The Jews in Babylonia in the Talmudic Era: A Social and Cultural History*, Monographs in Jewish History, ed. A. Grossman *et al.* (Jerusalem: Zalman Shazar Center, 1990), 185-203, 274-9.

ferent institutions, and the nature of the study carried on in each was correspondingly distinct. The synagogue was a house in which the all segments of the Jewish populace would congregate, whereas the *yeshivah* was an assembly of specialized scholars whose credentials presupposed mastery of the received written and oral traditions as well as sophisticated powers of halakhic analysis. It is inevitable that the respective literary productions should parallel their different places of origin. If the basic unit of aggadic midrash is the *derashah*, a rhetorically crafted literary homily, then its equivalent in the Talmud is the *sugya*, a dialectical halakhic commentary on the Mishnah or related text.[8]

Aside from the obvious dissimilarities in their subject-matters there are some specific differences in their respective uses of scripture that should be kept in mind as we proceed to study what is, in effect, a "talmudic midrash." Talmudic study, to the degree that it must involve itself with biblical passages, will strive to systematically interpret those words of scripture which have a bearing on the topic under discussion.[9] "Interpreting" is understood here in its broadest sense as comprising not only the clarification of the text, but also its application to various situations, the resolution of contradictions, the derivation of new and traditional teachings, etc. To a significant degree the role of the rabbi *qua* Talmudist will involve a confrontation with the text, in the course of which he will have to account for its meaning and implications according to the prevailing hermeneutical standards and assumptions.

The preacher's stance *vis à vis* the Bible is a different one. His primary purpose is to fashion a *derashah* which he will address to his

---

[8] The talmudic *sugya* was also perceived by its redactors as a literary form for which there were accepted aesthetic standards and conventions (especially with respect to their architectonic symmetry); see e.g., Shamma Friedman, "Some Structural Patterns of Talmudic *Sugiot*," in *Sixth World Congress of Jewish Studies in Jerusalem*, edited by A. Shinan (World Union of Jewish Studies, 1977), 389-402.

[9] I do not wish to imply that the Talmud is exclusively, or even primarily, a commentary on the Bible; the point is that when biblical texts are dealt with in the academic curriculum of the *yeshivah*, they will typically be examined as objects of study to be interpreted in a rigorous and consistent manner.

congregation. There are many different considerations that might enter into this *derashah*. These include such factors as the selection of a topic (a selection whose primary inspiration might come from a variety of stimuli, including the day's scriptural lection, some situation particular to his congregation, or from some standard set of sermon themes) and the adapting of the message to the prevailing rhetorical rules (e.g., proems or Messianic perorations). In accordance with the accepted literary conventions it is of course crucial that the homilist make frequent reference to biblical verses, whether in the formal sense of creating a connection to the current lection or with reference to the more general need to buttress his message with appropriate proof-texts. The centrality of the Bible to Jewish homiletics need not however contradict the claim that it is the homily itself that is central, and that whatever biblical exegesis will be produced thereby is subordinated to that central aim.[10] To put it another way, the role of the rabbi *qua* preacher is not to explain Scripture, nor to produce a commentary thereon, but rather to exploit it for an "extraneous" purpose.[11] It is natural that the ostensibly exegetical comments that do show up in the *derashah* would not be grasped as exegesis by an audience that is accustomed to this kind of rhetorical flourish.[12] It also follows naturally that the aggadic literature that derives from these homilies would not take the form of continuous or extended commentaries on books or lections of the Bible,[13] but of disconnected, "atomistic" comments on particular words

---

[10] *Contra* Daniel Boyarin, "The Song of Songs: Lock or Key? Intertextuality, Allegory and Midrash," in *The Book and the Text: The Bible and Literary Theory*, ed. Regina M. Schwartz, 214–30 (Oxford: Basil Blackwell, 1990), 228, n. 11.

[11] See Joseph Heinemann, "The Nature of Aggadah," in *Midrash and Literature*, ed. Geoffrey Hartman and Sanford Budick (New Haven: Yale University Press), 1986, 48–9.

[12] The perception that at least some midrashic "exegesis" was a literary fiction and not meant by its authors to be taken seriously was argued persuasively by Maimonides [*Guide of the Perplexed* 3:43]; see Eliezer Segal, "Midrash and Literature: Some Medieval Views," *Prooftexts* 11 (1991), 57–65.

[13] A slightly different formulation of this idea was proposed by B. De-Vries, "Ofyah ha-sifruti shel ha-'aggadah," in *Meḥqarim besifrut ha-talmud*, ed. E. Z. Melammed, 284-9 (Jerusalem: Mossad Harav Kook, 1968). This functional approach provides an

Continued on next page...

and verses.[14] In this sense as well, the redacted collections of aggadic midrash may have preserved with some measure of faithfulness a characteristic of the original homilies.

The above typology is of course an oversimplification to which many exceptions could easily be adduced. We unfortunately know too little about the "academic" (i.e., non-homiletical) aggadic study of the Bible in rabbinic circles to allow us to posit an alternative model for its origins.[15] It appears to me nevertheless that the fundamental division

...Continued from previous page

alternative to the more philosophical and anthropological explanations of midrashic "atomism" as proposed in such studies as Isaac Heinemann, *Darkhei ha-'aggadah* (Jerusalem and Tel-Aviv: Magnes and Masadah, 1970), especially 100-110 [referring to "the abandonment of the *logos*"]; Max Kadushin, *Organic Thinking* (New York: The Jewish Theological Seminary of America, 1938); *Idem.*, *The Rabbinic Mind* (New York: The Jewish Theological Seminary of America, 1952), 23, etc.; James Kugel, "Two Introductions to Midrash," in *Midrash and Literature*, ed. Geoffrey H. Hartman and Sanford Budick, 77-103 (New Haven: Yale University Press, 1986).

[14] It should follow from this the preachers would not usually strive for consistency between their own interpretations. This assertion (as distinct from the well-attested "polysemy" of redacted collections which necessarily have to assemble a variety of opinions by different rabbis) is a difficult one to prove in the light of the unreliability of the attributions in midrashic literature.

[15] The attempt to imitate the homiletical settings of the synagogue sermons is typical of the Amoraic midrashic collections. This situation stands in marked contrast to the aggadic component of the Tannaitic "halakhic" midrashim, whose institutional provenance is much more enigmatic. These texts do not demonstrate many explicit signs of homiletical origins (e.g., proems), and may likely be the record of academic sessions devoted to the elucidation of their respective Pentateuchal texts. Many of these passages do however exhibit elaborate rhetorical structures which seem to hearken back to sermons [For a perceptive literary analysis of passages from *Sifre* on Deuteronomy see Steven D. Fraade, *From Tradition To Commentary: Torah and Its Interpretation in the Midrash Sifre to Deuteronomy*, SUNY Series in Judaica: Hermeneutics, Mysticism, and Religion, ed. R. Goldenberg M. Fishbane and A. Green (Albany: State University of New York Press, 1991)]. While it is conceivable that the apparent differences between the Tannaitic and Amoraic aggadah owe more to the manner in which they were anthologized than to their original forms or content, the evidence remains ambiguous. The fact that the Palestinian Talmud and the classical midrashic compendia borrow regularly from one another also argues for a less polarized situation than that described above.

of roles between synagogue and yeshivah is a valid one both conceptually and in terms of the empirical evidence.[16]

This basic fact, that rabbinic midrash was not primarily an exegetical enterprise,[17] is one that has not always been fully appreciated either by specialists in midrashic literature or by those students of Western literature who have looked to rabbinic texts as a model for reader–centered hermeneutical models.[18] It does however lend a special importance to the study of the Babylonian Esther-Midrash.

---

16 For a concise and perceptive summary of the issues involved, see Isaiah Gafni, "Ha-yetzirah ha-ruḥanit-sifrutit," in *Eretz Israel: from the Destruction of the Second Temple to the Muslim Conquest*, ed. Tz. Baras, S. Safrai, Y. Tzafrir and M. Stern, 473-94, 1 (Jerusalem: Yad Yitzḥaq ben-Tzvi, 1982), 489-4.

17 A much stronger statement of this position is argued by William Scott Green, "Romancing the Tome: Rabbinic Hermeneutics and the Theory of Literature," *Semeia* 40 (1987), 147–68, who claims that the interpretation of the Bible was not a major concern of rabbinic culture at all. As will become evident from my presentation below, I consider that characterization to be exaggerated and one-sided if applied to the whole of rabbinic literature, though it does appear to apply to the major compendia of aggadic midrash. Note the similar views of Jacob Neusner, *The Oral Torah: The Sacred Books of Judaism* (San Francisco: Harper and Row, 1986), 128 (cited by Green, 153); *Idem., The Midrashic Compilations of the Sixth and Seventh Centuries: An Introduction to the Rhetorical, Logical and Topical Program*, Vol. 2, Brown Judaic Studies, ed. J. Neusner *et al.* (Atlanta: Scholars Press, 1989), 131-4; etc. See also De-Vries, "Ha-sugim ha-sifrutiyyim shel ha-'aggadah" (in *Meḥqarim besifrut ha-talmud*), 292-3.

18 At any rate, the existence of a phenomenon in the past cannot of itself constitute a claim for its inherent validity. See Green, 150. The underlying assumptions of midrash and deconstructionist hermeneutics are of course radically different. The hermeneutical precision with which the midrashic rabbis approached the words of the Bible was possible only because of their belief in its divine authorship and cannot credibly be applied to secular writings. The so-called "midrash of secular documents" that is mentioned occasionally in talmudic sources is of a decidedly different character; see *Tosefta Ketubbot* 4:9-12, ed. S. Lieberman [*The Tosefta...The Order Nashim* [1] (New York: The Jewish Theological Seminary of America, 1967)], 68-9, and Lieberman's short commentary there, as well as his remarks in *Tosefta ki-fshuṭah* (New York: The Jewish Theological Seminary of America, 1967), 6:246–7 and literature cited there]; see Susan Handelman, *The Slayers of Moses: The Emergence of Rabbinic Interpretation in Modern Literary Theory* (Albany: State University of New York Press, 1982), 79, 206, etc., and the critique of David Stern, "Moses-cide: Midrash and Contemporary Literary Criticism," *Prooftexts* 4 (1984), 203-4. In her

Continued on next page...

...Continued from previous page

"'Everything is in it': Rabbinic Interpretation and Modern Literary Theory," *Judaism* 35 (4 1986), 429–40 [reprinted in: J. Neusner, ed., *The Literature of Formative Judaism: Controversies on the Literature of Formative Judaism*, Vol. 13. Origins of Judaism (New York and London: Garland, 1990), 107–18], Handelman discusses the perception that indeed among some literary theorists "Language...has taken the place of God" (437).

In the more extreme instances, the deconstructionist methods are applied to the study of rabbinic literature itself, with the corollary that (following what they perceive to be the views of writers like Gadamer and, to some extent, Derrida), in our despair of entering into the minds of the original authors ["...what the rabbis 'intentions' were is impossible to know" —Handelman, "Fragments of the Rock: Contemporary Literary Theory and the Study of Rabbinic Texts—A Response to David Stern," *Prooftexts* 5 (1985), 89] there remain no valid criteria for preferring one interpretation over another, and hence all understandings of the meaning of a given text have equal validity [These claims are stated or implied in such studies as Handelman's *The Slayers of Moses*; and in several of the articles included in Hartmann and Budick's *Midrash and Literature*]. These epistemological assumptions, with their resultant disregard for the philological-historical method in favor of purely subjective appreciation of a text, are invalid and unproved. Even if we were to acknowledge the premise that we can never be certain of an author's intentions, we must nevertheless recognize that certain interpretations can be ruled out as impossible or unlikely on the basis of demonstrable facts (e.g., anachronisms, etc.). This, by the way, appears to be closer to the position of Gadamer, who does not rule out the possibility of meaningfully understanding texts on their own terms provided we do this with a consciousness of the initial gulfs that separate the reader from the author; see Hans-Georg Gadamer, *Truth and Meaning* translated by G. Barden and J. Cumming (New York: Crossroad Publishing, 1986), 245.

Several scholars with backgrounds in rabbinics have issued refutations of these theories. In addition to Green's article cited above, see: Steven D. Fraade, "Interpreting Midrash 2: Midrash and Its Literary Contexts," *Prooftexts* 7 (1987), 284–300; David Stern, "Midrash and Indeterminacy," *Critical Inquiry* 15 (1988), 132-61; as well as his "Moses-cide," *Prooftexts* 4 (1984), 193-213; Handelman, "Fragments of the Rock"; and Stern's rebuttal: "Literary Criticism or Literary Homilies? Susan Handelman and the Contemporary Study of Midrash," *Prooftexts* 5 (1985), 96–103. See also Gerald L. Bruns, "The Hermeneutics of Midrash," 209, n.3.

I strongly suspect that one of the chief reasons for the mis-application of literary models to midrashic texts has to do with the differing social settings in which aggadah and western literatures were produced. Post-modernism seems to take as its norm a literature which was produced by individuals and which reflects the private thoughts and feelings of those individual. Frequently these are individuals who stand at the peripheries of their societies. Rabbinic literature (like most non-Western and pre-

Continued on next page...

The reason why our Esther-Midrash takes on such importance lies precisely in the fact that it is not found in the expected context of a homiletical collection to a biblical work, but is incorporated into the Talmud itself. Unlike the normal Palestinian midrashic collections, the Talmuds did not originate in the synagogues but in the rabbinical academies where sacred texts (oral and written) were usually expounded in a systematic manner quite different from the literary homilies of the synagogue. The Esther-Midrash, in spite of its placement in the Talmud, is arranged along the lines of the classic Palestinian models.[19] The study of this text has thus come to serve as a means of focusing upon the difficult problem of the connection between literary-homiletical and systematic–exegetical interpretations of the Bible.

As will become evident at several stages in our commentary, what we have before us in the Babylonian Esther-Midrash is in large measure an originally homiletical midrash whose genesis was in Palestine but was afterwards, as a result of its inclusion in the curriculum of the Babylonian *yeshivah*,[20] transformed into an

...Continued from previous page

modern literatures) is, in contrast to that model, a collective undertaking, produced in the name of the community as a whole and addressed to the entire community. This basic distinction renders invalid the post-modernist dismissal of authorial intent. The solipsistic image of an alienated artist locked in her or his private feelings and inaccessible to others is probably unique to western literatures. [Similar criticisms have been leveled against the deconstructionist use of other traditional and non-western literary models; see Stern, "Midrash and Indeterminacy," 133–4; Bruns, *op. cit.*, 192.] Art that is addressed to a community must be composed according to a commonly recognized set of rules, values and assumptions of shared history and literary canon. Accordingly, the search for authorial intent need not involve the fathoming of the depths of the author's psyche, but merely an understanding of the language, culture and literary conventions according to which he or she is operating. With the aid of suitable historical and philological tools this is (at least in substantial part) an attainable goal.

19 This is exemplified most conspicuously in the introductory series of proems, but is also discernible in such phenomena as the division into *pisqa'ot* from the biblical verses.

20 The fact that the Esther-Midrash is a section of the Babylonian Talmud means that it is subject to the same analytical approaches that can be applied to other passages from

Continued on next page...

exegetical–style commentary. This metamorphosis, while most noticeable in the effects that it produced on the proems and their functions,[21] is perceptible as well in many other aspects of its presentation of the material, particularly when we compare the versions of traditions in our Esther-Midrash with the parallel traditions preserved in the Palestinian compendia, especially *Esther rabbah*.[22] The resultant changes in the treatment of the material are most instructive, and bear resemblances to later developments in the Palestinian aggadic literature such as the *Tanḥuma*-midrashim where the fragmentary comments of earlier collections began to be organized into continuous and coherent retellings of the biblical narrative.[23]

This difference in venue might also account for certain peculiarities which have hitherto been ascribed to the psychological or ideological make-up of the Babylonian rabbis, most notably their reputed inability to recognize or appreciate the "playful" and hyperbolic dimensions of aggadic exposition, which they approached with the same literalness and heavy-handed gravity with which they debated serious legal topics.[24] In light of our observations here it might be possible to account for the differences (at least in part) as stemming not so much from an essential divergence of outlooks but from the different institutional settings in which the traditions were transmitted.

...Continued from previous page
the Talmud, such as the investigation of terminological usages. With respect to what is perhaps the major preoccupation of current talmudic studies, the question of the relationships between the anonymous redactional strata ("anonymous Talmud") and the attributed dicta, the evidence of our midrash is somewhat anomalous, in that it includes anonymous Aramaic material that is clearly not redactional in character, much of which might be derived from an elaborate "rewritten" version of Esther (a Targum?). See the discussion of this issue in the concluding summary.

21 As described in Chapter Two.

22 E.g., in several of the examples we observe that what appears in the Esther-Midrash as a simple exegetical comment was incorporated by the Palestinian variants into a messianic peroration that is entirely absent from the Babylonian tradition.

23 On the continuation of this process into the post-Talmudic era see Joseph Dan, *The Hebrew Story in the Middle Ages*, Sifriyyat Keter (Jerusalem: Keter, 1974).

24 The issues are spelled out clearly by J. Heinemann, *Aggadah and Its Development*, 163-70.

While we are not always able to reconstruct fully the process of homiletical creation, we are able to deal meaningfully with the final product. Of course we must recognize that for a text which has undergone several stages of transmission and redaction "final" is necessarily a relative and ambiguous term. There are several "final" texts that can be studied; in particular: the original formulation of the tradition (which will often be no more than a tentative reconstruction), whether as a discrete dictum or as part of a homily; the way in which it has been incorporated into its current context as part of a midrashic pericope or, for that matter, as part of a full midrashic collection. At times we might have reason to posit one or more intermediate stages, as for example where a later sage made explicit use of a dictum of his predecessor or where a unit has been preserved in a variety of different redactional contexts. All of these strata are legitimate, even obligatory, subjects of study, provided that we make it clear to ourselves which stratum we are examining at any given moment.

Once having defined our "final" text, we can then proceed to explain and evaluate it. A proper explanation must begin by clarifying such necessary basics as the meanings of the words and the syntactic and logical relationships between the sentences and other units. The evaluation of the passage, on the other hand, will determine how effectively the authors and redactors have succeeded in accomplishing their goals.[25] In the present instance I view the literary commentary as the

---

25 The inclusion of an evaluative component in my commentary is something of a departure from the traditional models of scholarly midrashic studies. The commentaries which accompany the standard critical editions of midrashic collections, including those of Buber, Theodor and Albeck, Margulies and others have consistently confined themselves to descriptive explanation and citation of parallel and related material. This was understandable in light of the already cumbersome proportions of the text-critical apparatuses. [See Stern, "Literary Criticism or Literary Homilies?" 98]. Much of early midrashic scholarship, insofar as it dealt with literary questions, tended to adopt a stance of uncritical admiration, beginning from the assumption that the texts were perfect provided we had the philological tools to appreciate them. This attitude reflects the religious or apologetic sensibilities of the scholars or their perceived audiences. More recent work, as exemplified in the studies of Joseph Heinemann [e.g., in *Aggadah and its Development*], Avigdor Shinan [e.g., "The Opening Section of

Continued on next page...

primary purpose of my study, to which the other elements are subordinated.

As stated above, the literary commentary to be undertaken here will attempt to be faithful to what we understand to be the goals of their authors and redactors, as defined by the accepted conventions of the genre. No doubt the centuries which intervene between us and the texts will not always allow for full or certain appreciation of the aesthetic sensibilities and aims of the ancients; nevertheless I am convinced that the current state of literary midrashic studies has succeeded in furnishing us with a reasonably lucid picture of what the rabbis were trying to achieve in their homilies. We have already made reference to rhetorical forms which govern the structures of complete homilies; however these features do not figure prominently in the Babylonian Esther-Midrash, and are most likely to be mentioned in this commentary in cases where they are absent, especially when they appear in parallel pericopes in the Palestinian aggadic literature. Since our midrash shows a consistent preference for the commentary-form over the full literary homily, its literary success will inevitably have to be judged largely in terms of its successful and appropriate use of midrashic hermeneutic tropes in order to elicit religious and moral teachings from the words of the Bible. It is indeed possible to sense the difference between an interpretation which is based on a sound textual foundation—whether it be a technical device such as the *gezerah shavah* and the *heqesh*, or more general phenomena like redundancies, puns and contradictions[26]—and interpretations whose links to the scriptural word are fragile or questionable.[27] We can also appreciate how well individual

...Continued from previous page

Midrash Exodus Rabbah," in *Studies in Aggadah, Targum and Jewish Liturgy in Memory of Joseph Heinemann*, ed. Jacob J. Petuchowski and Ezra Fleischer, 175-83 [Hebrew section] (Jerusalem: Magnes Press and Hebrew Union College Press, 1981] and others, tends to be more outspoken in identifying some midrashic texts as inferior to others.

[26] See Bruns, "The Hermeneutics of Midrash," 196.

[27] E.g., as a word-play that fails to account for all the consonants in the word upon which it claims to be basing itself.

interpretations fit together into broader constellations of exegetical traditions, typologies and value–concepts. Additionally, we should be able to recognize that our inability to understand certain passages is not always to be blamed on our own ignorance, but that it may sometimes be a consequence of poor editing.

It is thus important never to lose sight of the fact that the authors of the aggadic midrashim were operating according to rules and conventions that were quitedifferent from those with which we are familiar in contemporary western literature.[28] Thus it would appear that simile and metaphor[29] were not defined as standard prosodic ornaments, but parables[30] were. If we do elect to look for literary parallels beyond those forms that were explicitly and consciously mentioned by the rabbis or which are immanent to the genre, then the first places where we look should be among those literatures which were contemporaneous and contiguous with that of the rabbis,[31] particularly those of the Hellenistic world.[32] Any further insights that might be applied from

---

[28] See Lou H. Silberman, "Towards a Rhetoric of Midrash."

[29] Cf. Boyarin, "The Song of Songs: Lock or Key?" 230, n. 35.

[30] When compared with midrashic exegesis, homiletics and anecdotal narratives, the parables have received remarkably little attention in literary studies of midrash, though they have figured prominently in works on the origins of Christianity [e.g., David Flusser, "Mishlei yeshu veha-meshalim besifrut ḥaza"l," in *Jewish Sources in Early Christianity: Studies and Essays*, ed. H. Safrai, 150-209, 2nd ed., (Tel-Aviv: Sifriyyat Po'alim, 1979)]; see David Stern, "Rhetoric and Midrash: The Case of the Mashal," *Prooftexts* 1 (1981), 261–91; *Idem.*, "The Function of the Parable in Rabbinic Literature," *Jerusalem Studies in Hebrew Literature* 7 (1985), 90–102; Daniel Boyarin, "Rhetoric and Interpretation: The Case of the Nimshal," *Prooftexts* 5 (1985), 269-76; "David Stern Responds," *Prooftexts* 5 (1985), 276–80; Dov Noy, "Mishlei ha-melakhim shel rabbi shimᶜon ben yoḥai," *Maḥanayim* (La"g baᶜomer 1961), 81-73.

[31] In this context we might also mention the comparison with "generic" folkloric patterns which is central to much of the typology of I. Heinemann's *Darkhei ha-'aggadah*; Louis Ginzberg, *The Legends of the Jews*, translated by H. Szold (Philadelphia: Jewish Publication Society of America, 1909-39) 1:vii–xv; as well as studies by Dov Noy and others.

[32] The importance of such comparative work has always been recognized by midrashic scholarship; see e.g. I. Heinemann's *Darkhei ha-'aggadah*; Lieberman, Saul, *Hellenism in Jewish Palestine: Studies in the Literary Transmission, Beliefs and*

Continued on next page...

the world of European literary criticism must build upon an understanding of aggadic midrash that is appropriate to its historical and ideological settings. Within this defined role, the discipline of literary criticism does have much to enrich midrashic studies.[33]

The above methodological assumptions should be regarded at this preliminary stage as no more than a working hypothesis that must be tested against the data provided by the Esther-Midrash itself. Like any other scholarly theory or theoretical model, their value will be proven by the extent to which they helps account for patterns of phenomena that would otherwise defy simple explanation. The results will be summarized in the concluding chapter of this study.

Midrash as an Oral Literature

Among the fundamental differences that distinguish rabbinic literature from our own are several that relate to the definition of its goals, the modes of its composition and publication, its social contexts and the place of this genre within the broader spectrum of Jewish life and literatures.

...Continued from previous page

Manners of Palestine in the 1st Century B.C.E.-4th Century C.E (New York: The Jewish Theological Seminary of America, 1962); David Daube, "Rabbinic Methods of Interpretation and Hellenistic Rhetoric," *HUCA* 22 (1949), 239–65; in many books and articles by E. E. Hallevy. See the selected bibliography in Hartman and Budick's *Midrash and Literature*, 384-5.

33 To put it another way, the methods of Western literary criticism cannot be used to *define* an aesthetic standard by which the rabbinic texts would be judged; they can however be profitably utilized in order to enhance our understanding of how the rabbis accomplished their own literary goals. This position is eloquently argued by David Stern, "Literary Criticism or Literary Homilies?" 97–8. In addition to several of the studies included in the Hartman-Budick collection cited above, we may mention the following very diverse examples of attempts to deal with aggadah in the context of general literary theory: Fraenkel, Jonah, "Hermeneutical Questions in the Study of the Aggadic Narrative," *Tarbiẓ* 47 (1977-8), 139–172; Marc Bregman, "Past and Present in Midrashic Literature," *Hebrew Annual Review* 2 (1978), 45–59; Jose Faur, *Golden Doves with Silver Dots: Semiotics and Textuality in Rabbinic Tradition* (Bloomington: Indiana University Press, 1986); Daniel Boyarin, *Intertextuality and the Reading of Midrash*, Indiana Studies in Biblical Literature (Bloomington: Indiana University Press, 1990); as well as previously cited works by Stern and Bruns.

Chief among the factors that distinguish rabbinic from conventional Western writing is the fact that the former, both the talmudic and the aggadic, are *oral* creations. This fact affects both the rhetorical presentation and the social setting in which the literature was meant to operate.

Many significant advances have been made over the last generations in our appreciation and understanding of the uniqueness of oral "literature." Several features which have been discerned as typical of the unwritten traditions of "primitive" societies can be applied with minimal modification to rabbinic texts. For example:

> In a primary oral culture, to solve effectively the problem of retaining and retrieving carefully articulated thought, you have to do your thinking in mnemonic patterns, shaped for ready recurrence. Your thought must come into being in heavily rhythmic, balanced patterns, in repetitions or antitheses, in alliterations and assonances, in epithetic and other formulary expressions, in standard thematic settings...in proverbs which are constantly heard by everyone so that they come to mind readily and which themselves are patterned for retention and ready recall, or in other mnemonic form... Mnemonic needs determine even syntax.[34]

Furthermore, the very existence of oral literature demands that it be delivered before an audience. This fact holds true for both halakhic and aggadic creations and it has a decisive influence on the content and goals of the literature. Unlike written or graphic art, which can be introspective and private and is expressed initially on an impersonal piece of paper or parchment, an oral narration will almost invariably be delivered within a living social setting. It is therefore much less likely to

---

34 Walter J. Ong, *Orality and Literacy: The Technologizing of the Word*, New Accents, ed. Terence Hawkes (London and New York: Methuen, 1982), 34, citing Eric A. Havelock, *Preface to Plato* (Cambridge, MA: Belknap Press of Harvard University Press, 1963). My thanks are extended to Prof. Harold Coward for calling my attentions to Ong's enlightening and readable summary of the "state of the art" in oral-culture studies. Although there is scarcely a single explicit reference in the book to rabbinic literature, there is little in there that could not have been observed on the basis of the study of aggadic midrash.

become a vehicle for the expression of individual feelings or to place contrived obstacles in the way of immediate comprehension. We are probably even justified in regarding excessive individualism or intimacy as an artistic flaw in an oral creation.[35] At any rate the aggadah, like all rabbinic literature, speaks in a collective voice of the Jewish people, in which both the literary methods and the conceptual vocabularies become generic, and it is rarely possible to discern individual personalities. There is no evidence that aggadah strives to represent itself as an autonomous profession of Judaism. On the contrary, it is much more likely that each work was composed in the awareness that it constituted a part of the rich constellation of a broader

---

35 See Ong, 74-5. Other features in rabbinic literature that typify oral transmission include: the eschewal of complex syntax and subordinate clauses in favor of simpler "additive" structures [Ong, 38–9. As a simple example of how this phenomenon expresses itself in rabbinic Hebrew we may point to the scarcity of relative pronouns in complex sentences, which are normally replaced by a question-answer construction. Thus, instead of "X awoke when the sun rose" we will find "When did X arise? At sunrise"]; full repetition of phrases, rather than the allusions to antecedents (e.g., "see above") that are possible only in a written document [*ibid.*, 40-1]; a preference for the concrete and human-related over the abstract or conceptual [*ibid.*, 42–3; 49–57. This could account for the well-known preference in rabbinic legal texts for "casuistic" rather than "normative" formulations; see M. Elon, *Jewish Law: History, Sources, Principles* (Jerusalem: The Magnes Press, 1973), 879–84]; a tendency towards sharp contrasts and conflicts, including exaggerated delineations of the good and evil characters and their fates [Ong, 43-5]; a general lack of objectivity, as the speaker tries to create among the listeners a clear-cut emotional involvement with the subject of the narration [*ibid.*, 45-6]; a "homeostatic" perception of time, which recalls history only to the extent that it is relevant to the present, and is reluctant to admit to changes in ideas, values or the use of language [*ibid.*, 46-9]. In addition, the perception of "memorization" of an oral tradition, which cannot be checked against an exemplar, appears to be psychologically distinct from the rote-learning of a written text, allowing for considerable flexibility and personalization of the "memorized" tradition, while not recognizing that this is any different from verbatim reproduction of the source [*ibid.*, 57-71].

See J. Heinemann, *Aggadah and Its Development*, 17-47 (especially the methodological observations on 44-7); Avigdor Shinan, "Sifrut ha-'aggadah bein higud ʿal peh umasoret ketuvah," *Jerusalem Studies in Jewish Folklore* 1 (1981), 44-60. We may have to modify this model of oral memorization with respect to Masorah and legal texts such as the Mishnah; see Saul Lieberman, *Hellenism in Jewish Palestine*, Ch. 5; Bruns, "The Hermeneutics of Midrash," 195–6.

"Oral Law" literature that included the Talmuds, halakhic midrash and other genres that were created by the same community of rabbinic sages. Each work or genre was designed to collect material appropriate to itself; taken together, they would preserve a full picture of the spectrum of rabbinic Judaism.[36]

Ultimately of course, what we will be striving for is to achieve as complete an understanding as is possible of the processes that gave rise to the text that lies before us. In our quest towards that elusive goal it is important not to lock ourselves into any single methodological school or doctrine, but rather (in keeping with the complexity of life, and the rich diversity of topics that finds expression in the literature) to be as liberal as possible in defining the methods and considerations that will be brought to bear on the subject. These will include the basic philological ground-work of collating and evaluating the textual evidence and familiarizing ourselves with pertinent languages and lexicographic data. Ideally it will involve the amassing of information about the world in which the authors lived, their religious and ideological world-views (and those of their opponents), the literature with which they would have been familiar; their hermeneutic assumptions; as well as the details of their material lives, including economics, politics, geography, technology and more. The likelihood of our understanding a text—and then appreciating it—will be proportional to our intimate familiarity with the world inhabited by its creators.

Midrash as Exegesis: Esther Retold

Given the above description of an exegesis that is subordinated to the requirements of literary homilies, we would not expect to find much consistency in the rabbinic interpretations of the Book of Esther. Since explanations of scriptural units were designed for incorporation into *derashot* on a variety of topics, the sum total of such comments

---

36 This view should be contrasted with that of Neusner's argument (see above) that each rabbinic "document" was composed by a single "author" in order to express a distinct and consistent ideology.

should have taken the form of disconnected and mutually contradictory expansions of the biblical narrative, lacking any conceptual or hermeneutical unity.

While this characterization might be applicable to much of the material in the Esther-Midrash, and to the midrashic expositions of Esther in general, it must be stressed that underlying this rich exegetical diversity is a firm infrastructure of thematic and narrative assumptions that appear to have been held in common by most of the midrashim to Esther. This foundation goes far beyond the information supplied by the original biblical text—in fact much of it involves a complete overturning of the thematic structure of the original story. Presumably this common exegetical tradition took shape during the early Tannaitic era or before.[37]

As we have already observed above, we shall frequently be called upon to speculate about which is the most likely explanation for the origin of a given midrashic interpretation: Was it inspired by a feature in the biblical verse (a striking turn of phrase or verbal parallel elsewhere in the Bible) or by an ideological outlook, is it a tradition that would have arisen spontaneously in the folk tradition,[38] or out of the interests of religious polemics, etc.? Each case will have to be examined and evaluated on its own merits.

The present commentary will record and examine the principal narrative themes which the authors introduced into the Esther story, at-

---

37 These motifs do not figure prominently in Josephus' expansion of the tale in the *Antiquities*.

38 This idea has been championed most vigorously by Louis Ginzberg in the introduction to his *The Legends of the Jews*.. The evidence of the Esther-Midrash furnishes very little support for such a thesis since virtually every comment in the midrash seems to be rooted at least in part in the application to the verse of elaborate midrashic hermeneutics. Ginzberg was of course aware of this "scholastic" dimension of most midrashic biblical interpretation, but argued that in many instances the hermeneutical sophistication is an *ex post facto* artifice for attaching traditions which existed already in the folk tradition. See also his "Jewish Folklore: East and West," in *On Jewish Law and Lore*, 61-76 (Philadelphia: Jewish Publication Society of America, 1955).

tempting to explain how they arose and comparing them to the exegetical traditions that appear elsewhere in Talmudic literature, especially in the Palestinian midrashic collections and the Targumim to Esther.

Use of Parallel Materials

In addition to the attempt to explain each passage on its own terms, both as independent comments and within the context of the Esther-Midrash as a whole, I have made extensive use of analogous materials scattered throughout the corpus of rabbinic literature and contemporary sources. The sources consulted range from the Mishnah, Tosefta, Tannaitic midrashim, through the Palestinian and Babylonian Talmuds, to the Aggadic midrashim, targums and more, as well as non-rabbinic authors such as Josephus and some Church Fathers.[39]

No single purpose or theory governs my use of this parallel material. On a case-by-case basis, each parallel should be allowed to tell us whatever it has to teach us about its relationship with the Babylonian Esther-Midrash. In some instances what will prove important is the similarity between the versions, as when an obscure statement in one text is illuminated by a clearer or better preserved version in a parallel passage. In many other places, what might strike us at first as essentially similar traditions will prove on closer inspection to have significant differences whether in their hermeneutical conclusions or in their literary formulations. Needless to say, both classes of phenomena must be examined if we wish to obtain a complete picture of the Esther-Midrash.

Although the chief purpose of this commentary is the elucidation of the Esther-Midrash, I have allowed myself to try to trace the comparative history of whatever exegetical or narrative traditions are encountered therein, even where this investigation is not, strictly

[39] Though it should be obvious from the notes in the commentary, I wish to acknowledge at the outset how indebted I am [as are all students of rabbinic literature] to Louis Ginzberg's indispensable *Legends of the Jews* for so many of my references to relevant passages throughout the corpus of talmudic, midrashic and other ancient and medieval literatures.

speaking, necessary for the understanding of the Esther-Midrash *per se*. One of the most profitable areas of midrashic studies has been the exploration of how exegetical traditions were transformed in the process of their oral retelling and how they were used in assorted literary, exegetical and ideological contexts, a process which can be reconstructed with varying degrees of certainty on the basis of comparisons between the different versions that have come down to us. These comparisons have much to teach us, provided we approach them with the appropriate methodological tools and questions.[40]

There have come down to us many midrashim devoted to the Book of Esther,[41] including two expansive Aramaic Targums and many incidental comments included in other midrashic compilations. Among all these, the one which appears to have the closest resemblance to the Babylonian Esther-Midrash is *Esther rabbah*, and particular attention will be devoted to the similarities and differences between the two works.[42] There is a strong impression that the two compilations represent divergent expansions of an original pool of common material.

---

[40] E. g.: What ideological or conceptual disagreement might account for the fact that Source A and Source B disagree about a given detail in the biblical story?

[41] See L. Zunz, *Die gottesdienstlichen Vorträge der Juden historisch Entwickelt (Hadderashot beyisrael)*, translated by Ch. Albeck (Jerusalem: Mosad Bialik, 1974), 128-30, 402-6; Menahem M. Kasher and Jacob B. Mandelbaum, ed., *Sarei ha-elef.* Vol. 1 (Jerusalem: Beit Torah Shelemah, 1978), 30; J. D. Eisenstein, ed., *Ozar Midrashim: Bibliotheca Midraschica*, reprint ed. ([Israel]: 1969), 51-66.

[42] In the absence, as of this writing, of a text-critical edition of *Esther rabbah*, I attempted to verify all readings against those of the *editio princeps* (a facsimile of the Pesaro 1519 printing). As with all citations from primary sources my translations of *Esther rabbah* are my own, though I did make profitable use of the English version included in H. Freedman and Maurice Simon, *The Midrash*, Vol. 9 (London: Soncino Press, 1939). Neusner's translation [*Esther Rabbah I: An Analytical Translation.* Vol. I, Brown Judaic Studies (Atlanta: Scholars Press, 1989)] is a curious affair, which seems to be based on the existing English version more than on the Hebrew-Aramaic original. I did not find it very useful. I made some use as well of the Yiddish edition of Samson Dunsky [*Midrash rabbah: Esther* (Montreal: Northern Printing and Lithographing Company, 1962)].

The Commentary

The commentary on the Babylonian Esther-Midrash will include the following components:

As in the previous volume, this segment of my commentary on the Babylonian Esther-Midrash will include the following components:

1. Presentation of text in translation:

The translation, given in indented paragraphs, will consist of a literal rendering with full punctuation. Though existing translations have been consulted,[43] the present one is my own. The text is based on the Yemenite manuscript Columbia University X893 T141 (designated as "MS **Y**"), which generally preserves the most faithful readings of any of the complete witnesses to the tractate.[44]

The following conventions will be adopted in the presentation of the text:

•All biblical verses are printed in italics. Since it is well-known that scriptural citations in midrashic texts are often abbreviated, I usually opt for the fullest citation that is preserved among the available witnesses, whether or not the verse is actually found in this way in MS Columbia.[45] The translations, where appropriate, follow the King James (Authorized Revised) version, which usually preserves faithfully the Hebrew word order and produces an impression of archaism that is analogous to the effect created when biblical Hebrew passages are quoted in rabbinic texts. All chapter and verse references to the Bible are given in full and without abbreviation. Except for those few instances where they affect the understanding of the text, I did not record variant readings of biblical verses.

---

[43] Principally that of M. Simon, ed., *The Tractate Megillah*, Mo'ed:4, The Soncino Talmud (London: Soncino Press, 1948).

[44] See E. Segal, "The Textual Traditions of Ms. Columbia University to TB Megillah," *Tarbiẓ* 53 (1 1983), 41-69.

[45] Though it should be noted that MS **Y** does normally give full citations of biblical passages.

•In those instances where the differences between textual traditions are too great to be conveyed as "variant readings" in the footnotes, the traditions are recorded in parallel columns. The witness which forms the basis of the main text will be identified at the beginning of the column, and the distribution of the other witnesses will be indicated in the notes.

•In those instances where it is clear that MS Columbia has absorbed extraneous material that is not part of the Talmudic text (usually from Midrash *Panim aḥerim* B), the addition will be indicated with a vertical line to its left.

•Square brackets indicate additions and emendations that are found in the textual witness. Parentheses indicate a deletion in the text. Braces ({ }) normally designate explanatory phrases added in the translation.

•Following a useful convention employed in the Soncino translations of the Babylonian Talmud, answers to questions or objections are usually preceded by a dash (—).

•The Hebrew הקדוש ברוך הוא , which should literally be translated as the cumbersome "the Holy One Blessed Be He," will be rendered simply as "the Holy One," more in keeping with the naturalness of the phrase in Hebrew or Aramaic.

•Proper names which appear in the Bible are usually given in their standard English forms, except where a more precise transliteration is required for word-plays etc.

•The title "Rabbi" is normally abbreviated as "R." in those places where the equivalent abbreviation (ר') is employed in MS Columbia.

•In a departure from the conventions adopted in most translations of rabbinic texts, the word אמר, used to introduce rabbinic dicta, is treated as an Aramaic participle rather than a Hebrew perfect, and translated accordingly as a present-tense verb ("says"), following the prevailing norms of the Mishnah and other Tannaitic works.[46]

2. Variant readings:

The variant readings accompanying the text are not intended to constitute a proper critical edition, which would at any rate be an absurdity in a translated text. They are expected to provide an idea of the variety that exists in the textual witnesses, insofar as this variety can be reflected in English translation. The listings do not record all the textual information. For example, one cannot know from this apparatus whether the omission of a witness from the listing of variants indicates that its reading agrees with MS Columbia or that there is a gap in the manuscript.[47]

The following conventions are adopted for the presentation of the variant readings.

•Variants are listed in footnotes. As a rule, I have tried never to mix textual variants and other information in the same paragraph, and usually not in the same footnote. The information in the footnote relates to the text preceding the footnote reference (in the case of variants) as defined in the lemma, or (in the case of additions) to the place where the footnote reference is inserted.

---

46 That this is the proper translation was proven by Hyman Klein, "Gemara and Sebara" *JQR* 38 (1 1947), 87 [reprinted in Abraham Goldberg, ed. *Collected Talmudic Scientific Writings of Hyman Klein* (Jerusalem: Akademon, 1979), 84], who notes how it appears in parallel with בעי, which is unquestionably a participle. Shamma Friedman, ["A Critical Study of *Yevamot X* with a Methodological Introduction," in *Texts and Studies, Analecta Judaica*, ed. H. Z. Dimitrovsky, 275-442 (New York: The Jewish Theological Seminary of America, 1977), 37, n. 110] notes further that the plural in these contexts is usually "אמרי."

47 I have generally tried to minimize the size of the listings. Thus if only one or two witnesses preserve a certain reading, it will be recorded as "Thus only in **X** and **Y**; all other witnesses read: '…'," without identifying all the witnesses which support the majority reading.

•The textual information is provided in complete English sentences, rather than in technical notation.[48] Accordingly, both the lemma and the variant reading are placed in quotation-marks, separated by a dash (—). The variant readings are understood to replace everything in the lemma.

•Variants to a single lemma are separated by semi-colons (;). Separate lemmas are separated by periods (.).

•In cases where lemmas are abbreviated (with a "..."), I have tried to remove any ambiguity about the extent of the citation. Where the opening word or phrase of the abbreviated lemma appears more than once in the passage, the reference may be presumed to be to the last occurrence.

•The tilde (~) indicates that the content of the lemma is missing in the designated witness or witnesses.

•I have not identified the Genizah fragments, which are referred to generically in the apparatus; nor can it be assumed that two reference to Genizah fragments in the same passage refer to the same fragment.[49] (Hence, the words "Genizah fragment" do not appear in bold typeface like the rest of the sigla.)

The listing of sigla normally follows the following order:

1. Variants themselves are listed according to what I felt to be a logical order.[50]

---

[48] As such there is some flexibility in the syntax. E.g., the sigla may appear before the readings (followed by a colon) or after them (preceded by a dash or the word "in" etc.).

[49] For a description of the Genizah fragments to *TB Megillah* see Eliezer Segal, "The Textual Traditions of Tractate Megillah in the Babylonian Talmud," Ph. D., Hebrew University of Jerusalem, 1981, 254-69.

[50] E.g., if there were two primary traditions the order would be: (1) tradition #1 (that most similar to MS Columbia), (2) tradition #2, (3) conflations of the two traditions and, lastly, (4) witnesses which omit the text in question. For reasons of space, I have not usually commented on the significance or history of each reading, though the interested reader will be able to draw conclusions from the manner in which I record the material.

2. The witnesses to each reading are listed according to the following order: (1) complete manuscripts; (2) partial texts (including aggadic compendia in manuscript and print); (3) printings; (4) fragments.[51]

3. Within each of these classes the witnesses are listed according to textual type: Oriental, Spanish, Ashkenazi. Where possible the readings are grouped into "families" (see below).

3. Transliteration:

The transliteration system used here for Hebrew and Aramaic is, for the most part, standard. The following idiosyncrasies should be noted, most of which reflect my use of "Sepharadic" pronunciation:

ו is normally rendered *v* (not *w*), as is undotted ב.

Left-dotted שׂ is not distinguished from ס, both of which are rendered *s*.

No distinctions were made between long, short or "half" (*ḥaṭaf*) vowels. Similarly, *sheva mobile* (*naʿ*) is indicated simply by an *e*.

No distinctions were made between dotted and undotted ג, ד, or ת, which are rendered indiscriminately as *g*, *d* and *t* respectively.

Right-dotted שׁ is represented as *sh*, and undotted כ as *kh*. Where the transliteration is referring to two separate consonants, they are separated by a hyphen (*s-h*, *k-h*).

Following current bibliographical conventions, a less precise transliteration system is employed for modern Hebrew (mostly in titles of books and articles). In such references, the definite article is rendered as "*ha-*" with hyphen and no doubling of the following consonant; and צ is transliterated as *tz* rather than *ṣ* as in classical texts. א at the beginning of a word is not indicated.

---

51 Only actual manuscripts are designated as such ("MS" or "MSS") in the apparatus.

Where a European-language translation is provided in a Hebrew book or article (in an alternative title-page or table of contents, etc.), I refer to it by that title rather than by a transliteration.

4. The Textual witnesses and their sigla:

The following witnesses to the text of the Esther-Midrash are cited in the apparatus:[52]

Oriental types:

Manuscripts:

Y	MS Columbia University X893 T141

Partial texts and fragments:

N	MS New York (JTS.ENA) 84
AgE	*Aggadat esther* (ed. S. Buber)
MhG	*Midrash haggadol* to the Pentateuch, cited according to the Mossad Harav Kook editions (no page references are supplied)
Genizah fragment	[see above]

52 Fuller descriptions may be found in "The Textual Traditions of Tractate Megillah in the Babylonian Talmud."

Spanish types:

Manuscripts:

O	MS Oxford Bodlean 366 (Oppenheim fol. 23)
G	MS Göttingen 13
B	MS Munich 140

Partial texts:

EY	R. Jacob Ibn Ḥabib's *ʿEin yaʿaqov*, cited from *editio princeps*, Salonika 1516-22
HgT	*Haggadot hattalmud*. The following two versions were consulted. Where no superscript is supplied their readings may be presumed to be identical:
HgT¹	MS Parma 3010
HgT²	Constantinople 1511 printing
P	MS Parma 427

Ashkenazic types:

Manuscripts:

L	MS London (British Library) 400 (Harl. 5508)
M	MS Munich 95
R	MS Vatican 134

Partial texts:

W	MS Warsaw (Jewish Historical Institute) 260
Mf	MS London Montefiore 88
V	MS Vatican 49/2
Z	MS Vienna (Dominican Monastery) 10

YS *Yalquṭ shimʿoni*, cited according to MS Oxford (Neubauer 2637) and *editio princeps*. Passages from Genesis and Exodus were compared as well to the Mossad Harav Kook editions]. Precise references are not provided.

Printed editions:

Printings Pesaro (c. 1510) and Venice (Bomberg, 1521) printings of the Babylonian Talmud.

In those few places where variants exist between these two texts, they are indicated in the apparatus; otherwise they may be presumed to be identical.

In order to simplify the presentation of the textual data, readings common to certain groups were recorded as "families" according to the following criteria:

•"**Yemenite family**": Where there was agreement between MS **Y**, **AgE** and **MhG** (or MS **G**, which has close affinities with this family).

•"**Spanish family**": The special readings of this tradition are very distinctive, consisting largely of explanatory glosses and expansions. The grouping was used to designate agreement among any three of the following witnesses: **O**, [**B**], **EY**, **HgT**, **P**.

•"**Ashkenazic family**": This tradition is less consistent. I grouped the readings as a family only when there was agreement among all three complete manuscripts: **L**, **M** and **R**.

Square brackets ([]) around either a reading or a siglum indicate that the reading in question is found in an emendation or gloss to that witness.

Chapter One

Prologue

"*Vayhi*" Means Sorrow

[10b] "[1]*And it came to pass* [vayhi] *in the days of Ahasuerus*" (Esther 1:1).

R.[2] Levi; and if you should say: R. Joḥanan:[3] This matter is a tradition in our hands[4] [5] from the Men of the Great Assembly: Every place in which it says "*and it came to pass*" is none other than a reference to sorrow.

The Esther Midrash is found at the end of Chapter One of *TB Megillah*, following the conclusion of the pericope expounding the chapter's final mishnah. A. Weiss[6] is correct, to my mind, in his assertion that the formal connection to the Talmudic pericope was furnished by the phrase "this matter is a tradition in our hands[7] from the Men of the Great Assembly...," which bears a resemblance to the formula "every town concerning which you possess a tradition[8] from your fathers[9]..." in the preceding pericope (Note however that MS **R** inserts

---

[1] MS **R** adds: "End of Gemara."

[2] "R." — Only in MS **Y** and **EY**; in all other witnesses: "Says R."

[3] "Joḥanan" — Thus in MSS **Y**, **O**, **W**, **L**, **M**, **EY**; in all other witnesses: "Jonathan."

[4] **Spanish family**, MSS **N**, **W**, **M**, **R** and **V** add: "from our fathers."

[5] MS **W** adds: "and."

[6] A. Weiss, *Studies in the Literature of the Amoraim*, 280. Ibn Ḥabib has already noted in the **EY** that the pericope about *mishloaḥ manot* and gifts to the poor on 7a-b most probably originated as a part of the Esther Midrash (where it is to be inserted at 16b).

[7] Note the variant readings cited in the notes to the text, above.

[8] Several witnesses add: "in your hands."

[9] "from your fathers" — ~ in MS **B**.

the phrase "End of Gemara" before the start of the midrash). The "Great Assembly," often mentioned in rabbinic literature as the earliest known phase of post-Prophetic tradition, refers in its narrowest sense to the assembly of returned exiles convened by Ezra in order to publicly read and accept the authority of the Law of Moses, as described in Nehemiah 8–10. Such attributions are unlikely to have much historical value, but rather reflect the desire of the tradent to link his dictum to the most ancient stages of the post-biblical oral tradition.[10]

The exegesis builds upon the similarity between the Hebrew word for "and it was" or "and it came to pass"—"*vayhi*"— and a common expression of grief, "*vay*" or "*way*."[11] Accordingly, the word is read as

---

[10] My interpretation of the talmudic evidence concurs in most respects with that of Ira J. Schiffer, "The Men of the Great Assembly," in *Persons and Institutions in Early Rabbinic Judaism*, ed. William Scott Green, 237-83, 3 (Missoula: Scholars Press for Brown University, 1977) [see summary on 266-70], that the "Assembly" in question is most likely the one-time event in Jerusalem [and the "*Men* of the Great Assembly" were the participants or veterans of that event], rather than a permanent institution that served as a prototype of the later Sanhedrin; though later rabbinic sources are not consistent on that point. The quantity of secondary scholarly literature on the subject is in inverse proportion to the amount of information provided in the primary sources. Some standard studies include: L. Finkelstein, *Ha-perushim ve-'anshei keneset ha-gedolah* (New York: Jewish Theological Seminary of America, 1950) [with bibliography of earlier studies on p. 51, n. 144]; G. Alon, *Toledot ha-yehudim be'eretz yisra'el bitequfat ha-mishnah veha-talmud*, fourth ed., Vol. 2 ([Israel]: Hakibutz Hameuchad, 1975), 223-4; E. Urbach, *The Sages: Their Concepts and Beliefs*, translated by I. Abrahams (Cambridge, Mass. and London, England: Harvard University Press, 1987), 567-8; H. Mantel, "The Nature of the Great Synagogue (Knesset ha-Gedolah)," in *Fourth World Congress of Jewish Studies in Jerusalem*, edited by S. Shaked and Y. Shenkman, World Union of Jewish Studies, 81-88, 1967; *Idem., Anshei keneset ha-gedolah* (Jerusalem: 1983).; M. Elon, *Jewish Law: History, Sources, Principles*, 454-5. As we shall note below, the Palestinian versions of this tradition do not speak at all of the Men of the Great Assembly, but rather of a tradition brought from the "*Golah*" of Babylonia. In *Pesiqta rabbati*, 5 [M. Friedmann, ed., *Pesikta rabbati* (Vienna: 1880), 19b] the reading is "from Babylonia." Both terms allude roughly to the same historical era. See also: Jacob Neusner, *A History of the Jews in Babylonia*, 2nd ed. (Leiden: E. J. Brill, 1965-1970), 205.

[11] The interjection "*vay*" appears with some frequency in Amoraic texts, especially in the Babylonian Talmud [e.g., *TB ʿAvodah zarah* 11b; *TB Megillah* 16a; *TB Moʿed qaṭan* 28b, and many more], but also in Palestinian works such as: *Genesis rabbah*, 26:4 [J. Theodor and Ch. Albeck, ed., *Midrasch Bereschit Rabbah* (Berlin: 1903-36),

Continued on next page...

a combination of two words, "*vay hi'*'": "It is 'Woe!'" implying that the content of the verse will involve something unfortunate.

The Talmud continues to cite instances in support of R. Levi's rule that the formula "and it came to pass" invariably serves as a prelude to trouble or grief:

...Continued from previous page

247], 65:22 (742); 93:8 (1158); *Pesiqta derav kahana*, 10:4 [Bernard Mandelbaum, ed., *Pesikta de Rav Kahana* (New York: The Jewish Theological Seminary of America, 1962), 165; transl. William G. Braude and Israel J. Kapstein, *Pesikta de-Rab Kahana* (Philadelphia: Jewish Publication Society of America, 1975), 190, and n. 18]; and *Lamentations rabbah*, 1:5 (ed. S. Buber, 66), etc. In all the above passages, unlike our own, the word is used in contexts where there is no need to produce a word-play on a biblical form [as distinct from passages such as *Genesis rabbah*, 36:4 (p. 339) where the *vay* is employed to produce a series of puns on past-tense verbs similar to those in our current pericope]. In biblical Hebrew, other forms are used more commonly, particularly "אוי"; see E. Kautzsch and A. Cowley, ed., *Gesenius' Hebrew Grammar* (Oxford: The Clarendon Press, 1910), 307; S. Mandelkern, *Veteris Testamenti Concordantiæ* (Leipzig: Veit et Comp., 1896), 40. Note that in two verses in Ecclesiastes (4:10; 10:16) the variant form "אִי" is employed, a form which would become the standard one in reliable texts preserving the Palestinian tradition of the Mishnah, as noted by E. Y. Kutscher, *The Language and Linguistic Background of the Isaiah Scroll (I Q Isa*[a]*)*, English ed., Vol. 6, Studies on the Texts of the Desert of Judah, ed. J. Van der Ploeg (Leiden: E. J. Brill, 1974), 390; *Idem.*, "Leshon ḥaza"l," in *Sefer Ḥanokh Yalon*, 246-80 (Jerusalem: 1963), 266-7 [It does not however appear in the reliable Babylonian tradition of MS Vatican of the *Sifra*; see *Idem.*, "Some Problems of the Lexicography of Mishnaic Hebrew and its Comparison with Biblical Hebrew," in *Archive of the Dictionary of Rabbinical Literature*, ed. E. Y. Kutscher, 29-82, 1 (Ramat-Gan: New Dictionary of Rabbinical Literature Project, 1972), 48, 68; A. Bendavid, *Biblical Hebrew and Mishnaic Hebrew*, revised expanded ed., Vol. 1 (Tel-Aviv: Dvir, 1967), 77, 200]. As noted in the above examples אי does not appear to have carried over to the same extent into Amoraic Hebrew and Aramaic even in Palestine; e.g., *Genesis rabbah*. Cf. however *ibid*. 46:10 (467-8) and 89:6 (1088) where "*'i*" is used, and see Theodor's and Albeck's notes to the respective passages; in *Genesis rabbah*, 93:10 (1160) and *ibid*., 93:11 (1170) where the "אי" and "אוי" alternate in two citations of the same dictum in MS London; *Exodus rabbah*, 17:5. This phenomenon may perhaps be explained as a consequence of Greek and Latin influences. Both these languages use interjections that transliterate as "*vay*"; Greek: ὀυαι [which appears often as the Greek rendering of biblical "*'oi*" or "*hoi*"; e.g., Numbers 21:29, Amos 5:1]; Latin: *vae*.

> [10b] "*And it came to pass in the days of Ahasuerus*" —there was Haman.
>
> "*And it came to pass in the days when the judges judged*" (Ruth 1:1) —there was a famine.

The connection between the *vayhi* and the famine is spelled out clearly in the verse.[12]

> [10b] "*And it came to pass, when men began to multiply on the face of the earth...and the sons of God saw the daughters of men...*" —"*and the Lord said: My spirit shall not abide in man forever*" (Genesis 6:1-3).[13]

The above verses describe the mating of the "sons of God" with human women, and conclude with the "sorrow" of God's decision to shorten the mortal life-span to one hundred and twenty years.[14] It is possible that the passage was meant to be read as a single unit with the following verses, in which God decides to bring a flood upon all flesh.[15]

> [10b] "*And it came to pass, as they journeyed east, that they found a plain in the land of Shinar...*" —"*and they said... Come let us make brick...Come, let us build us a city...*" (Genesis 11:2-5).[16]

This *vayhi* verse leads up to the erection of the Tower of Babel.[17]

> [10b] "*And it came to pass in the days of Amraphel...*" (Genesis 14:1;) —they waged war.

---

12 MS **M** actually cites the continuation of the verse (in the Hebrew, the difference between that and the paraphrase contained in the other witnesses is a small one).

13 **Spanish family** adds: "There was a flood."

14 Jewish legends surrounding this episode are collected by Ginzberg, Louis, *The Legends of the Jews*, translated by H. Szold (Philadelphia: Jewish Publication Society of America, 1909-39), 1:148–51, 5:169-72, nn. 10–13.

15 As understood in the texts of the "Spanish family" recorded above.

16 "'*And it came to pass, as they journeyed...city*'" —Thus in MSS **Y**, **N**, **Printings** and **AgE**; ~ in all other witnesses.

17 R. Solomon Edels, the "Maharsha," observes that it seems more logical in this context to cite Genesis 11:1.

The reference is to the "War of the Four Kings Against the Five Kings," in which Lot was taken captive and had to be rescued by Abraham. While the outcome is a favorable one from Abraham's perspective, the war itself is generically regarded as an evil.

MS **Y**	All other witnesses
[10b] "*And it came to pass, when Isaac was old*" —"*and his eyes were dim*" (Genesis 27:1).[18]	

As described here, it is the affliction of blindness in itself that is regarded as the sorrow,[19] without reference to the more pronounced theme of Esau's and Jacob's struggle for the blessing which dominates the subsequent verses.

MS **Y**	All other witnesses
[10b] "*And the Lord was* [vayhi] *with Joseph...*" —"*and his master's wife cast her eyes*, etc." (Genesis 39:2-7).[20]	

Joseph's rejection of the advances of Potiphar's wife results in his being cast into prison.[21]

---

18 "'*And it came to pass, when Isaac...dim*'" — Thus in MSS **Y**, **G**, **N*** and **AgE**; ~ in all other witnesses.

19 For rabbinic interpretations of Isaac's blindness see Ginzberg, *Legends*, 1:328-9; 5:281–2, n. 74.

20 "'*And the Lord...eyes*, etc.'" —Thus in MSS **Y**, **G**, **N** and **AgE**; ~ in all other witnesses.

21 He languished there for ten years; see Ginzberg, 2:58; 5:341, n. 136.

MS **Y** and **MhG**	All other witnesses
	[10b] "*And it came to pass, when Joshua was by Jericho, that he lifted up his eyes and looked, and, behold, there stood a man over against him with his sword drawn in his hand*, etc. (Joshua 5:13)"

"*So the Lord was* [vayhi] *with Joshua*" (Joshua 6:27) —"*But the children of Israel committed a trespass in the accursed thing*" (Joshua 7:1).

In this version of the text, the occasion for sorrow is Achan's theft from the spoils of Jericho. This act will provoke God's anger, leading to the defeat at Ai (7:5) and the stoning of Achan (7:25).[22]

---

22 However, according to the reading of the majority of textual witnesses, where the citation begins at Joshua 5:13 with Joshua's encounter with the "captain of the host of the Lord," certain difficulties arise. The incident described is not a "sorrowful" one, since it relates how the angel assured Joshua of the coming victory over Jericho which is described in Chapter 6. Most likely the intention was to see this passage as the *vayhi* verse leading up (through Chapter 6!) to 7:1, though this in turn raises the further difficulty, that the latter verse already commences with *vayhi*. It is probably for this reason that the Yemenite texts dropped the reference to 5:13. It is nevertheless possible that the redactor of the pericope interpreted the verse in light of the midrashic traditions which state that the angel had come to chastise Joshua and the people for neglect of Torah study and sacrificial offerings, as in described in *TB ʿEruvin* 63b, and above 3a. On the last-mentioned passage see Segal, E., "'The Goat of the Slaughterhouse...'—On the Evolution of a Variant Reading in the Babylonian Talmud," *Tarbiẓ* 49 (1-2 1979-80), 43-51. Other unfavorable interpretations of the incident are listed by Ginzberg, *Legends*, 4:7; 6:173, nn. 19-20. Accordingly, it is not entirely inconceivable that Joshua 5:13 and 7:1 are being cited as separate incidents. In the Palestinian midrashic parallels (see references below) the citations are from Joshua 6:27 and 7:5. There are two principal textual traditions there as regards the nature of the "sorrow": (1) "On that day he was compelled to rend his garments" (referring to Achan's transgression); (2) "because on that day Jair was killed" (on the significance of this detail see Ginzberg, *Legends*, 6:175, n. 23).

> [10b] "*And there was* [vayhi] *a certain man of Ramathaim*" —"*...for he loved Hannah, but the Lord had shut up her womb*" (1 Samuel 1:1-5).[23]

The touching story of Hannah's barrenness and the taunting of her rival Peninah represents a more personal kind of suffering than the religious and national sorrows mentioned in most of the examples. This is true as well of the story of Samson's mother, the wife of Manoah, as recounted in the following example:

MS **Y**	All other witnesses
[10b] "*And there was a certain man of Zorah*, etc." —"*and his wife was barren, and bore not*" (Judges 13:2).[24]	

> "*And it came to pass, when Samuel was old, that he made his sons judges...*" —"*And his sons walked not in his ways*" (1 Samuel 8:1, 3).

MSS **Y** and **P**	All other witnesses
	"*And David had* [vayhi] *great success in all his ways*" (I Samuel 18:14).

MS **Y**	All other witnesses
	—"*And Saul eyed David from that day and forward*" (I Samuel 18:9).

23 MS **W** adds: "'*And it came to pass, when Isaac was old, and his eyes were dim.*'"

24 "'*And there was a certain...bore not*'" —Only in MS **Y**, **AgE** and Genizah fragment; ~ in all other witnesses.

It is noteworthy that the "sorrow" verse here precedes the "*vayhi*" verse instead of coming after it, as would normally be expected.[25] The midrash does not seem to attach importance to the order of the items, as long as the two components appear in the same episode.

> [10b] "*And it came to pass when the king dwelt in his house,* etc." (2 Samuel 7:1) —"*Nevertheless thou shalt not build the house…unto my name*" (1 Kings 8:19).[26]

The "*vayhi*" passage serves as an introduction to God's message to David (through the prophet Nathan) that the king would not be permitted to construct a sanctuary.[27]

Exceptions

Following the list of proof-texts in support of the proposition that *vayhi* invariably presages misfortunes, the Talmud proceeds to

---

25 Rashi is probably alluding to this difficulty when he comments that "It is also written there '*And Saul eyed David*' because of the latter's successes." His point seems to be that verse 14 precedes verse 9 *logically*, if not physically.

26 MS **B** adds: "'*And it came to pass, when Isaac was old, and his eyes were dim*'—'*And the Lord was* [vayhi] *with Joseph…*'—'*and his master's wife cast her eyes,* etc.'"

27 It is very curious that all the witnesses here are as one in citing the verse from the secondary context of 1 Kings, where it figures in Solomon's recounting of the event, rather than in its original locus, 2 Samuel 7:5, as part of the original report of Nathan's prophecy, whose wording is almost identical: "*Shalt thou build me an house for me to dwell in*?" If this is not an instance of an early scribal error in the transcription of the verse (an error common to all witnesses!), then it might reflect an editorial preference for 1 Kings' clearly negative formulation over 2 Samuel's rhetorical question, which is more susceptible to misreading in an unpunctuated Hebrew text. The 1 Kings verse is also the one quoted in all the Palestinian versions of the pericope; see below. For an additional instance of a misquoted biblical citation in *TB Megillah*, see 4a and commentators. R. Hai Ga'on already reports that the "non-verse" had found its way into the manuscript tradition. See S. Shneurson, ed., *Ḥemdah genuzah* (Jerusalem: 1903), #78; cited in B. M. Lewin, ed., *Otzar Hageonim* (Haifa and Jerusalem: 1928-43) to *Megillah* 4a and *Berakhot* 48a; J. N. Epstein, *Introduction to Amoraitic Literature*, ed. E. Z. Melamed (Tel Aviv and Jerusalem: Dvir and Magnes Press, 1962), 138.

compile a list of passages that contradict the rule; i.e., where *vayhi* seems to accompany joyous occasions:

> [10b] [28] [29] *"And it came to pass on the eighth day, that Moses called Aaron and his sons ..."* (Leviticus 9:1).
>
> And it was taught:[30] On that very day there[31] was a great[32] rejoicing[33] before the Holy One,[34] as[35] on the day when the heavens and the earth were fashioned.[36]
>
> Here[37] it is written: *"And it came to pass on the eighth day,"*[38] and there it is[39] written[40] *"And there was evening and there was morning one day"* (Genesis 1:5)!

---

[28] MS **G** adds: "And where it is written *vayhi* it denotes sorrow?"; MSS **N**, **R*** and **Mf** add: "Do you say that all *vayhi*s have negative connotations?"; MS **V** adds: "But can you say that they all have negative connotations?"; MS **W** adds: "And is this indeed so?"

[29] All witnesses except MSS **Y**, **N**, **AgE** and **MhG** add: "And is it not written."

[30] "was taught" — **Spanish family**: "taught" (ותאנא).

[31] "On that very day there" — MS **L**: "That very day."

[32] "a great" — ~ in MS **G** and **Printings**.

[33] MS **R*** adds: "for Israel."

[34] "Holy One" — **AgE**: "'Place [*Maqom*], Blessed be He'; **MhG**: "'Place.'" The epithet *Maqom* to designate the immanence of God is an ancient one which was often removed from the textual traditions of rabbinic works in favor of the more prevalent later usage of "Holy One Blessed Be He." See: S. Esh, הק(בה) *Der Heilige <Er sei gepriesen>* (Leiden: 1957); Urbach, *The Sages*, 66-7, 711-2.

[35] "as" — ~ in MS **N** (before emendation) and **HgT**^{2}.

[36] **MhG** adds: "Did not Nadab and Abihu die?"

[37] "Here" — ~ in MS **B** (before emendation).

[38] "Here...'...*day*'" — ~ in **MhG**.

[39] "and there it is" — **MhG**: "And is it not."

[40] The Talmud formulates the expressions "here it is written" and "there it is written" in Aramaic, indicating that this passage is an Amoraic or editorial addition, not part of the original *baraita*. As noted below, the verse comparison itself is attested in the *Sifra*, and its Aramaic appearance in our pericope might simply be the result of the expressions having been abbreviated and subsequently re-expanded.

—Nevertheless, Nadab and Abihu died.[41]

The *baraita* comparing the consecration of Aaron and his sons with the creation[42] appears in the *Sifra Shemini*, 1:15, to Leviticus 9:1, in precisely the same formulation.[43] The anonymous comment of the Talmud points out correctly that the joy of that day was ultimately marred by the deaths of Aaron's sons Nadab and Abihu.[44]

Concluding its attack on the initial hypothesis, the Talmud now presents a series of joyous "*vayhi*" verses for which it is not able to

---

41 "Nevertheless...died" — Thus only in MSS **Y** and **G**; all other witnesses read: "Did not Nadab and Abihu die?"; **AgE**: "Nadab and Abihu (were burned) [did they not die?]"; ~ in **MhG**.

42 The motif of comparing the sacrificial service to the creation of the world, thereby making it a condition for the existence of the universe, is found in several ancient Jewish sources. It is for example implied in the observances associated with the *ma'amadot*, when the Creation passages of Genesis 1 would be read because "had it not been for the *ma'amadot*, then the heavens and the earth could not exist" (See *TB Ta'anit* 27b; *Megillah* 31b, etc.; cf. *TP Ta'anit* 2:2 (68a), *TP Megillah* 3:7 (74b); *Pesiqta derav kahana* 19:6 [ed. Mandelbaum, 309; transl. Braude and Kapstein, 329]: "When did the world become established? —When they arrived at your holy habitation"; *Mishnah Avot* 1:18). This theme underlies the classic formula of the *'Avodah* liturgies of the Day of Atonement, which commence with the account of creation and culminate in the selection of Aaron as priest to perform the atoning rituals, such that only with the institution of the Tabernacle did the Creation reach full completion. As has been noted by several scholars [S. J. Rappoport, *Toledot rabbi el'azar ha-kalir*, reprint ed. (Warsaw: Tevunah, 1913), 225; Cecil Roth, "Ecclesiasticus in the Synagogue Service," *JBL* 71 (3 1952), 171-8], the *piyyuṭ* tradition known best from the works of Yose ben Yose can be traced back to Ben-Sirah's progression from Creation (42:15) to his glorification of the priesthood of Simon (Ch. 50). The phenomenon is discussed by Aharon Mirsky, ed., *Yosse ben Yosse: Poems* (Jerusalem: Bialik Institute, 1977), 26-9.

43 It begins: "What does it come to teach us when it says '*And it came to pass*'? —It teaches that there was rejoicing...'" Additional aggadic traditions about this event are found in Ginzberg, *Legends*, 3:184; 6:73-4, n. 380.

44 Cf. Maharsha, who has trouble justifying the Talmud's choice of this objection from among many possible alternatives. On the episode itself see: Avigdor Shinan, "The Sins of Nadab and Abihu in Rabbinic Literature," *Tarbiẓ* 48 (3-4 1979), 201-14 [reprinted in: Avigdor Shinan, ed., *Likkutei Tarbiz 4: The Aggadic Literature—A Reader*, Maslul Series: Studies Textbook Publishing Projects (Jerusalem: The Magnes Press, 1983), 174-87].

find any unpleasant connotations. The first of these involves the completion of Solomon's Temple:

> [10b] And is it not written: "*And it came to pass in the four hundred and eightieth year after the children of Israel were come out of the land of Egypt...that he began to build the house of the Lord*" (1 Kings 6:1)?[45]

Yemenite family	All other witnesses
	And is it not written: "*And it came to pass, when Jacob saw Rachel*" (Genesis 29:10)?[46]

> And is it not written:[47] "*And there was evening and there was morning*" (Genesis 1:5, 8, 13, 19, 23, 31)[48]

> And are there not many "*vayhi*," "*vayhi*"[49] that we have omitted![50]

Rather than resort to case-by-case objections, the Talmud at this point seems to revert to a "common-sense" approach to the subject, recognizing that there are so many non-sorrowful "*vayhi*"s in the Bible that R. Levi, etc.'s dictum is utterly unacceptable.[51]

---

45 MS **G** adds: "(And according to your reasoning there are many more *vayhi*s)."

46 Maharsha: "This is difficult: I might have argued that we are justified in seeing this verse as expressing sorrow since it introduces '*And when Rachel saw that she bare Jacob no children...*' (Genesis 30:1), which qualified as a sorrowful instance in the case of Hannah below... —It can be replied that in Rachel's case there is an interruption between the verses, which was not the case with respect to Hannah."

47 "And...written" — ~ in **Yemenite family**.

48 All witnesses except **Yemenite family** add: "'*one day*'. And is there not '*the second day*'? And is there not '*the third day*'? ["And is there not '*the fourth day*'?"——only in MS **G***]."

49 "'*vayhi*' '*vayhi*'" —All but MS **Y**: "*vayhi*."

50 "which we have omitted" —MS **Y**, **AgE** and **MhG**; MS **N**: "which we have not counted"; MSS **W**, **R**, **Mf** and **HgT**: "which come {to indicate} favorable {contexts}"; ~ in MSS **G**, **B**, **P**, **O**, **L**, **M**, **EY**, **Printings**, **V**.

51 Cf. *Genesis rabbah*, 38:14 (365), where a similarly audacious midrashic rule is proposed by R. Levi for the word "*ein*" =("is not"), which (according to his principle)

Continued on next page...

Rav Ashi's Solution

[10b] Rather,[52] says Rav Ashi: {As regards}[53] "*vayhi*"[54] there are instances like this and there are instances like this.[55]

[56]"*Vayhi*[57] *bimei*" (*And it came to pass in the days of*) is assuredly[58] an indication of[59] sorrow.

And there are five:[60]

MS **Y**	All other witnesses
	"*And it came to pass in the days of Amraphel*"

...Continued from previous page
always implies that the matter in question actually "*is*" (i.e., eventually comes to realization)!

52 "Rather" — ~ in **Printings**.

53 MSS **N**, **M**, **Mf**, **EY**, **MhG**, **AgE** add: "All."

54 "*Vayhi*" —only in **Yemenite family**; in all others: "All '*vayhi*'s."

55 "there are instances like this and there are instances like this" — MSS **G** and **N**: "it can mean this and it can mean this."

56 MSS **L**, **HgT**, Genizah fragment add: "Rather"; MS **B** and **EY** add: "All"; MS **G** adds: "Rather, all"; MSS **Mf** and **V** add: "However."

57 "*vayhi*" — ~ in **AgE** and **MhG**.

58 "assuredly" — MS **M** and **Printings**: "none other than."

59 "an indication of" — ~ in MS **R**.

60 All witnesses except MSS **Y**, **B** (before emendation), **P**, **L** (before emendation), **M**, **EY** and **AgE** add: "*vayhi* ["*vayhi*" — ~ in MS **G**] *bimei*."

	(Genesis 15:1); "*And it came to pass in the days when the judges judged*" (Ruth 1:1); "*And it came to pass in the days of Ahaz son of Jotham*" (Isaiah 7:1); "*And it came to pass in the days of Jehoiakim the son of Josiah, king of Judah, etc.*" (Jeremiah 1:3); "*And it came to pass in the days of Ahasuerus*" (Esther 1:1).[61]

Yemenite family etc.	Most witnesses
"*And it came to pass in the days of Amraphel*" —they waged war.[62] "*And it came to pass in the days when the judges judged*" —"*that there was a famine.*"[63]	

61 "'*And it came to pass in the days of Amraphel'...'...Ahasuerus*'"— Thus in MSS **G**, **N** and Genizah fragment; MSS **B**, **W**, **Mf**, **V**, **Spanish family** (**HgT** reverses Jehoiakim and Amraphel), **Ashkenazic family**, **Printings**: "'*And it came to pass in the days of Ahasuerus...And it came to pass in the days of Amraphel...And it came to pass in the days when the judges judged...And it came to pass in the days of Ahaz...And it came to pass in the days of Jehoiakim*'"; MS **N**: "'*And it came to pass in the days of Amraphel...And it came to pass in the days when the judges judged...And it came to pass in the days of Ahasuerus...*[*And it came to pass in the days of Ahaz...And it came to pass in the days of Jehoiakim*].'"

62 "they waged war" — MS **V**: "there was a war."

63 "'*that there was a famine*'"—**AgE** and MS **V**: "There was a famine."

"And it came to pass in the days of Ahaz son of Jotham"—"Rezin the king of Aram...went up [to Jerusalem to war against it] (Isaiah 9:11)."[64][65]

And it came to pass in the days of Jehoiakim the son of Josiah, king of Judah, etc." —"*I beheld the earth and, lo, it was waste and void*" (Jeremiah 4:23).[66]

"*And it came to pass in the days of Ahasuerus*"—there was Haman.[67]

Rav Ashi rejects the original formulation of the tradition, substituting for it a more modest version of the rule. It is not every one of the hundreds of instances of *vayhi* that have unfortunate associations, but rather the more unusual *vayhi bimei*, "and it came to pass in the days of," which actually occurs only in the five places listed here, and which can readily be seen to introduce unfortunate situations or developments.[68] Three of the verses (Genesis 14:1, Ruth 1:1, Esther, 1:1),

---

64 **AgE** adds: "And what sorrow was there here?"

65 MSS **G**, **V**, **AgE** and Genizah fragment add: "'*The Arameans on the east, and the Philistines on the west*' (Isaiah 9:11)"; MS **W** adds: "'*And they devour Israel with open mouth*' (Isaiah 9:11)." The citation from Isaiah 9:11 is probably copied from the Palestinian parallels cited below. Those sources introduce a different, aggadic explanation, according to which Ahaz weakened Israel by closing down the religious schools. See Ginzberg, *Legends*, 4:264; 6:360, n. 40; *Genesis rabbah* 63:1.

66 "'*I beheld the earth and , lo, it was waste and void*'" — **AgE**: "The Sanctuary was destroyed and the Holy One wished to return the world to waste and void."

67 "'*And it came to pass in the days of Amraphel*'...Haman" — This section is found here only in MSS **Y**, **G**, **AgE**, **V** and Genizah fragment; ~ in all other witnesses.

68 Unlike the midrashic exegesis of *vay*, *vah*, duplicated names, etc., it is impossible to discern here any specific play on the sound or meaning of "*bimei*" that would justify its association with the idea of sorrow or misfortune. Cf. other midrashic pseudo-

Continued on next page...

already figured in the original statement of the *vayhi* rule, and have been explained above. The two new additions are: Isaiah 7:1, which speaks of the Israelite-Syrian alliance that coalesced against Jerusalem;[69] and Jeremiah 1:3, which effectively foretells the destruction of Jerusalem.[70]

The basic elements of our pericope are also found in a number of Palestinian midrashic sources,[71] where the materials are arranged in a different manner. The structure of the Palestinian pericope is as follows:

> R. Tanḥuma in the name of R. Ḥiyyah the Great; R. Berakhiah in the name of R. Eleazar [Hammodaʿi]:[72] This is a midrash that came to us from the Captivity: Every place in which it says "*and it came to pass in the days of*" refers to trouble.
>
> Said R. Samuel [or: Ishmael][73] bar Naḥman: There are five:[74] [There follows a listing of the five *vayhi bimei* verses, and a discussion of

...Continued from previous page

rules, such as "Says R. Simon: Everywhere where it states '*And it came to pass after* [aḥarei]' [it implies] that the world had returned to its previous state" [*Genesis rabbah*, 62:4 (675), where the sense of "reversion" is actually suggested by the root אחר.

69 The misfortune was of limited extent, consisting merely of the threat itself, since the invasion was ultimately thwarted and turned to a Judean victory, as Isaiah reassures Ahaz in the subsequent verses, and as recounted in 2 Kings 16. As we shall note below, the Palestinian midrashic tradition derives a different lesson from the episode.

70 See Maharsha, who discusses (on the basis of the Palestinian parallels) whether or not a specific "sorrow" verse is being alluded to. The seemingly arbitrary choice of Isaiah 4:23 as the complementary verse is also found in the Palestinian traditions discussed below; note also the expanded version in *Tanḥuma Shemini*, 9, where the episode is developed into a discourse on repentance.

71 The most important passages include: *Genesis rabbah* 41 (42):3 (399–407); *Leviticus rabbah*, 9:1 [Mordecai Margulies, ed., *Midrash wayyikra rabbah* (Jerusalem: Wahrmann, 1972), 228–37]; *Ruth rabbah*, Proems #1; *Esther rabbah*, Proems #11. Additional parallels are listed in Theodor's and Margulies' notes to their respective editions.

72 Thus in *Leviticus rabbah* only.

73 *Leviticus rabbah*, etc. The reading is not necessarily corrupt. An Amora of the same name is mentioned also in manuscripts of *Genesis rabbah*, 51:6 (531); see Theodor's notes, and W. Bacher, *Die Agada der palästinischen Amoräer*, Vol. 1 (Strasbourg:

Continued on next page...

> each[75] beginning:] What trouble was there? [followed by an illustrative parable, and concluding:]...they began crying "*vay*! *vay*!—"*vayhi*: "*And it came to pass in the days of...*"!
>
> Simeon b. Abba in the name of R. Joḥanan: Every place in which it says "*vayhi*" can refer to either trouble or joy. If it is trouble, then there is no trouble like it; if it is joy, then there is no joy like it.
>
> They objected:
>
> [There follows a series of objections from the following verses: Genesis 1:3; Genesis 1:5; Genesis 1:8; Genesis 1:13; Genesis 1:19; Genesis1:23; Genesis 1:31; Genesis 39:2; Leviticus 9:1; Numbers 7:1; Joshua 6:27; 1 Samuel; 18:4; 2 Samuel 7:1;[76] each of which is

...Continued from previous page

1892-99), 484. Cf. J. N. Epstein, *Mavo' lenosaḥ ha-mishnah* (Jerusalem: Magnes Press, 1948), 1191-1202.

[74] This is not the only place where R. Samuel bar Naḥman limits a midrashic generalization to five instances. Cf. *Genesis rabbah*, 30:8 (274) and parallels, where he proposes a similar explanation to R. Levi's rule "Any one concerning whom it says 'was' sees a new world." In that instance of course, as distinct from our current one, there are far more than five "was" verses in the Bible.

[75] On the midrashic treatment of Jeremiah 1:23 see Saul Lieberman, "Roman Legal Institutions in Early Rabbinics and in the Acta Martyrum," *JQR* 35 (1944-45), 1-57; *Idem., Hellenism in Jewish Palestine: Studies in the Literary Transmission, Beliefs and Manners of Palestine in the 1st Century B.C.E.-4th Century C.E.* (New York: The Jewish Theological Seminary of America, 1962), 7 ff.

[76] The resemblances between the lists of proof-texts in the respective Palestinian and Babylonian pericopes suggest that they may have exerted some sort of influence on each other (verses which are cited in the midrashim as objections followed by their justifications are treated in the Bavli as simple "sorrow" verses), whether in the redaction or in the later manuscript traditions, as reflected in the major divergences between the readings in MS **Y** and other witnesses. It is however difficult to discern any consistent pattern. If we exclude the five "*vayhi bimei*" verses, we are left with only three verses which are cited in the Palestinian midrashim but are absent from one or both of the Babylonian traditions: Genesis 1:3; 39:2 (only in MS **Y**, etc.) and Numbers 7:1 (not in any text of *TB*). On the other hand, there are several verses found in the Babylonian Esther-Midrash which are not cited in the Palestinian texts. Of these four (Genesis 6:1; 1 Samuel 1:1; 8:1; 1 Kings 6:1) are common to both Babylonian traditions, whereas the others are found in only one or the other of the Babylonian families (in MS **Y**: Genesis 11:2; 27:1; 39:2; Judges 13:2. In the majority tradition: Genesis 29:10; Joshua 5:13). This situation would seem to preclude any likelihood that one of the Babylonian textual traditions had been "filled in" in any systematic way on the basis of one of the Palestinian midrashic parallels. Even in those verses which are

Continued on next page...

refuted by R. Simeon b. Abba with an argument that "this was not [true] joy, because...[of some imperfection attached to the occasion].

It is worth summarizing some of the more significant differences between these related traditions:[77]

In the Palestinian midrashic collections, there is appended to each of the "*vayhi bimei*" verses a long and elaborate midrash beginning with the formula "What sorrow was there then?" Then a parable is adduced, leading up to the conclusion "As soon as they saw this, they all began to cry '*vay!*' '*Vayhi*'"—It was 'woe' that there was (*vay shehayah*) in the days of..." Not only is the resulting pericope much more sophisticated and symmetrically crafted, but the midrashic elaboration of the respective biblical episodes results in significant alterations of their thematic content, which does not focus on the events as described in Scripture, but rather on a variety of homiletical motifs that were introduced by the midrashic process.[78]

After expounding all five "*vayhi bimei*" verses, these midrashim all go on to adduce the dictum of Simeon bar Abba in the name of R. Joḥanan: "Every place in which it says '*vayhi*' [indicates] sorrow and joy...R. Samuel bar Naḥman came and made a distinction: Every place in which it says '*vayhi*' [indicates] sorrow; every place in which it says

...Continued from previous page

cited by all the traditions, the formulation is usually so substantially different as to rule out any copying.

77 Cf. the overview of Jacob Neusner, *The Midrashic Compilations of the Sixth and Seventh Centuries: An Introduction to the Rhetorical, Logical and Topical Program*, Vol. 2, Brown Judaic Studies, ed. J. Neusner *et al.* (Atlanta: Scholars Press, 1989), 24-31.

78 Several of these passages reflect topics which were undoubtedly of practical concern in contemporary congregations and communities. Thus in the hands of the homilists, the War of the Four and the Five Kings (Genesis 14:1 ff.) is transformed into a personal campaign waged by the forces of heathenism against Abraham and his faith (see Ginzberg, *Legends*, 1:230); the attack against Ahaz in Isaiah 7:1 turns into a discourse on the need for schools of Torah (Ginzberg, 4:264, 6:360, n. 40); Ruth 1:1 is developed into a lesson on the proper respect for judicial authority (Ginzberg, 4:30, 6:187, n. 32); etc.. This tendency to introduce extra-scriptural midrashic motifs is required in order to refute the more obviously non-sorrowful meanings of several of the unadorned proof-texts.

'*vehayah*' [indicates] joy." At this point, objections are raised (as in the Bavli) from various "*vayhi*" verses whose simple meanings indicate joy. Here however, they succeed in fending off all the objections.[79] The midrash concludes: "They say to him: We have said ours. Now say yours." This provides the homilist with an opportunity to cite a series of verses[80] in which "*vehayah*" indicates joy, drawing the midrash to a conclusion of messianic consolation:

> ...They objected: "*And he was there* [vehayah] *when Jerusalem was taken*" (Jeremiah 38:28)!
>
> He said to them: This too is not a sorrow, because Israel thereby received a pardon[81] for their sins.
>
> For R. Samuel bar Naḥman says: Israel received a compete pardon for their sins on the day when the Temple was destroyed. This is what is written: "*The punishment of thine iniquity is accomplished, O daughter of Zion; he will no more carry thee away into captivity*" (Lamentations 4:22).

In contrast to the Palestinian versions, which preserve features that are appropriate to the *Sitz im Leben* of the synagogue sermon,[82] whether in their criticisms of the community's religious standards or in their striving to conclude on an inspiring note of consolation, the Babylonian Esther Midrash is noticeably lacking in any of these homiletical elements, and appears to have restricted itself to the recording of comments that bear directly on the meaning of the biblical texts. As long as we do not know with precision what sources were available to the redactors of our Babylonian pericope, it would be premature to draw any far-reaching conclusions from this fact.[83] We can

---

[79] Cf. the similarly structured pericopes in *Genesis rabbah*, 30:4 (271) and 38:12 (361), etc.

[80] For a review of the variations in the lists of verses see Theodor's notes, 407.

[81] ἀποχή; see Samuel Krauss, *Griechische und lateinische Lehnwörter im Talmud, Midrasch und Targum* (Berlin: 1899), 100.

[82] See Joseph Heinemann, *Derashot betzibbur bitequfat ha-talmud.*

[83] The detailed explanations of the five "*vayhi bimei*" verses in the Palestinian midrashim, with their elaborate use of parables and concluding formula, would appear

Continued on next page...

however note that such differences between the Babylonian and Palestinian collections will recur often in the course of the present study.

As regards the general structure of the two traditions, they are of course very different in the manner in which they organize the material. In the Bavli, the "*vayhi bimei*=sorrow" position is not adduced until the conclusion of the discussion, only after the Talmud has been forced, in the face of the numerous objections, to reject the version that spoke of "*vayhi*" alone indicating sorrow.

The comparison between the Palestinian and Babylonian traditions invites the following question: Was Rav Ashi actually familiar with the earlier Palestinian tradition regarding "*vayhi bimei*" and yet he intentionally ignored its existence in order to allow the construction of a pericope in which that view could be brought at the end, as the only acceptable reading of the R. Levi's tradition? Though the state of the evidence does not permit us to give a clear answer to that question, the fundamental structural difference between the two *sugyot* is at any rate quite clear: In the Babylonian version, the "*vayhi* =sorrow" position is rejected in favor of the "*vayhi bimei*=sorrow" position; whereas in the Palestinian midrashim the two versions are set against each other as the rabbis labor—through the use of hairsplitting dialectics that we might otherwise have characterized as 'typically" Babylonian—to defend the "*vayhi* =sorrow" position.[84] In the face of our ignorance of the sources that were available to the redactor of the Babylonian pericope (or Rav Ashi), it is impossible to fully evaluate or appreciate his aims or contributions to the structure of the current passage.

...Continued from previous page

to belong to the later redactional strata, and hence are unlikely to have been known to the redactors of the Babylonian Esther Midrash.

[84] J. Heinemann, *Aggadah and Its Development*, 169, recognizes this passage as an exception to the general rule that Palestinian sources (unlike their Babylonian counterparts) do not raise objections against aggadic traditions.

Amoz and Amaziah Were Brothers

The Talmud proceeds to cite a second aggadic dictum in the name of the same tradent(s),[85] introduced by a similar formula indicating its antiquity:

> [10b] And says R. Levi:[86] This matter is a tradition in our hands from our ancestors:[87] Amoz and Amaziah were brothers.[88]

The reference is to Amoz the father of the prophet Isaiah[89] and to Amaziah son of Joash, king of Judah.[90] Though there is of course no scriptural basis for the assertion, from a chronological perspective this would not be impossible, since Isaiah is reported (Isaiah 1:1) to have been active "*in the days of Uzziah, Jotham, Ahaz, and Hezekiah, kings of Judah.*" Since Uzziah is the same as Azariah, son of Amaziah, we may presume that the fathers of the king and the prophet were contemporaries.[91]

Rabbi Levi's tradition is also found in the Tannaitic *Seder ʿolam*[92]

> In the time of Amaziah, "*there came a man of God to him*, etc." (2 Chronicles 25:7). Lastly he said to him: "*I know that God hath*

---

[85] See variants listed below.

[86] MSS **G**, **N**, **Spanish family** and Genizah fragment add: "and if you should prefer: R. Jonathan ["Jonathan"—MSS **O** and **P**: "Nathan"]."

[87] "from our ancestors" — ~ in some Ashkenazic witnesses.

[88] "were brothers" —Hebrew in MSS **Y**, **N**, **AgE**, **MhG** and Genizah fragment. Others witnesses formulate it in Aramaic.

[89] The name appears in the Bible exclusively as Isaiah's patronymic.

[90] His reign is described principally in 2 Kings 14:1-16, 2 Chronicles 25.

[91] For the chronology of the later Judean rulers see: M. Cogan and H. Tadmor, eds., *II Kings*, The Anchor Bible (Garden City: Doubleday, 1988), 11-12; with a review of chronological difficulties in dating Amaziah's reign on p. 154. Amaziah's dates are given as 798-69 B.C.E. and Isaiah (I)'s as 745-81.

[92] Ch. 20; B. Ratner, ed., *Midrash seder olam*, S.K. Mirsky ed. (New York: Moznaim, 1988), 86; Chaim Milikowsky, "Seder Olam: A Rabbinic Chronology," Ph.D., Yale University, 1981, 351, 508.

> *determined to destroy thee*, etc." (25:16). It is said that this was Amoz his brother.

Although R. Levi's statement is chronologically possible, and may in fact derive from an old exegetical tradition, this does not in itself constitute sufficient midrashic grounds for making such an assertion. By midrashic standards there should be a practical point to a rabbinic dictum, beyond the mere clarification of past events.[93] And this is the challenge that is raised by the Talmud immediately:

> [10b] What does this teach us?[94]
>
> —Like this {dictum} of R. Samuel bar Naḥmani.[95]
>
> For R. Samuel bar Naḥmani[96] says: R. Joḥanan[97] says:[98] Every bride who is modest in her father-in-law's house is worthy that kings and prophets should issue from her.
>
> Whence do we know this? —From Tamar.[99]
>
> For it is written: "*And Judah saw her and he thought her to be a harlot, for she had covered her face*" (Genesis 38:15).
>
> Because she had covered her face "*he thought her to be a harlot*"!

---

93 On the rabbinic lack of concern for one-time historical events, as distinct from the eternal truths which were to be learned from these events, see Isaac Heinemann, *Darkhei ha-'aggadah*, 5-7, 11, 122, 177; Joseph Heinemann, *Aggadah and Its Development*, 11–12. The classic expression of this attitude in the Babylonian Talmud is the phrase " מאי דהוה הוה ": "What happened happened!"

94 "What...us" — MS **O**: "This teaches us"; MS **V**: "What."

95 "Naḥmani" —MS **R**: "Rav Isaac."

96 "For...Naḥmani" —only in MS **Y**, **AgE** and **MhG**.

97 "Joḥanan" — Only in MS **Y**; in all other witnesses: "Jonathan."

98 "R. Joḥanan says"— ~ in MS **R** and **EY**.

99 "From Tamar" — ~ in MS **N**.

—And[100] says R. Eleazar:[101] That[102] she covered her face in her father-in-law's house,[103] she was worthy[104] that[105] kings and prophets should issue from her.[106] [107]

"Kings" from where? [108]—From David.[109]

"Prophets"[110] from where?[111]

—As[112] says R. Levi:[113] [114] Amoz and Amaziah were brothers.[115]

---

100 "And" —Only in MSS **Y**, **N**, **R**, **MhG**; MS **V**: "Because" (reading doubtful); all other witnesses read: "Rather."

101 "says R. Eleazar"— ~ in **Printings**.

102 "That" — MSS **G**, **B**, **EY**, **Printings**, Genizah fragment: "Because"; MSS **N**, **L**, **Mf**, **R**, **V**, **YS**: "This teaches that."

103 **Printings** add: "and he did not recognize her."

104 "she was worthy" —only in **Yemenite family**; MS **B**:"and now she revealed it; "others: "therefore."

105 "She was worthy and" —MS **L**, **EY**, **HgT**: "for this reason."

106 "she was worthy...from her" — ~ in MSS **N***, **O**, **R**, **P**, **YS**, **AgE**; MS **B**: "and now she uncovered it."

107 "that kings...from her" — MS **G**: "Kings and prophets."

108 "'Kings' from where?"—MSS **N**, **B**, **R**, **P**, **Mf**, **YS**: "Whence 'kings'?"; MSS **O**, **L**, **M**, **V**, **EY**, **HgT**, **Printings**, "'Kings.'"

109 "From David" —in MSS **G**, **R***: "From Amaziah."

110 "Prophets" — MSS **L**, **P**, **Mf**, **V**, **EY**, **YS**, **AgE**: "And prophets."

111 "from where" — Only in MS **Y** and Genizah fragment; MSS **B**, **L**, **V**, **Spanish family**, **YS**, "From Amoz"; MS **R**: "From Amoz (and Amaziah)"; MSS **B**, **Mf** and Genizah fragment: "From Amoz and Amaziah"; MS **M**: "from Isaiah."

112 "As" — MS **N***: "From what"; MSS **R** and **Mf**: "And."

113 **MhG** and **AgE** add: "since the Master said."

114 MSS **L**, **M**, **V**, **Spanish family**, **Printings**, Genizah fragment add: "This matter is a tradition in our hands from our ancestors ["from our ancestors" — ~ in MS **Mf**]."

115 "were brothers" —Hebrew in MS **Y**, **N**, **AgE**, **MhG** and **Printings**; other witnesses formulate it in Aramaic.

> And[116] it is written: *"The vision of Isaiah son of Amoz, which he saw…"* (Isaiah 1:1).[117]

The Talmud justifies R. Levi's dictum by noting that it helps to corroborate R. Samuel bar Naḥman's homiletical reading of the rewards for Tamar's modesty. In a rather roundabout way it establishes that Isaiah was related to the Judean royal house[118] and hence, like them, was counted among the progeny of Judah and Tamar.[119] This serves as an effective homiletical incentive for modest behavior.

The pericope as found before us is assembled from a number of separate components, including: (1) R. Levi's dictum; (2) R. Eleazar's homily on Genesis: 38:15; (3) R. Samuel bar Naḥman's use of (1) to explain (2).[120] We should note that the structure is a circular one since R. Levi's statement, which forms the basis of the original question, is ultimately quoted again as part of the solution. This is due to the fact that our passage is citing an existing exegetical pericope from *TB Soṭah* 10b, which starts out from the verse in Genesis.[121]

In spite of the claims of the Talmud and R. Samuel bar Naḥman we cannot take it for granted that the traditions concerning

---

116 "And" — MSS **B**, **L**, **HgT**: ~.

117 "And it is… '…*saw*"— ~ in MS **M**. **EY** adds: "'*which he saw*' and wherever a prophet is identified by his father's name, it is an accepted premise that his father was prophet like himself."

118 Much of the midrashic treatment of the Judah and Tamar episode is concerned with the birth of Perez, seen as the ancestor of the House of David, and hence the precursor of the Messiah; see Ginzberg, *Legends*, 5:336, n. 92. In the current passage, the connection to David is barely mentioned, perhaps because it is so obvious.

119 See Rashi here and to *TB Soṭah* 10b. Maharsha correctly raises the point that David and Solomon, also among Tamar's descendants, are enumerated among the ranks of prophets as well, making it unnecessary to introduce Amoz into the discussion.

120 These three Palestinian *Amora'im* were roughly contemporary; see Ch. Albeck, *Introduction to the Talmud, Babli and Yerushalmi* (Tel-Aviv: Dvir, 1969), 224-7, 256, 266. See also *TP Sanhedrin* 3:13 (21d).

121 For enlightening textual notes and references to medieval commentaries see Liss, Abraham, ed., *The Babylonian Talmud with Variant Readings…: Tractate Sotah*, Vol. 1 (Jerusalem: Institute for the Complete Israeli Talmud, 1977), 239-40.

Amoz/Amaziah and Tamar were originally interdependent. The very fact that they are attributed to different rabbis calls that claim into question. Though midrashic tradition does not supply us with a better justification for R. Levi's dictum,[122] there are observations on Tamar's covering her face which serve to demonstrate that this detail was used for very different homiletical ends from those of our pericope. Note for instance the following passage from *Genesis rabbah*, 85:8:[123]

> "*When Judah saw her*, etc."— Says R. Aḥa:[124] A man should familiarize himself with his wife's sister and to his female relations. Why? —In order that he should not stumble with regard to one of them. And from whom do you learn this? —From Judah: "*When Judah saw her, he thought her to be a harlot; because she had covered her face*." He said: If she were a harlot, would she have covered her face!

This passage builds upon the same anomaly in the story, namely the fact that the covering of Tamar's face would seem to be an unlikely practice for a harlot. Whereas R. Eleazar arrives at the clever solution that Tamar covered her face not while posing as a harlot, but previously while at home, R. Aḥa accepts the obvious sense of the verse, understanding that Tamar disguised herself not to make herself look more like a harlot, but merely to avoid being recognized.[125] The lesson to be learned from the story is diametrically opposite: For R. Eleazar, approaching it with an emphasis on Tamar's behavior, it teaches us an admirable lesson in domestic modesty; whereas R. Aḥa, focusing on

---

122 On purely hermeneutical grounds we may point to the similarity of the names, and the widespread midrashic tendency to identify minor characters. None of these considerations, however, appears sufficient to account for the ceremonious introduction of R. Levi's dictum as an ancient tradition.

123 Pp. 1041-2.

124 On his identity see Albeck's notes.

125 See Maharsha to *TB Soṭah* 10b. Rashi in an alternative explanation in **EY** to *Soṭah*, and in his commentary on the Pentateuch explains otherwise: Since Tamar had demonstrated such modesty in her home, Judah did not suspect her (*in spite of the fact* that she now veiled her face in an un-harlot-like manner). See Liss's edition of *TB Soṭah*, p. 129.

Judah's mistake, deduces that excessive modesty in the home can lead to potentially fatal errors.

In spite of these basic differences, it is clear that R. Eleazar's exegesis, which builds upon the lack of contact between Judah and Tamar prior to the incident on the road to Timnath, would have fit at least as well into the homiletical purposes of the *Genesis rabbah* passage. This raises the likelihood that the dictum did in actuality originate in some such context,[126] where the concern was for explaining the Judah and Tamar story without any reference to Tamar's descendants.[127] In its current form in *TB Megillah*, however, the allusion to kings and prophets is explicitly attributed to R. Eleazar.

The Place of the Ark

The Talmud now proceeds to cite its third ancient tradition, on a completely unrelated topic.

> [10b] And says R. Levi—and if you should say: R. Jonathan:[128]
>
> This matter is a tradition in our hands from the Men of the Great Assembly:[129]
>
> The place of the ark is also[130] not included in the measurement.[131]

---

[126] As we do in fact find in *Tanḥuma* (Buber) [Solomon Buber, ed., *Midrash Tanḥuma*, Vilna: 1885), *Vayyeshev*, 17], where R. Eleazar's explanation of the covering of Tamar's face (cited there in R. Joḥanan's name) is grafted on to R. Aḥa's conclusion: "For this reason our rabbis have said: A man should be familiar with his daughter-in-law."

[127] A different connection between Tamar's wearing a veil and her bearing children is observed in the previous paragraph of *Genesis rabbah*, (85:14, p. 1040); also in *Tanḥuma* (Buber), *ibid.*: "There were two women who covered themselves with veils and gave birth to twins: Rebecca and Tamar..."

[128] "and if ... Jonathan" — ~ in MS **N**, **V**, **Mf**, **Ashkenazic family**, **Printings**, **AgE**; **Spanish family**: "and if...Rav Pappi [**HgT**: "Pippi"]."

[129] "from...Assembly" —Thus only in MS **Y** and Genizah fragment; in all other witnesses: "from our fathers."

[130] "also"—Thus only in MS **Y**; as an Aramaic word in an otherwise Hebrew sentence, it is presumably an error.

[131] "measurement"—MS **G**: "count."

Since it is says: "*And in front of the Sanctuary was twenty cubits in length and twenty cubits in breadth and twenty cubits in the height thereof*" (1 Kings 6:20).[132]

And[133] it was also taught thus[134] {in a *baraita*}: The ark which Moses[135] fashioned has[136] ten cubits[137] in every direction.[138][139][140][141][142]

Where was the ark itself standing?

—Hear[143] from this: It was standing miraculously.[144]

The measurements of the Ark of the Covenant are, according to Exodus 25:10, "*two cubits and a half...the length thereof, and a cubit and a half...the breadth thereof, and a cubit and a half the height thereof.*" It was to be set in the Holy of Holies both during the period when the Tabernacle was in use (Exodus 26:34) and later in Solomon's

---

132 "since it...thereof"—only in MSS **Y** and **G**; ~ in all other witnesses.

133 "And" — ~ in MSS **G**, **N** (before emendation), Genizah fragment.

134 "And it...thus"— MSS **G**, Genizah fragment read: "It was taught."

135 "Moses" —**HgT**: "Solomon."

136 "has" — ~ in MS **M** (and added in emendation).

137 Some texts add: "space."

138 **HgT** adds: "as it is written: '*And the house, that is, the temple before it, was forty cubits long*'" (1 Kings 6:17).

139 MS **L**, **HgT** and Genizah fragment add: "and ["as" —Genizah fragment] it is written: '*And he prepared the Sanctuary in the midst of the house within, to set there the ark of the covenant of the Lord*'" (1 Kings 6:19).

140 All MSS except MSS **Y** and **G** add: "And [MSS **M**, **V**: "As"] it is written: '*And before the Sanctuary which was twenty cubits in length, and twenty cubits in breadth, and twenty cubits in the height thereof, overlaid with pure gold*'" (1 Kings 6:20).

141 "Where was the ark itself?"—**Spanish family** adds: "set"; **Ashkenazic family** adds: "standing."

142 **Printings** add: "And it is written: '*and ten* [sic] *cubits was the one wing of the cherub, and ten* [sic] *cubits the other wing of the cherub*'" (cf. 1 Kings 6:24).

143 "Hear"— **Spanish** and **Ashkenazic families**: "Rather, hear."

144 MSS **L**, **Mf** and **HgT** add: "{Indeed}, hear from this."

Temple (1 Kings 8:6). This is the section known as the "*devir*" (Sanctuary), described in 1 Kings 6:20[145] as a twenty-cubit cube.[146]

The information contained in the biblical passages does not by itself present any difficulties or contradictions. What is perceived by our talmudic section as problematic[147] is the *baraita* which speaks as it were of the ark having ten cubits in each direction; understood to mean that there were ten cubits of *unfilled space* in each direction, which of course implies that the ark itself did not occupy any measurable space! We have here a remarkable sort of miracle involving an overruling of the laws of geometry.[148]

---

145 Cf. S. Wilman, ed., *Tosefot ha-rosh ha-shalem* (Tel-Aviv: 1971): "...We do not read there [in the texts of *Bava batra*; see below] '*And in front of the Sanctuary...*' And it would appear that here too we should not read it." He argues that the verse is necessary to establish the height of the Sanctuary in the *Bava batra* passage, but is not necessary here in *Megillah*. This is a very strange assertion since the verse is equally necessary here, as our source for its twenty-cubit breadth, without which the "miracle" makes no sense. Rashbam, "R. Gershom," R. Meir Abulafia and other commentators to *Bava batra* all introduce the verse into that discussion, on the understanding that without it there is no basis for the Talmud's reasoning. It is possible that the *Tosefot ha-rosh* was referring not to verse 6:20, but to some other verse which had found its way into the *Megillah* texts, such as 6:24 (cited [incorrectly] in the **Printings**): "*And [five] cubits was the one wing of the cherub*, etc.," a verse which connects to the following pericope in *Bava batra*, but not to *Megillah* [as was recognized by R. Arieh b. Asher, *Ṭurei Even*, Vol. *Megillah* (Vilna: 1836)]. As we see in the above textual notes, in spite of the great confusion in the ordering of the material 1 Kings 6:20 is cited in all the witnesses, whether before or after the *baraita*.

146 For further details see: S. Z. Zevin, *Talmudic Encyclopedia*, fifth ed., Vol. 2, ed. J. Hutner (Jerusalem: Talmudic Encyclopedia Foundation, 1979), 174-9.

147 The wording of MS **Y**, in which the *baraita* appears to be cited in *support* of the verse, is difficult. Perhaps the introductory formula was meant to apply to the entire subsequent discussion, but this would be an inappropriate use of the terminology. See *Ṭurei even*.

148 Cf. Maharsha to *Bava batra* 99a: "They are not included in the measurement because the *Shekhinah* rests there... and they are not made of physical substance, and not contained by space or measurement." The nature of the miracle perceived by the Talmud is not clearly defined. It might presumably mean that the ark was hovering in the air, while the measurement was taken from the floor. A similar usage is implied in the dictum "the *mem* and *samekh* in the tablets were standing miraculously" (*TB Megillah* 2b; *TB Shabbat* 104a). An object's not occupying space is characterized as a

Continued on next page...

This strange reasoning demands that we direct our attention to the *baraita* that gave rise to the perceived difficulty. A similar tradition is contained in the *Baraita dimelekhet hammishkan* Chapter 7:[149]

> The ark was placed inside the Temple, with ten cubits on each side of it.

This brief passage is much more modest in its claims than the talmudic versions, making no references to miracles or mathematical difficulties. It is not unlikely that its author was speaking in round numbers without wishing to put too fine a point on the issue.[150] It is nonetheless easy to understand how the rabbis, accustomed to dealing with texts that were formulated with exacting precision, might have read such a statement in its most literal sense, as implying that there were ten cubits aside from the ark itself.

...Continued from previous page

miracle in the discussion on the wing-spans of Solomon's cherubs in *TB Bava batra* 99a (see below), which is attached there to our own passage ("Says Rabinai: Says Samuel: The cherubs stood miraculously"), as well as in the traditions about how the Temple never became crowded in spite of the throngs of people, found in Mishnah *Avot* 5:5 (a source which is linked to out pericope in *TB Yoma* 21a). See also Ginzberg, *Legends*, 6:64, n. 330. It seems most likely that the "miracle" interpretation of the ark measurements is a later development (unknown in the *TP* version, see below) which crept in under the influence of the *Bava batra* parallel. Cf. the criticism leveled by Galen against the Jewish reluctance to recognize any act as impossible by its nature, cited in Urbach, *The Sages*, 119 (and 730, n. 64).

149 The work has been published in a number of different editions, including the Venice 1602 printing (as an appendix to Hai *Ga'on*'s *Mishpeṭei shevuʿot*); Vilna 1902 edition (with Buber's *Aggadat bereshit*); in Adolph Jellinek, ed., *Bet ha-Midrasch* (Jerusalem: Wahrmann, Reprint:1967), 3:144-54 [our quote is on 149]; ed. M. Friedmann (Vienna, 1908); and in J. D. Eisenstein, ed., *Ozar Midrashim: Bibliotheca Midraschica*, reprint ed. ([Israel]: 1969), 298-304 [our quote on 301]. Whether or not it is a true *baraita*, the passage in question strikes us as a source independent of the Talmud. On the dating of the work see: L. Zunz, *Die gottesdienstlichen Vorträge der Juden historisch entwickelt (Ha-derashot beyisra'el)*, translated by Ch. Albeck (Jerusalem: Mosad Bialik, 1974), 43 and 26, n. 13; Friedmann's introduction.

150 This possibility has a greater likelihood with respect to the width of the ark, which involves subtracting less than a cubit on each side, than with respect to its length, where a discrepancy of a cubit and a quarter (1/8 of the total) is harder to pass off as a rounding-off of the number.

A pericope from elsewhere in Talmud suggests another route through which the Talmud might have arrived at its surprising conclusion. The following is found in *TB Bava batra* 98b-99a:[151]

> Rabbi Ḥanina went out to the villages. They would throw together contradictory verses for him.
>
> It is written: "*And the house which king Solomon built for the Lord, the length thereof was threescore cubits, and the breadth thereof twenty cubits, and the height thereof thirty cubits*" (1 Kings 6:2).
>
> And it is also written: "*And in front of the Sanctuary was twenty cubits in length and twenty cubits in breadth and twenty cubits in the height thereof.*"
>
> He said to them: What it is measuring is from the edge of the cherubs upwards.
>
> What does this come to teach us?
>
> —That above is like below: Just as above[152] there is nothing in the way, so too below[153] there is nothing in the way.
>
> [154]For says R. Levi—and if you should say: R. Joḥanan: This matter is a tradition in our hands from the Men of the Great Assembly: The place of the ark is also not included in the measurement.
>
> And[155] it was also taught thus {in a *baraita*}:
>
> The ark which Moses fashioned has ten cubits in every direction.

R. Ḥanina is trying to resolve an apparent discrepancy between two verses, one of which measures the height of the Temple at thirty cubits, while the other speaks of the *devir* as being only twenty cubits

---

[151] Cited according to L. Goldschmidt, ed., *The Babylonian Talmud Seder Nezikin Codex Hambourg 165 (19)*, reprint of Berlin 1914 ed. (Jerusalem: Makor, 1969). Cf. *Diqduqé soferim ad loc.*

[152] I.e., from the top of the ark and upward to the ceiling.

[153] I.e., from the sides of the ark to the wall.

[154] Most witnesses add: "This supports R. Levi."

[155] "And" — ~ in MSS **G**, **N** (before emendation), Genizah fragment.

high.[156] He reconciles the contradictory texts by stating that both structures were in fact thirty feet high, but that the *devir* was being measured not from the floor, but from the top of the Cherubs of the ark, which extended to a height of ten cubits. The Talmud then concludes that in employing this unusual manner of measurement,[157] Scripture was trying to draw an analogy to the twenty-cubit measurement of the *breadth* of the Holy of Holies; i.e., that it is referring to empty space, exclusive of the ark itself, and sees this as equivalent to R. Levi's dictum and to the *baraita* which speaks of ten cubits on each side.

There is no certainty that R. Ḥanina's explanation accurately reconstructs the deductive process that underlies the *baraita* or R. Levi's tradition. Nor for that matter is the point of his explanation an obvious one. It could be taken as a mere technical note about the use of measurements in the respective verses,[158] or—as our pericope has it—the appreciation of its miraculous nature.[159] The perception that the

---

156 The commentators to this verse dealt with the difficulty in a variety of ways. Rashi was satisfied to accept that the ceiling of the Holy of Holies was simply lower than the rest of the structure; cf. *Tosafot*, who glibly observe that Rashi had not paid attention to the talmudic discussion (!). Qimḥi argues that the verse is only speaking of the portion that was overlaid with gold (as described in the following verse).

157 Rashbam: "Why did it have to measure it in this way, from the edge of the cherubs upwards? It ought to have merely written: 'and thirty cubits in the height thereof'!"

158 This would at any rate invite the objection: Why do we ignore the ark in the horizontal measurements, but not in the vertical ones?

159 This particular is not found in the *Bava Batra* pericope, though a similar "miracle" is discerned with respect to the measurements of the Cherubs' wings in the following passage there. A lengthy series of objections to that assertion is raised by several Babylonian *Amora'im*. It is likely that the redactor of the *Megillah* pericope was influenced by that context.

Note as well the aggadic traditions about Solomon's attempts to pass his enlarged ark through the gates of the Temple (e.g., *Exodus rabbah*, 8:1 and parallels cited by Shinan, 198): "He fashioned an ark of ten cubits into which he placed the first one and carried it. Upon reaching the entrance to the Temple, the entrance itself was ten cubits and the ark was ten cubits, and ten cubits cannot enter through ten..." The commentators express their surprise that there does not seem to be any textual basis for the construction of a second ark (see *Yefeh to'ar*).

Continued on next page...

positioning of the ark—like that of the cherubs—was a miracle is also accepted by the anonymous objector in *TB Yoma* 21a, who wishes to have the positioning of the ark and cherubs included in the Mishnah's (*Avot* 5:5) list of miracles that transpired in the Temple.

An interesting variant on these Babylonian traditions is recorded in *TP Bava batra* 6:2 (15c):[160]

> Says R. Tanḥuma: I am in possession of an aggadic tradition to the effect that the place of the *devir* is not included in the measurement.
>
> Says R. Levi: Nor is the place of the ark included in the measurement.
>
> And so does it teach in the name of R. Judah bar Lʿai: The ark would stand in the middle of the Temple, dividing the Temple into ten cubits in each direction.

The Palestinian tradition of R. Tanḥuma is introduced in terms that resemble those of R. Levi's dictum in *TB*. R. Levi in the Yerushalmi is not transmitting a separate tradition, but adding to R. Tanḥuma's. Neither of these statements speaks of a miracle, but merely point out that according to the convention adopted by the *baraita* the dimensions of the ark are ignored when measuring the distance between it and the walls.

...Continued from previous page

Cf. the various midrashic passages on "the small containing the large" [המועט מחזיק את המרובה]: *Genesis rabbah*, 5:7 (36), *Exodus rabbah*, 11:4 (241), *Leviticus rabbah*, 10:9 (215), *Tanḥuma Va'era*, 14, *Mishnat rabbi eliʿezer* (ed. Enelow, New York, 1934), 207, etc. The examples adduced there seem to refer to miraculous "compression" of the objects in question rather than to an alteration of the laws of geometry as in our current passage.

160 E. S. Rosenthal and S. Lieberman, eds., *Yerushalmi Neziqin*, Texts and Studies in Rabbinic Literature (Jerusalem: Israel Academy of Sciences and Humanities: Section of Humanities; The Institute for Advanced Studies, The Hebrew University of Jerusalem; The American Academy for Jewish Research, 1983), 96-7, and Lieberman's notes on 208. The passage is preceded by a parallel to the *TB Bava batra* passage, involving Rav Hamnuna the Scribe, R. Ḥaninah, R. Jeremiah and R. Abbahu. While the solution is clearly the same as that in the *TB* pericope, the meaning of the narrative framework is obscured by textual and linguistic difficulties.

Concluding Remarks

The passage that linked the Esther-Midrash to the talmudic material of *TB Megillah* is built around three dicta cited in the name of "R. Levi, and if you should say: R. Jonathan":

> 1) This matter is a tradition in our hands from the Men of the Great Assembly: Every place in which it says "*and it came to pass*" is none other than a reference to sorrow;
>
> 2) This matter is a tradition in our hands from our ancestors: Amoz and Amaziah were brothers;
>
> 3) This matter is a tradition in our hands from the Men of the Great Assembly: The place of the ark is not included in the measurement.

All three of these traditions were expanded and discussed in the normal talmudic manner; in the case of the latter two traditions the redactors appeared to be drawing to a considerable extent upon material found elsewhere in the Babylonian Talmud.[161] Only the first of these traditions relates to the subject-matter of the tractate, and indeed it is also found at the beginning of *Esther rabbah*, Proem #11 (and parallels). We have noted at length how the basic dicta related to the first tradition were developed in different ways by the redactors of the respective collections.

We do not find these three dicta appearing as a collection in any of the Palestinian parallels, nor do they demonstrate any discernibly common features, other than their introductory formulæ. In *Esther rabbah* the first passage constitutes a pivotal moment in the progression of the proem section, since each of the proems concludes with the formula "As soon as they saw this, they all began to cry '*vay*!' '*Vayhi*'—It was 'woe' that there was (*vay shehayah*) in the days of Ahasuerus." In the Bavli, on the other hand, R. Levi's dictum does not connect directly to the proem collection, but is interrupted by the other two sub-peri-

---

[161] For #2: from *TB Soṭah* 10b on the story of Judah and Tamar; for #3 from *TB Bava batra* 99a.

copes. At any rate, the connection to Esther is not pronounced in the Talmud's presentation of the *vayhi* tradition.

Chapter Two

The Proems[1]

In addition to furnishing us with a unique opportunity to investigate the functions of the *petiḥtot*[2] as they were perceived in Babylonia, the current passage also allows us to conduct comparisons with parallel material in the Palestinian aggadic midrashic collections. As we shall see, what we encounter here is not primarily native Babylonian aggadah (since most of the material that appears here is attributed to Palestinian

---

1 Much of the material in the current chapter was originally published in Hebrew, in somewhat different form, as Eliezer Segal, "The *Petiḥta* (Proem) in Babylonia," *Tarbiẓ* 54 (2 1985), 177-204.

2 In Joseph Heinemann's seminal article "The Proem in the Aggadic Midrashim: A Form-Critical Study" can be found bibliographical references to earlier studies of the midrashic proems, including the various Hebrew articles from which the English one was compiled. See also Mayer Lerner, *Anlage und Quellen des Bereschit Rabba* (Berlin: 1882); Some subsequent studies are listed by Avigdor Shinan, "Letorat hapetihta," *Jerusalem Studies in Hebrew Literature* 1 (1981), 133 n. 2 [see also *Idem.*, ed., *Midrash Shemot Rabbah Chapters I-XIV* (Jerusalem and Tel-Aviv: Dvir, 1984), 14-6]; Marc Bregman, "Circular Proems and Proems Beginning with the Formula '*Zo hi shene'emra beruaḥ haq-qodesh*,'" in *Studies in Aggadah, Targum and Jewish Liturgy in Memory of Joseph Heinemann*, ed. J. Petuchowski and E. Fleischer, 34-51 [Hebrew section] (Jerusalem: The Magnes Press and Hebrew Union College Press, 1981), 34 n. 1; Harry Fox, "The Circular Proem Composition: Terminology and Antecedents," *PAAJR* 49 (1982), 1-33; Martin S. Jaffee, "The 'Midrashic' Proem: Towards the Description of Rabbinic Exegesis," in *Approaches to Ancient Judaism*, ed. William Scott Green, 95–112, 4: Studies in Liturgy, Exegesis, and Talmudic Narrative (Chico: Scholars Press, 1983); David Stern, "Midrash and the Language of Exegesis: A Study of Vayikra Rabbah, Chapter 1," 105–24; H. Basser, "Pesher Hadavar: The Truth of the Matter," *Revue de Qumran* 13 (1988), 389-8 (especially 396-8).

sages), so much as the reworking of aggadic sources at the hands of Babylonian Talmud.

The midrash apparently contains fourteen proems, as indicated in a mnemonic *siman* found in MS Columbia, *Aggadat esther* and Genizah fragment.[3]

> [10b] Jonathan[4] Rose Instead of Samuel. Joshua Rejoiced in the Priest.[5] He Redeemed His Throne in the Blood of His Servants. He Waved, He Caused to Ride. Joḥanan Remembered, He Heard a Lion. A Slothful One Helped. Naḥman. If It Had Not Been. Rava. Righteous. Gift. Nation. The Man of God. A Sign.[6]

---

[3] The full text of the mnemonic is found in MS **Y** and **AgE**, which usually represent virtually identical textual traditions (i.e., "**Yemenite family**"). MSS **L**, **Mf**, and Genizah fragment extend only as far as the words כהן הטוב. However fragment Vatican 49/2 (MS **V**) contains a separate *siman* before Proem #4:

ס י מ' טוב כיון <!> וקפץ תליסר תתקלקל

which I am unable to decipher. MS **Mf** inserts before Proem #5:

סימן כסאי ברב עבדים חנן הרכיב יוחנן זכר

which covers Proems #5-#8; and before Proem #9 it reads:

שמע ארי אלעזר עצל נחמן לולי רבא צדיק מתן גוי אשר ניסא סימן

for the conclusion of the collection. These facts raise the possibility that what we have here is really a series of units of four proems a piece. It is possible that the scribes were unable to finish copying the unit פדה כסאו owing to the difficulties in determining the reading of the name Afdon–Efron (see below). A complete listing of all the *simanim* in the known textual witnesses to *TB Megillah* may be found in: E. Segal, "The Textual Traditions of Ms. Columbia University to TB Megillah," *Tarbiẓ* 53 (1 1983), 41-69.

[4] "Jonathan"—Some texts: "A Sign: Jonathan."

[5] "Jonathan...priest"—found only in some MSS.

[6] "He Redeemed...a Sign"—only in **Y**, **AgE**.

Reference in *Siman*	**Name of Rabbi**	**Verse**
1. יונתן קם Jonathan rose	R. Jonathan	Isaiah 14:22: *And I will rise up against them...*
2. תחת שמואל Instead of Samuel	R. Samuel bar Naḥmani	Isaiah 55:13: *Instead of the thorn...*
3. יהושע שש Joshua rejoiced	R. Joshua ben Ḥananiah[7]	Deuteronomy 28:63: *...as the Lord rejoiced over you...*
4. בכהן הטוב In the good priest	R. Abba bar Kahana	Ecclesiastes 2:26: *...For the man that is good in his sight...*
5. פדה כסאו He redeemed his throne	Rabbah bar Afdon[8]	Jeremiah 49:38: *And I will set my throne...*

---

7 See variant readings discussed below.

8 See variant readings below. This is the reading in MS **Y** and **AgE** and it is supported by the reading פדה in these Yemenite texts as well as the Spanish tradition of **HgT** (and MS **P**). The Ashkenazic MSS **L**, **R** and **Mf** read בר עפרון, as do MSS **B**, **G** and a Genizah fragment; this was also the reading in the texts of the *Tosafot* who emended it to עופרן— "for '*the name of the wicked shall rot,*' (Proverbs 10:7 [See *Genesis rabbah*, 49:1 (496-7); *Midrash Samuel*, 1:2]) and their names should not be used," an emendation which was introduced, as usual, into the printed Talmuds and **EY**. In the Geonic responsum about the names Rava and Rabbah (Shraga, Abramson, ed., *Tractate 'Abodah Zarah of the Babylonian Talmud, Ms. Jewish Theological Seminary of America*. (New York: The Jewish Theological Seminary of America, 1957), 128 and 117 (Heb.) ff., which also contains a résumé of previous research) it reads: "ראבה בר עפרון דמגלה רבה" (see the editor's notes) p. 121. However it is not altogether certain that the *Ga'on* is referring to our proem, seeing as Rabbah bar Efron appears again below on 15a. The reading "Efron" is also attested in J. L. Maimon, ed., *Yiḥusei tanna'im ve'amora'im me'et rabbi yehudah berabbi qalonimos mishpeira* (Mosad Harav Kook, Jerusalem, 1963), 220. However, in Z. Fillipowsky, ed., *Yuhasin* (*Hashalem*) *by R. Abraham Zakut* (Frankfurt a/M, 1925), 186b the reading is עפראן. Note also the Arabic commentary to Esther attributed to Maimonides (Livorno, 1800), 48. On the wickedness of the Biblical Ephron see L. Ginzberg, *The Legends of the Jews*, 5:257 and n. 267; S. Buber, ed., *Midrash sekhel tov by R. Menahem b. Solomon* (Berlin, 1900-01), Exodus 326.

6. בדם עבדיו In the blood of his servants	Rav Dimi bar Isaac	Ezra 9:9: *For we are bondmen...*
7. הניף הרכיב He waved. He caused to ride	Rav Ḥanina bar Pappa	Psalms 66:12: *Thou hast caused men to ride over our heads...*
8. יוחנן זכר Joḥanan remembered	R. Joḥanan	Psalms 98:3: *He hath remembered his mercy and his faithfulness...*
9. שמע ארי He heard a lion	R. Simeon b. Laqish	Proverbs 28:15: *As a roaring lion and a ravenous bear...*
10. עזר עצלן A slothful one helped	R. Eleazar	Ecclesiastes 10:18: *By slothfulness he that lays rafters sinks...*
11. נחמן לולי Naḥman. If it had not.	R. Naḥman bar Isaac	Psalms 124:2: *If it had not been for the Lord...*
12. רבא צדיק Rava. Righteous.	Rava	Proverbs 29:2: *When the righteous are increased...*
13. מתן גוי Gift. Nation.	Rav Mattanah	Deuteronomy 4:7: *For what great nation...*
14. איש אלקים Man of God	Rav Ashi	Deuteronomy 4:34: *Or hath God assayed...*

The last two proems in the collection differ in their formats from the rest, because of their abbreviated introductory formulas: "R. X said: From here," instead of "R. X opened a proem to this lection from here." If this is interpreted as a sign that they derive from a different literary source, then we should regard the main collection as containing twelve units.[9] A rough division could be made between Proems #1-#10

[9] Abraham Weiss, *Studies in the Literature of the Amoraim*, p. 280 n. 24, does not enumerate these last two as proems at all. Apparently he is placing emphasis on the fact that the wording "R. X said: From here" does not strictly speaking reflect an actual public sermon, but only a suggestion of a verse that *could* serve as the text for the

Continued on next page...

and #11-#14, the former being attributed to sages from the Land of Israel, while the latter are cited in the names of Babylonian rabbis. As regards Rabbah bar Afdon, who is presumably to be identified with the Rabbah bar Efron who transmits a dictum of R. Eleazar in *TB Megillah* 15b, it is probable that he is also a Palestinian scholar. This may be true as well of Rav Dimi bar Isaac, who is mentioned nowhere else in talmudic literature; this in spite of the fact that the title "Rav" (supported by all witnesses) should normally serve as an identifier for Babylonian sages.[10]

...Continued from previous page

proem. On the phenomena of seven- or fourteen–unit collections in rabbinic literature, see: Shamma Friedman, "Some Structural Patterns of Talmudic *Sugiot*," in *Sixth World Congress of Jewish Studies in Jerusalem*, edited by A. Shinan, World Union of Jewish Studies, 389-402, 1977, especially pp. 396 ff. The combination לדאי פרשתא , with its feminine noun and masculine adjective, is attested in all textual witnesses, except for the early printed editions, which read להא from Proem #5 onwards. The Genizah fragment consistently uses the abbreviations 'לה or 'להא.

10 Regarding Rabbah bar Afdon, see Ch. Albeck, *Introduction to the Talmud*, 378: "He was apparently a Babylonian"; however cf. A. Weiss, *op. cit.* nn. 21, 23. R. Dimi bar Isaac is also enumerated by Albeck (ibid. 280) among the Babylonian Amora'im of the third generation, though Albeck is unable to cite other instances where this scholar appears. He is apparently identifying him with the Rav Dimi bar Joseph whose name appears in his stead in the printed editions of *TB Ḥullin* 55b (so too in MS Hamburg 169 to *Ḥullin*). Other biographers relied on the printed readings in *Ḥullin* and state simply that Rav Dimi lived during the third Amoraic generation. See: Raphael Halperin, *Atlas 'ets-ḥayyim*, Vol. 4 (Tel-Aviv: 1980), 166; *Yuḥasin Hashalem* 123; Jehiel Halperin, *Seder hadorot* (Jerusalem: reprint: 1956), *ad loc*; cf. Aaron Hyman, *Toledot tanna'im we'amora'im* (reprint: Jerusalem: 1964), 332. Cf. R. N. N. Rabbinowicz, *Diqduqé Soferim, Variæ Lectiones in Mishnam et in Talmud Babylonicum* (New York: M.P. Press, reprint: 1976) to *Ḥullin* 45b n. ו. MS Munich reads here: Rav Avdimi bar Joseph. Under the circumstances, we should seriously consider the suggestion of the *Seder hadorot* (*s.v.* "R. Dimi") that the scholar normally referred to as "Rav Dimi" without patronymic is identical with Rav Dimi bar Joseph; note however the objections raised against this view by Z. W. Rabinowitz, *Sha'are torath babel: Notes and Comments on the Babylonian Talmud*, ed. E. Z. Melamed (Jerusalem: The Jewish Theological Seminary of America, 1961), 374. Basing ourselves on the evidence from our passage, there are grounds for arguing that Rav Dimi bar Isaac is Rav Dimi *naḥota* who standardly conveys Palestinian traditions to Babylonia. Accordingly, he might be responsible for transmitting the original collection of proems (including, presumably, the Palestinian kernel of the Esther Midrash) from the land of Israel to Babylonia, where it was subsequently incorporated into the talmud of Rava and R. Naḥman b. Isaac.

In the following pages we shall attempt an examination of each of the proems in the Babylonian Esther Midrash, with a view to obtaining an understanding of the ways in which they were fashioned, their use of verses and motifs, and how they compare to parallel traditions in the Palestinian midrashic literature.

Proem #1

[10b] R. Jonathan opened a proem to this lection from here:

"*And I will rise up against them, saith the Lord, and cut off from Babylon name and remnant, and offshoot and offspring, saith the Lord*" (Isaiah 14:22).

"*Name*" —This refers to script[11]

---

[11] Rashi interprets: "'This refers to script' —Their only script derived from another nation." This explanation follows from the characterization of the Romans found in *TB ʿAvodah zarah* 10b ("'*Thou art greatly despised*' (Obadiah 1:2) —because they have neither language nor script"); and *Giṭṭin* 80a ("What is an unworthy empire? —The Roman empire. And for what reason does he refer to it as an unworthy empire? —Because they possess neither a script nor a language"). Rashi to *ʿAvodah zarah* explains: "The script and the language of the Romans came to them from another people (Others established all their scriptures for them)." The words in parentheses are missing from MS Parma; however in the version of Rashi cited in the *editio princeps* of the **EY** (cf. *D.S.*) we read the following continuation: "Others established for them all the books of their error: John, Paul, Peter; and they were all Jews. 'Language' means 'grammatica,' the language spoken by the monks. They altered and twisted [emending עקמו from עמקו —E.S.] the language and fashioned for themselves an absurdity so that they would be considered apart, and in order to remove them from Israel. Not that they were heretics; for they had in mind the welfare of Israel. Rather, it was because they observed that Israel was in trouble and difficulty because of Jesus' deceptions, that they presented themselves as if they supported him in his whoredom, they therefore ordered all these things, as related in the book of the Crucifixion of Jesus..." The reference is probably to a tradition like the following: "And [Elijah] said: The main thing that Jesus requires of you is that you separate yourselves from the Jews with respect to the Torah, language and society... And they asked his name, and he said it was St. Paul. So the disciples separated from each other, and the wicked separated themselves from being Jews, and the world was at peace..." (Jellinek's *Bet ha-Midrasch* 6:9-14; see also *ibid.* 5:60 ff.; Samuel Krauss, *Das Leben Jesu nach jüdischen Quellen* (Berlin: 1902); Joseph Dan, *The Hebrew Story in the Middle Ages*, Sifriyyat Keter (Jerusalem: Keter, 1974), 122 ff., and bibliographical references on p. 274). If this addition is an authentic part of Rashi's commentary, then it demonstrates that he regarded the statement about the language of the Romans having been "derived

Continued on next page...

"*And remnant*" —This refers to language.

"*And offshoot*" —This refers to coinage.[12]

"*And offspring*"—This refers to Vashti.

The various interpretations given here to the expressions in Isaiah's prophecy do not reflect a consistent exegetical approach. Whereas "name," "remnant" and "offshoot" are explained as aspects of royalty, "offspring" is identified with a historical figure. Furthermore, the logical connection between "offshoot" and coinage not explained adequately.[13]

A comparison with Proem #12 of *Esther rabbah* reveals a different arrangement of the material:

> Rav said: Everything which the Holy One said was with reference to him.[14] This is what is written: "*And cut off from Babylon name and remnant, and offshoot and offspring, saith the Lord.*"

...Continued from previous page

from another nation" as referring not to the Latin tongue as such, but to the Latin Christian writings that had been translated into that language in order to maintain a separation between Christians and Jews. On the attitudes of the ancient Jewish sages to Latin see, e.g., *Genesis Rabbah*, 16:4 (p. 148); *TP Megillah* 1:11 (71c); *Esther rabbah*, 4:12 [and the comments of Issachar Ber ben Naftali Hakohen. "*Mattenot kehunnah*," in *Midrash rabbah* (Vilna: Romm, 1878.)]; Samuel Krauss, *Griechische und lateinische Lehnwörter*, Introduction, 14-19; M. D. Herr, *Ha-shilṭon ha-romi besifrut ha-tanna'im*, Ph. D., Hebrew University, 1970, 90 n. 4. In light of all the above, it is not clear on what basis Rashi applied these traditions, which speak explicitly about Latin, to a Babylonian context, especially when the context makes reference to a script that was in the possession of the Babylonians, but was afterwards cut off from them in fulfillment of Isaiah's prophesy. See also *Tosafot ad loc.*, *s.v.* שאר.

12 "coinage"— **Printings** and **EY**: "royalty." The reading "royalty" is probably influenced by Rashi's interpretation of *Nin*: "referring to dominion, etc.", though it is difficult to reconstruct Rashi's precise reading in the Talmud. On the importance of coinage as a political symbol see: Samuel Krauss, *Paras veromi batalmud uvamidrashim* (Jerusalem: 1948), 65.

13 Cf. Rashi, and previous note.

14 *Mattenot kehunnah*: "concerning the King of Media"; cf. Samuel Jaffe, *Yefeh ʿanaf*, in: *Midrash rabbah* (Vilna: Romm, 1878). Note also the observations of Ze'ev Wolf Einhorn ("Maharzu") in *Midrash rabbah* (Vilna: Romm, 1878) regarding the structure

Continued on next page...

"*Name*" —This refers to Nebuchadnezzar.

"*And remnant*" —This refers to Evil-merodach.

"*And offshoot*" —This refers to Belshazzar.

"*And offspring*"—This refers to Vashti.

An alternate explanation:

"*Name*" —This refers to their script.

"*And remnant*" —This refers to the language.

"*And offshoot and offspring*" —son and grandson.

The relationship between these two sources is difficult to define with precision.[15] At any rate, we can note that *Esther rabbah* contains two separate and alternative lists; one of them applies the verse to individuals, whereas the second one proposes a more general interpretation, relating the items to various royal and national symbols. The significance of the expression "son and grandson," cited from the Aramaic, is particularly perplexing. It is possible that the homilist or redactor, having no original material to add here, merely copied the Targum in order to fill in the exposition of the verse, a common practice in midrashic works.[16] A similar midrash is found in *Aggadat bereshit*:

"*Name*" —This refers to its coinage.

"*Remnant*" —"*And there shall not be any remaining* [*of the house of Esau*]" (Obadiah 1:18).

"*And offshoot*" —This refers to dominion.

...Continued from previous page

and text of the proem. It is conceivable that "to him" refers to Ahasuerus, and that the unit is attached to Esther 1:1.

15 Nor can we rule out entirely the possibility that the text of the *Esther rabbah* passage as we have it has been influenced by the Bavli.

16 There may be a word-play between the words of the Targum "*bar bera*" and the concept of "barbarian." The *Yefeh ʿanaf* explains that the author's intention was to reject the previous identification with Vashti, emphasizing the masculine forms of the Aramaic rendering. Cf. the other traditional commentators.

"*And offspring*" —This refers to a prince [אלוף ?].[17]

Midrash Panim aḥerim B[18] cites the same verse in connection with Vashti: "...And the Holy One said '*And [I shall] cut off from Babylon name and remnant, and offshoot and offspring*.' For this reason this befell her, in order to fulfill the word of the Holy One. And when he commanded her to enter, she said: I shall not enter. '*But the queen Vashti refused...*' (Esther 1:12)."

In the Bavli the verse from Isaiah does not connect to the opening verse of Esther; at most we might argue that it relates to the first *chapter*, which is concerned principally with the Vashti episode. This structural flaw does not apply to the parallel in *Esther rabbah*, since there Rav's dictum was not really intended to be an independent proem, but rather it was embedded within a complex proem that goes on to cite a dictum by Samuel, and then concludes as follows:

> R. Samuel bar Naḥman said: "*The Lord shall bring you and your king*" (Deuteronomy 28:36) —If you should say "to Babylonia," were they not already in Babylonia! If so, then why does it say "*unto a nation which neither you nor your fathers have known*"?
>
> —Rather, this refers to Media. Hence: "*And it came to pass...*"[19]

From a thematic perspective, this proem performs a vital function in liberating the Esther narrative from historical isolation, inserting it into the process of the fulfillment of the prophecies concerning the fall of Babylonia and the restoration of Judæa. Thereby it underscores the conviction that the events of the Megillah are the continua-

---

[17] Solomon Buber, ed., *Aggadat Bereshit* (Cracow: Fischer, 1902). The biblical Hebrew word "'*aluf*" is not a normal part of the rabbinic vocabulary and its significance here is unclear [but cf. *Genesis rabbah*, 70:15 (814), and Albeck's notes]. It is most likely a scribal error of some sort.

[18] In: Salomon Buber, ed., *Sifre de-aggadeta al megillat ester* (Vilna: Romm, 1886), 60-1.

[19] It is possible that the author of the Babylonian pericope was not cognizant with the convention current in Palestinian midrashic collections, of expounding a verse according to alternative interpretations. Hence he combined the two units into a single one.

tion of the story of the destruction of the Temple at the hands of Nebuchadnezzar[20] and the first stage in the unfolding of the redemption of the Return to Zion.

Proem #2

[10b] R. Samuel bar Naḥman opened a proem to this lection from here: "*Instead of the thorn shall come up the cypress* {*and instead of the brier shall come up the myrtle*, [hadas] *and it shall be to the Lord for a name*" (Isaiah 55:13).

"*Instead of the thorn shall come up the cypress*"} —Instead of the wicked Haman who made himself into an idol—as it is written: "*and upon all thorns and upon all brambles*" (Isaiah 7:19)—

"*Shall come up the cypress*" —Shall come up the righteous[21] Mordecai, who was called the chief of the spices; as it is written: "*And do thou take to thee the chief spices, flowing myrrh*" (Exodus 30:23), and we render it in the Targum as "*mor daki*"[22] [=pure myrrh].

"*And instead of the brier* [ha-sirpad] *shall come up the myrtle*" —Instead of[23] the wicked Vashti, the daughter of the son of the wicked Nebuchadnezzar, who burned[24] the house of the throne [*repidato*][25] of the Holy One;[26] as it is written: "*its top* [*repidato*] *was gold*" (Song of Songs 3:10)—

---

[20] This motif is an important one, which finds expression in the narrative sections of the midrash, in such episodes as the messianic speculations attributed to Belshazzar, Ahasuerus and Daniel (11b-12a below); the removal of the Temple vessels at Ahasuerus' feast; and in the tradition that identifies Vashti as Belshazzar's daughter (this last tradition was widespread in the midrashim to Esther; cf. Ginzberg, *Legends*, 6:455, n. 3).

[21] "the righteous"— ~ in MS **M** and **Printings**.

[22] "*mor daki*" —All witnesses except MSS **Y**, **B**, **Printings** and Genizah fragments: "*mera dakia*."

[23] "Instead of"—MSS **M**, **R**, **P**, **EY**, **YS**: "This is."

[24] MS **M** adds: "with fire."

[25] "house ...throne"—**Printings**: "throne of the house of God"; MSS **G** and **Mf**: "throne."

[26] "of the...One" —Only in MS **Y** and Genizah fragment; **Printings**: "of the Lord"; other witnesses: "of our God."

"*Shall come up*" [27]—the righteous Esther, who is called Hadassah; as it says:[28] "*And he brought up Hadassah*" (Esther 2:7).[29]

"*And it shall be to the Lord for a sign*" —these are Purim.[30]

"*For an everlasting sign that shall not be cut off*"—This is the reading of the Megillah[31] [32]

This proem, for which there is no parallel in any of the other known works of aggadic midrash, turns out to be one of the most successful in the present collection. Its structure is simple: The verse from Isaiah (55:13) provides the darshan with an opportunity to emphasize the victory of the righteous over the wicked in the Esther narrative, and to mention the feast of Purim which was established in commemoration of that miracle. In this instance, as in the others, the proem is not connected explicitly to the opening verse of Esther.

It seems likely that this passage evolved in two stages and that R. Samuel bar Naḥmani himself is not to be credited with the citation of the various verses brought in support of his identifications; nor did he posit verbal midrashic connections or word-plays between Haman and the thorn, Mordecai and the cypress, or Vashti and the brier, other than devising the pairs of righteous and wicked figures. The attempt to invent specific verbal connections between the items in the verse and the figures in the Megillah likely belongs to a later stage in the evolution of the material.

The above hypothesis is supported by several facts. For example, the connection between Mordecai and the cypress is founded, so it

---

27 MSS **G**, **O**, **L**, **M**, **EY**, **Printings** and Genizah fragment add: "'*the myrtle*'—shall come up"

28 "says"—MSS **G**, **B**, **O**, **Mf**, **HgT**, **L**, **AgE**: "is written."

29 **Spanish family** adds: "And it is written: '*and he stood among the myrtle-trees that were in the bottom*' (Zechariah 1:8)."

30 "these are Purim"—**Ashkenazic family**: "This is the reading of the Megillah"; MS **P**, **EY** and **AgE**: "These are the days of Purim."

31 "This...Megillah"—MSS **N**, **B**, **HgT**, **L**, **M**, **R***, **Mf**, **V**, **Printings**, **YS**: "These are [the days of—MS **N**, **HgT**, **M**, **R***, **Mf**, **V**, **Printings**] Purim."

32 MSS **R***, **Mf**, **V**, **HgT** add: "As it is written [concerning them—**HgT**: '*And that these days of Purim should not fail from among the Jews* etc.'(Esther 9:28)."

appears, upon a conversation between Rav Mattanah and the Papponeans whose source is in *TB Ḥullin* 139b.[33] The remark about Haman "who made himself into an idol" may also be a quotation from the talmudic passage on 19a below.[34] Such quotations from other places in the Talmud are generally considered a sign of late redactional strata. The selection of the proof-texts also seems forced. R. Solomon Edels (the Maharsha) has clearly described the difficulty implicit in the citation from Isaiah:7:19: "According to its simple meaning, this verse also is speaking about thorns and briers, and I have no idea why it is perceived as a more explicit reference to idolatry."[35] A similar objection could probably be directed against the reference to "*reṗidato*" in Song of Songs, whose literal meaning has nothing to do with the Temple, though this particular interpretation is firmly entrenched in the traditions of the midrash and targums.[36] It would therefore appear that we are justified in positing two stages in the development of this proem:

---

33 The midrash makes sense only according to the Onkelos Targum, but not according to the Palestinian versions (e.g., MS Neofiti).

34 Though this is more doubtful: The clause appears there in Aramaic, and it is just as likely to be paraphrasing this proem. Cf. *TB Sanhedrin* 61b ("worshipped like Haman"). On the motif of Haman's making himself into an idol, see Ginzberg, 6:463, n. 100; Ibn Ezra's (first) commentary to Esther 3:2 [cited by Barry Walfish, "The Two Commentaries of Ibn Ezra on the Book of Esther," *JQR* 79 (4 1989), 337].

35 It is likely however that the interpretation presupposes the explanation of Targum Jonathan to the verse: "And in all the wastelands of thorns and in all their houses of praise" (Cf. *Tanḥuma* (Buber) *Ḥuqqat*, 1 [50b]: "...And in future times the Holy One...will exact punishment from the idolatrous nations by means of trivial things, as it says: '*And it shall come to pass in that day...*')." The interpretation in Targum Jonathan is of course based on a reading of נהלול in the verse as deriving from הלל, praise; cf. Rashi and Qimḥi on the verse. The idea of interpreting Isaiah 55:13 with respect to the righteous and the wicked is in itself consistent with Targum Jonathan there: "Instead of the wicked shall arise the righteous..."; cf. Rashi to the verse. In *Song of Songs rabbah*, 1:1:6 the verse is cited as evidence that "a wicked person begets a righteous one".

36 The interpretation [see variants listed above; note that most texts read "of our God" (*Eloheinu*), rather than the more conventional "Holy One Blessed Be He"] also follows the Targum to Song of Songs: "King Solomon erected a Holy Temple," as well as many midrashic traditions, e.g. *Song of Songs rabbah*, 3:15-17 (where the verse is applied to the Tabernacle and the ark); *Numbers rabbah*, 12:4 (about the Temple); *Baraita dimelekhet hammishkan* Ch. 6; *Pesiqta derav kahana*, 1 (ed. Mandelbaum, 3

Continued on next page...

1. Initially, the original Palestinian *petiḥta* consisted of the selection of an appropriate verse, each element of which was identified with a personality or precept associated with the Book of Esther.
2. Subsequently, basing himself on these identifications, the Babylonian redactor appended several verses according to his own ingenious and intricate methods, with the aim of demonstrating specific connections between the items mentioned in the *petiḥta* verse and the references to Esther.

It is probable that the association between "myrtle" (*hadas*) and Esther (=Hadassah) [and perhaps even that between "*shall not be cut off*" and "*so as it should not fail*" (Esther 9:27)][37] were in the mind of the original author, and underlay his selection of the proem verse.

Proem #3

[10b] R. Joshua son of Ḥananiah[38] opened a proem to this lection from here: "*And it shall come to pass that as the Lord rejoiced over you to do you good, so the Lord will rejoice* [yasis] *over you to cause you to perish*, etc." (Deuteronomy 28:63).

And does the Holy One indeed rejoice over the downfall of the wicked? And is it not written: "*As they went out before the army, and say, Give thanks unto the Lord, for his mercy endureth for ever*" (2 Chronicles 20:212)—

And said R. Joḥanan[39]: For what reason does it not say "for He is good" in this thanksgiving?[40] —Because the Holy One does not rejoice over[41] the downfall of the wicked.

...Continued from previous page

ff.), [regarding the Tent of Meeting]; Mordecai Margulies, ed., *Midrash haggadol on the Pentateuch: Exodus* (Jerusalem: Mosad Harav Kook, 1956) to Exodus 25:1, p. 566 [regarding the Temple; the editor notes that "the source is unknown"]. Cf. Ibn Ezra, Rashi and Sforno to the verse.

37 See variant readings.

38 "son of Ḥananiah" — ~ in MS **M**; **Printings**: "son of Levi."

39 "Joḥanan" — MS **R***: "Nathan."

40 "thanksgiving"—In **MhG** and **AgE**: "passage."

41 "rejoice over" —**MhG**: "desire."

And said R. Samuel bar Naḥmani: Said R. Jonathan:[42] What is it that is written "*And one came not near the other all the night*" (Exodus 14:20)?

—At that moment[43] the ministering angels wished to recite song before the Holy One.[44] The Holy One[45] said to them:[46] The work of my hands are drowning in the sea and you are reciting song before me!

Said R. Yose b. R. Ḥaninah:[47] He Himself does not rejoice; however he causes others to rejoice.

Note carefully as well, that it is written: "*yasis*" [=normally: He shall cause to rejoice], and it is not written "*yisos*" [Usual form for "He shall rejoice"].

Hear from this.[48]

This proem raises a number of fundamental questions which must be addressed before we can properly evaluate it.

Firstly, what is the precise extent of the proem? In addition to the verse itself, the Talmud raises an objection ("And does the Holy One indeed rejoice over the downfall of the wicked, etc.") along with its solution ("Said R. Yose b. R. Ḥaninah, etc."),[49] neither of which connects very neatly to the topic of Purim.[50] True, we could view the entire

---

42 "Jonathan"—MS **G** and **Printings**: "Joḥanan."

43 "At...moment" —thus in MS **Y**, **AgE** and **Spanish family**; ~ in other witnesses.

44 "before...One"— ~ in MSS **N**, **B** (before emendation) **L**, **Mf**, **Printings**, **YS**.

45 "The Holy One"—MSS **G**, **R EY**: "He."

46 "to them" — ~ in MS **P**, **Printings, YS**.

47 "Yose b. R. Ḥaninah"—**Printings**: "Eleazar."

48 **EY** adds: "But with reference to love and consolation it is written: '*For the Lord will again rejoice over thee for good*'" (Deut. 30:9). MS Vat. 49/2 (**V**) adds a *siman* whose reference is unclear.

49 We shall ignore, for the moment, the obvious problems of chronology.

50 Cf. however *Genesis rabbah*, 53:10 (565): "R. Judan in the name of R. Yose b. R. Ḥaninah: '*Then the king made a* great *feast*' (Esther 2:18)—The Eternally Great One was present there, as it is written: '*For the Lord will again rejoice* [lasus] *over thee for good, as he rejoiced* [sas] *over thy fathers*' (Deuteronomy 30:9)." This verse is the complement of the one upon which the proem is founded, and it is not unlikely that an earlier version of the homily should have built upon the contrast between the two,

Continued on next page...

passage as a single unit, which comes to make a statement about God's feelings when he has to punish the wicked; however, it is also possible that the original proem consisted of no more than the citation of Deuteronomy 28:63,[51] and that the additional discussion was attached tangentially through the association with the verse, in spite of the fact that it has no intrinsic connection to the verse's function within the proem. There exists a parallel to this discussion in *TB Sanhedrin* 39b, only there the question "And does the Holy One indeed rejoice over the downfall of the wicked?" is directed at 1 Kings 22:36: "*And there went out a proclamation throughout the host,*" referring to the death of Ahab. The question therefore arises: Is this discussion an integral part of R. Joshua ben Ḥananiah's proem, or was it transferred from another context, such as that of *TB Sanhedrin*?

It would appear at first that this question can be solved through a careful reading of the wording of R. Yose b. R. Ḥaninah's dictum, which is undoubtedly crucial to the pericope: "He Himself does not rejoice; however He causes others to rejoice." Now these words allude to the words of the verse "*so the Lord will rejoice,*" and yet the verse is not cited at all in the *Sanhedrin* passage! This would seem to lead us to the conclusion that the discussion originated in *Megillah* and was subsequently transferred to *Sanhedrin*, where the redactors neglected to adapt it completely to the context of 1 Kings 22:36. This argument however is not to be regarded as conclusive. The received text of *Sanhedrin* may represent no more than an accidental deletion of the verse at some later stage in its textual transmission, and R. Yose b. R. Ḥaninah himself might very well have used the Deuteronomy verse in order to resolve the difficulty from 1 Kings. At any rate, it would be unfair to base a complete reconstruction of the two pericopes on this single detail.

...Continued from previous page

producing a more optimistic proem than the one preserved in the Babylonian tradition. See also *Lamentations rabbah*, 2:17 [Salomon Buber, ed., *Midrasch Echa Rabbati* (Vilna: Wittwe & Gebrüder Romm, 1899), 120, and n. 212]; *Tanḥuma* (Buber), *Devarim*, 1.

51 This chapter describes the evils of exile, and was expounded in *Esther rabbah* with respect to the events of the Purim story. See below.

On the other hand, there are a number of phenomena which favor the view that the passage originated in *TB Sanhedrin*:

1. In the parallel pericope in *TP Sanhedrin* (end of Ch. 4), we encounter the identical motifs: "It is written '*And there went out a proclamation throughout the host.*' And what is 'the proclamation (*harinnah*)'? —Peace (?)[52] And so it says: '*As they went out before the army*, etc.' This comes to teach you that even the downfall of the wicked is not an occasion for joy before the Holy One" —And none of this is connected to Deuteronomy 28:63.

2. According to the wording in *TB Megillah* the objection does not correspond to the context of the verse. The expression "downfall of the wicked" is hardly an appropriate characterization of the fate of the Jews in the days of Haman, whom aggadic tradition does not regard as wicked.[53] Consequently it would appear more likely that the redactors have transposed to *Megillah* a phraseology that originated elsewhere; namely, in *TB Sanhedrin*, in connection with the death of Ahab.

For these reasons, it seems that the discussion about God's lack of joy at the downfall of the wicked is not an original constituent of the

---

52 Heb.: הריני. Cf. N. Brüll, "Die Entstehungsgeschichte des babylonischen Talmuds als Schriftwerkes," *Jahrbücher für jüdische Geschichte und Literatur* 2 (1876), 34, n. 8; B. Z. Bacher, *Aggadat amora'ei eretz yisra'el* (Tel-Aviv: 1930) 3:1:79, n. 2; Alexander Kohut, *Aruch Completum.* (Vienna-New York: 1878-92), 3:244; Bernard Mandelbaum, ed. *Pesikta de Rav Kahana*, 474-5 (notes by S. Lieberman); *Pesiḳta de-Rab Kahana*, translated by W. G. Braude and I. J. Kapstein (Philadelphia: Jewish Publication Society of America, 1975), 332, n. 3.

53 There is a reference on 11a to "laziness that inhered in Israel because they did not occupy themselves in the Torah"; similarly, on 12a, in the conversation between R. Simeon b. Yoḥai and his disciples, a number of suggestions are proposed as to why the Jews of that generation should have deserved destruction (see our discussion of the pericope in Chapter 5 below). However none of these explanations would warrant the use of the epithet "wicked." See further discussion of this below.

proem in *TB Megillah*,[54] but was transferred from *TB Sanhedrin*, presumably by virtue of R. Yose b. R. Ḥaninah's use of the proof-text from Deuteronomy in order to resolve the objection to the verse from 1 Kings.

Scholars have already noted an additional difficulty in this passage.[55] According to the context of the Bavli—where the dictum "The work of my hands are drowning in the sea and you are reciting song before me!" is used to illustrate the claim that "the Holy One does not rejoice in the downfall of the wicked"—we are forced to understand that "the work of my hands" refers to the wicked; i.e., the Egyptians. This reading stands in opposition to all the Palestinian versions of the midrash, in every one of which God's concern is for the fate of the Israelites, not the Egyptians.[56]

---

54 Joseph Heinemann, *Aggadah and Its Development*, 241, n. 35, determines that "in *Sanhedrin* the beginning of the homily is truncated; from its conclusion it is evident that it also was based originally on Deuteronomy 28:63, in spite of the fact that the verse was omitted from the beginning." It is clear at any rate that the proem preached by R. Joshua b. Ḥananiah (in the generation of Jamnia) could not have contained the remarks of R. Yose b. R. Ḥaninah, nor those of R. Joḥanan or R. Jonathan. See also: B. Moran, "*Le'arikhatah shel masekhet megillah*," Ph. D., Bar-Ilan University, 1971, 81 ff.

55 Heinemann, *op. cit.*, 175-9; Menahem Kasher, *Torah shelemah* (Jerusalem: 1927-81), *Beshallaḥ*, p. 63, n. 126; note especially his citation from Shabazi's *Ḥemdat Yamim*.

56 *Exodus rabbah*, 23:8: "My legions are in peril..."; H. S. Horovitz and I. A. Rabin, ed. *Mechilta d'rabbi ismael*, 2nd ed. (Jerusalem: Wahrmann, 1970), *Wayhi beshallaḥ* #3 (p. 97): "My beloved ones are drowning in the waters"; *Tanḥuma* (Buber) *Beshallaḥ*, 13: "My children are in peril" (Heinemann, *op. cit.* 178, n. 40). It is equally evident that the verse (Exodus 14:20) "*the one came not near the other all the night*" cannot refer to the drowning of the Egyptians, since it appears before the account of the parting of the Red Sea (Heinemann, *ibid.*, and n. 41). Kasher attempted to force the meaning of the Palestinian parallels into the text of the Bavli: "...And accordingly, we ought to say that when the Gemara states here 'And said R. Joḥanan, etc.' [following the reading of the printed editions —E.S.] ...it does not mean to say that here too it is expounding that the Holy One has no joy in the downfall of the wicked. Rather, it is merely bringing by way of association [*derekh agav*] another similar exposition in the name of R. Joḥanan. And furthermore, it deals with the same theme, for if he does not rejoice in the downfall of the wicked, all the more so when his own children are in danger." However, all but two of the witnesses to the text of the Gemara read "R. Jonathan" rather than "Joḥanan" as the author of the tradition (See text-critical notes to the passage). It is therefore clear that Kasher's ingenious

Continued on next page...

Joseph Heinemann[57] argued that the Babylonian version of R. Jonathan's dictum came about "...as a result of ...a mistaken understanding of the statement's content and language—albeit a mistake that also resulted, as it appears, from an attitude that is peculiar to Babylonian Jewry." Later in his discussion[58] Heinemann deals with this question at greater length.

> And furthermore, this sermon for Purim, which is brought in the Babylonian Talmud, appears to express a distinctly Babylonian attitude. The feast of Purim was undoubtedly a problematic and embarrassing festival for the Jews of the Babylonian Diaspora. How was it possible for Jews living in the Persian empire to express unqualified joy at the killing, at their hands, of thousands of subjects of the King of Persia? The *derashah* before us testifies to hesitations and to mixed feelings regarding the joy of Purim, and it gives expression to a pronounced ambivalence... There can be no doubt that the sage who preached this sermon on Purim was a Babylonian Rabbi, and even if he was making use of Palestinian *aggadot* that were available to him, he gave to them, by combining them in this particular manner and assembling them into a different context, a significance that was radically new when compared with what had, presumably, been their original meanings...[59]

It seems that Heinemann himself was not altogether certain whether what we have here is an unconscious misunderstanding of the source, or an intentional act of editorial manipulation in which the redactor, motivated by apologetic considerations, reworked the

...Continued from previous page

reconstruction is unacceptable, as was noted already by Heinemann (*ibid.*, 241, n. 47). The reading quoted by Kasher in the name of R. Solomon ben Hayatom [Z. P. Chajes, ed., *Perush masekhet mashqin lerabbi shelomo ben hayyatom*. 2nd ed. (Jerusalem: 1910), 120, and Introduction, 30] is not supported by any of the witnesses to the text of the Bavli.

57 *Op. cit.*, 175

58 *Op. cit.*, 179.

59 Heinemann's words give the impression that in the original (Palestinian?) version of the proem the verse "*so shall he rejoice*, etc." had been applied to Israel's enemies, including the Persians. If this was truly his intention, then the claim is quite astonishing, since the simple sense of the verse speaks so unambiguously of Israel. I have found no other commentator who suggests a similar interpretation (cf. Rashi to the Talmud and the biblical verse; Maharsha, and the commentators to the **EY**).

Palestinian sources that stood before him. He astutely observed that if the redactor was utilizing the same versions of R. Jonathan / Joḥanan's words that have come down to us in assorted midrashic works, speaking as they do of "my beloved ones," "my sons," or "my legions" that stand in danger, then there is no escaping the conclusion that this was an intentional change.[60] There can at any rate be no doubt that the verse "*the one came not near the other all the night*" has been removed from its original sequence, which speaks of the eve of the parting of the Red Sea, prior to the drowning of the Egyptians.

Heinemann's analysis presupposes that the entire unit in the Bavli, including the verse and the discussion about the question "does the Holy One rejoice, etc.," was originally formulated in order to serve as a proem. Our own view, as we have already stated, tends towards the opposite conclusion, that the discussion is a secondary transposition of a pericope that originated in *TB Sanhedrin*. Nor has it been confirmed from other evidence that the Babylonian Jews held more "universalistic" opinions about their gentile neighbors.

It seems more likely that the editor of our pericope was led astray because he understood the expression "drowning in the sea" in an overly literal manner. This could not be perceived as a reference to the Israelites, since they did not actually drown in the sea! Once the redactor had determined that the reference was to the Egyptians (who were ultimately drowned), he overlooked the fact that Exodus 14:20 speaks of the night before the miracle of the Red Sea.

Proem #4

[10b] R. Abba bar Kahana[61] opened a proem to this lection from here:[62] "*For to the man that is good in his sight he giveth wisdom*

---

[60] However, he also suggests the possibility that "my beloved ones" (ידידי) became transformed in the course of oral transmission to "מעשה ידי." This solution seems most unlikely. Even allowing that the Babylonian redactor was familiar with a Palestinian source that read "מעשה ידי" or some such neutral wording, we have still not resolved the difficulty of the use of "*the one came not near the other all the night*" in an inappropriate context.

[61] "bar Kahana"— ~ in MS **R**.

[62] "a proem...here"—MS **O**: "this proem."

> *and knowledge and joy {but to the sinner he giveth the task, to gather and heap up, that he may leave it to him that is good in the sight of God*" (Ecclesiastes 2:26).
>
> "*For to the man that is good in His sight He giveth wisdom and knowledge and joy*"}[63] —This is Mordecai.
>
> "*But to the sinner he giveth the task, to gather and heap up*" —This is Haman.
>
> "*That he may leave it to him that is good in the sight of God*" —This is Mordecai;[64] as it is written:[65] "*And Esther set Mordecai over the house of Haman*" (Esther 8:2).

The structure of this proem is neat and symmetrical. To each item in the "generic" verse from Ecclesiastes the darshan has added a set of specific identifications.

A parallel version of this homily found in *Ecclesiastes rabbah* (2:26) is virtually identical to R. Abba bar Kahana's proem. In *Ecclesiastes rabbah* the verse is expounded with reference to assorted pairs of righteous and sinful figures from the Bible: Abraham and Nimrod, Isaac and Abimelech, Jacob and Laban, the Israelites in Egypt and the Canaanites, Hezekiah and Sennacherib, and finally Mordecai and Haman:

> Another explanation: "*For to the man that is good in his sight*" —This is Mordecai. "*He giveth wisdom and knowledge and joy.*"
>
> "*But to the sinner he giveth the task, to gather and heap up*" —This is Haman.
>
> And to whom does it say "*that he may leave it to him that is good in the sight of God*?" —This is Mordecai, as it says (Esther 8:1): "*On that day did the king Ahasuerus give the house of Haman …unto Esther the queen.*"[66]

---

63 Bracketed passage included according to MSS **G**, **W** and **V**.

64 **Printings** add: "and Esther."

65 "is written"—MSS **G**, **L**, **EY**: "says."

66 On the simple meaning of the *Ecclesiastes rabbah* passage, see the traditional commentators. In general, it does not seem that the *midrashim* have gone very far beyond the simple sense of the biblical text, which speaks of the sinner who spends his whole life amassing wealth, only to have to ultimately hand it all over to the

Continued on next page...

We cannot state with certainty whether the midrash in *Ecclesiastes rabbah* originated as a proem to Esther,[67] especially when we keep in mind that both texts conclude with verses from the end of Esther, rather than the opening verse.[68]

...Continued from previous page
Godfearing sage. There are however a number of factors that cast doubts on the originality of this passage to *Ecclesiastes rabbah*: In MS Vatican 291 of *Ecclesiastes rabbah* the reading of the final segment is:

> Another explanation: "*For to the man that is good in his sight*" —This is Mordecai. "*he giveth wisdom and knowledge and joy*'"—"*But to the sinner*"—This is Haman. "*That he may leave it to him that is good in the sight of God*" —This is Mordecai: "*On that day did the king Ahasuerus give...unto Esther.*"

This formulation deviates from the symmetry and uniformity that characterize the previous segments of the midrash. A similar version may have stood before the *Mattenot kehunnah* (though the Pesaro printing is the same as the standard editions). In *Kohelet zuṭa* (and in the *Yalquṭ shimʿoni*) are found all the segments that are contained in *Ecclesiastes rabbah* (without the proof-texts), except for the last one dealing with Mordecai and Haman! All these factors give rise to the suspicion that the passage in *Ecclesiastes rabbah* was filled in later on the basis of the Bavli, and is not original to the Palestinian midrash.

67 It is a frequent occurrence that midrashim in *Ecclesiastes rabbah* that appear to be arranged around verses from Ecclesiastes actually originated as proems to other lections in the Bible. Of the verses quoted in the current passage, possible candidates for the role of *petiḥta* lection include Genesis 22:1, which begins a unit in the Palestinian cycle, as well as (apparently) Numbers 26:52-3 [cf. Menahem Zulay, ed., *Piyyute yannai*, Publications of the Research Institute for Hebrew Poetry (Berlin: Schocken, 1938), 225; Zvi Meir Rabinovitz, ed., *The Liturgical Poems of Rabbi Yannai According to the Triennial Cycle of the Pentateuch and the Holidays: Critical Edition with Introduction and Commentary* (Jerusalem: Mosad Bialik and Tel-Aviv University), 1985-7, 115; *Encyclopedia Judaica* 15:1388 (and the bibliographical references listed there)]. This is not however true of Genesis 31:11 or 2 Chronicles 32:23.

68 The concluding verse of the *Ecclesiastes rabbah* passage does not quite fit the context to which it is appended: "...This is Mordecai, as it says: '...*did the king give...unto* **Esther** *the queen.*'" The following verse, which is cited in the Bavli, would have been more appropriate: "*And Esther set Mordecai over the house of Haman*" (cf. Esther 8:17). Perhaps we are meant to take seriously the "etc." ('וגו) in *Ecclesiastes rabbah* which points ahead to verse 2. See also R. Josiah Pinto's commentary ("Rif") to the **EY**: "...for first it says '*For to the man that is good*' —This is Mordecai. And afterwards it says: '*that he may leave it to him that is good in the sight of God*' —This is Mordecai and Esther..." See also *Tanḥuma Lekh lekha*, 8, where the verse is expounded with reference to a slave who acquires property. Cf. *TB*

Continued on next page...

Proem #5

[10b] Rava[69] bar Afdon[70] opened a proem[71] to this lection from here: "*And I will set my throne in Elam, and will destroy from thence king and princes, saith the Lord*" (Jeremiah 49:38).

"*King*" —is Vashti.

"*And princes*" —this is Haman and his ten[72] sons.

A parallel version of this proem is found among the *petiḥtot* to *Esther rabbah* (#12). The beginning of that proem has been cited in our discussion of Proem #1 above.

...and Samuel said: Everything which the Holy One said was with reference to him. This is what is written: "*And I will set my throne in Elam, and will destroy from thence the king and the princes*" (Jeremiah 49:38).

"*The King*" —This is Vashti .

"*And the princes*" —These are the seven princes of Media and Persia.

According to the Bavli, the verse from Jeremiah functions as a proem to the entire Megillah, with Haman's defeat being grasped as the central event of the book.[73] However Samuel's remarks in *Esther rab-*

...Continued from previous page

Megillah 15a in the matter of "a slave who is purchased for a loaf" and the sources cited by Ginzberg, *Legends*, 6:464, n. 105 (see also *ibid.*, 4:397 ff.), with regard to Haman's becoming enslaved to Mordecai. The episode is found in several texts of the Bavli (including Genizah fragments), whether in the body of the text or in marginal glosses. It is certain however that it is not an original part of the Bavli text.

69 "Rava"— variants: MSS **O**, **V**, **EY**, **Printings**: "R. Abba"; MSS **G**, **B**, **R**, **Mf**, **HgT²**: "Rabbah"; **HgT¹**: "{ }Abba"

70 "bar Afdon"— MSS **G**, **L**, **R**, **Mf**, Genizah fragment: "bar Efron": **EY**, **Printings**: "bar Ofran"; MSS **O**, **V**: "bar Afron"; MSS **B**, **W**: "bar Ada"; MS **M**, **HgT²**: ~.

71 "a proem"— ~ in MS **G**.

72 "ten"— ~ in MS **G** and **EY**.

73 It is more difficult to understand how Vashti's fall would also occupy such a central position in the narrative. However there is no other real "king" in the story aside from Ahasuerus, and he of course does not suffer any defeat in the course of the plot. We

Continued on next page...

bah only relate to the events recounted in Esther Chapter One regarding Vashti, an episode which is perceived as the realization of Jeremiah's prophecies about Elam.[74] Samuel's dictum is not presented in *Esther rabbah* as a separate proem, but as an interpretation to the verse in Jeremiah. It connects neither to the opening verse of Esther nor to the Megillah as a whole.

Proem #6

> [10b] Rav Dimi[75] bar Isaac opened a proem to this lection from here:[11a] "*For we are bondmen; yet hath God not forsaken us in our bondage, but hath extended mercy unto us in the sight of the kings of Persia...*" (Ezra 9:9).[76]

Rav Dimi bar Isaac's proem seems to consist only of the verse from Ezra, without any additional explanation or comments. Among the manuscript variants we find several glosses appended to the verse in order to create an explicit connection to the subject-matter of Esther.[77] It would appear that this situation was necessitated by the fact that the verse, taken by itself, speaks of the narrowly defined historical context of the Return to Zion and the building of the Second Temple. It is clear

...Continued from previous page
have already observed above in our analysis of Proem #1 that Rav also regarded Vashti's execution as the fulfillment of Isaiah's prophecies about the end of Nebuchadnezzar's line. As we shall observe especially in Chapter 6 below, this was a widespread and important motif in the midrashic retelling of Esther.

74 The reference to "the seven princes of Persia and Media" is to a tradition found in several aggadic sources; e.g.: "'*After these things, when the wrath of king Ahasuerus was appeased*' when he sobered up from his wine...'And who advised him to have her executed?' They replied to him: The seven princes of Persia and Media. He immediately killed them, and for this reason they are not mentioned again" [*Midrash Abba gorion* 9:1, in: Salomon Buber, ed., *Sifre de-aggadeta al megillat ester* (Vilna: Romm, 1886); see the full passage there]; other sources are listed in Ginzberg, *Legends*, 6:457 ff., n. 52.

75 "Dimi"—MS **M**: "Avidimi."

76 For the reading of MS **G** see below; MSS **L**, **W** add: "When '*hath* [*he*] *extended mercy unto us*'? —in the days of Mordecai and Esther"; MSS **R**, **Mf**, **V**, **EY**, **HgT** add: "When '*hath* [*he*] *extended mercy unto us*'? —in the days of Mordecai"; **Printings** add: "When? —In the days of Haman."

77 See the variants listed above. MSS **Y**, **M**, **B**, **P** and **AgE** contain no additions to the verse.

that the "kings of Persia" mentioned in this verse are Cyrus and his court, such that it cannot readily be applied to other situations. This historical context is even more pronounced in the continuation of the verse, which is cited in full in several textual witnesses: "*To give us a reviving, to set up the house of our God, and to repair the ruins thereof, and to give us a fence in Judah and in Jerusalem.*"[78] As we shall be observing in much of this study, much of the midrashic version of Esther is dominated by a historical perspective according to which Ahasuerus actively stalled the project that had been initiated by Cyrus.

Proem #7

[11a] R. Ḥanan[79] bar Pappa opened a proem to this lection from here: "*Thou hast caused men to ride over our heads, we went through fire and through water, but thou didst bring us out into abundance*" (Psalms 66:12).

"*We went through fire*" —in the days of[80] Nebuchadnezzar.[81]

"*And through water*" —in the days of[82] Pharaoh.

---

[78] Note the explanation of Rabbi Jacob Ibn Ḥabib in his comments to the **EY**: "What it means is that we are still the slaves of Ahasuerus, and for this reason we do not recite Hallel on Purim…" (cf. *TB Megillah* 14a, *ʿArakhin* 10b). MS **G** preserves a unique reading: "…'*For we are bondmen*' —in the days of Pharaoh; '*yet our God hath not forsaken us in our bondage*' —in the days of Nebuchadnezzar; '*but hath extended mercy unto us*' —in the days of Haman." According to this reading, the verse is midrashically being broken up into several topics, as though Ezra himself were reviewing the nation's history. We might complete the thought ourselves: "'…*and to give us a wall in Judah and Jerusalem*' —in the days of Cyrus." This version of the proem, which strongly resembles the next one in the collection, presents the fewest difficulties. Nonetheless, it seems most likely that the original text comprised only the Biblical citations without any interpretations.

[79] "Ḥanan"—only in MS **Y**; MSS **B**, **Spanish family**, **AgE**, **V**: "Ḥanina"; MSS **G**, **M**, **L**, **Mf**, **Printings**, **YS**: "Ḥinena"; MS **R**: "Joḥanan."

[80] "in the days of"— MSS **M** and **R**: "This is."

[81] "Nebuchadnezzar"—MSS **M**, **W**, **Printings** and **YS**: "the wicked Nebuchadnezzar"; **AgE** and **Y***: "Chaldeans."

[82] MSS **L**, **M** and **YS** add: "the wicked."

> "*But thou didst bring us out into abundance*" —in the days of Mordecai and Esther.[83]

R. Ḥanan bar Pappa is expounding a verse from Psalms with reference to national redemption, such that "*men*" becomes translated into "nations." The Psalm itself can be interpreted in terms of either national or individual redemption.[84] The standard Targum to Psalms does not greatly enhance our understanding of the issue. However, Palestinian midrashic works cite a version of a targum[85] that renders the verse in Aramaic as "You have caused the nations to ride over our heads."[86]

---

[83] "Mordecai and Esther"—Only in MS **Y**; in all other witnesses (including **Y***): "["the wicked"—MS **L**] Haman."

[84] The first part of the Psalm contains expressions of national thanksgiving such as the following: "*Make a joyful noise unto God, all ye lands...All the earth shall worship thee...He turned the sea into dry land; they went through the flood on foot; there did we rejoice in him: He ruleth by his power forever; his eyes behold the nations...O bless our God, ye people...*" etc. However, from our verse onwards, the tone becomes one of personal thanksgiving, formulated in first-person-singular.

[85] See Albeck's notes to *Genesis Rabbah*, p. 444: "...It is rendered in some targum." Cf. next note.

[86] To the best of my knowledge there is no actual parallel to this proem in Palestinian midrashic literature. However, we do encounter an analogous use of this verse in some midrashic sources, also in connection with a dictum of R. Ḥanina bar Pappa. Owing to conflicting textual traditions in the transmission of the source, it remains unclear how we ought to interpret the data. In *Genesis rabbah*, 44:21 (444) we read as follows:

> "*Behold a smoking furnace and a burning lamp*" (Genesis 15:17). Simeon bar Abba in the name of R. Joḥanan: Four things did {God} show {Abraham}: Gehenna, the empires, the giving of the Torah, and the Temple. He said to him: By which do you prefer that your children be oppressed, by Gehenna or by the empires? R. Ḥinena bar Pappa said: Abraham selected for himself the empires. R. Judan and R. Idi and R. Ḥama b. Ḥaninah: Abraham selected for himself Gehenna, and the Holy One selected for him the empires... We have come to the dispute of R. Ḥanina bar Pappa and R. Idi and R. Ḥama bar Ḥaninah. R. Ḥanina bar Pappa said: Abraham selected for himself the empires, and R. Judan and R. Idi and R. Ḥama b. Ḥanina said in the name of a certain elder in the name of Rabbi: The Holy One selected for him the empires. This is what is written: "*Thou hast caused men to ride over our heads*" —{In Aramaic:} "Thou hast

Continued on next page...

The structure of this proem is simple and effective. The darshan chose a verse that dealt with a general topic, and then identified each item in the verse with a specific Biblical figure, culminating in a connection to the Book of Esther.

...Continued from previous page

caused the nations to ride over our heads as we come through fire and through water."

According to the text as cited here, Ps. 66:12 is being adduced in support of R. Judan and R. Idi, etc., as against the view of R. Ḥanina bar Pappa (stressing "***Thou** hast caused to ride*" —i.e., it was God, not Abraham, who caused the nations to ride). The pericope is brought in roughly identical form in *Exodus Rabbah*, 51:7, and in *Pesiqta derav kahana*, 5:2 ("*Haḥodesh hazzeh*," ed. Mandelbaum, 81; trans. Braude-Kapstein, 91-3), Midrash on Psalms 40:4 (S. Buber, ed., *Midrash tehillim* (Vilna: 1891) [based on *Pesiqta derav kahana*]), etc.; see also the observations of M. Friedmann in his notes to *Pesiqta rabbati* [M. Friedmann, ed. *Pesikta rabbati* (Vienna: 1880)] "*Haḥodesh*" #15 (67a, n. 14). However, an alternate tradition, preserved in the standard printings of *Genesis rabbah* as well as in MSS Vatican 30 and 60, etc., omits the sentence (at the end) "R. Judan and R. Idi and R. Ḥama...the Holy One selected for him the empires." From this version it seems that the verse is being brought in support of R. Ḥanina bar Pappa's view, or of both views. According to this reading the verse should be understood as implying that the enslavement to the empires comes instead of the fire and waters of Gehenna. However, we are not expected to deduce from this whether it was God or Abraham who was responsible for the selection. A reading similar to this one is brought in *Tanḥuma Pequdei*, 8. Indeed, were it not for the fact that the abbreviated version is attested by the most reliable witnesses to *Genesis rabbah* and supported by the *Tanḥuma*, we would have written it off easily as a simple homoioteleuton, especially when we consider that without R. Judan's opinion the pericope must at all events be considered textually defective [after stating "we have come to the *dispute*," the midrash brings only a single position!]. Such was the determination of Theodor in his edition. However, in light of the structural complexity of the pericope, with its apparent joining of two separate sources one of which is quoting the other, there might still be room for a different reconstruction of its textual evolution. At any rate, aside from any outstanding textual questions, it remains possible (as we suggested above) that the verse from Psalms was not intended to connect to the issue of the dispute, but only to the idea that enslavement to the nations is a substitute for Gehenna. If so, then it is possible that it was R. Ḥanina who cited the verse in that context, and that the Bavli's attribution of the proem to R. Ḥanina bar Pappa was based on the fact that it was he who introduced the rendering of "*men*" as "nations"; or at least, that they retained some recollection of R. Ḥanina's having expounded that verse.

Proem #8

[11a] R. Johanan opened a proem to this lection from here: "*He hath remembered his mercy and his faithfulness to the house of Israel, all the ends of the earth have seen the salvation of our Lord*" (Psalms 98:3).

When did[87] "*all the ends of the earth see the salvation of our Lord*?"[88] —In the days of Mordecai and Esther.

This proem (for which there are no known parallels in the Palestinian midrashic literature) has a structure similar to the preceding one: It draws a thematic connection from a verse that speaks in a general way about redemption, to the specific redemption of the Jews of the Persian empire in the days of Mordecai and Esther. This verse could easily have served as a proem to any other scriptural lection involving a national salvation.

Proem #9

[11a] [89]R. Simeon b. Laqish opened a proem to this lection from here: "*As a roaring lion and a ravenous bear, so is a wicked ruler over a poor people*" (Proverbs 28:15).

"*As a roaring lion*" —This is[90] Nebuchadnezzar; concerning whom it is written: "*A lion is gone up from his thicket*" (Jeremiah 4:7).

"*And a ravenous bear*"—This is Ahasuerus; concerning whom it is written regarding the kingdom of Persia:[91] "*And behold another beast, a second, like to a bear*" (Daniel 7:5).

And Rav Joseph taught [in a *baraita*]: These are the Persians who eat[92] like a bear[93] and drink like a bear[94] and are enveloped in flesh[95]

---

87 "When did"— ~ in MSS **O**, **R** **HgT1**, .

88 "did…'…*Lord*'"— ~ in **HgT2**. MSS **O**, **P**, **EY** add: "This is."

89 MS **V** adds: "Heard Eleazar Slothful Naḥman Would Rava Righteous Dotan (?) Nation Which Miracle: Sign"; MS **R**: "Sign."

90 **Spanish family** and **Printings** add: "the wicked."

91 "regarding ...Persia"— ~ in **Printings**.

92 **YS** (*editio princeps*, not in MS Oxford) adds: "flesh."

93 "like...bear"— ~ in MSS **M**, **R**, **Mf**, **EY**, **Printings**, **YS**.

94 "and drink like a bear" — ~ in MS **L** and **YS**.

95 "in flesh"— ~ in MSS **G**, **B**, **O**, **R**, **W**, **Mf**, **P**, **V**, **EY**, **HgT**.

like a bear, and grow their hair long[96] like a bear, and they have no rest[97] like a bear.[98]

"*A wicked ruler*" —This is Haman.[99]

"*Over a poor people*" —These are Israel, who became impoverished[100] of the commandments.[101]

This proem also follows the method of supplying specific interpretations to a general verse.[102] Rav Joseph's comment is not original to the proem, but was transferred in the later redaction from its original context in *TB Qiddushin* 72a (perhaps *via ʿAvodah Zarah* 2b).

Proem #10

[11a] R. Eleazar opened a proem to this lection from here: "*By slothfulness he that lays rafters sinks* [yimakh], *and through idleness of the hands the house leaketh*" (Ecclesiastes 10:18).

Through the slothfulness that inhered in Israel, that they did not occupy themselves in the Torah,[103] as it were,[104] he[105] became the enemy[106] of the Holy One.

---

96 See J. Preuss, *Julius Preuss' Biblical and Talmudic Medicine*, 2nd ed., translated by Fred Rosner (New York: Hebrew Publishing Company, 1978).

97 "grow...rest"— MS **B**: "have no rest...grow their hair long."

98 On the identification of Persia with a bear see: Jay Braverman, *Jerome's Commentary on Daniel: A Study of Comparative Jewish and Christian Interpretations of the Hebrew Bible*, Vol. 7, The Catholic Biblical Quarterly Monograph Series, ed. B. Vawter *et al.* (Washington: The Catholic Biblical Association of America, 1978), 86-9.

99 "This is Haman" — ~ in MS **B**.

100 "became impoverished" —MSS **G**, **B**, **R**, **Mf**, **V**, **Printings**,: "who are poor."

101 MSS **R**, **Mf** and **V** add: "in the days of Haman." **AgE** adds: "which are in the Torah."

102 The identification of the "*poor people*" with Israel may be influenced by the frequently cited dictum of R, Joḥanan: "Every place where it says *dakh*, *ʿani* or *evion*, Scripture is speaking of Israel, since poverty has inhered in them ever since the Temple was destroyed." See *Genesis rabbah*, 71:1, *Midrash on Psalms*, 9:19, etc.

103 "that they...Torah"—in Aramaic only in MS **Y**; all others, in Hebrew.

104 "as it were"—only in MS **Y**, **EY**: "in the days of Haman"; ~ in all other texts.

105 "he"—MS **M** and **YS**: "they."

106 "enemy"—**YS:** "enemies."

> "*Sinks*" —the one who is called "He who lays the rafters."[107]
>
> And "*makh*" [sink] means nothing other than impoverished, as it says: "*And if he is too poor* [makh] *for thy valuation*" (Leviticus 27:8).
>
> And the layer of rafters [*ha-meqareh*] is none other than the Holy One, as it says: "*Who layest the rafters* [ha-meqareh] *of the upper chambers in the waters*" (Psalms 104:3).

The interpretation "through the slothfulness that inhered in Israel, etc." is found verbatim in *TB Taʿanit* 7b, where it is adduced as an explanation of Rav Qaṭina's dictum: "Rain is withheld only on account of slothfulness [variant: neglect][108] of the Torah, as it says: '*By slothfulness*, etc.'" Following this dictum, the passage continues: "Rav Joseph said: From here..." indicating[109] that the pericope (or at least the citation from Ecclesiastes) was already known to him. The subject-matter of the verse, "*Who layest the rafters of the upper chambers in the waters*," also seems more appropriate to the context of *Taʿanit*, which deals with the subjects of rainfall and drought. Taken together, all these facts indicate that the homily originated in *Taʿanit*. It is however hard to imagine that at any stage in its evolution the proem had consisted of nothing more than the scriptural citation, without any explanatory transition to Esther. There appear to be two possible explanations for the current state of the pericope: (1) The verse might have been expounded independently by two separate preachers in two different contexts (one with reference to drought, and the other with reference to Purim), after which the later redaction correlated the wordings of the two traditions, creating the illusion of parallel traditions. Or alternatively: (2) It is conceivable that the very transposing of the dictum from *Taʿanit* to *Megillah* was the creative act that constituted the Esther proem; i.e., the darshan constructed his

---

107 MS **R** adds: "As it is written: '*Who layest the rafters of thy upper chambers in the waters*' (Psalm 104:3)."

108 בימול; see Henry Malter, ed., *The Treatise Taʿanit of the Babylonian Talmud*, Vol. 1, Publications of the American Academy for Jewish Research (New York: American Academy for Jewish Research, 1930), 23.

109 The conection is not proven however, and may be the result of editorial manipulation.

petiḥta around Ecclesiastes 10:18 *as interpreted by Rav Qaṭina.* It is also possible that R. Eleazar himself was making conscious use of Rav Qaṭina's interpretation.[110]

Proem #11

> [11a] Rav Naḥman bar Isaac opened a proem to this lection from here:[111] "*A song of ascents: If it had not been for the Lord who was for us, let Israel now say, If it had not been for the Lord who was for us when man rose up against us*" (Psalms 124:1-2).
>
> "*If it had not been for the Lord who was for us when man rose up against us*" —a[112] "*man*," and not a king.

The intent of Rav Naḥman bar Isaac's comment is obscure. The traditional commentators understood "a man" to be an allusion to Haman. This would appear to imply that the homilist is trying either to deny any active role on Ahasuerus's part in Haman's plot or to assert that, had the initiative actually come from the king, then the Jews could not have been saved (thereby enhancing the miraculous dimensions of the story). It is however also possible to view the comment as a questioning of the legitimacy of Ahasuerus' claim to the throne, in the same vein as the opinions brought on 11a below: "He was not fit [to be king]; It was that he gave more money, and was appointed."

However we might choose to interpret R. Naḥman bar Isaac's comment, there is no doubt that Psalm 124 is by itself a perfectly appropriate text upon which to build a proem to Esther.

---

[110] In *Leviticus rabbah*, 19:4 [Mordecai Margulies, ed., *Midrash wayyikra rabbah* (Jerusalem: Wahrmann, 1972, 424 ff.], the verse from Ecclesiastes is expounded in a variety of ways, but two of the interpretations follow the pattern "because Israel were slothful…'*he that lays rafters sinks.*'" This fact gives further support to the likelihood that two homilists might have independently arrived at similar interpretation of the same verse, though applying it to different topics. It appears that the principal reading in both *Taʿanit* and *Megillah* is מד שנקרא מקרה , though I am not certain of its correct translation. Cf. the notes in *Diqduqé Soferim* to *Megillah* here.

[111] "to this…here"— ~ in MS **O**.

[112] **HgT** adds: "wicked."

Proem #12

> [11a] Rava[113] opened a proem to this lection from here: "*When the righteous are increased the people rejoice,* {*but when the wicked beareth rule the people sigh*" (Proverbs 29:2).
>
> "*When the righteous are increased the people rejoice*}"[114] —This is[115] Mordecai.[116]
>
> As it is written: "*And Mordecai went forth from the presence of the king in royal apparel ...and the city of Shushan shouted and was glad*" (Esther 8:15).[117]
>
> "*But when the wicked beareth rule the people sigh*" —This is Haman, as it is written: "[*And the king and Haman sat down to drink*], *but the city of Shushan was perplexed*" (Esther 3:15).

The same verse is expounded among the Proems to *Esther rabbah* (#6):

> R. Isaac opened: "*When the righteous are increased the people rejoice, but when the wicked beareth rule the people sigh*" —When the righteous enjoy greatness, there is joy and happiness in the world: *Vah vah*[118] in the world. But when the wicked enjoy greatness, there are *vay* and sighing and wrath in the world ... Among the nations of the world, as it says: "*And it came to pass* [vayhi] *in the days of Ahasuerus*" —*Vay* that Ahasuerus reigned!

The only feature common to these two proems is the verse that they cite. More significant are the differences between them: Rava's proem elaborates the contrast between the righteous and the wicked, exemplified in Mordecai and Haman. The proof-texts are from Esther chapters 3 and 8, and the conclusion "*but the city of Shushan was perplexed*" (Esther 3:15) does not lead to a proper *petiḥta*. By contrast, R.

---

113 "Rava" —MSS **B**, **V**: "Rabbah"; MS **P**: "Rav"; **AgE**: "R. Abba."

114 Bracketed section added according to most witnesses; ~ in MSS **Y**, **G** and **B**.

115 MS **Mf** adds: "the righteous."

116 Most witnesses (other than MSS **Y**, **L**, **Mf AgE**) add: "and Esther."

117 **Spanish family** and MS **R** add: "And it is written: '*The Jews had light and gladness and joy and honor*' (Esther 8:16)."

118 On "*vah*" as an expression of joy see Kohut, 3:254. He notes that, like its counterpart "*vay*," the term was in use in both Latin (*vah*) and Greek (οὐά). See our discussion at the beginning of Chapter 1 above.

Isaac's homily in *Esther rabbah* restricts the interpretation of the verse to righteous and wicked *kings*. The first part of the verse is interpreted with reference to David,[119] Solomon and Asa among Israelite monarchs, and Cyrus among the Gentile rulers; the last part is applied to Ahab, Hosea son of Elah and Zedekiah among the Israelite monarchs, and Ahasuerus among the Gentile rulers. By means of this exegetical approach, the darshan is able to lead up to a conclusion that ties in with the verse "*And it came to pass in the days of Ahasuerus.*"[120]

Proems #13-#14

[11a] Rav Mattanah[121] said: From here: "*For what great nation is there that hath God so nigh to them* [*as the Lord our God is whensoever we call upon him*?]" (Deuteronomy 4:7).

Rav Ashi[122] said: From here:[123] "*Or hath God assayed to go and take him a nation from the midst of another nation* [*by trials, by signs, and by wonders*]" (Deuteronomy 4:34).

---

119 See *Yefeh ʿanaf*: "He expounds '*increased*' (ברבות) in the sense of '*and the elder* (ורב) *shall serve the younger*' (Genesis 25:23); i.e.: when the righteous become great and powerful." Cf. Maharsha to the Bavli: "...Or maybe the word '*increased*' implies importance..."

120 In *Aggadat bereshit* (Buber) end of Ch. 35, the same theme is developed from a different verse (in which a king is explicitly mentioned): "...Another interpretation: '*Now king David was old and stricken in years*' (1 Kings 1:1). This is what Scripture has said: '*A king that sitteth in the throne of judgment scattereth away all evil with his eyes*' (Proverbs 20:8). Come and see, when the wicked become great in the world, an evil beast comes to the world. But when the righteous become great in the world, all are joyous and glad. When Zedekiah was appointed king, all commenced saying '*vay*!' —'*And* [*Zedekiah*] *the son of Josiah reigned* [vay-yimlokh]...' (Jeremiah 37:1)." Cf. Ch. Albeck, ed., *Midrash bereshit rabbati* (Jerusalem: 1940), 165. Proverbs 29:2 is also expounded in *Midrash on Psalms* (47), but there the theme that is developed is that "when the wicked rule over the world everyone sighs, etc.," and no illustrations are adduced.

121 "Mattanah"—**EY**: "Mottena"; ~ in MS **M**.

122 "Rav Ashi"—MS **O**: "Rav Mattanah"; MS **R***: "And Rav Assi"; MS **V**: "And Rava"; MS **L**: "Rav."

123 "From here"— ~ in MSS **G** and **B** (before emendation).

Rav Mattanah and Rav Ashi bring two verses that could serve as proems to Esther.[124] R. Mattanah's verse speaks of the special closeness between Israel and the God who hurries to respond to the prayers of his people. Rav Ashi's verse emphasizes (so, presumably, did he understand the text) God's power to deliver the Jews during their exile among the nations of the world, as well as his ability to gather them up from their dispersion as he did at the time of the Exodus.[125] The two verses are quoted without any accompanying commentary. Possibly it is being assumed that these verses could be expounded. However in light of the preceding instances, it appears more likely that the Babylonian *Amora'im* really understood that the verse (provided that it comes from a different book of the Bible) can by itself constitute a proem. It would have been a simple procedure to attach the verses to the lection through the addition of a formula such as "When? —In the days of Ahasuerus."

These two verses seem to have held a special importance for Rav Ashi as expressions of the divine love for the Jewish people. In *TB Berakhot* 6a he identifies them as the passages inscribed in God's phylacteries.[126]

---

124 Syntactically the expression has to be read elliptically, as: "[A proem can be constructed] from here" or something of the sort. The inconsistency in the terminology implies that the previous units were used as actual proems, whereas the present ones are only hypothetical. From a source-critical perspective it would appear that Rav Mattanah (?) and Rav Ashi (possibly in some sort of editorial capacity) were adding "appendices" or glosses to proem-lists which had been transmitted to them. I discern in this fact no suggestion on the part of the talmud's redactors that these two units could not have served as proper proems (e.g., because they contain only unexpounded biblical verses).

125 Maharsha: "He is comparing their redemption in the days of Mordecai and Esther to their redemption from Egypt... and this is the point of saying '*Or hath God assayed to go and take him a nation from the midst of another nation*, etc.' —referring to a nation that is subject to another nation seeking to harm it."

126 Cf. *Mekhilta Shirata* [ed. Horovitz-Rabin 126; Jacob Z. Lauterbach, ed., *Mekilta de-rabbi ishmael* (Philadelphia: Jewish Publication Society of America, 1961), 2:23]; *Mekhilta derabbi shimʿon ben yoḥai*, p. 78; D. Hoffmann, ed., *Midrasch Tannaïm zum Deuteronomium* (Berlin: Itzkowski, 1909), 221. *Esther rabbah*, 7:13 contains the following:

> ...Immediately [Ahasuerus] sent and assembled all the wise men of the nations of the world. They all came before him. Ahasuerus said to

Continued on next page...

Rav's "Proem"

> [11a] [127]"*And it came to pass* [vayhi] *in the days of Ahasuerus*" (Esther 1:1)—
>
> Says Rav:[128] *Vay hayah* [Woe came to pass]![129] There was a fulfillment of[130] what is written:[131] "*And there ye shall sell yourselves unto your enemies for bondmen and for bondwomen, and no man shall buy you*" (Deuteronomy 28:68).

At the conclusion of the proem-collection we encounter a puzzling phenomenon. Following Rav Ashi's proem is inserted a second *pisqa* to Esther 1:1: "*And it came to pass in the days of Ahasuerus*," in spite of the fact that the same *pisqa* has already appeared before the dicta of R. Levi / R. Jonathan on the previous leaf.[132] Rav interprets the opening verse of Esther with reference to Deuteronomy 28:68 And yet immediately afterwards we read: "And Samuel said: From here:[133] '*And yet for all that, when they are in the land of their enemies...*'"

...Continued from previous page

> them: Is it your will that we cause this nation to perish from the world? They all said to him as one: ... And furthermore, all the nations are termed "strangers" before the Holy One...but Israel are termed "close"... And no nation is close to the Holy One except Israel, as it says: "*as the Lord our God is whensoever we call upon Him.*"

This portion of *Esther rabbah* belongs to a later midrash, which already made use of the Babylonian Talmud; see Zunz–Albeck, *Hadderashot beyisra'el*, 129-30, and n. 35.

127 MSS **M** and **Mf** add: "Another matter."

128 "Says Rav"—MSS **B** (after emendation), **Mf**, **AgE**: "Rav says"; MS **L**: "Says Rav Judah"; MS **P**: "Says [Rav]"; MS **M**: ~.

129 "*Vay hayah*"—MSS **M** and **W**: "*Vay havah*" (Aramaic); **EY** and **Printings**: "*vay vehi*"; MS **O**: "*vay*"; **AgE**: "*Vayhi—vay hayah*"; ~ in MS **P** and **HgT[1]**.

130 "There...fulfillment"– ~ in most texts (other than MS **Y**, **Spanish family** and **AgE**); MS **B**: "in his days"; Genizah fragment: "in the days of Ahasuerus."

131 Most texts (other than MSS **Y**, **B**, **W**, **V**, **Printings**, **AgE** and Genizah fragment) add: "in the Torah."

132 Note that two Ashkenazic manuscripts precede the second *pisqa* with the formula דבר אחר ("Another matter"), as if to introduce an alternative midrash to the first pericope. It is true that Rav's dictum does follow naturally from the first pericope.

133 See variant readings listed above.

In other words, the Talmud is presenting Samuel's comment as a continuation of the sequence of proems, notwithstanding the fact that Rav's dictum has already taken us into the next phase of the midrash, the actual exposition of the first verse of Esther. The Vilna *Ga'on* in his glosses to the Talmud was sensitive to this incongruity, and concluded that Rav's words should be considered as part of the proem-list and that the *pisqa* was inserted here mistakenly. According to him, the *pisqa* should properly be moved forward to the end of the proem-list, where it ought to serve as an introduction to the various explanatory comments to Esther 1:1. Therefore, his version of Rav's dictum reads only "Said Rav: From here: '*And there ye shall sell yourselves unto your enemies for bondmen and for bondwomen, and no man shall buy you*' (Deuteronomy 28:68)." Now this explanation would indeed seem very persuasive[134] were it not for the fact that it finds no support in any extant textual witnesses, all of which read (with minor variations) "Says Rav: *Vay hayah* [Woe came to pass]! There was a fulfillment of what is written '*And there ye shall sell yourselves...*'"[135] It would appear nonetheless (as we shall have occasion to observe below) that the *Ga'on*'s explanation does reflect accurately the state of Rav's dictum as it existed at the time of the midrash's earliest redaction.

The verse cited by Rav (Deuteronomy 28:68) is not altogether appropriate to its current midrashic context, opening as it does with "*And the Lord shall bring you into* ***Egypt*** *again with ships*" —hardly the best choice for a homily about the days of Ahasuerus in Persia and

---

[134] This is especially true when we consider the fact that the passage to which the *Ga'on* wants to attach Rav's dictum also begins with the words "Said Rav: [the brother of the 'Head'...]," increasing the likelihood that a scribe had confused the two instances.

[135] An explanation similar to that of the Vilna *Ga'on* is suggested by H. D. Azulai, *Petaḥ ʿeinayim* (Livorno: 1790). He proposes that Samuel's dictum be moved to the end of the proem-collection. He also notes difficulties in the chronological progression of the collection: "It requires serious consideration, why Samuel and his contemporaries are cited after Rav Ashi." See also the observations of Arieh b. Asher, *Ṭurei Even*: "I do not know why the Gemara interrupted the proems with this homily, seeing that it continues afterwards to bring more proems by several Amora'im. Perhaps Rav's dictum is also a proem." Note that witnesses from the Spanish family insert a *pisqa* citing Esther 1:1 before the dictum about "brother of the Head," though most of the texts have only the single word "Ahasuerus."

Media. The selection of this verse does become somewhat more acceptable when we compare our text to the opening of *Esther rabbah*, which contains an exposition of the entire Deuteronomy passage, beginning with verse 66: "*And your life shall hang in doubt before you.*" These curses, which can be understood to have been fulfilled in the Babylonian exile, speak of the tribulations of *all* exiles.[136] In keeping with its scriptural context, the passage was expounded with reference to Egypt, but also with reference to other exiles. Accordingly we find the following passage at the beginning of *Esther rabbah*:

> "*And it came to pass in the days of Ahasuerus*"—
>
> Rav opened: "*And your life shall hang in doubt before you.*" Rav interpreted the verse with reference to Haman: "*And your life shall hang in doubt before you*" —from one moment to the next.[137] "*And you shall fear day and night*" —at the time when the documents fly off.[138] "*And shall have no assurance of your life*" — "[*The copy of the writing, to be given out for a decree in every province, was to be published unto all the peoples*] *that they should be ready against thee that day*" (Esther 3:14).[139]
>
> "*In the morning you shall say: Would that it were evening*" —In the morning of Babylonia, you shall say: Would that it were its evening! In the morning of Media, you shall say: Would that it were its evening!...
>
> An alternative interpretation: ...In the morning of Babylonia, you shall say: Would that it were the evening of Media! And in the morning of Media, you shall say: Would that it were the evening of Greece!...

---

[136] E.g., verse 63: "*...so the Lord will rejoice over you to destroy you...and you shall be plucked from off the land whither you go to possess it* (64) *...And the Lord will scatter you among all the people, from the one end of the earth even unto the other...*(65) *And among these nations you shall find no ease, neither shall the sole of your foot have rest...*"

[137] Cf. Esther 3:9 and glosses of R. David Luria; *Numbers rabbah*, 14:12.

[138] Cf. Esther 3:15.

[139] For detailed discussion of some other segments of the passage, see: Daniel Sperber, *Roman Palestine 200–400: The Land*, Bar-Ilan Studies in Near Eastern Languages and Culture (Ramat-Gan: Bar–Ilan University Press, 1978), 57, and the exhaustive bibliographical references in n. 29. See also *Genesis rabbah*, 91:6 (1122); *Tanḥuma Miqqeṣ*, 7; *Tanḥuma* (ed. Buber) *Miqqeṣ*, 10 (195). Cf. Neusner, *The Midrashic Compilations of the Sixth and Seventh Centuries*, 2:19-24, 49-50.

> "*And no man shall buy you.*" Why will no man buy you? —Rav says: Because you did not transmit הקניתם the words of the covenant,[140] for there is among you none who will "buy" the words of the five books of the Pentateuch, the numerical value of "קונה."[141]
>
> And says R. Judah: You are Imperial property (ταμιακός),[142] and is it not true that anyone who acquires a slave from the Imperial Treasury is liable to the death penalty! Even so did Ahasuerus say to his wife: "*Behold, I have given Esther the house of Haman*" (Esther 8:7), and R. Judah b. R. Simon said: Thus was the fate of anyone who laid his hand on the Imperial Treasury...
>
> And Rabbi Isaac says: As slaves and maidservants you are not bought; however you are bought to destroy, to slay, and to cause to perish (cf. Esther 3:13; 7:4, etc.). For so does Esther address Ahasuerus: "*But if we had been sold for bondmen and bondwomen...*" (Esther 7:4). For thus did Moses our Teacher write for us in the Torah: "*And there ye shall sell yourselves unto your enemies for bondmen and for bondwomen, and no man shall buy you*" (Deuteronomy 28:68). Perhaps "*to be destroyed, to be slain, and to perish.*" —As soon as they all observed this, they commenced crying "*Vay vay!*" —"*Vayhi*" —Woe that it was in the days of Ahasuerus!

The proem in *Esther rabbah* is a complex one, and we cannot be altogether certain of its original structure, nor about which of its segments were included in Rav's original homily. At any rate, we may presume that Rav expounded verse 66 in connection with Esther; his *derashah* on verse 68, which does not allude directly to the Purim story, is also cited by the redactor of *Esther rabbah*. However, the central moment of the proem is contained in the words of R. Isaac at the conclusion of the passage, as he builds upon the verbal similarities between "*And there ye shall sell yourselves unto your enemies for bondmen and for bondwomen, and no man shall buy you*" and "*But if we had been sold for bondmen and bondwomen I had held my peace*"

---

140 Cf. the following verse (Deut. 28:69): "*These are the words of the covenant which the Lord commanded Moses*, etc."

141 The meaning is very obscure; see the traditional commentators.

142 See Krauss, *Griechische und lateinische Lehnwörter*, 268.

(Esther 7:4).[143] A cursory comparison of the Palestinian and Babylonian traditions reveals that the former is at once more coherent and more elegantly crafted. There can be little doubt that the original version of the passage was founded upon the link to Esther 7:4—and yet this pivotal verse is not even mentioned in the Esther-Midrash. Furthermore, by moving the "*vayhi–vay hayah*" ahead to the beginning of the dictum rather than placing it at the conclusion, the Babylonian proem-collection has been divested of its unified *petiḥta* structure and its original symmetry has been destroyed. However it is precisely the anomalous placement of Rav's exegetical dictum in the midst of a collection of proems that provides us with a strong indication (as the Vilna *Ga'on* recognized) that the dictum's original form must have resembled that of *Esther rabbah*, where it constitutes a proem to the Book of Esther, not an explanation of its opening verse. The later redactors of the Babylonian *sugya* were no longer sensitive to how inappropriate the dictum had become in its new context.[144] The transformation of Rav's dictum from a proem into an explanatory gloss also affected the functions assigned to the subsequent dicta of Samuel, R. Levi and R. Ḥiyya bar Abba. We shall return to this topic below when we discuss those dicta in detail.

This instance points to a weakening in the understanding of the function of the *petiḥta* among the Babylonian redactors of the Esther–Midrash, a phenomenon that becomes readily apparent when we examine the connection between the "proem verse" and the opening verse of Esther, a connection that should lie at the crux of a proper *petiḥta*. We have already observed that in *Esther rabbah* there is a uniform conclu-

---

[143] The content of this passage is also incorporated into the Second Targum to Esther 1:1; see also L. B. Paton, *A Critical and Exegetical Commentary on the Book of Esther*, International Critical Commentary, ed. S. R. Driver, A. Plummer and C. A. Briggs (Edinburgh: T & T Clark, 1964), 122.

[144] It is possible that the connection between Deuteronomy 28:68 and Esther 7:4 is being alluded to in Rashi's remarks to the Talmud here; cf. Maharsha, and the "*Ḥiddushim*" section of the **EY** editions. The fact that the original context of Rav's dictum resembled that of *Esther rabbah* is further borne out by the fact that in both sources Samuel's proem is cited immediately following it (in very similar wordings). R. Levi's proem is also found in an expanded version among the proems to *Esther rabbah*.

sion to all the proems: "As soon as they all observed this, they commenced crying '*Vay vay!*' —'*Vayhi*' —Woe that it was in the days of Ahasuerus!" This structure provides the homilist with considerable flexibility for the development of his various themes. In order to tie his *derashah* in with the first verse of Esther all he is required to do is to lead up to any topic that has something to do with the dangers and sufferings (*Vay!*) that befell or threatened the Jews during the reign of Ahasuerus.

This is of course radically different from the situation in our Babylonian midrash. There, not a single one of the proems actually creates a transition to the opening verse of Esther, or even concludes with the mention of the name "Ahasuerus." In many of the instances, such a connection could have been created with no difficulty, but the redactors felt no compulsion to do so.

Following is a list of the conclusions of the *petiḥtot*:

1. "*...and offspring*"—This refers to Vashti.
2. "*...that shall not be cut off*"—This is the reading of the Megillah.[145]
3. "*...so the Lord will rejoice* [yasis] *over you to cause you to perish*, etc."[146]
4. ...This is Mordecai;[147] as it is written: "*And Esther set Mordecai over the house of Haman.*"
5. "*...and princes*" —this is Haman and his ten sons.
6. "*...but hath extended mercy unto us in the sight of the kings of Persia*, etc." (Ezra 9:9).[148]

---

[145] Cf. the variant readings listed above, some of which are very significant. See also Heinemann, *Derashot beṣibbur bitequfat ha-talmud*, p. 43.

[146] This is presumably the conclusion of the proem *per se*. See our discussion above.

[147] Cf. variant readings.

[148] Note the additions found in the various texts, as recorded in detail above: "When [*hath he extended mercy unto us*]? In the [days] [time] of [Haman] [Mordecai] [Mordecai and Esther].

7. "*But thou didst bring us out into abundance*" —in the days of Mordecai and Esther.[149]
8. When did "*all the ends of the earth see the salvation of our Lord*"? —In the days of Mordecai and Esther.
9. "These are Israel, who became impoverished of the commandments".[150]
10. "He became the enemy of the Holy One.[151]
11. "'*A man*,' and not a king."
12. "This is Haman, as it is written: '*but the city of Shushan was perplexed.*'"[152]

As regards most of the conclusions in our list, it would have been easy to have added a passage like "When? In the days of Ahasuerus: '*And it came to pass in the days of Ahasuerus*,'" in order to transform the units into proems to the opening verse. In numbers #6, #7, #8, etc., the situation is even more surprising. In all of these instances the unit ends with the words "in the days of Haman / Mordecai /Mordecai and Esther" —precisely in places where the wording "in the days of Ahasuerus" would have supplied us with a satisfactory transition. In other instances (#4, #12, etc.) the darshan concluded with other verses from Esther. Taken together, all these phenomena furnish us with abundant evidence that, unlike their Palestinian colleagues, the redactors of our Babylonian pericope did not insist on the connection between the *petiḥta* and the first verse of the lection.

---

149 Or: "Haman." See critical apparatus.

150 Cf. the reading of MS **R** cited above.

151 This appears to be the conclusion of the proem proper. The complete unit concludes "And the layer of rafters is none other than the Holy One, as it says: '*Who layest the rafters* [hammeqareh] *of thy upper chambers in the waters*.'" Note **EY**'s addition of "in the days of Haman."

152 The remaining examples consist only of verses, without any literary or exegetical embellishment. That of Samuel, concluding "in the days of Gog and Magog," (or: "For the future times, when no nation or language will hold power over you") obviously does not connect formally to Esther.

Samuel's Proem

[11a] And[153] Samuel said: From here:[154] "*And yet for all that, when they are in the land of their enemies, I will not reject them, neither will I abhor them, to destroy them utterly, and to break my covenant with them*" (Leviticus 26:44).[155]

"*I will not reject them*" —in the days of the Greeks.

"*Neither will I abhor them*" —in the days of Vespasian Caesar.[156]

"*To destroy them utterly,*[157] *and to break my covenant with them*" —in the days of Haman.[158]

"*For I am the Lord their God*"[159] —in the days of Gog and Magog.

There follows a *baraita* on a theme similar to that of Samuel's dictum.

YSMG: a sign[160]

In a *baraita* it teaches:

KNMR: a sign[161]

---

153 "And" —Thus in all direct witnesses; see our analysis of the significance of this fact to the literary structure of the pericope. Only in **MhG** to Leviticus [A. Steinsaltz, ed., *Midrash haggadol ʿal ḥamish-shah ḥumshei torah sefer vayyiqra* (Jerusalem: Mosad Harav Kook, 1975), 752]: "Said Samuel."

154 "From here" —Thus in the MSS **Y, M, Mf, AgE,** as well as before Rashi; MS **W**: "from the verse:"; ~ in MSS **G, L, R*, V, Printings, Spanish family** and Genizah fragment.

155 **MhG** and **AgE** add: "YSM'G: a sign."

156 "Caesar"— ~ in MSS **B, O, R*, P, V, HgT**.

157 Thus in MSS **Y, AgE** and **MhG**; MSS **G, B** (before emendation) and **R*** add: "in the days of the Romans"; all other witnesses (including **Ashkenazic** and **Spanish families**, MS **B** after emendation and Genizah fragment) add: "in the days of Haman".

158 "Haman"— Thus in **Yemenite family**, MSS **B** (before emendation), **O, R***; all other witnesses [including MS **B** (after emendation) and Genizah fragment]: "the Romans."

159 "*God*" —MS **L** adds: "in the days of the Messiah and"; MS **M** adds: "In the future to come and."

160 "YSMG: a sign" — found only in MS **Y**.

161 "KNMR: a sign" —found only in **Yemenite family**.

"*I will not reject them*" —in the days of the Chaldeans, when I appointed[162] for them Daniel "*the man greatly beloved*" (Daniel 11:12),[163] Ḥananiah, Mishael and Azariah.

"*Neither will I abhor them*" —in the days of the Greeks, when I appointed for them Simeon the Righteous[164] and Mattathias[165] son of Joḥanan[166] the High Priest[167] and[168] Ḥashmonai and his sons.

"*To destroy them utterly*" —in the days of Haman, when I appointed for them Mordecai and Esther.[169]

"*To break My covenant with them*" —in the days of the Romans, when I appointed for them those of the House of Rabbi and the Sages of his generation.[170]

"*For I am the Lord their God*" —For the future times, when no nation or language will[171] hold power over you.[172]

The Talmud continues:

R. Levi said:[173] From here:

"*But if you will not drive out the inhabitants of the land from before you,* [*then shall those that you let remain of them be as thorns in your eyes...*]" (Numbers 33:55).

---

162 "appointed"—**HgT²**: "did not appoint."

163 "Daniel...'*...beloved*'"—only in **Yemenite family**; MS **M**: "Simeon the Righteous"; MSS **G**, **B** (before emendation), **O**: ~; others: "Daniel."

164 "Simeon the Righteous" — ~ in MSS **O**, **M**.

165 "and Mattathias" — ~ in MS **O** and **YS**.

166 "son of Joḥanan" — ~ in MSS **B**, **O**, **W**, **Printings**, **YS**.

167 "the High Priest" — ~ in MSS **B**, **O**, **HgT¹**.

168 "and" — ~ in MSS **G**, **O**.

169 "Greeks... Simeon the Righteous... Haman...Mordecai and Esther" —**EY**, **YS** reverse the order: "Haman [=**EY**; **YS**: Media] ...Mordecai and Esther ...Greeks ...Simeon the Righteous (and Mattathias son of Joḥanan the High Priest the Hasmonean and his sons — ~ in **YS**)."

170 "his generation" —thus in MS **M**, **MhG**; all other witnesses: "the generations."

171 MSS **G**, **B**, **Mf**, **W**, **V**, **EY**, **Ashkenazi family**, **YS**, **Printings**, Genizah fragment add: "be able to."

172 MSS **B**, **M** and Genizah fragment add: "any more."

173 "said" —**EY** and **HgT** add: "opened a proem to this lection [last three words ~ in **HgT¹**]."

R. Ḥiyya bar Abba[174] said: From here:

"*Moreover it shall come to pass, that I shall do unto you, as I thought to do unto them*" (Numbers 33:56).[175]

There are two possible ways of understanding how the dicta of Samuel, R. Levi and R. Ḥiyya bar Abba were meant to fit into the structure of the pericope, and it seems as if the respective choices between these explanations influenced the wording of the talmudic textual traditions.

According to one possibility the comments are attached to Rav's statement: "There was a fulfillment of what is written: '*And there ye shall sell yourselves unto your enemies for bondmen and for bondwomen, and no man shall buy you.*'" Each of these *Amora'im* is proposing a Pentateuchal verse of castigation that was fulfilled in the days of Mordecai and Esther. An interpretation along these lines is reflected in those textual witnesses that omit the expression "from here" (which does not connect to Rav's dictum) from Samuel's comment. It is evident that, unlike Rav, Samuel wished to underscore the idea of consolation, rather than the trouble and "*vay*."

However it appears that this reading, and its implied interpretation, are not original to the pericope. The words "from here" appear in all witnesses to the dicta of R. Levi and R. Ḥiyya bar Abba.[176]

---

174 "bar Abba" — ~ in MSS **B** (before emendation), **W**, **M**, **Printings**. **Spanish family** (including MS **B***) and MS **V** add: "said R. Joḥanan."

175 **MhG** to Numbers [Z. M. Rabinowitz, ed., *Midrash haggadol on the Pentateuch: Numbers* (Jerusalem: Mosad Harav Kook, 1973), 567] adds: "When did they seek to destroy them utterly? —In the days of Haman."

176 If Rav and Samuel were indeed explaining Esther 1:1, then it would be unlikely for the subsequent statements to revert back to the proem-sequence. This point was alluded to by Rashi, who seems to have had the reading "from here" in Samuel's dictum as well (cf. the glosses of R. Joel Sirkes, who tried to harmonize Rashi's comments with the text of the printed editions). The reading in Rashi's commentary is supported by MS New York-J.T.S. Rab. 382. However in MS Munich 216 (see *D.S.* n. *q*) of Rashi's commentary the word "proem" is omitted. According to this reading, Rashi may have read Samuel's comment as attached to Rav's. See W. Bacher, *Die Agada der babylonischen Amoräer* (Frankfurt a/M: 1913), 119, n. 26.

The second possibility is that the dicta of Samuel, R. Levi and R. Ḥiyya bar Abba all originated as proems to the Book of Esther.

A comparison with the parallel passages in *Esther rabbah* provides further evidence that all these Amoraic comments originated as proems. Samuel's dictum is brought there almost verbatim (Proem #4) immediately following the parallel to Rav's dictum (cited above). The introductory formulæ are: "Samuel opened ...R. Hiyya taught (תני)..."[177] In *Esther rabbah* as well the unit does not connect to the opening verse, as is required by a "proper" *petiḥta*. Rather, Samuel's dictum appears to be the first segment of a complex proem which also includes #5, and which goes on to dwell on the theme of the historical progression of empires. This unit concludes "And when they saw this they all began to cry '*vay!*' — '*And it came to pass* [vay hayah] *in the days of Ahasuerus.*'"[178]

A version of Levi's dictum is also included among the proems to *Esther rabbah* (#7):[179]

---

177 Jacob Neusner, *From Literature to Theology in Formative Judaism: Three Preliminary Studies*, Vol. 199, Brown Judaic Studies, ed. Jacob Neusner *et al.* (Atlanta: Scholars Press, 1989), comments on the *Esther rabbah* passage in the context of a study of "*davar aḥer*" pericopes in aggadic midrash, noting with respect to R. Ḥiyya's and Samuel's interpretations that "There is no way that the two *davar aḥers* can be read apart from one another, because only together do they make the point the compositor wanted to make. The two readings are of course complementary, the one invoking times of trouble in ages past, the other in the perceived present." The evaluation is a curious one: Both sources—neither of which is introduced as a *davar aḥer*!—speak of past and present [as well as future], overlapping more than they complement one another. The fact is that each of the traditions can exist perfectly well without the other.

178 See our discussions in the previous chapter.

179 A discussion of this passage is included in Jacob Neusner, *The Midrashic Compilations of the Sixth and Seventh Centuries: An Introduction to the Rhetorical, Logical and Topical Program*, Vol. 2, 19-24. The conclusions there are so trivially obvious as to be puzzling. They include: the fact that the midrashic passage employs a commentary-form; that some sections employ a proposition-form; that the conclusion of the proem is the basis for the connection to the base verse (Esther 1:1); and that the attributions are not integral to the content. As regards the last-mentioned item, Neusner seems to be using this fact as part of his general argument for the spuriousness of all attributions. While I share much of his skepticism regarding the reliability of attributions of dicta, it seems to me that, taken in isolation, the data adduced here

Continued on next page...

R. Levi opened: "*But if you will not drive out the inhabitants of the land from before you, then shall those that you let remain of them be as thorns in your eyes*" —This speaks of Saul. When Samuel said to him (1 Samuel 15:3) "*Now go and smite Amalek*" he said to him: You went out innocent and you returned guilty, and you took pity on him,[180] as it says (verse 9): "*But Saul and the people spared Agag.*" And behold, a shoot survives from him who will do to you harsh things, "*thorns in your eyes and goads in your sides.*" And who is this? —This is Haman, who thought to destroy, to slay, to cause to perish. And when everyone saw this they began to cry "*vay*!" "*And it came to pass* [vayhi] *in the days of Ahasuerus.*"

There can be little doubt that R. Levi's statement in the Bavli ought to be interpreted in the light of *Esther rabbah*,[181] except that the Babylonian tradition has once again preserved only the verse, without the exegesis or formal structure of the *petiḥta*.[182] The choice of verses in itself presents some problems. What we have here is two consecutive verses, conveying the identical message, namely that unless the Israelites drive out the inhabitants of the land (a category that can be extended to include Amalek), they are doomed to suffer at their hands. Why, then, should the verses be offered as two distinct (and perhaps contrasted) proems? It would appear rather that R. Ḥiyya bar Abba is actually reacting to R. Levi's suggestion and adding to his message: not only will the nations themselves become "thorns in your eyes and goads in your sides, etc." (as specified in verse 55), but God himself will

...Continued from previous page

would serve more effectively in *support* of their authenticity; i.e., on the face of it the only reason for introducing an attribution, if it is unnecessary to the presentation of the content *per se*, would be that it happens to be true. Furthermore, several of the attributions in the *Esther rabbah* proem (e.g., Rav, Levi) *are* actually corroborated by the (presumably independent) traditions of the Babylonian Esther-Midrash, a fact with which Neusner does not deal.

180 See *Mattenot kehunnah* and glosses of R. David Luria.

181 Rashi: "'*But if you will not drive out*, etc.' —They too were punished because of Saul's compassion on the Amalekites." See also Maharsha.

182 In *Pesiqta derav kahana* (ed. Mandelbaum, 228-9) and in the parallels listed in Buber's notes to *Eikhah zuṭa* [in: S. Buber, ed., *Midrash Zuṭa* (Berlin: 1894), 75, n. 6], there is found a proem by R. Samuel bar Naḥman to Jeremiah 1:1 in which Deuteronomy 33:55 is applied to Rahab, whom the midrash believed to be an ancestor of Jeremiah. Cf. the *Yefeh ʿanaf* to *Esther rabbah* "'It speaks of Saul' — i.e., we can expound it *also* with reference to the Amalek and Saul; however the primary sense of the verse concerns the 'seven nations.'"

bring upon you the destruction that he had originally intended to bring upon those nations. It is further possible that beneath the surface of this innocent-looking difference in the selection of proem-verses lies a fundamental divergence over the theological dimensions of the Purim story: Should Haman be regarded as a villain acting on his own initiative or as an instrument employed by God to punish the Jews for their transgressions?[183]

Concluding Remarks

1. Sources of the Proem-List:

It seems that the entire collection is based on Palestinian sources, including those that are cited in the Bavli in the names of Babylonian *Amora'im*. Several of the proems have parallels (full or partial) in *Esther rabbah*[184] or other midrashic compilations.[185] In general, the sources available to the Bavli were similar to those used by the redactors of *Esther rabbah*, though each of these works reworked the materials in its own distinctive manner. The resemblance to *Esther rabbah* is particularly notable when we take into consideration the relatively large number of midrashim that have survived to Esther, and observe that none of the others demonstrates such a consistent similarity to the Babylonian Esther Midrash.

---

183 See Eliezer Segal, "Human Anger and Divine Intervention in Esther" *Prooftexts* 9 (1989), 247-56.

184 These include those of R. Joḥanan, Rabbah bar Afdon, Rava, Rav, Samuel, R. Levi, as well as the tradition of R. Levi / R. Jonathan in the "Prologue." We have excluded from this count references to the second part of *Esther rabbah*, which is a separate and later work that makes use of the Babylonian Talmud; see, e.g.: *Esther rabbah*, 10:13; 7:13.

185 R. Abba bar Kahana's proem.

2. Ideological Themes:

The principal ideological motifs that are underscored in the proem collection include:

1. The incorporation of the Megillah narrative into the process of changing empires, as understood from prophetic tradition.[186] This theme emphasizes Vashti's role as Nebuchadnezzar's granddaughter and Ahasuerus's attempts to interfere with the erection of the Second Temple.[187]
2. Disasters befall the Jews only because of their sins.[188]
3. The righteous triumph over the wicked (and, by implication, Israel over the heathen nations).[189]
4. The exile to Elam and the decrees of Haman are the fulfillment of admonitions that were addressed to Israel in the Torah.[190]

The choices of these particular themes were dictated to some extent by the *petiḥta* form itself: The use of a verse from the Prophets will understandably lead the darshan to develop historical or eschatological ideas.[191] Verses from the Wisdom Literature lend themselves to discourses on the contrasts between the righteous and the wicked (or the

---

[186] This is true of the proems of R. Jonathan, R. Samuel bar Naḥmani, Rabbah bar Afdon, Rav Dimi bar Isaac, R. Ḥanina bar Pappa, R. Simeon b. Laqish and Samuel.

[187] Based on Ezra 4:6. This theme recurs in several places in the Esther Midrash; e.g., 11a ("Nebuchadnezzar destroyed and he wished to destroy; as it says '*And in the reign of Ahasuerus...wrote they an accusation* etc.'" (11a); 15b: "'*Even to the half of the kingdom it shall be performed*' —Half the kingdom, but not all the kingdom, and not something that drives a wedge in the kingdom. And what is this? —The building of the Temple"; etc. See Ginzberg, *Legends*, 6:457, nn. 47-8; 474, n. 150.

[188] As in the proems of R. Joshua b. Ḥananiah, R. Simeon b. Laqish and R. Eleazar.

[189] Proems of R. Samuel bar Naḥmani, R. Abba bar Kahana, R. Naḥman bar Isaac and Rava.

[190] Proems of R. Joshua b. Ḥananiah, Rav, Samuel, R. Levi, R. Ḥiyya bar Abba.

[191] The popularity of this subject probably owes to the fact that it lends itself to themes of consolation: Just as empires have risen and fallen in the past, according to an order that was predetermined by a divine plan, so will this last empire ultimately pass from the world.

wise man and the fool, etc.).[192] By contrast, those midrashim which emphasize the transgressions of the Jews in the generation of Ahasuerus are usually based on patently non-literal readings of the scriptural texts. This fact suggests that it was the ideological factors, more than the literary conventions or exegetical considerations, which led to the development of this motif. As to the tendency towards viewing the Megillah story in the light of the Pentateuchal admonitions, it is more difficult to determine with certainty whether it was the ideological concerns which influenced the choice of proem-verses or *vice versa*; however there can be no doubt that the graphic descriptions of Leviticus 26 and Deuteronomy 28-9, etc., do lend a distinctive perspective to the events that transpired in the days of Mordecai and Esther.

It should be emphasized that few of the motifs which we have enumerated among the Babylonian proems are in any way unique when compared with parallel passages in Palestinian midrashic works. A long passage in *Esther rabbah*[193] contains discourses that were composed about the assorted empires and kings that ruled over Israel.[194] Even the perception of the woes of exile as the fulfillment of the admonitions and warnings in the Torah is founded upon a motif which occupies a central place in *Esther rabbah*.[195] This is also true about the drawing of contrasts between the wise and the righteous, as against the fools and the wicked, one of the most widespread themes in the *petiḥta* corpus, especially those built around verses from Proverbs, Ecclesiastes and Psalms.

---

192 "The Aggadah 'interprets' the general philosophies of life of the Hagiographa in terms of historical protagonists, and thereby applies the sharp contrasts in the Wisdom Literature to the stories of the fathers, which are not dealt with explicitly by the Torah, etc." [from: Isaac Heinemann *Darkhei ha'aggadah*, 47; note carefully his full discussion there]; on the contrasts between Israel and the nations of the world in the Aggadah see *ibid.* 48 ff. See also Ch. Albeck, *Einleitung und Register zum Bereschit Rabba*, Second Printing, Vol. 1: Einleitung, Veröffentlichen der Akademie für die Wissenschaft des Judentums (Jerusalem: Wahrmann, 1965), 18.

193 Proems # 4-5; #12.

194 See our discussion above.

195 The first Proem is devoted to this theme.

Nonetheless, it appears possible to point to some element of novelty or originality in the thematic structures of the Babylonian Esther-Midrash; namely in the underscoring of the connection between the Jews' observance of the commandments and their fate at the hands of the ruling empires. Accordingly, they were imperiled by Haman's decrees because they became "impoverished of the commandments," on account of "the slothfulness that inhered in Israel because they did not occupy themselves in the Torah." This idea recurs in subsequent portions of the midrash.[196] While it is true that we can find in the Palestinian sources parallels to the traditions which ascribe the threat facing the Jews of that generation to the fact that they participated in Ahasuerus' feast, or that they had bowed down before the image in the time of Nebuchadnezzar,[197] I am not familiar with other sources which

---

[196] 13b: "They slumbered from the commandments" [the motif appears in midrashic interpretations of Song of Songs 5:2: "*I sleep* (ישנה), *but by heart waketh*"; see *Exodus rabbah*, 2:5 (110), and parallels cited by Shinan]; 14a: "...The removal of the ring caused them to return to the right course"; etc. To some extent this may be viewed as a by-product of the widespread tendency to place the Esther story within halakhic parameters. An illustration of this tendency would be the important function assigned to the Sages in the midrashic retelling of the Megillah, to the point where Mordecai takes on the appearance of a talmudic rabbi. E.g., 12b: "'*Then the king said to the wise men*' —Who are the wise men (*ḥakhamim*)?– the rabbis. '*Which knew the times*' —Who know how to calculate leap-years and to fix months etc."; 13b: "...Because she used to show menstrual blood to the sages"; *ibid.*: "Mordecai would sit in the Chamber of Hewn Stone, and was proficient in seventy languages"; "...Initially to Mordecai alone, but in the end, to the people of Mordecai; and who are they? —The rabbis..."; "He went and found the rabbis sitting before him, and he was demonstrating for the rabbis the laws of 'taking a fistful' etc."; 16b: "'*and accepted among the greater part of his brethren*' —among the greater part of his brethren, but not among all his brethren; this teaches that a part of the sanhedrin withdrew from him." The authors of the midrash also employed other means in order to introduce halakhic categories into the story. We may note, for instance, the halakhic questions that are raised concerning aspects of Esther's behavior; e.g.: sabbath observance (13a; cf. 12b); her relations with Ahasuerus and Mordecai (13b); her observance of dietary laws while in the royal court (13a), etc. These topics will be examined in greater detail in the following chapters of this commentary.

[197] *Song of Songs rabbah*, 7:8: "...If so, then why did Israel become endangered in the days of Haman? The rabbis and R. Simeon b. Yoḥai: The rabbis say: Because Israel worshipped idols, and R. Simeon said: Because they ate food cooked by gentiles..." See also *Esther rabbah*, 7:18 and other sources listed by Ginzberg, *Legends*, 6:154, n. 17; 467 ff., n. 122.

link the dangers to a general laxity in the observance of the commandments. This departure might plausibly have been introduced by the Babylonian homilists, inspired by the *Sitz im Leben* of public preaching, in hopes of improving the quality of congregational religious observance.

3. Literary Perspectives:

The proems in the current collection did not impress us with the variety or imaginativeness of their literary construction. In several of them, particularly in those *petiḥṭa*s that were cited in the names of Babylonian *Amora'im*, the whole proem consisted of nothing more than the reference to a verse from elsewhere in Scripture which had some connection to the Book of Esther. At most, simple identifications were appended to the verses: "This is Mordecai," "This is Haman," or "...When? In the days of Mordecai and Esther," etc. In the few proems that did merit more elaborate treatment, this was limited to the addition of proof-texts for the identifications.[198] And though Proem #3 appears to have undergone more extensive literary crafting, our analysis of its construction suggests that what we have there is merely a mechanical copying of a pericope from *TB Sanhedrin*, with no direct connection to the proem structure. We did not encounter, for example, any "complex proems," wherein a verse is expounded according to a variety of alternative methods until the final "*davar aḥer*" creates a connection to the beginning of the lection,[199] or any systematic presentation of subjects or ideas that were learned from the verses.

---

[198] As in Proem #2: "'*Shall come up*'—the righteous Esther, who is called Hadassah; as it says: '*And he brought up Hadassah.*'" See also the other units in this proem, as well as Proems #9 and #10.

[199] It is doubtful whether proems of this sort actually represent the preaching that took place in the synagogues during the talmudic era. More likely, most or all of them are the creation of the editors of literary midrashic compilations, who found in this method a convenient vehicle for combining several interpretations into a literary unit. For an overview of the methodological questions involved, with extensive references to previous studies, see: R. S. Sarason, "Toward a New Agendum for the Study of Rabbinic Midrashic Literature," in *Studies in Aggadah, Targum and Jewish Liturgy in Memory of Joseph Heinemann*, ed. J. Petuchowski and E. Fleischer, 55-73

Continued on next page...

Notwithstanding, the most conspicuous phenomenon to impress itself upon us at several points in our analysis was the fact that, of all the "*petiḥta*s" in the collection, there was not a single one that conformed to the standard definition of a *petiḥta*: "in which the preacher uses as his starting-point a verse taken from another place in the Bible ...and not from the lection that is to be read on the occasion of his current discourse... From this 'far-off' verse he leads his homily along its course until he creates a link to the beginning of today's lection and concludes with its first verse..."[200] As noted already, there is not a single instance among the eighteen or so in our collection about which we can truthfully say that it "creates a link to the beginning of today's lection."

We may speculate that what reached the Babylonian redactors of the Esther-Midrash was merely an abbreviated list of Palestinian proems, which included only the verses themselves, and perhaps some comments on the verses, but not complete proems. Everything that we have seen in our study of the collection points towards the conclusion that the Babylonian sages were not familiar with the function of the *petiḥta*, and therefore did not feel the need to rework the sources in order to restore their original structures as introductions to the opening verses of the lections. It appears that they had a different perception of the function of the *petiḥta*, defining it as a verse from another book which helps elucidate (even without being expounded) the current lection (not necessarily its opening verse).[201] Possibly, this state of affairs

...Continued from previous page

(Jerusalem and Cincinnati: The Magnes Press and Hebrew Union College Press), 1981 (especially 61-6).

200 Joseph Heinemann, *Derashot beṣibbur bitequfat ha-talmud*, 12.

201 Ironically it is Rav's proem, which presents the most successful connection to the opening verse, that was changed by the redactors into an explanatory comment. The fact that most of the proems relate to Esther as an integral unit, and not just to the first verse, recalls the "topical *petiḥta*" as identified by A. Goldberg, review of B. Mandelbaum's edition of pesiqta derab kahana, *Kiryat Sefer* 43 (1967-8), 69-79, though I do not feel that the two phenomena are really related. The two *petiḥta*s to Deuteronomy 19 found in *TB Makkot* 10b do not conclude with the opening verse of the lection. This pericope deserves a separate detailed analysis which would take into account comparisons with parallel material. For the moment see: M. Friedmann, ed., *Bavli masekhet makkot* (Vienna: 1858), 26, nn. 6-9.

is the consequence of the fact that the classical *petiḥta* structure was not in active use among the Babylonian preachers,[202] and was known to the Babylonian Talmud only *via* Palestinian sources. While the redactors of the Bavli included the proems that they received as part of the Babylonian Esther-Midrash, the manner of their treatment of these proems demonstrates that they were not very knowledgeable about the distinctive character of this midrashic form.

---

202 This might be because of their preference for the "*Yelammedenu*" form, as exemplified in a work like the *She'iltot*. Much material bearing on the structure of the "*pirqa*," the public discourse in Babylonia during the Amoraic era, was collected by S. K. Mirsky, ed., *Sheeltot de rab ahai gaon* (Jerusalem: Sura Research and Publication Foundation and Mosad Harav Kook, 1959-77), 1:2 ff. Basing himself on passages such as *TB Berakhot* 28b (about Rav Avia and Rav Joseph), Mirsky argues that the *pirqa* lesson was delivered after the reading from the Torah, prior to the *Musaf* service (*ibid*., 2-3 and n. 6). If this is correct, then it may provide us with a good reason for the neglect of the *petiḥta* by Babylonian preachers, since that form is appropriate only to a derashah before the Torah reading. See: Joseph Heinemann, "The Proem in the Aggadic Midrashim: A Form-Critical Study," 100-22, who proves "that the proems were originally sermons delivered before the scriptural lesson itself" (p, 109).

Chapter Three

Ahasuerus

Etymologies

[11a] [1]RShNY: a sign[2]

"*Aḥashverosh*" (Esther1:1):

Says Rav:[3] The brother of the "Head" [*aḥiv shellarosh*] and under the same sign as the "Head."

The brother of the "Head" — The brother of[4] the wicked Nebuchadnezzar, who is called "Head";

as it is written: "*Thou art this head of gold*" (Daniel 2:38).

And of the same constellation as the "Head"—[5] Nebuchadnezzar[6] killed and he[7] wished to kill. Nebuchadnezzar[8] [9] destroyed[10] and he wished to destroy;

as it says:[11] "*And in the reign of Ahasuerus, in the beginning of his reign, wrote they unto him an accusation against the inhabitants of Judah and Jerusalem*" (Ezra 4:6).[12]

---

1 **Spanish Family** adds: "*And it came to pass in the days of Ahasuerus.*"

2 "RShNY: a sign" —only in MS **Y** and **AgE**. MS **Mf**: "'*Ahasuerus*' RShWN: a sign."

3 "Says Rav" —**EY**: "R. Levi says."

4 "The brother of" —MS **G** and **HgT**: "This is"; ~ in MSS **B**, **V**, **YS**.

5 MS **L** adds: "Of the same constellation as the wicked Nebuchadnezzar."

6 "Nebuchadnezzar" — **Printings**: "He."

7 "And he" —MS **N**: "(And this one) [And destroyed, and he wished]."

8 "Nebuchadnezzar" — **Printings**: "He."

9 "killed...Nebuchadnezzar" — **YS**: "who destroyed the Temple."

10 MS **O** adds: "the abode [*repidato*] of our God"; MS **W** adds: "the Temple."

11 "as it says" — Some members of **Spanish family**: "And so it says."

12 MS **G** adds: "And it is written: '*Then ceased the work of the house of God*' (Ezra 4:24)."

And Samuel says: Because the faces of[13] Israel[14] were blackened [*hosh-ḥaru*] in his days[15] like the bottom of a pot.[16]

And[17] R. Ḥanina[18] says:[19] Because[20] everyone who recalls him says "*Ach*" for his[21] head [*aḥ lerosho*].

And[22] R. Joḥanan says: Because all became poor [*rashin*] in his days;[23]

as it says[24] "*And the king Ahasuerus laid a tribute upon the land, and upon the isles of the sea*" (Esther 10:1).[25]

The Esther-Midrash is replete with similar "etymologies" on the names of figures from the book of Esther. The use of fanciful interpretations of names is a well-known midrashic device.[26] If we

---

13 MSS **G** and **N*** add: "the enemies of."

14 "the faces of Israel" — MSS **O** and **R**: "their faces."

15 "in his days" — ~ in MSS **G, Mf, YS.**

16 MSS **G** and **Mf** add: "in his days."

17 "And" — ~ in most witnesses.

18 "Ḥanina" — MS **B, Printings**: "Joḥanan"; MS **B***: "Jonathan."

19 MS **B** adds: "'*Aḥashverosh*' (and of the same constellation as the Head)."

20 "Because" — ~ in MSS **G, M, Printings**.

21 "his" — MS **N** and **HgT¹**: ~; **HgT²**: "my."

22 "And" — ~ in some witnesses.

23 "in his days" — ~ in MS **P**.

24 "as it says" — Some texts: "for it is written."

25 Matters related to taxation and customs duties are read into several details of the story, reflecting what were probably universal economic concerns. Note, e.g., 12a (where the king declares an exemption from taxes); 13a (where he offers exemptions in return for Esther's revealing her origins); etc. On the possibility that the Babylonian rabbis enjoyed exemptions from certain taxes, see: Moshe Beer, *The Babylonian Amoraim: Aspects of Economic Life* (Ramat-Gan: Bar-Ilan University Press, 1974), 225-41. On the commercial activities of the Babylonian rabbis see *ibid.*, 156-221. Beer presents an exhaustive review of earlier literature on all the questions which he discusses.

26 A concise but penetrating discussion of the topic may be found in Isaac Heinemann's *Darkhei ha-'aggadah*, 110-2 (he cites our passage among his illustrations). Heinemann notes that analogous usages are found in the Bible, Philo and ancient literatures; and (to the extent that the names are both given at birth and describe the later deeds of their bearers) presuppose a belief in some divine guidance of the naming process. For an exhaustive survey of the use of "midrashic name derivations"

Continued on next page...

were to take such explanations in full seriousness, the authors would have to be understood as implying that none of the names in question are really names at all, but epithets that were attached to their bearers for assorted reasons, whereas the real names were not revealed to us.[27] It is doubtful however whether the etymologies were intended to be taken so seriously.[28] In the present instance (as in most other examples in the literature), this is rendered obvious when we observe how forced the similarities are between the word אחשורוש and the various explanations which are supposedly derived from it, all of which involve (even after we have made allowance for the ephemeral status of Semitic vowels) the addition of extra consonants, or the metathesis of key radicals, etc.

Rav's comment, equating Ahasuerus with Nebuchadnezzar in their antagonism to the Temple, is based on the now familiar identification of the Ahasuerus of Esther with his namesake in Ezra Chapter 4. While there remain some dissenting opinions, most historians would agree that the monarch in both stories is Xerxes I, who reigned from 486-65 B.C.E.[29] However, the Ezra passage tells us no more than that a complaint was issued to Ahasuerus, without recording the royal response. Verse 7 immediately moves along to a similar

...Continued from previous page

in the Hebrew Bible, see: Moshe Garsiel, *Biblical Names: A Literary Study of Midrashic Derivations and Puns*, translated by P. Hackett (Ramat Gan: Bar-Ilan University Press, 1991); see especially his discussion of rabbinic materials on pp. 28-32.

27 Variations on this approach can be discerned in the many instances where two Biblical figures are identified with one another, alongside the midrash's explanation that one of the names was a real name, whereas the other is intended as a description of some sort. Interpretations of this sort are very frequent in the Esther-Midrash, and we shall encounter several below.

28 See Ibn Ezra's inconsistent stand (in his two commentaries to Esther) on the etymologies, described by B. Walfish, "The Two Commentaries of Abraham Ibn Ezra on the Book of Esther," 342.

29 E.g., Carey A. Moore, ed. *Esther*, the Anchor Bible (Garden City: Doubleday, 1971), 3-4; W. J. Fuerst, ed., *The Books of Ruth, Esther, Ecclesiastes, the Song of Songs, Lamentations: The Five Scrolls*, the Cambridge Bible Commentary (Cambridge, London, New York, Melbourne: Cambridge University Press, 1975), 44; Jacob M. Myers, ed., *Ezra, Nehemiah*, Anchor Bible (Garden City, N.Y.: Doubleday, 1965), xxxi-xxxxiii.

event in the time of Artahshasta (Artaxerxes I; 465-24).[30] The midrashic tradition may have deduced that unless Ahasuerus had done something to intentionally sabotage the erection of the Temple it should have been completed during his reign,[31] and lays a heavy emphasis on the king's determination to foil its rebuilding. As we have already observed above, this theme is used to great advantage in order to inject traditional Jewish cultic values into the apparent secularism of Esther.

Alternative etymologies are brought in other midrashic works.[32] *Esther rabbah*, 1:1[33] cites in the name of R. Joshua ben Qorḥah an explanation that is substantially identical to Samuel's. In addition there is an interpretation by a R. Taḥlifa bar bar Ḥanah (?) that is a variation of Rav's:[34]

---

[30] *Seder ʿolam* Ch. 30 [B. Ratner, ed., *Midrash seder olam.*, S.K. Mirsky ed. (New York: Moznaim, 1988), 136] seems to argue that Artahshasta is a generic title, given to Cyrus and Darius. Ratner assembles considerable medieval testimonies to the fact that this passage is a later interpolation copied from *TB Rosh hash-shanah* 3b (where it is cited as a *baraita*). It is however found in the best witnesses, as recorded by Chaim Milikowsky, "Seder Olam: A Rabbinic Chronology," Ph. D., Yale University, 1981, 436, 544. According to the accepted chronology there was no king between Ahasuerus and the Darius who completed the construction, hence Ezra 4:23-24 ("*Now when the copy of king Artaxerxes'* [Artaḥshasta's] *letter was read... Then ceased the work of the house of God... So it ceased until the second year of the reign of Darius...*" would also have been taken as a reference to Ahasuerus. See Shinan, *Midrash Shemot Rabbah*, 213.

[31] Cf. Myers, op. cit., 34-5. The identification is central to the presentation in *Seder ʿolam* Ch. 29 . Ratner deals at great length with a textual tradition in the *Seder ʿolam* according to which Haman's sons were responsible for instigating the protest against the building of the Temple.

[32] See L. Ginzberg, *The Legends of the Jews*, 6:451, n. 4.

[33] See Jacob Neusner, *The Midrashic Compilations of the Sixth and Seventh Centuries: An Introduction to the Rhetorical, Logical and Topical Program*, Vol. 2, 36-7.

[34] *Panim Aḥerim* A, p. 46, has a conflation of the Bavli texts: "Rav says: It was *vay*. And Samuel says: '*Aḥashverosh*,' because the faces of Israel became blackened like the bottom of a pot, and they all became poor in his days, as it says: '*And the king Ahasuerus laid a tribute...*'" See Buber's notes.

And R. Taḥlifa bar bar Ḥanah says: Because he was the brother of the "head," the brother of Nebuchadnezzar.[35]

And was he indeed his brother? Was not the one a Chaldean and the other a Median?

—Rather, the one abolished the service of the Temple, while the other destroyed it. For this reason, Scripture equated them.

This is what is written: "*He also that is slothful in his work is brother to him that is a great waster*" (Proverbs 18:9).

"*He also that is slothful in his work*" —This is Ahasuerus, who abolished the service of the Temple.

"*Is brother to him that is a great waster*" —This is Nebuchadnezzar, who destroyed the Temple.

The etymologies of Samuel and R. Ḥanina might both be viewed as analogous the following passage, which relates to the two motifs of headaches[36] and fasting.[37] If it is true that one tradition is copying from the other, there is no easy way to determine its direction.[38]

R. Berakhiah says: Because he weakened the head [*shehikh-ḥish roshan*] of Israel with fasts and afflictions.

The other etymologies proposed by *Esther rabbah*, while similar in their use of farfetched word-play, are new:

And Rabbi Levi says: Because he caused them to drink gall [*rosh*] and wormwood.

---

35 See also *Panim Aḥerim* B, p. 56. In addition to bringing the "brother of the Head" interpretation, it also explains: "The head of [*reshehon*] of all the Jews."

36 On this topic see J. Preuss, J., *Biblical and Talmudic Medicine*, 305.

37 Cf. *Exodus rabbah* 1:17 (66) where a similar etymology is proposed for the name "Ash-ḥur" in 1 Chronicles 4:5: "And why was he [identified by the midrash as Caleb] called Ash-ḥur? —Because his face was blackened with fasting" (See Shinan's notes, which include several examples of rabbinic references to blackening (normally of teeth) through fasting.

38 In light of the general unreliability of the attributions, and the ambiguities as regards their significance (i.e., do they indicate the original author, or the last link in the transmission, etc.?), I am not attaching much weight to the names of the rabbis as indicators of the ages of the traditions.

And Rabbi Judah b. R. Simon says: Because he wished to uproot the "egg" of Israel.[39]

"This is Ahasuerus..."

The Babylonian Esther Midrash continues its meticulous reading of the opening verse of Esther:

> [11a] *"This is Ahasuerus."* —He continued in his evil from his beginning until his end.
>
> *"This is that Dathan and Abiram"* (Numbers 26:9). —They continued in their evil from their beginning until their end.
>
> "*...This is that king Ahaz*" (2 Chronicles 28:22). —He continued in his evil from his beginning until his end..
>
> " *He is Esau the father of the Edomites*" (Genesis 36:43). —He continued in his evil from his beginning until his end.[40] [41]
>
> "*Abram, the same is Abraham*" (1 Chronicles 1:27). —He continued in his righteousness from his beginning until his end.[42]
>
> "*These are that Moses and Aaron*" (Exodus 6:27) —They continued in their righteousness from their beginning until their end.[43]
>
> "*And David was the smallest*" (1 Samuel 17:14) —He persisted in his smallness[44] [=humility] from his beginning until his end. Just as when he was small he humbled[45] himself before one who was

---

[39] While the Hebrew text does not explicitly indicate any verbal similarity with the name Ahasuerus, the traditional commentators are obviously correct in positing an allusion [!] to the word "*shoresh*" (root); see the commentaries of Luria, Maharzu, *Mattenot kehunnah*, etc.

[40] "'*This is that Dathan...Esau*'" —The order varies in the witnesses: "'*Dathan...Esau...Ahaz*'" —MS **G**, **Printings**, Genizah fragment; "'*Dathan* ... [*Esau* ... *Ahaz*]'" —MS **N**; "'*Esau...Ahaz* ... *Dathan*...'" —**EY**; "'*Esau* ... *Dathan* ...'" —MSS **M**, **P**; "'*Dathan...Esau*'" —**HgT**[1]; "'*Ahaz*...'" —**HgT**[2].

[41] MSS **G***, **B***, **P**, **EY** add: "And so too with respect to the righteous."

[42] On the relevance of this comparison see Ibn Ezra's commentaries to Esther 1:1 [discussed by Barry Walfish, "The Two Commentaries of Abraham Ibn Ezra on the Book of Esther," *JQR* 79 (4 1989), 329].

[43] "'*Abram...Moses*'" **MhG**: "'*...Moses...Abraham.*'"

[44] "smallness" —MS **O** and **EY**: "righteousness"; **MhG** and **AgE**: "faith."

[45] "humbled" — **Pesaro Printing**: "humbles."

greater than himself[46] in order to learn Torah,[47] so when he was king[48] he humbled[49] himself before one who was greater than himself[50] in order to learn Torah.[51] [52]

Another explanation: "*This is Ahasuerus*" — This is the head of all the Jews.[53]

In spite of the variations in order, the witnesses to the Bavli seem to be relatively consistent in citing a total of seven examples of figures who continued from their beginnings to their ends, four of them wicked and three righteous.[54] The criteria for entry into the list consist

---

46 **Spanish family** adds: "in wisdom"; MS **W** and **Printings** add: "in the Torah."

47 "in...Torah" — ~ in MSS **G** (before emendation) and **R**; MS **Mf**: "(in the) [in order to learn] Torah."

48 "when he was king" —MSS **B** and **O**: "in his greatness."

49 "humbled" — **Pesaro Printing**: "humbles."

A similar tradition about David's humility is recorded in *TP Sanhedrin* 2 (20b-c). See also the sources listed by Ginzberg, *Legends*, 6:263, n. 86. Cf. *Exodus rabbah*, 15:20: "What is the meaning of '*The sluggard is wiser in his own conceit than seven men that can render a reason*' (Proverbs 26:16)? —That Solomon would control his mouth so as not to speak before one who was greater than he."

50 **Spanish family**, **Printings** add: "in wisdom."

51 "before ... Torah" — MS **B**: "in order to learn Torah (from) [before] one who is lesser than himself in all things."

52 "in...Torah" —MS **N** and **EY** add: "from him." ~ —MS **W**, **Printings**.

53 "Another ... Jews" — found only in MS **Y**. The addition originates in *Panim Aḥerim* B, p. 56, from which it was included in **AgE**. See Buber's notes to **AgE** p. 6 n. 41. On the tendency of MS **Y** to insert such additions, see: E. Segal, "The Textual Traditions of Ms. Columbia University to *TB Megillah*." *Tarbiẓ* 53 (1 1983), 45-6, and n. 6 (to which the current instance should be added).

54 Note also *Sifre Deuteronomy* par. 334 (ed. Finkelstein, 384), where similar exegesis is applied to Joshua (on the basis of Deuteronomy 32:44), Joseph (Exodus 1:5) and David : "And do we not know that David was the youngest! It is to inform you of the righteousness of David who used to shepherd his father's sheep. Now even though he was granted the position of King over Israel, he was still David in respect to his 'youngest' types of behavior" (I have used the translation of Herbert Basser, *Midrashic Interpretations of the Song of Moses*, Vol. 2, American University Studies: Series 7, Theology and Religion (New York, Frankfort on the Main, Berne: Peter Lang, 1984). See his comments on 262, n. E3. In *Exodus rabbah*, 1:7 the rule is brought with reference to Joseph only; see Shinan's notes to the passage (p. 43).

of a proper name immediately preceded or followed by a copulative הוא.[55]

A similar list can be found in a variety of Palestinian sources,[56] only there the numbers are unambiguously defined in the introductory formula: "There are five for goodness ... and five for evil."[57] The individuals included are:

Evil: Nimrod (based on Genesis 10:9), Esau, Dathan and Abiram, Ahaz, Ahasuerus.

Righteous: Abra(ha)m, Moses [and Aaron] (Exodus 6:27), Aaron [and Moses] (Exodus 26:6);[58] Hezekiah (2 Chronicles 32:30), Ezra (Ezra 7:6).[59]

In these texts, unlike the Bavli, the passages are developed so as to lead up to a homiletic conclusion with an optimistic and rhetorical flourish:

> Rabbi Berakhiah in the name of the Rabbis there [i.e. in Babylonia]: They have an additional one which is the best of all: "*He is the Lord our God*" (Psalms 105:7).

---

55 See E. Kautzsch, ed. *Gesenius' Hebrew Grammar*, 453-4.

56 The significance of the *Esther rabbah* parallel was completely misconstrued by Jacob Neusner, *Esther Rabbah: An Analytical Translation*, Vol. I, Brown Judaic Studies (Atlanta: Scholars Press, 1989), 50, who summarizes that the passage "means to designate two distinct figures or two distinct reigns." He has obviously misunderstood both the text of the midrash and the notes from M. Simon's translation (cited by Neusner on p. 46) upon which his own comments claim to be founded. In his *The Midrashic Compilations of the Sixth and Seventh Centuries*, 2:38, he uses the same explanation.

57 The passage is found in *Genesis rabbah*, 37:3; *Esther rabbah*, 1:2; *Midrash on Psalms*, 105:2; *Panim Aḥerim* B; Second Targum to Esther here, as well as in several medieval midrashic anthologies, such as **YS** to Genesis and Esther, Makiri and **AgE**. See detailed discussions in Theodor's commentary to *Genesis rabbah* (p. 345) and Buber's notes to **AgE**, 55-6; D. Heimann, I. Lehrer and I. Shiloni, ed., *Yalquṭ shimᶜoni lerabbenu shimᶜon hadarshan* (Jerusalem: Mosad Harav Kook, 1973-), (Genesis 1), 225. Cf. the citation from the *Mas'et Moshe* commentary cited in the *Ḥiddushei ge'onim* section of the **EY**.

58 Theodor observes that the midrash departs from the scriptural verse order because of Moses' greater importance.

59 See Theodor's notes. He refers to texts that replace the seemingly redundant Aaron and Moses reference (cf. *Yefeh to'ar*) with David.

The Bavli simply states the exegetical principle and some examples, without exploiting it for the fashioning of a literary homily.

All the above passages should be regarded as variations on the basic *gezerah shavah* format, and are probably intended to imitate interpretations like that of R. Samuel bar Naḥman above,[60] which claim to discern consistent patterns in the occurrences of common forms of the Hebrew verb "to be." In the present case, the emphasis is on the pattern "this is X" as an indication of permanence or sameness.[61]

"Which Reigned..."

> [11a] [62] "...*Which reigned*..."
>
> Says Rava:[63] {This implies} that he reigned by himself.
>
> Some say this as praise; and some say this derogatorily.[64]
>
> Some say this as praise: That there was no one who was as worthy[65] as he.
>
> And some say this derogatorily: He was not fit.[66] It was that he gave more money,[67] and was appointed.[68]

---

60 **AgE** alone introduces the lists with: "Said R. Samuel." This fact underscores the structural similarity to R. Samuel bar Naḥman's famous list of *vayhi bimei* verses discussed above. See also: E. L. Segal, "'The Same from Beginning to End' — On the Development of a Midrashic Homily," *JJS* 32.2 (1981), 158-65.

61 Cf. L. B. Paton, *A Critical and Exegetical Commentary on the Book of Esther*, International Critical Commentary, ed. S. R. Driver, A. Plummer and C. A. Briggs (Edinburgh: T & T Clark, 1964), 121.

62 MS **Mf** inserts: "A sign: Reigned, (?), And sat, Despised, and Rested, in Months (?), Was Exiled in Seven Women After The Next (?) Hallel, Break of Rabbah." The text is difficult to read or interpret.

63 "Rava" —MS **B**, **YS** and **Printings**: "Rav."

64 "as praise...derogatorily" —MS **B**: "derogatorily...as praise."

65 "who was as worthy"—Thus in MSS **Y** and **R**; other witnesses add: "as [MS **G**: "to be"] king"; MS **M**: "who was like him"; **AgE**: "no one who was as plentiful (נפיש ?) as he."

66 MSS **B**, **L**, **M**, **R***, **Mf** add: "as king"; MSS **G**, **O**, **W**, **P**, **EY**, **HgT**, **Printings**, Genizah fragments add: "for royalty."

67 "It was...money"—MSS **O**, **P**, **HgT**: "And he gave more money"; MS **N**: "[The reason why he was considered worthy of royalty was on account of] the extra money

Continued on next page...

Rava is paying close attention to the Hebrew phraseology of the verse, noting that the unusual use of the participle "המלך" seems to indicate a more dynamic and willful activity of reigning or becoming king,[69] not merely a factual identification of the name of the monarch. The implication seems to be that Ahasuerus did not accede to the throne in the natural manner, but had to take active measures in order to install himself in power. The anonymous talmudic traditions observe that this exegesis can be interpreted in two opposite directions. On the one hand it can be understood that, but for his act of bribery, Ahasuerus would not have been considered a legitimate claimant to the throne.[70] Alternatively, the scriptural author might be suggesting that,

...Continued from previous page

that he gave [that he became king] and was appointed"; MS **L**: "Rather, because of the extra money that he gave, he became king."

68 "Some say this as praise: That there .... And some say this derogatorily: He was not fit...appointed" —MS **B**: "Some say this derogatorily: That the man was not fit as king, and he gave extra money and was appointed. Some say this as praise: There was no one who was as worthy as king as he."

69 See Maharsha. On the differences in usage of participles between biblical and rabbinic Hebrew, see Abba Bendavid, *Biblical Hebrew and Mishnaic Hebrew*, Vol. II (Tel-Aviv: Dvir, 1971), 545-6. Bendavid observes that, though in the Bible participles can denote a variety of times and modes, in mishnaic Hebrew it has become virtually restricted to present-tense, and instances that do not fit the later usage must be explained by the rabbis, as in our case, as having special significance, denoting repeated or immediate actions, etc. Note in particular his example from *Genesis Rabbah*, 63:10: "*And Rebecca loved* [lit.: *loves*] *Jacob*" (Genesis 25:28)—Whenever she would hear her voice her love for him would increase." Bendavid's conclusions could fit our text as well: "This entire interpretation is made possible only because it does not say 'And Rebecca loved' but rather 'loves,' which has a different meaning in the Sages' spoken language than it does in Scripture." Additional examples of exegesis based on changes in Hebrew usage may be found in Isaac Heinemann, *Darkhei ha-'aggadah*, 116-7. Walter J. Ong, *Orality and Literacy: The Technologizing of the Word*, 46-9, observes that "Oral cultures of course have no dictionaries and few semantic discrepancies. The meaning of each word is controlled by... 'direct semantic ratification,' that is, by the real-life situations in which the word is used here and now."

70 In our analyses of the proems we have already encountered a number of sources that express the rabbis' esteem for legitimate succession of monarchs (see for example our discussion of Proems #1 and #11). In this belief they were presumably sharing the concerns of their non-Jewish contemporaries, and perhaps relating to the chaotic transfers of power in the Roman Empire. On the question of whether Ahasuerus

Continued on next page...

even had he not been the favored candidate in the normal order of succession, Ahasuerus' qualifications and abilities would have gained him the position.

This dispute over whether Ahasuerus was a wise or stupid king is a recurrent one in our midrash. It is difficult to surmise whether this is a purely exegetical problem brought about by the text's silence on the issue, or whether there is some ideological consideration at play.[71]

"From India Even Unto Ethiopia..."

[11a] *"From India even unto Ethiopia* (Esther 1:1)"

Rav and Samuel:

One says: India is at {one} end[72] of the world, and Ethiopia is at {the other} end of the world[73].

And the other says: India and Ethiopia stand[74] next to each other.[75]

...Continued from previous page

inherited or usurped the throne, see Ginzberg, *Legends*, 6:451. Cf. Samuel Krauss, *Paras veromi battalmud uvammidrashim*, 36, 43.

71 The midrashic tradition had good grounds to vilify the king for opposing the construction of the Temple, as we have already remarked frequently above. It is not uncommon for figures whom the Bible depicts as religiously or morally indeterminate, or even admirable (e.g., Noah or Job), to be criticized by at least some of the rabbis, possibly for no other reason than that the rabbis in question could not conceive that heathens were capable of true righteousness.

72 "end" —**EY**: "beginning."

73 "end of the world" —MSS **O** and **P**: "its end."

74 "Stand" —Thus in MSS **N**, **L**, **R***, **P**, **Mf**, **EY**, **AgE**, **Printings**; MSS **O**, **W**, **HgT**, **YS**: "used to stand"; MS **G**: "used to sit"; ~ in "MS **M**.

75 "India is at {one} end ... next to each other" —MS **B**: "India and Ethiopia stood next to each other. And one said: India [stands] at {one} end of the world and Ethiopia at the {other} end [of the world]."

And[76] just as he reigned over India and[77] [78] Ethiopia,[79] so did he reign over the entire world.[80] [81]

In a similar vein it says: "*For he had dominion over all the region on this side of the river, from Tiphsah even to Gaza*" (1 Kings 4:24).

Rav and Samuel:[82]

One says: Tiphsah is at {one} end of the world, and Gaza is at {the other} end[83] of the world.[84]

And the other says: Tiphsah and Gaza[85] stand[86] next to each other.[87]

And[88] just as he reigned over Tiphsah and[89] [90] Gaza,[91] so did he reign over the entire world.

Rav and Samuel disagree here over the significance of the biblical narrator's mention of India and Ethiopia when defining the

---

76 "And" —Thus in **Yemenite family** and **Ashkenazic family**; MS **B**; "Those who interpret it as praise say"; **Spanish family**: "Rather"; MSS **N**, **W**: ~

77 MSS **B**, **M**, **R***, **Mf**, **W**, **HgT**[1], **YS** add: "over."

78 "over India and" —**HgT**[2]: "from India to."

79 "India and Ethiopia" — MS **O**: "these."

80 "over the entire world" —**Printings**: "From {one} end of the world until its {other} end"; MS **Mf**: "over one hundred and seven and twenty provinces, or over the entire world."

81 MS **B** adds: "And some interpret it derogatorily: He reigned only over India and over Ethiopia."

82 "Rav and Samuel" — ~ in MSS **R*** and **P**.

83 "end" —**EY**: "beginning."

84 "Rav...of the world" — ~ in MS **O**.

85 "Tiphsah and Gaza" — ~ in MSS **O**, **P**.

86 "stand" —Thus in MSS **P**, **Mf**, **EY**, **Printings**; MSS **O**, **W**, **L**, **R***, **AgE**, **HgT**, **YS**, **Printings**: "used to stand"; MS **G**: "used to sit"; ~ in MS **M**.

87 "Tiphsah is at {one} end ... next to each other" —MS **B**: "Tiphsah and Gaza lie next to each other. And one said: Tiphsah is at {one} end of the world and Ethiopia at the {other} end."

88 "And" —Thus in MS **Y** and **Ashkenazic family**; MS **B**: "Those who interpret it as praise say"; **Spanish family**: "Rather"; ~ in MSS **G**, **W**, **EY**, **Printings**.

89 MSS **B**, **R***, **W**, **Printings** add: "over."

90 "over Tiphsah and" —MS **P** and **HgT**[2]: "from Tiphsah until."

91 "Tiphsah and Gaza"—MS **O**: "these."

extent of Ahasuerus' dominions. According to one view, the purpose of this detail is to show the vastness of the empire, extending as it does from one end of the world to the other. According to the second view, the verse is describing the *power* of the king. It has chosen to name two neighboring provinces as a way of indicating that just as Ahasuerus was in absolute control over these two nearby regions, such was his hold over the (undefined) farthest reaches of his domains. An identical dispute is recorded concerning a verse in 1 Kings that describes the territories ruled by King Solomon.

It is relatively easy to reconstruct a hypothetical chain of reasoning which would have given rise to this exegesis: The darshan was stimulated by the question of what importance there is in knowing the precise borders of this pagan monarch, especially when we are also informed explicitly the total number of his provinces. Hence the respective rabbis try to discover an additional purpose for the inclusion of these superfluous details.

While the above reconstruction adequately accounts for the hermeneutical process at work here, at this point it seem more difficult to trace a convincing *homiletical* purpose for the interpretations. It appears that some insight on this question is supplied by a reading of the unique version of our text contained in MS Munich 140 (**B**).

> Rav and Samuel: One says: India and Ethiopia stood next to each other, and one says: India stands at one end of the world and Ethiopia at the other end.
>
> Those who interpret it as praise say: Just as he ruled over India and Ethiopia, so did he reign over the entire world.
>
> And some interpret it derogatorily: He reigned only over India and Ethiopia.

As distinct from the standard printed texts, this version states that the second position, which holds that India and Ethiopia are neighboring provinces, is open to a negative interpretation as well, that Ahasuerus ruled only over the two provinces. The presumable implication is that the king ruled over the rest of the 127 provinces in name only, but exerted effective control only over the two closest.

I doubt that this reading is an authentic one. Not only is it virtually neutralized by the unanimous testimony of the other witnesses, but it would destroy the symmetrical parallelism with the Tiphsah and

Gaza clause, for which no such negative interpretation is supplied. Nevertheless, I believe that we can learn something from a consideration of *why* someone would have invented such a text. The simplest explanation seems to be that he was bothered precisely by the fact that the existing version expressed such an unambiguously favorable attitude towards Ahasuerus. In order to overcome this difficulty our "scribe" prefers to read the dictum as if it were susceptible to either approving or disapproving interpretations, along the lines of analogous disputes between Rav and Samuel that are scattered through the Esther-Midrash, where various details about Ahasuerus are read as indications of both of his wisdom and his folly, his virtue and his wickedness. Accordingly the author of the emendation is quite correct in perceiving that an unambiguously favorable assessment of Ahasuerus' statecraft runs headlong against the prevailing approach of the Esther-Midrash.

I believe that in this perception lies one of the keys to reconstructing the evolution of our pericope.

As the next step in our investigation, let us focus on the geographical assertions in our passage:

The basic geographical premise of this midrash seems factually untenable. By ancient standards India and Ethiopia cannot be viewed as neighboring states,[92] nor for that matter was the distance between Gaza and Tiphsah a trivial one.[93] While we need not expect too much

---

92 Moore in the Anchor Bible Commentary to Esther (p. 4): "'India' refers to the north-western part of the Indus River, which Darius had conquered... the [Kush] here is Ethiopia..."; see also Paton, *The Book of Esther*, 123-4 and 132–3. The text of Xerxes' "foundation table" is cited in Moore's commentary. See Ibn Ezra's commentaries. As noted by B. Walfish, "The Two Commentaries of Abraham Ibn Ezra on the Book of Esther," 336, 339, Ibn Ezra seems to accept the rabbinic view in his first commentary, but rejects it in his second [published in vol. 5 of the Jerusalem 1972 edition of *Kol kitvei r. avraham ibn ʿezra*].

93 See C. H. Kraeling, *The Rand-McNally Bible Atlas*, 2nd ed. (New York: Rand McNally, 1962), 214, who presents the scholarly consensus that Tiphsah is the place known to later geographers as Thapsacus, which probably lay "on the left bank of the Euphrates near the point where the Balikh River enters it from the north. ... 'From Tiphsah to Gaza' comprises the sphere of the whole caravan route from the Euphrates to the border of Egypt."

precision in the geographical knowledge of the midrashic rabbis, it nevertheless strikes us as unlikely that they would not have had some familiarity with the locations of such well-known places as India, Ethiopia and Gaza.[94] The weak link in this respect is the obscure Tiphsah, which, from its context in the biblical passage, might easily have been presumed to lie somewhere west of the Jordan.[95] This consideration increases the likelihood that the midrash originated as a comment on 1 Kings, and was only secondarily applied to the context of Esther.[96] This impression receives further confirmation from the fact that, contrary to our expectations and to the general pattern of the exegesis in this section, the biblical text is interpreted only as a glorification of the respective kings' conquests[97] and is not turned into a belittling or minimizing of their achievements.[98] This makes better

---

[94] Cf. the comments of the Rabbi Josiah Pinto to **EY** "...They are not arguing about the facts, that these are neighboring places..." His solution, that it is a question of how one measures along the earth's spherical surface, is of course not to be taken seriously; it is a variation on the explanation brought in S. Buber, ed., *Midrash mishlei* (Vilna: 1893), 20:9 [=*Song of Songs zuṭa* 1:1, in: S. Buber, ed., *Midrash zuṭa ʿal shir ha-shirim rut eikhah veqohelet* (Vilna: 1925)], that "Just as a man departs from Tiphsah and travels to the east, and from the east to the north, and from the north to the south, he keeps circling as he ascends until he goes up to Gaza—so did Solomon progressively attain dominion as he encompassed the whole world from beginning to end."

[95] Rashi appears to have understood that the midrash was built around a contradiction between the Tiphsah-Gaza axis and the claim (in the same verse) that Solomon also ruled beyond the Jordan. According to the Talmud's solution, "what it is saying is that he ruled over the entire region beyond the Jordan just as he did from Tiphsah to Gaza." This explanation appears to fit the text in our midrash far better than that of the *Midrash mishlei* and *Song of Songs zuṭa* cited above about Solomon's wandering around the world until he came back to Gaza.

[96] In the absence of other exegetical or homiletical considerations, the syntactic structure of "Place #1 ועד Place #2" is too common to justify the specific association with Esther 1:1 .

[97] The strangeness of this fact underlies the unique reading of MS **B** (see the above discussion). Cf. Neusner, *The Midrashic Compilations of the Sixth and Seventh Centuries* 2:43.

[98] As suggested by Maharsha, in light of the explicit mention of the one hundred and twenty-seven provinces it is not a simple matter to limit Ahasuerus' dominions to India and Ethiopia. The implication therefore is that his control over the remainder of the

Continued on next page...

sense if we assume that it was applied originally to Solomon[99] than if it was said about Ahasuerus.

When applied to Solomon the interpretation makes a superior homiletical device. Extolling the greatness of a religious hero is in itself a sufficient, if not ideal, subject for a sermon. As we shall see below, a commonly elaborated theme in homilies on books ascribed to Solomon, especially Ecclesiastes, was the legend of how Solomon, at the peak of his earthly power, was so overcome by pride that God punished him by having him deposed from his throne, and he was compelled to wander in the guise of an unrecognized beggar. Our midrash of course would fit neatly into such a sermon that dwelled on the unfortunate consequences of human pride by dramatically contrasting the situations before and after Solomon's fall from greatness.

Some further indirect support for this hypothesis may be found in the fact that when we compare our passage with parallel materials in Palestinian midrashic literature it becomes evident that it is the 1 Kings passages that attracted the exegetical attentions of the rabbis.[100] Thus, in *Song of Songs zuṭa* and *Midrash mishlei*, 20:9[101] the 1 Kings verse is expounded without any reference to Esther. Each of these midrashim includes some additional exegetical material about Solomon that is not found in our passage. In contrast, the midrashim on Esther [*Esther rabbah* (1:4) and *Panim aḥerim B*] both include discussions of the 1 Kings verse, and yet neither adds any exegesis to the Esther verse beyond what is found in our passage in the Babylonian Esther-Midrash.

To put it another way: What the Babylonian Esther-Midrash has done is to take a piece of "*pseudo*-exegesis" that was originally composed with reference to King Solomon, and applied it as a *real*

...Continued from previous page

empire was in name only. Cf. Samuel Krauss, *Paras veromi batalmud uvamidrashim*, 5-6.

99 It is not improbable that the exegesis was originally formulated in the context of the legends which describe Solomon's absolute fall from absolute power, where it indeed appears in several of the midrashic collections; cf. Ginzberg, *Legends of the Jews* 4:165-72; 6:299-302.

100 See also *TB Sanhedrin* 20b.

101 See previous notes. The passages links up to the subject of Solomon's authorship of the respective biblical works.

exegetical rule to Ahasuerus. In its new context the interpretation has lost the homiletical thrust that it had in the original sermon.[102]

As a closing observation to our discussion of this pericope, we shall note a further instance of a phenomenon that appears to typify the relationship between the Esther-Midrash and its Palestinian relations. We refer to the fact that, while the Bavli limits its exposition here to an exegetical explanation of the scriptural text, *Esther rabbah* goes a step farther and incorporates the material into a more elaborately literary homiletical framework. Thus we find, following the interpretations of the same verses from Esther and 1 Kings, the following continuation:

> In a similar vein it says: "*From the temple to Jerusalem*[103] *shall kings bring presents unto thee*" (Psalms 68:30).
>
> But is not from the temple to Jerusalem a negligible matter?
>
> Rather, just as the offerings are common from the temple to Jerusalem, so will there be a procession of messengers[104] bringing gifts for King Messiah.
>
> This is what is written: "*Yea, all kings shall prostrate themselves before him*" (Psalms 72:11).
>
> R. Kohen the brother of R. Ḥiyya bar Abba said: Just as the divine presence [*Shekhinah*] is found between the Temple and Jerusalem, so shall the divine presence fill up the earth from one end to the other.
>
> This is what is written: "*And let the whole earth be filled with his glory, Amen and Amen*" (Psalms 72:19).[105]

Unlike the Esther and 1 Kings verses, the last two verses from Psalms, direct us towards the future messianic epoch, thereby supplying

---

102 For a discussion of a similar phenomenon, see: E. L. Segal, "'The Same from Beginning to End' — On the Development of a Midrashic Homily."

103 ARV: "*Because of thy temple at Jerusalem.*"

104 On διαδοχή see J. Levy, *Neuhebräisches und chaldäisches Wörterbuch über die Targumim und Midrashim* (Leipzig: 1876-89), 2:340; J. Perles, *Etymologische Studien* (Breslau: 1871), 115; Kohut, *Aruch Completum*, 3:25-6; and the standard talmudic dictionaries.

105 Cf. Jacob Neusner, *The Midrashic Compilations of the Sixth and Seventh Centuries* 2:39.

a suitable and climactic conclusion for a public discourse.[106] Now it is not clear what would be the liturgical occasion for such a reading, seeing as the Book of Psalms is not read formally in the synagogue,[107] and 1 Kings 4 is not known to comprise a *hafṭarah* in the triennial cycle. It would appear most likely that what has the appearance of a homiletical discourse was in reality fashioned by the redactor of *Esther rabbah* as an artificial structure, following the standard literary convention, but not necessarily with a view to its oral delivery as a sermon in the synagogue.[108]

"...*Over Seven and Twenty and a Hundred Provinces*"

[11a] "...*Over seven and twenty and a hundred provinces.*"

---

[106] On this phenomenon see E. Stein, "Die homiletische Peroratio im Midrasch," *HUCA* 8-9 (1931-2), 353 ff.; Marc Bregman, "The Triennial Hafṭarot and the Perorations of the Midrashic Homilies," *JJS* 32 (1981), 74-84 (Note in particular his remark on p. 75 that the "happy ending" convention typifies both classical and *Tanḥuma-Yelammedenu* midrashim); D. Stern, "Midrash and the Language of Exegesis: A Study of Vayikra Rabbah, Chapter 1," 113-7.

In general the literary study of midrashic perorations has yet to attract the scholarly attention that has attended the proems. I note here one particular issue that demands consideration: In light of Heinemann's view (which I find persuasive) that the proem was a self-contained homily culminating in the opening verse of the lection, what place was there for the perorations at all. If they were restricted to alternate sermon structures (e.g., *Yelammedenu* homilies), then this fact would seem to have far-reaching implications on form–critical attempts to reconstruct the *Sitz im Leben* of homiletic fragments which include messianic perorations. Alternatively, it can be argued that two (separate or related) sermons were normally preached, one (the *petiḥta*) before the Torah reading and one following it. On this question note the incisive observations of Marc Bregman, "Circular Proems and Proems Beginning with the Formula '*Zo hi shene'emra beruaḥ haq-qodesh*,'" in *Studies in Aggadah, Targum and Jewish Liturgy in Memory of Joseph Heinemann*, ed. J. Petuchowski and E. Fleischer, 34-51 [Hebrew section] (Jerusalem: The Magnes Press, Hebrew Union College Press, 1981), 50-51.

[107] Psalm 72 is however "*A Psalm of Solomon*," and connects naturally to a lection concerning Solomon.

[108] The connection to Esther is too tenuous, in my judgment, to indicate that this was a derashah on Esther or Purim.

> Says Rav Ḥisda: At first he reigned over seven, and in the end he reigned[109] over[110] twenty; and in the end he reigned[111] over one hundred..
>
> But according to this,[112] what is written[113] "*And the years of the life of Amram were seven and thirty and a hundred years*" (Exodus 6:20) —How do you expound this?[114]
>
> —Here it is different, because the verse is redundant: Seeing as it is written "*From India to Ethiopia*," why do I need "*seven and twenty and a hundred provinces*"? Learn[115] from this: For the exposition.[116]

The exegetical foundation of Rav Ḥisda's comment is far from obvious. Our first inclination would be to explain it as another reaction to a change in Hebrew usage between the biblical and rabbinic sources. In the present instance, the change would involve the order of compound numerals, which the Bible normally[117] lists from smaller to larger units, whereas rabbinic texts follow the reverse order.[118] Hence Rav Ḥisda explains that the "seven and twenty and a hundred" is not merely the *number* of Ahasuerus' provinces, but a description of the *order* of their acquisition.

The above reconstruction, while it is probably correct in its essentials, nonetheless requires some modification: While it is probably correct to say that the hundred-tens-units order is universal in rabbinic

---

109 "he reigned" — ~ in MSS **G, R*, YS**.

110 "in the end...over" — ~ in MS **M**.

111 "he reigned" — ~ in MSS **G, O, M, R*, YS, Mf**.

112 "but...this" — ~ in **HgT¹**.

113 "what is written" — ~ in MSS **G, N, W, HgT, Ashkenazic Family, Mf**; "that which is written" — **AgE, P**.

114 MSS **G, N, B, O, L, R*, Mf, W, YS** add: "there"; MS **P, AgE, HgT** add: "So too."

115 "Learn" — MSS **O, B***: "Rather: Learn."

116 MSS **O, B** add: "as we have said."

117 But by no means inevitably; see the discussion in *Gesenius' Hebrew Grammar*, §134 h-i (p. 434).

118 See M. H. Segal, *A Grammar of Mishnaic Hebrew* (Oxford: Clarendon Press, 1927), 196; Abba Bendavid, *Biblical Hebrew and Mishnaic Hebrew*, Vol. 2, 470.

Hebrew, there is no equivalent uniformity in biblical syntax.[119] This flaw in the hermeneutical logic[120] likely underlies the Talmud's insistence on seeking a further justification in the supposed *redundancy* of the numbers.

Rav Ḥisda's comment does not have an explicit homiletical point. One is tempted to supply it with a continuation, in the spirit of "Some interpret it as praise, while some interpret it derogatorily." As praise, the midrash would be pointing out that the king himself was responsible for creating his empire rather than merely inheriting it. Derogatorily, it questions his legitimacy: the empire had to be acquired [perhaps by questionable means, such as bribes] piece by piece.

Similar interpretations, understanding the components of the number as denoting a progression, are recorded in *Esther rabbah*, 1:1:

---

119 See S. Herner, *Syntax der Zahlwörter im Alten Testamentum* (Lund: 1893), 73. Cf. Ibn Ezra to Genesis 23:1: "It is the grammatical norm for the larger unit to precede the smaller; but one finds the opposite as well, as in Genesis 47:28." See also his second commentary here, cited by B. Walfish, "The Two Commentaries of Abraham Ibn Ezra on the Book of Esther," 339. Maharsha (in his second explanation) suggests that Rav Ḥisda attached significance to the fact that, whatever inconsistencies may exist with regard to the placement of the hundreds, tens normally follow units in the Bible. Gesenius, *ibid.*, notes that this is not always the case.

120 An instructive exegetical literature has accumulated around Genesis 23:1 "*And Sarah was a hundred years and twenty years and seven years*," which was expounded in the midrash in a manner similar to Rav Ḥisda's interpretation here [see *Genesis rabbah* 58:1 (ed. Theodor-Albeck p. 618) and parallels cited in notes]. The verse was midrashically linked to Esther 1:1 [see *Genesis rabbah*, 58:3 (621) and parallels cited by Theodor, relating a public discourse by Rabbi Akivah; E. L. Segal, "'The Same from Beginning to End,'" 65]. Rashi to Genesis observes that "it is because 'years' is inserted after each number that each unit is able to be expounded individually." Naḥmanides raises an objection from Genesis 25:17 where the same pattern is employed ("*And these are the years of the life of Ishmael, a hundred years and thirty years and seven years*"), and concludes that the repetition of the noun between the numerical units is actually the norm in biblical Hebrew, and therefore the pattern cannot serve as a basis for midrashic interpretation (like our Talmud passage, he ascribes the midrashic exegesis of Genesis 23:1 to a redundancy in the structure of the verse). Maharsha applies this approach to our passage in *TB Megillah.* He argues that what the Talmud finds unusual in Esther 1:1 (as well as in Exodus 6:20) is the fact that Scripture does not repeat the noun between the numerical units. See also the remarks of the *Yefeh ʿanaf* commentary to *Esther rabbah*, 1:7.

Another interpretation: "*Seven and twenty and a hundred provinces.*"—

R. Judah and R. Nehemiah:

R. Judah said: He conquered seven that were as difficult as twenty. He conquered twenty that were as difficult as a hundred.

R. Nehemiah said: He took the inhabitants from seven and [with them] conquered twenty. He took the inhabitants of twenty and conquered a hundred.

Both of these interpretations seem to present Ahasuerus' progressive expansion in a favorable light, as indicators of his tenacity and strategic skills. There might be some implied topical allusion to the contemporary Roman practice of conscripting colonials into the army in order to serve as the basis for subsequent conquests.[121]

"Three Reigned in the Vault"

[11a] Our masters taught: Three[122] kings[123] reigned in the vault:[124]

Ahab the son of Omri[125] and Nebuchadnezzar and Ahasuerus.[126]

This list of three kings who ruled over the whole world[127] appears to be based on purely exegetical foundations, without any

---

121 The phenomenon of the "barbarization" of the Roman army is familiar to historians of the period; see e.g., M. Rostovtzeff, *The Social and Economic History of the Roman Empire*, 2nd ed. (Oxford: Clarendon Press, 1957): 107, 127, 129, 468, 511-2, 710-1.

122 **EY** and **HgT¹** add: "kings."

123 "Three...reigned" — **EY**: "There were three kings who reigned."

124 Spanish family, MSS **N**, **L**, **P**, **Mf**, **Printings**, **AgE** add: "And they are:."

125 "the son of Omri" — ~ in MS **M**, **Printings**, **AgE**.

126 "Nebuchadnezzar and Ahasuerus"—**Printings**: "Ahasuerus and Nebuchadnezzar."

127 The metaphor of "ruling over the vault" (of the heavens) is, as far as I know, not found elsewhere in rabbinic literature, though the commentators all seem to in agreement about its meaning (see Rashi here, *Aruch Completum* 4:289, etc.). The notion that the heavens constitute a vault or arch (כיפת הרקיע) is attested [e.g. *Genesis Rabbah*, 4:5 (28-9); 48:12 (432), 48:6 (p. 481); *Tanḥuma Shofeṭim*, 11; etc.]. MS **M** reads: בקופה (normally: basket); for a similar variant see *Tosefta ʿEruvin*

Continued on next page...

obvious homiletical point, nor will the subsequent talmudic discussion of the respective monarchs make any effort to set them in a uniform homiletical context. The *baraita*[128] has assembled a number of apparently unrelated texts which, through midrashic interpretation, are taken to refer to universal dominion. The selection of these particular three does not follow any obvious pattern. If we accept that Ahasuerus is being classified as a wicked king, then it is probably safe to presume that the author of the *baraita* was restricting his list to such evil monarchs, which might be the real reason for the exclusion of some of the other candidates mentioned by the Talmud and in parallel passages discussed below. Such an interpretation might lend additional homiletical significance to the metaphor of "ruling in the vault" or "arc," as we are given assurances that their respective ascents to success will inevitably be followed by resounding falls from power.[129]

...Continued from previous page

7(5):3 [The *Tosefta*: *Mo'ed*, ed. S. Lieberman (New York, 1962), 111], noted by Kohut, *Aruch Completum*, *loc. cit.*, n. 7. This interpretation is further supported by the wording in parallel sources (see below) where the expression used is "from one end of the world to the other." The Greek ἀψις is sometimes used in this sense (also as the orbit of a heavenly body; see the entry in Liddell and Scott's Lexicon). Note also *TP 'Avodah zarah* 3:1 (42c): "Says R. Jonah: When Alexander of Macedon wished to ascend upwards he would rise up above until he could view the world as a ball and the sea as a bowl..." It is not unlikely that "ruling in the vault" originated as a Hebrew translation of κοσμοκράτωρ (see below). Cf. Samuel Krauss, *Paras veromi batalmud uvamidrashim*, 87.

We should nevertheless seriously consider the possibility that the reference in this passage is architectural rather than cosmological, referring to the dome at the top of a standard basilica (e.g., *Mishnah 'Avodah zarah* 1:7), in which case the meaning would be roughly that they ruled at the highest level. Several talmudic sources suggest that domes were regarded as common features of buildings; e.g., *Mishnah Sanhedrin* 9:5 [On its interpretation see: Saul Lieberman, "Interpretations in Mishna," *Tarbiẓ* 40 (1 1970), 10-13].

128 On the usage of the תנו רבנן form, see Ch. Albeck, *Meḥqarim bivrayta vetosefta veyaḥasan lattalmud*, 2nd ed. (Jerusalem: Mossad Harav Kook, 1969), 5-12; *Idem.*, *Introduction to the Talmud*, 21-4; cf. I. H. Weiss, *Dor dor vedoreshav*, 2:214; W. Bacher, *Tradition und Tradenten* (Leipzig: 1914), [203, n. 4; 235]; Abraham Weiss, *Leqorot hit-havvut ha-bavli*, reprint: Jerusalem, 1970 ed., Publications of the Institute of Jewish Studies in Warsaw (Warsaw: Institute of Jewish Studies in Poland, 1929), 79, n. 1.

129 According to a tradition preserved in the Second Targum to Esther, "There were four who ruled from one end of the world to the other, two from the nations of the

Continued on next page...

While our tradition about the three kings is not attested elsewhere in rabbinic literature,[130] there is a similar tradition which is brought in the Second Targum to Esther,[131] as well as in *Pirqei derabbi eli'ezer* and some related texts,[132] which speaks of *ten* kings who ruled from one end of the world to the other.[133] The identities of the ten kings vary in the different traditions, which are summarized in the following list:[134]

...Continued from previous page

world and two from Israel, Solomon and Ahab from Israel...and from the nations of the world Nebuchadnezzar and Ahasuerus..." The Targum is translating a dictum of R. Levi that is cited in *Panim aḥerim* B (p. 56) [which adds: And some say: Cyrus etc.]. There can be little doubt that both these traditions are elaborations of our text from *TB Megillah.*

130 Cf. *Pesiqta derav kahana*, 2:5 (ed. Mandelbaum, 24; transl. Braude and Kapstein, 29), *Esther rabbah*, 1 (Proems to Esther 1:9) and *Song of Songs rabbah*, 3:3, where God promises Merodach-baladan that he will beget three "world–conquerors" (κοσμοκράτωρ): Nebuchadnezzar, Evil-merodach and Belshazzar, all of whom will rule "from one end of the world to the other." Note also the various texts which speak about "four kings who were too proud" and which enumerate Pharaoh, Sennacherib, Nebuchadnezzar and Hiram [assembled by H. M. Horowitz in *Beit 'eqed ha-'aggadot* 3:Appendix 2; Eisenstein's *Ozar Midrashim* 69].

131 See also: A. Sperber, ed., *The Bible in Aramaic*, Vol. IV A (Leiden: E. J. Brill, 1968), 173.

132 Ch. 11; G. Friedlander, ed., *Pirke de rabbi eliezer*, 4th ed. (New York: Sepher-Hermon Press, 1981), 80-83. The *Midrash 'aseret melakhim* is a late text, based primarily on *Pirqei derabbi eli'ezer*. It was first published from a De Rossi manuscript by H. M. Horowitz in his *Beit 'eqed ha-'aggadot* 1 (Frankfort a/M., 1881), 16-33, 38-55, and subsequently reprinted by J. D. Eisenstein, ed., *Ozar Midrashim*, 461-6. On the basis of historical references contained in the work Horowitz judges that the *Midrash 'aseret melakhim* was composed in the mid-8th century. See also: M. Gaster, ed., *The Exempla of the Rabbis* (Philadelphia: Jewish Publication Society of America, 1934), beginning.

133 See also: Mordecai Margulies, ed., *Midrash haggadol on the Pentateuch: Genesis* (Jerusalem: Mosad Harav Kook, 1967), 194-5 (to Genesis 10:8) and the parallel sources cited in the notes; Paton, *The Book of Esther*, 121.

134 See the overview of the traditions in L. Ginzberg, *Legends*, 5:199-200, n. 82. His attempt to read the list of ten kings into the text of Esther rabbah is not persuasive.

Second Targum	***Pirqei derabbi eliʿezer, Midrash ʿaseret melakhim***	***Mekhilta*** (See below)	***Leviticus rabbah*** (See below)
God	God		
			Adam
Nimrod	Nimrod		
Pharaoh[135]	Joseph	Pharaoh (of Moses' time)	
Israel	Solomon		Hiram
	Ahab		
		Assyria	Sennacherib
Nebuchadnezzar	Nebuchadnezzar		Nebuchadnezzar
	Cyrus		
Ahasuerus		Medes (Darius)	
Greece	Alexander	Greece	
Rome	[Augustus Caesar][136]	Rome	[Esau]
			Israel
Messiah Son of David	King Messiah		

135 With respect to Pharaoh, cf. *Exodus rabbah*, 5:14 (2) [ed. Shinan, p. 168] *Tanḥuma Va'era*, 5: "...and all the kings would come and crown him, so that he would be a κοσμοκράτωρ." See also the sources cited by Shinan in his notes. The same title is given to Joseph in *Pesiqta rabbati*, 3 (ed. Friedmann p. 10b).

136 The reading "Augustus Cæsar" instead of Alexander is found only in Midrash *Bereshit rabbati* of R. Moses Hadarshan [Ch. Albeck, *Midrash bereshit rabbati* (Jerusalem: 1940)], cited by Horowitz, p. 19.

God	God[137]		

Note that none of these traditions includes all three of the monarchs mentioned in our *baraita*. Ahab is missing from the Targum's list, and Ahasuerus from the *Pirqei derabbi eliʿezer*.[138] Of the additional kings mentioned by the Talmud, Sennacherib and Darius are missing in both the Targum and the *Pirqei derabbi eliʿezer* traditions, and Solomon and Cyrus from the Targum. It is therefore unlikely that what we have here is a mere copying from one source to the next.

As regards both its context and its content the *Pirqei derabbi eliʿezer* tradition bears a striking resemblance to a passage in *Leviticus rabbah*, 18:2[139] which consists of a composite proem to Leviticus 15:2 based on Habakkuk 1:7: "*They are terrible and dreadful; their judgment and their dignity shall proceed of themselves.*"[140] The midrash offers a list of alternate expositions of the verse, most of which reiterate the theme that the respective subjects, all sinners, ultimately proved to be the sources of their own "judgment" (i.e., punishment). The examples mentioned are: Adam (whose punishment was caused through his wife);[141] Esau[142] (berated in the prophesies of the Edomite convert[143]

---

137 Not mentioned explicitly in *Midrash ʿaseret melakhim*.

138 He is however classified as a κοσμοκράτωρ in *Esther rabbah*, 1 (to Esther 1:2).

139 Ed. Margulies 400-4; see the editor's notes. Parallels are found in *Tanḥuma* (standard [#8] and Buber [#10] editions) to the same section of Leviticus (*Tazriaʿ*) Cf. Zvi Meir Rabinovitz, ed., *The Liturgical Poems of Rabbi Yannai*, etc., 420 (#88, l. 8). See also David Stern, "Midrash and Indeterminacy," *Critical Inquiry* 15 (1988), 132-61, who comments on the heterogeneity of the figures in the *Leviticus rabbah* list.

140 The context of the verse clearly refers to the Chaldean armies (see verse 6), a fact which is stubbornly ignored by most of the midrashic exegetes. It is thus an excellent example of the atomism noted by James Kugel, ["Two Introductions to Midrash"], who observes that "midrash is an exegesis of biblical verses, not of books. The basic unit of the Bible, for the midrashist, is the verse: this is what he seeks to expound, and it might be said that there simply is no boundary encountered beyond that of the verse until one comes to the borders of the canon itself"; see especially pp. 93-100; and cf. I. Heinemann, *Darkhei ha-'aggadah*, 131-6. See my comments above in the Introductory Remarks chapter.

141 "She caused his death" (*Tanḥuma*).

142 The *Tanḥuma*s derive this detail from Daniel 7:7, in which the "fourth beast" is depicted as "dreadful and terrible." The treatment is thus exclusively of a national

Continued on next page...

Obadiah); Sennacherib (punished through his sons); King Hiram of Tyre (punished through Nebuchadnezzar); Nebuchadnezzar (punished through Evil-merodach); Israel (punished for slander through fluxes and plagues).

While this discourse is not primarily concerned with the enumeration of kings who ruled the world, kings and other national archetypes (i.e., Esau who is treated here in his capacity as the ancestor of Rome) do figure prominently in the list, the only apparent exception being Adam. It is therefore of particular interest that the midrash goes on at considerable length to apply the "*terrible and dreadful*" phraseology of Habakkuk to Adam by citing traditions about the "Primordial Man" who filled the entire world. In "composite proems" of this sort, we need not always insist on finding a thematic unity between the different interpretations of the "proem verse";[144] it is nonetheless understandable that a later darshan or redactor[145] would

...Continued from previous page

symbol, not of Esau the individual. This differs from *Leviticus rabbah*'s citation of Genesis 27:15, which relates [in a manner that is not entirely clear; see sources cited by Margulies] to the deeds of Esau the person. The theme of Nimrod's miraculous garments is elaborated in great detail in *Midrash ʿaseret melakhim*. See Ginzberg, *Legends*, 1:177-8, 318-9; 2:139; 5:199, nn. 78-9; 5:276-7, nn. 38-9; 5:366, nn. 377-9. The sources for this legend all appear to be very late, and hence I consider it very unlikely that it is actually being alluded to in the *Leviticus rabbah* passage.

143 On this tradition, see Margulies' notes; Ginzberg, *Legends*, 5:31, n. 91; and especially 6:344, n. 6.

144 For a different approach to the subject, see Joseph Heinemann, "Profile of a Midrash: The Art of Composition in *Leviticus Rabbah*," *JAAR* 39 (1971), 141-150; [=Heinemann, Joseph, "Ommanut ha-qompozitziyyah bemidrash vayyiqra rabbah," *Hasifrut* 2 (1971), 150-160]. Cf. the critical observations of R. S. Sarason, "Toward a New Agendum for the Study of Rabbinic Midrashic Literature," in *Studies in Aggadah, Targum and Jewish Liturgy in Memory of Joseph Heinemann*, ed. J. Petuchowski and E. Fleischer, 55-73 (Jerusalem and Cincinnati: The Magnes Press and Hebrew Union College Press, 1981), especially pp. 64-7.

145 Typically, we can discern the beginnings of this process in the *Tanḥuma*, which takes the trouble to spell out explicitly that "the verse speaks of the first man, Pharaoh, Edom, Sennacherib and Nebuchadnezzar." In describing Adam, it states that he "ruled over the entire world, as it says: '*and have dominion*, etc.'... It seems likely that the differences in the *Tanḥuma*'s choice of examples are to be understood in connection with its desire to produce a more symmetrically arranged proem which would deal only with world-dominating [i.e., "terrible and dreadful"] kings [note, e.g., how it identifies Pharaoh as a κοσμοκράτωρ, a detail whose relevance to the story is not

Continued on next page...

have tried to uncover precisely such a unifying thread. In our case, Adam was treated as a paradigm of royal power in subsequent generations.[146]

None of the above passages are from Tannaitic texts. There is however a tradition preserved in the *Mekhilta* of Rabbi Ishmael which, though not manifestly an enumeration of kings, demonstrates significant affinities with our text. It is found in *Mekhilta Beshallaḥ*, #1:[147] This midrash is attached to Exodus 14:5: "...*and the heart of Pharaoh and of his servants was turned against the people, and they said, Why have we done this that we have let Israel go from serving us?*" and explains that the Egyptians feared that the precedent of the Hebrew rebellion would invite rebellions of other subject peoples. The *Mekhilta* concludes:

> This comes to teach you[148] that Pharaoh ruled from one end of the world to the other, and that he had governors from one end of the world to the other, for the sake of Israel's honor...

...Continued from previous page

obvious]. In this light the final example "this refers to Humanity" should be seen as a separate homily, as might be implied by its exclusion from the introductory list cited above [though it does appear in the Buber edition]. The redactor could not jettison that unit since he would thereby have lost the formal connection to the lection.

146 The implication of the above discussion is that the *Leviticus rabbah* list eventually evolved into the enumeration of "ten kings." This is suggested in spite of the obvious fact that the actual list of monarchs in *Pirqei de-rabbi eliᶜezer* is completely different from that of *Leviticus rabbah*, the only common element being Nebuchadnezzar.

We should note two other traditions found in several *Tanḥuma* collections (see *Exodus rabbah*, 8:2, and parallels listed by Shinan, 201-4) which bear significant resemblances to our current texts: (1) One passage speaks of "four mortals who made themselves into gods and caused harm to themselves" [in the *Tanḥuma*s (*Va'era*, 9; ed. Buber, 8(23-4))] and goes on to list Hiram, Nebuchadnezzar, Pharaoh and Joash; (2) R. Berakhiah speaks of "those vain ones who make themselves into gods, and the Holy One turns them into objects of ridicule in the world," applying this to Nebuchadnezzar and Sennacherib.

147 Ed. Horowitz-Rabin, 87; ed. Lauterbach, 197 (Section #2 in Lauterbach's division). See also: J. N. Epstein and E. Z. Melamed, eds., *Mekhilta d'rabbi šimᶜon b. jochai*, 50.

148 The reasoning is less than satisfactory, being based on a midrashic embellishment of the story that is not justified on hermeneutical grounds. It is only the midrash that makes mention of the pivotal fact that "all the nations of the world" would challenge Egyptian rule. Aside from the possibility that the text suffers from a lacuna (a hypothesis for which there is, at any rate, no evidence in the apparatuses of Lauterbach

Continued on next page...

> And thus do you find, that each nation and tongue that subjugated Israel ruled from one end of the earth to the other, for the sake of Israel's honor.

The *Mekhilta* goes on to cite additional instances of this general rule, supporting each with an appropriate verse: Assyria (Isaiah 10:14), Babylonia (i.e., Nebuchadnezzar, citing Jeremiah 27:8), the Medes (i.e., Darius, citing Daniel 6:26), Greece (Daniel 7:6), the "fourth kingdom" (=Rome,[149] citing Daniel 7:23). In the end it restates the principle: "Thus you have learned that each nation and tongue that subjugated Israel ruled from one end of the earth to the other, for the sake of Israel's honor."

It is easy to discern that, while the midrash is couched in a terminology that speaks of nations and tongues rather than individual kings (a situation which is promoted by its heavy reliance on the apocalyptic vocabulary of Daniel), virtually all of its references to Biblical nations can easily be translated into specific monarchs. In fact, it is noteworthy that in the very first example reference is made only to "Pharaoh" and not to "Egypt." It therefore seems very probable that this passage should be regarded as the earliest instance of the manifold lists of kings who ruled the world. As with the other traditions (other than that of the Babylonian Esther-Midrash), it has a clear homiletical purpose, namely to point out the correlation between the importance of

...Continued from previous page

of Horovitz), the most likely explanation would seem to be that the *Mekhilta* is basing itself on Psalm 105:20 and 22, (the former verse is not actually cited until farther on), which refers to the Pharaoh of Joseph's time as "a ruler of nations" who authorizes Joseph "*to bind his kings and princes at his pleasure*." The *Midrash on Psalms*, 105 (transl. Braude 183) associates this theme with such verses as Genesis 27:29 (Jacob's blessing "*Let peoples serve thee and nations bow down to thee*"). It would accordingly seem that the *Mekhilta*'s exegesis originated in a proem based on Psalm 105 (probably intended to introduce a reading from the Joseph story, but possibly a lection from the Exodus narrative). In attempting to transform the dictum into an exegetical comment on Exodus 14:5, the redactor overlooked the fact that, in its current form, the midrash is making reference to a verse that has not yet been quoted.

149 Possibly an early censor's gloss; cf. the reading of *Midrash ḥakhamim* recorded by Horovitz and Lauterbach: "the guilty kingdom."

Israel and the magnitude of the world powers that have taken the trouble to conquer it.[150]

The most glaring contrast between the version in the Esther-Midrash and the others probably lies in the fact that, unlike our text, the other midrashim incorporate the theme of the ten kings into homiletical discourses. In the case of the Targum this is achieved by demonstrating that, just as Ahasuerus and his empire eventually fell, so shall be the fate of all other kingdoms that will subjugate Israel, until the dominion returns to its rightful Master, God. *Leviticus rabbah* and *Tanḥuma* derive the lesson that people's actions contain the seeds of their own punishment. *Pirqei derabbi eli*ʿ*ezer* attaches the "ten kings" passage to the legends about the Primordial Adam,[151] who was appointed by God as His "agent" to rule the earth on his behalf. Here as well the implication is that the post-Messianic return to direct divine rule is to be viewed as a reversion to the original conditions of Creation, and that temporal empires rule in the interval either through usurpation or by partaking of the sovereignty originally vouchsafed to Adam. The *Midrash* ʿ*aseret melakhim* appears to have expanded the material in *Pirqei derabbi eli*ʿ*ezer* so as to produce a work which is essentially a "messianic tract."[152] The Esther-Midrash, by contrast, seems to arbitrarily link together a few names of the kings who ruled the world, without applying this exegetical information to any edifying purpose.

We should however take note of the similar-sounding passage in *Esther rabbah*, 1:1 to our verse,[153] where we read as follows:

"...*Seven and twenty and a hundred*"

---

150 Lauterbach (p. 196, n. 5): "It is less of a humiliation to be oppressed by a mighty empire."

151 See p. 79 n. 1 of Friedlander's edition; cf. L. Ginzberg, *Legends*, 1:59, 5:79, etc.

152 On the genre, see Joseph Dan, *The Hebrew Story in the Middle Ages*, Sifriyyat Keter (Jerusalem: Keter, 1974). Horowitz speculated, on the basis of the midrash's expansive treatment of the destructions of the two Temples and Betar, that the midrash originated as a discourse for "*Shabbat Ḥazon*," the sabbath preceding the Ninth of Av, when Isaiah 1 is the Prophetic reading.

153 See Neusner, *The Midrashic Compilations of the Sixth and Seventh Centuries*, 2:39-43.

> Rabbi Eleazar in the name of R. Ḥaninah: But are there not two hundred and fifty hyparchies in the world?
>
> > And David reigned over all of them...
> >
> > And Solomon reigned over all of them, as it is written: "*And Solomon reigned over all the kingdoms*, etc." (1 Kings 5:1).
> >
> > And Ahab reigned over all of them, as it is written "*As the Lord liveth...*"; and is it possible for a man to impose an oath in a place where he does not hold power?
> >
> > And further, from the following: "*Then he numbered the young men of the princes of the provinces, and they were two hundred and thirty-two*, etc." (1 Kings 20:15).
>
> Where were the remainder? ...

While the names of the kings in the *Esther rabbah* passage are not identical with those in the *baraita* in the Babylonian Esther-Midrash, the similarity is certainly strong enough to arouse the suspicion that our passage in *TB Megillah* evolved out of a pericope that had a similar purpose to that of *Esther rabbah*, in which the number of Ahasuerus's provinces was contrasted with those of other monarchs who, in the eyes of the midrash, ruled over larger dominions. The above impression is strengthened by our analysis of the Talmud's discussion of Ahab, in the subsequent passage:

> [11a] Ahab the son of Omri,[154] as it is written:[155] "*As the Lord God liveth, there is no nation or kingdom whither my lord hath not sent to seek thee; and when they said, He is not there; he took an oath of the kingdom and nation, that they found thee not*" (1 Kings 18:10).
>
> And were it not that he reigned over them,[156] would[157] he have been able to take an oath of them?[158]

---

154 "the son of Omri" — ~ in MS **W**, **Printings**, **YS**, **AgE**.

155 "as it is written" —**Spanish family**: "This is what Obadiah says to Elijah."

156 "that ...them" — MS **B**: ~, and filled in in **B***.

157 "would" — All other witnesses, except **AgE** and **YS**: "how could."

158 **YS** adds: "Ahasuerus, as it is written *'From India to Ethiopia.'*"

This proof that Ahab reigned over the whole world is also brought in *Pirqei derabbi eli'ezer* and its derivatives.[159] Other than the exegetical stimulus of the verse itself, it is not clear what the practical homiletical point of the observation might be.[160]

However a possible homiletical context for the tradition might be reconstructed in light of what we have observed in *Esther rabbah*, 1:1 and its parallels, where a contrast is drawn between the two hundred and thirty young men of the princes of the provinces slain by Ahab in his battle against Ben-hadad—taken as indicating the total number of countries in the world—and the "mere" one hundred and twenty-seven provinces ruled by Ahasuerus. It is thus possible that the midrashic interest in the extent of Ahab's dominions originated as a by-product of a discussion of the size of Ahasuerus's empire.[161] When we take into account the fact that the discussion in *Esther rabbah* is attributed entirely to *Amora'im*, this would suggest that the "*baraita*" should probably be considered a fictitious one.

The Esther-Midrash now continues its explication of the *baraita* about kings who "ruled in the vault":

> [11a] Nebuchadnezzar, as it is written:[162] "*And it shall come to pass that the nation and the kingdom which will not serve the same Nebuchadnezzar [king of Babylon and will not put their neck under*

---

[159] In Friedlander's edition of *Pirqei de rabbi eli'ezer*, p. 81 n. 11 he discusses the differences between the readings of the first printed edition and the Vienna manuscript upon which his own translation is based. Though the Vienna MS omits explicit reference to Ahasuerus it is clear that the discrepancy between the two verses regarding the number of provinces is of concern to both traditions. So too in *Midrash 'asaret melakhim.*

[160] The following possibility deserves consideration: The darshan might be trying to enhance the absoluteness of Ahab's evil by associating it with his absolute power. This would serve to underscore Elijah's courage in opposing such a formidable antagonist, and to emphasize the miraculousness of his success in eluding such a mighty king. Cf. *Seder eliahu rabbah*, in: L. M. Friedmann, ed., *Seder Eliahu rabba und Seder Elijahu zuta [Tanna d'be Eliahu]* (Vienna: Achiasaf, 1902), Ch. 9, p. 49. For a summary of midrashic perspectives on Ahab see Ginzberg, *Legends*, 4:186-9; and especially 6:310 n. 31, where he cites the Septuagint rendering of 1 Kings 18:10 as evidence of Ahab's reputed absolute power.

[161] See Ginzberg, ibid., 6:310-1, n. 32.

[162] "as it is written" — **EY**: "about whom it is written."

> *the yoke of the king of Babylon, that nation will I punish, saith the Lord, with the sword, and with the famine, and with the pestilence, until I have consumed them by his hand*]" (Jeremiah 27:8).

Nebuchadnezzar is included in virtually all the traditions about kings who ruled throughout the world, a claim for which there is ample scriptural support,[163] and which serves to heighten the universal significance of the destruction of the Temple.[164] The juxtaposition to Ahasuerus serves to underscore the midrashic affinity between the king who destroyed the Temple and the king who obstructed its reconstruction.

> [11a] Ahasuerus — That which[165] we have said.[166]

This usage of the formula "as we have said" has some unusual features. The expression is usually taken to be a redactional or scribal abbreviation for a full repetition of a previously cited *talmudic* passage.[167] Rashi refers us in the present instance to the "from India to Ethiopia" pericope above.[168] Now, if the "as we have said" is indeed an abbreviated citation of the "India to Ethiopia" pericope, then we would

---

163 Maharsha astutely observes that the Talmud's proof-text refers not only to Nebuchadnezzar himself, but also to his progeny.

164 See Ginzberg, *ibid.*, 6:422, n. 96.

165 "That which" — MS **P**: "As."

166 "Ahasuerus...said" — ~ in **YS**. **Printings** add: "A sign: שסדך."

167 A modest variation on the גרש phenomenon so familiar to students of the Palestinian Talmud, a usage which wavers on the borderline between redactional and scribal activity; see: J. N. Epstein, ed. E. Z. Melamed, *Introduction to Amoraitic Literature: Babylonian Talmud and Yerushalmi* (Jerusalem and Tel-Aviv: The Magnes Press and Dvir, 1962), 322-32; E. S. Rosenthal, "Leshonot soferim," in *Yovel shai: sefer ha–yovel leSha"Y Agnon*, 293-324 (Ramat-Gan, 1958); E. S. Rosenthal and S. Lieberman, eds., *Yerushalmi Neziqin*, Texts and Studies in Rabbinic Literature (Jerusalem: Israel Academy of Sciences and Humanities: Section of Humanities; The Institute for Advanced Studies, The Hebrew University of Jerusalem; The American Academy for Jewish Research, 1983), 26-28; Michael Sokoloff, ed., *The Geniza Fragments of Bereshit Rabba*, Texts and Studies in Rabbinic Literature (Jerusalem: Israel Academy of Sciences and Humanities, 1982), 22-3, 45–50.

168 It might be argued the reference here should have been to the biblical verse by itself, since the interpretations of Rav and Samuel do not really strengthen the proof to any appreciable extent. The terminology indicates quite unambiguously however that the allusion is to a talmudic text.

find ourselves in a situation where the full text of the "*baraita*" contained a reference to an Amoraic discussion! In light of the above observations and difficulties, it seems more acceptable to modify our understanding of the use of "as we have said"; it is not intended to allude to a longer text of the *baraita*, but merely to introduce an explanatory gloss: The *baraita* itself did not contain a proof-text, so the Talmud is explaining its reasoning through a reference to a similar conclusion reached above.[169]

Thus far the citation from the *baraita*. Now the anonymous Talmud subjects it to a series of objections, asking why various other kings were excluded from the list of monarchs who ruled "in the vault."

> [11b] And are there no more?[170]
>
> Is there not Solomon?
>
> —[171] His reign did not last, because Ashmedai came and banished him.[172]
>
> Now this is fine for him who says that he was a king and a commoner and nothing more.[173] However, for him who says that he was a king and a commoner and a king, what is there to say?
>
> —Solomon was different, because[174] he had an additional[175] quality, that he reigned over the upper and lower realms; as it says: "*And Solomon sat upon the throne of the Lord as king instead of David his father, and prospered; and all Israel obeyed him*" (1 Chronicles 29:23).

---

169 Cf. Malachi b. Jacob Hakohen, *Yad malakhi* (reprint: Israel, no date), 1:80b:#346.

170 MS **M** adds: "Is there not שסדך"; MS **Mf** adds: "שסדך: Solomon, Sennacherib, Darius, Cyrus."

171 Most texts (other than MSS **Y**, **W**, **Printings**) add: "Solomon." MS **Mf** adds: "Solomon is different because."

172 "because...him" — Only in **Yemenite family**.

173 "and nothing more" — MS **N**: "These things and nothing more"; MSS **G**, **O**, **W**, **EY**, **Printings**, **AgE**: ~.

174 "was...because" — ~ in MS **L** and **Printings**. "because" — ~ in MSS **L**, **R**, **AgE**.

175 "additional" —only in MS **Y** and **AgE**; in all other witnesses: "different."

The anonymous pericope resolves its own objection initially by alluding to an aggadic legend in *TB Giṭṭin* 68b. The legend relates how King Solomon, after capturing the demon Ashmedai in order to make use of his powers in building the Temple, was eventually tricked by the demon into releasing him and giving him the ring inscribed with God's name through which Solomon had hitherto been able to control the spirit world.[176] Armed with the magical ring, Ashmedai was then able to hurl Solomon four hundred parsangs and depose him from his throne. Ashmedai then commenced impersonating the king while Solomon was forced to wander as a beggar. With reference to this tale the Talmud records the following dispute:

> Rav and Samuel—One says: He was a king and a commoner. And one says: He was a king and a commoner and a king.

The reference to Solomon's dominion over the upper and lower realms is based on another passage in *TB*, this one in *Sanhedrin* 20b. The passage is based on a dictum of Resh Laqish:

> Says Resh Laqish: In the beginning Solomon ruled over the upper realms and in the end over the lower realms.
>
> "Over the upper realms,"[177] as it says: "*And Solomon sat upon the throne of the Lord*, etc."
>
> "And in the end[178] he ruled over the lower realms," as it says: "*For he had dominion over all the region on this side of the river, from Tiphsah even to Gaza*" (1 Kings 4:24).
>
> And in the end he ruled only over Israel, as it says: "*I Kohelet was king over Israel*, etc." (Ecclesiastes 1:12).

---

[176] For textual variants see: M. S. Feldblum, *Diḳduḳe Sopherim Tractate Gittin* (New York: Horeb, Yeshiva University, 1966). This version of the legend is told in identical manner in S. Buber, ed., *Midrash tehillim* (Vilna, 1891) #78:12 [W. G. Braude, transl., *The Midrash on Psalms*, 3rd ed., Yale Judaica Series (New Haven: Yale University Press, 1976), 31-6].

[177] This longer reading, attested (with minor variations) by MS **M**, appears authentic; see *Diqduqé Soferim* ad loc., n. פ.

[178] This awkward phraseology is supported by most witnesses, and has the advantage of being a *lectio difficilior* in comparison with the ostensibly smoother reading of MS **M**: "and afterwards."

And in the end he ruled only over Jerusalem, as it says: "*The words of Kohelet the son of David, king in Jerusalem*" (Ecclesiastes 1:1).

And in the end he ruled only over his bed, as it says: "*Behold his bed, which is Solomon's*, etc." (Song of Songs 3:7-8).

And in the end he ruled only over his staff, as it says: "*and this was my portion of all my labor*" (Ecclesiastes 2:10).[179]

Rav and Samuel— One says: This refers to his staff, and one says: This refers to his flask (?)[180]

Did he return or did he not return?[181]

Rav and Samuel— One said: He returned, and one said he did not return.

The one who says that he did not return [is saying that] he was a king and a commoner.

The one who says that he did return [is saying that] he was a king and a commoner and a king.

This pericope, which was used by the redactor of the *Giṭṭin* passage, is the Esther-Midrash's source for the interpretation that the throne of God mentioned in 1 Chronicles 29:231 refers to Solomon's dominion over the supernatural worlds, an interpretation of the verse that appears to be exclusive to Babylonian sources.[182]

---

179 Some traditions cite Ecclesiastes 1:3; see *Diqduqé Soferim*.

180 See dictionaries, especially Kohut, *Aruch Completum* 7:63-4 and 2:317. Several witnesses (see *Diqduqé Soferim* n. ר) have the reading "קודו" or "קורו." For a detailed philological analysis, see: J. N. Epstein, ed., *The Gaonic Commentary on the Order Toharot Attributed to rav Hay Gaon* (Jerusalem and Tel-Aviv: Dvir and Magnes Press, 1982), 42. Cf. S. Krauss, ed., *Additamenta ad Librum Aruch Completum* (Reprint ed., Jerusalem: Makor, 1969), 126, 357.

181 I.e., to the throne.

182 While many midrashic passages take note of the powerful expression "throne of God," interpreting it as a sign of God's readiness to share power with mortals or as an indication of the absoluteness of Solomon's (earthly) dominion or judicial authority, few use it in the sense in which it is interpreted in the above passages from the Babylonian Talmud. See *Song of Songs rabbah* [S. Dunsky, ed., *Midrash shir ha-shirim: midrash ḥazita* (Jerusalem and Tel Aviv: Dvir, 1980), 8-9].

A similar tradition is brought in *Song of Songs rabbah* (1:1:10)[183] and *Ecclesiastes rabbah* 1:1:12:

> "*I Kohelet was king over Israel in Jerusalem*" (Ecclesiastes 1:12)—
>
> He saw three worlds in his days and in his life.
>
> R. Judan[184] and Rabbi [Ḥ]oniah:[185]
>
> R. Judan said: He was a king and a commoner and a king; a wise man and a fool and a wise man; a rich man and a poor man and a rich man.
>
> What is the reason? —"*All things have I seen in the days of my vanity*" (Ecclesiastes 7:15).
>
> A person never relates his distress until the time of his relief, after he has reverted to his wealth.
>
> And R. [Ḥ]oniah said: He was a commoner and a king and a commoner; a fool and a wise man and a fool; a poor man and a rich man and a poor man.
>
> And what is the reason? —"*I Kohelet was king over Israel in Jerusalem.*" [I was once, but now I am nothing].[186]

The *TB Giṭṭin* passage upon which our own text is based can be readily seen to be composed of several discrete traditions about Solomon that developed independently in connection with various

---

[183] *Ibid.* In this collection, our passage is preceded by one which speaks of Solomon's "ten falls," as his kingdom was whittled away. The king, after ruling initially over the entire world (see above), came to rule only over Israel, then over Jerusalem, then merely over his house, and finally not even over his bed. Note that there is no reference to ruling over the upper or spirit world.

[184] Presumably the fourth-century Palestinian sage; see Ch. Albeck, *Introduction to the Talmud*, 332.

[185] Identity unclear. It is improbable that the reference would be to the first-generation Amora R. Ḥoniah Divrat Ḥawran (see Albeck, *op. cit.*, 164-5).

[186] The bracketed section appears at the beginning of the *Ecclesiastes rabbah* passage; see the detailed discussion in Maharzu's commentary.

biblical verses, especially from Ecclesiastes [notably: 1:12;[187] 2:7;[188] 7:15; as well as *Song of Songs* 3:7]. Such narrative traditions may have developed in connection with the individual verses, or as parts of proems to the biblical books which were ascribed to Solomon. The sophisticated combining of the different elements in the *Giṭṭin* pericope —especially those of the dethroning of Solomon and the Ashmedai story[189]—shows signs of late and developed editorial activity; and hence the citation in our Esther-Midrash of both the *Giṭṭin* and *Sanhedrin* pericopes likely belongs to the advanced redactional ("Saboraitic") strata.[190]

The Talmud now continues its discussion of the *baraita*.

> [11b] But is[191] there not Sennacherib, as[192] it is written: "*Who are they among all the gods of those countries that have delivered their country out of my hand*" (Isaiah 36:20)?

---

[187] See Louis Ginzberg, "Die Haggada bei den Kirkenvätern V," in *Abhandlungen zur Erinnerung an Hirsch Perez Chajes*, ed. A. Z. Schwarz and V. Aptowitzer, 22-50 (Vienna: The Alexander Kohut Memorial Foundation, 1933), 23; *Idem.*, "Jewish Folklore: East and West," 65, 70, 243.

[188] The association of Solomon with the demonic realm seems to date back to ancient legends, not necessarily in connection with this verse. See the extensive literature utilized by Ginzberg, *Legends*, 4:149-54,165-69; 6:291-9.

[189] This feature of the legend is unique to the Babylonian versions. In the Palestinian traditions of the story [e.g. *TP Sanhedrin* 2, 20c; *Pesiqta derav kahana*, 26:2 (ed. B. Mandelbaum, 386, transl. W. Braude and I. Kapstein, 394-5); E. Grünhut and J. Ch. Wertheimer, eds., *Midrash shir hashirim*, 2nd ed. (Jerusalem: Ktav Yad Vasefer Institute, 1981), 3:7-8 (pp. 71-2); *Tanḥuma Aḥarei*, 1; *Tanḥuma* (Buber), *Aḥarei*, 2], Ashmedai does not play an active role in the story, but it is God who removes Solomon from the throne in punishment for excessive pride, whereupon an angel occupies the throne. In the Targum to Ecclesiastes and in E. Grünhut, ed., *Midrash al yit-hallal* [in *Sefer ha-liqquṭim* (Jerusalem, 1898-1902), 20b-21a] we find a hybrid tradition, in which God directly appoints Ashmedai to replace Solomon, without any mention of Ashmedai's capture or the Temple building episode. Cf. *Lamentations rabbah*, 19:2 (421). An extensive list of parallels, including references to a variety of medieval anthologies, may be found in Ginzberg, Legends, 6:299-300, n. 86.

[190] See Shamma Friedman, "A Critical Study of Yevamot X with a Methodological Introduction," in: *Texts and Studies, Analecta Judaica*, ed. H. Z. Dimitrovsky, 275-442, 1 (New York: The Jewish Theological Seminary of America, 1977), especially criteria #1 (Aramaic; p. 301) and #7 (citation of other pericopes; p. 304).

[191] "is" —**Printings**: "was."

[192] "as" —**EY**: "concerning whom."

—There was Jerusalem which he did not conquer,[193] as it is written: "*that the Lord should deliver Jerusalem out of my hand*" (ibid.).[194]

As noted above, Sennacherib[195] does not appear in the various midrashic lists of kings who ruled "from one end of the world to the other," although Isaiah 36:20 is cited in several midrashic texts as evidence of Sennacherib's universal dominion.[196] Our anonymous passage does not appear to be quoting directly from any other talmudic or midrashic text;[197] rather, it is alluding to the unmediated biblical verses.

[11b] But is[198] there not Darius, as it is written: "*Then king Darius wrote unto all the peoples, nations and languages that dwell in all the earth, Peace be multiplied unto you*" (Daniel 6:26)?

—There were seven over which he did not reign, as it is written: "*It pleased Darius to set over the kingdom a hundred and twenty satraps* [*which should be over the whole kingdom*]" (Daniel 6:1).

Daniel 6:26 is cited as evidence for Darius's ruling over the entire world[199] in *Mekhilta Beshallaḥ*, 1[2][200] (quoted above) and in *Esther rabbah*, 1:1:4, where Darius's empire is contrasted with that of Ahasuerus, which was incomplete by comparison. This reading is the

---

193 "which…conquer" — **AgE**: "over which he did not reign."

194 "as…hand" — Only in **Y** and **AgE**.

195 For a composite of his portrayal in rabbinic literature, see Ginzberg, *Legends*, 4:267-70.

196 See Ginzberg, *Legends*, 6:361-2, n. 51. Isaiah 36:20 is cited as evidence of Sennacherib's insolent power in *Leviticus rabbah*, 7:6 (ed. Margulies, p. 162) and *Ecclesiastes rabbah*, 5:1. In *Leviticus rabbah*, 18:2 (p. 402) and *Tanḥuma Tazriaʿ*, 8 [=*Tanḥuma* ed. Buber, Leviticus (*Tazriaʿ*, 10), p. 38] the verse is incorporated into an account of Sennacherib's failed attack on Jerusalem, as part of a complex proem based on Habakkuk 1:7. See our discussion of this passage above.

197 The talmudic tradition that Sennacherib had confused "all the nations," used to justify intermarriage with converts from biblically forbidden peoples, may have been based on exegesis of the same verse, though I am not aware of its being cited in that connection. Cf. *Tosafot Soṭah* 9a s.v. מנימין.

198 "is" — MS **G**: "was."

199 Or the Median empire.

200 As well as in *Mekhilta derabbi shimʿon ben yoḥai*, 50.

reverse of our own passage.[201] It is not clear whether the author of our passage was thinking of a midrashic parallel, or relating directly to the biblical verses.[202]

> [11b] And is there not Cyrus, as it is[203] written: *"Thus saith Cyrus king of Persia, All the kingdom of the earth hath the Lord given me"* (Ezra 1:2)?
>
> —There[204] he is glorifying himself.

In spite of the Talmud's refutation Cyrus figures in the list of ten kings in *Pirqei derabbi eliʿezer* and *Midrash ʿaseret melakhim.*[205] The former confines itself to a citation of Ezra 1:2, while the latter fills in an aggadic tradition about how Nehemiah persuaded the king to permit the rebuilding of Jerusalem.[206] The Talmud does not seem to be citing any other talmudic passage.

Concluding Remarks

When taken on its own terms, the structure of this brief passage was not found to demonstrate any unusual complexity. The biblical descriptions of the vastness of Ahasuerus empire raised associations with a *baraita* that listed him among kings who ruled throughout the world. The anonymous redactors challenged the coherence of that list by suggesting the names of some other kings who had been excluded from it in spite of the fact that they too ruled the world. In each of the cases the Talmud was able to produce a reason to justify the exclusion.

It was when we began to investigate some more critical issues that the passage was seen involve some more fundamental questions. Our own pericope displayed some of the features which typify the

---

201 The enumeration of satrapies in Daniel 6:2 seems to invite comparison with the number of Ahasuerus' provinces, hence it is particularly surprising that the verse is apparently not cited elsewhere in rabbinic literature (as evidenced by Aaron Hyman and Arthur Hyman, *Torah hakethubah vehamessurah*, Second revised edition ed. (Tel Aviv: Dvir, 1979), 3:226.

202 On Darius in the aggadah see Ginzberg, *Legends*, 4:343-8; 6:434-9.

203 "as it is"—**HgT** and **EY**: "concerning whom."

204 "There" — ~ in MS **O**.

205 See Friedlander's edition, p. 82, n. 4.

206 Ed. Horowitz p. 44; Eisenstein's edition p. 463.

redactional activity of the "anonymous Talmud," the late strata of scholars who cement together the disparate units of the Babylonian Talmud.[207] This process was discernible in the citation of developed pericopes about Solomon's fall from greatness taken from *Sanhedrin* 20 and *Giṭṭin* 68b. We noted also that rabbinic literature records a number of similar-looking discussions about the cosmocrators of history, which were used in a variety of homiletical contexts. With respect to our passage, it seemed most likely that the Babylonian "*baraita*" of the three kings is actually a reformulation of an Amoraic passage in *Esther rabbah* in which the extent of Ahasuerus' dominions is contrasted with those of several kings who supposedly ruled over vaster empires. We observed in passing how various scattered talmudic discussions about great monarchs of history were gradually synthesized, embellished and systematized in later midrashic works like *Pirqei derabbi eli'ezer* and *Midrash 'aseret melakhim* as they were incorporated into the detailed quasi-apocalyptic messianic scenarios of the medieval era. As in previous chapters, we were repeatedly faced with the fundamental difference between the Babylonian midrash and its Palestinian counterparts: the Bavli displays a repeated tendency to ignore or eliminate the homiletical contexts and literary structures that define Palestinian midrashic activity, and to treat the midrash as an academic exegetical enterprise.

---

207 On the sources of the passages discussed in the present chapter see the summary by A. Weiss, *Studies in the Literature of the Amoraim*, 282, who observes that it is composed of: "...midrashic comments on almost every word in Esther 1:1. Most of these comments are by Rav and Samuel. Among them is relevant material, both Tannaitic and Amoraic... With regard to both its content and sources, this material bears the stamp of a distinct unit."

Chapter Four

Ahasuerus' Calculations

"His Mind Became Settled"

[11b] "*In those days, when the king Ahasuerus sat...*" (Esther 1:2).

And it is also written: "*In the third year of his reign*" (Esther 1:3)![1] [2]

—Says Rava:[3] What is {the meaning of} "*when the king Ahasuerus sat*"?[4] —When[5] his mind became settled.

He[6] said: Belshazzar counted[7] and made an error. I shall count[8] and not make an error.

The textual stimulus to this midrash is the apparent redundancy[9] of the phrase "*when the king Ahasuerus sat on the throne of his majesty.*" Under other circumstances the Talmud's expected response might have been to understand the verse as saying that this was the *first time* that he sat on the throne; i.e., at the start of his reign. In this case however such an interpretation is impossible, since the text itself goes

---

1 "And it...'...*reign*'" — ~ in MSS **B** and **Mf**, and filled in in **B***.

2 MS **G** adds: "What is {the meaning of} '*when {the king} sat*'?"

3 "Rava" — MS **N**: "Rabbah."

4 "What... '...*sat?*'" — ~ in MS **G**.

5 "When" —**Spanish family**, **Printings**: "After."

6 "He"—MS **W**, **HgT**: "Ahasuerus."

7 "counted" —**AgE**, **Spanish family** and MS **W**: "calculated."

8 "count" —**AgE**, **Spanish family** and MS **W**: "calculate."

9 The difficulty is not a contrived one, and has been discussed by biblical scholars. See Carey A. Moore, *Esther*, The Anchor Bible (Garden City: Doubleday, 1971), 5: "Many scholars of the past and present see the word as meaning 'when he sat *securely*,' thereby alluding to the fact that Xerxes had to put down uprisings in Egypt...and in Babylon"; Paton, 124–9; Cf. Rashi to the verse: "When his kingdom became secure in his hands"; and midrashic sources cited in notes below.

on to state explicitly that this was the third year of his monarchy. Hence Rava's reading that the verb "*sat*" should be read not in the sense of physical sitting, but of mental settling.

It is not clear that Rava himself had in mind the explanation that the Talmud goes on to supply, about the king's conviction that the seventy-years prophesied by Jeremiah for the redemption of Israel had expired. Rabbinic literature supplies a number of different variations of why Ahasuerus would have become secure in his reign or settled in his mind. For example, there are traditions that explain that following his futile attempts to seat himself upon the miraculous throne of Solomon he commissioned an inferior imitation which, after three years, was now ready;[10] or that he convened his feast in order to celebrate the suppression of a rebellion.[11] The Bavli however, consistent with its thematic reading of Esther, opts for an interpretation that would assert the centrality of the fate of the Temple and Ahasuerus' role in obstructing its reconstruction.

Belshazzar's Error

The midrash assumes that Belshazzar and Ahasuerus were familiar with Jeremiah's prophecy (29:10) that Israel would be "visited" after seventy years were "accomplished for Babylon." Both monarchs took Jeremiah's words seriously enough to refrain from tampering with the Temple's vessels before they had satisfied themselves that the promise was not going to be carried out.[12]

---

[10] *Abba gorion*, 8; *Panim aḥerim* A (55) and B (58); *Esther rabbah*, 1:12; both Targums to Esther; see L. Ginzberg, *Legends*, 6:451, n. 5; Paton, 129.

[11] *Abba gorion*, 8, *Panim aḥerim*, B 58 and both Targums (the interpretation is not connected there to the sitting / settling on the throne, but proposed as an occasion for the feast); *Ginzberg*, *ibid.*, 6:452, n. 6. The danger of rebellion is alluded to later on in the Esther-Midrash. See Ibn Ezra's (first) commentary and B. Walfish, "The Two Commentaries of Abraham Ibn Ezra on the Book of Esther," 337-8.

Esther rabbah 1:11 takes a different approach, emphasizing that "*as* he sat" (כשבת) indicates less permanence than would "*when* he sat," and hence inspiring a homiletical contrast between the ephemeral nature of heathen rule and the permanence of Jewish settlement (On the passage see commentaries of Luria and *Yefeh ʿanaf*).

[12] Rashi: "At first he was worried that the Jews might be freed from his control upon the conclusion of the seventy years of the Babylonian captivity. Now however his

Continued on next page...

The notion that gentile kings would be learned in the words of the Hebrew prophets is of course a commonplace in the midrashic perception of history,[13] deriving at least in part from the ethnocentric certainty that world history is a mere by-product of Jewish history, and that Jewish history itself takes on significance as the embodiment of the divine plan and covenantal relationships described in scriptural prophecy.[14]

> [11b] What is this?[15] That which is written: "*For thus saith the Lord, That after seventy years be accomplished for Babylon I will visit you*" (Jeremiah 29:10).[16]
>
> What is "*for Babylon*"? —To the reign of Babylon.[17]
>
> Subtract[18] forty-five[19] of Nebuchadnezzar,[20] twenty-three of Evil-merodach and two of his own— Behold: seventy.

...Continued from previous page

mind was put at rest." According to Rashi's explanation the king's antipathy towards the Temple was pragmatic and selfish, rather than religious or simply malicious, as appears more likely from the midrashic sources.

13 Isaac Heinemann, *Darkhei ha-'aggadah*, 40, brings a wealth of examples (including our own passage, mentioned on p. 212, n. 55), noting that the phenomenon is just as likely to occur in anachronistic contexts; (i.e., where the citation is of a biblical text that has supposedly not been written yet), and that the assumption is utilized to produce dramatic literary effects.

14 On the midrashic assumption that it is the Bible and its concepts that bestow meaning on history, see the perceptive observations of: James Kugel, "Two Introductions to Midrash," especially 84-90.

15 "What...this" —MS **N***: "What did Belshazzar count?" MS **B** adds: "which Belshazzar calculated and made an error?"

16 MS **M** and **Printings** add: "And it is written: '*That he would accomplish for the desolations of Jerusalem seventy years*" (Daniel 9:2).

17 "What...reign of Babylon" —Found only in MSS **Y** and **W** and **AgE**; MS **N**: "How long did Nebuchadnezzar rule? Forty-five years"; MS **B**: "He took out the sacred vessels and made use of them. He calculated:."

18 "Subtract" —only in MS **Y** and **AgE**; Most witnesses: "He calculated."

19 MSS **N** and **W**, **AgE** and **EY** add: "years."

20 Several texts add: "and."

> Immediately[21] he took out the vessels of the Holy Temple and made use of them.[22]

In order to understand the calculations described in this passage we must appreciate the traditional chronology of the post-exilic era, as modified in the book of Daniel and systematized in the Tannaitic *Seder ʿolam*. This chronology differs in several important respects from that of the conventional histories. Thus, according to the accepted scholarly reading of the evidence Nebuchadnezzar began his rule in 605/4 B.C.E., while Belshazzar was left as temporary ruler of Babylon during the absence of his father, the usurper Nabonidus, beginning in 552; with the reigns of two other Neo-Babylonian emperors intervening between Nebuchadnezzar's son Evil-merodach and the accession of Nabonidus.[23] The author of Daniel,[24] on the other hand, treats Belshazzar as the son of Nebuchadnezzar. Aware that Evil-merodach, the real son of Nebuchadnezzar, is mentioned in Jeremiah 52:31 and 2 Kings 25:27,[25] the *Seder ʿolam*[26] turns Belshazzar into Nebuchadnezzar's grandson.

Accordingly, from Belshazzar's perspective there would have been three reigns to be accounted for in order to fill in Jeremiah's seventy years from the beginning of the Babylonian empire. The Talmud now proceeds to demonstrate its reasons for assigning the

---

21 "Immediately" — only in MS **Y** and **AgE**. MS **W** adds: "Now that he saw that seventy years had expired and they had not been redeemed he said: Since they have not been redeemed now, they will no longer be redeemed."

On the use of this expression in midrashic narratives see Ch. Albeck, *Einleitung und Register zum Bereschit Rabba*, Vol. 1: Einleitung, 30; M. H. Segal, *Mishnaic Hebrew Grammar*, 241-2.

22 "Immediately...them" — ~ in MS **B**.

23 On the whole question see: L. F. Hartmann and A. Di Lella, eds., *The Book of Daniel*, Vol. 23, The Anchor Bible (Garden City, New York: Doubleday & Company, 1978), 29-43, 46-54.

24 5:2,11, 18, 22.

25 The omission of Evil-merodach from Daniel is explained homiletically in *Genesis rabbah* 65:2 (according to Albeck's interpretation on p. 1032). Cf. *Tanḥuma* ed. Buber, *Vayyeshev*, 11 (p. 183).

26 Ed. Ratner, Ch. 28, p. 126 (see note 15 there); ed. Milikowsky, 422, 537

respective lengths of the reigns of each king. It begins with Nebuchadnezzar:

> [11b] Whence do we know that Nebuchadnezzar ruled for forty-five years?
>
> —Because the master says: They were exiled in the seventh. They were exiled in the eighth. And they were exiled in the eighteenth. And they were exiled in the nineteenth.[27]
>
> "They were exiled in the seventh" —after the conquest of Jehoiakim,[28] which is "the eighth"[29] to the reign of[30] Nebuchadnezzar.[31] "They were exiled in the eighteenth" of the conquest[32] of Jehoiakim,[33] which is the nineteenth year[34] of the reign of[35] Nebuchadnezzar; as the master says:[36]

The reference introduced here by the formula "the master says"[37] appears to be (at least its first part) from *Seder ʿolam* Chapter 25,[38] which reads as follows:

---

27 **Spanish family** add: "But were there four [MS **B***: three] exiles? There were two exiles! Rather:" The reading in MS **B*** is cited by the *ʿArukh* (Kohut, 2:279) in the name of both the *Megillah* and *ʿArakhin* passages.

28 "Jehoiakim"—MS **N** (after emendation) and **Printings**: "Jehoiachin."

29 MSS **O** and **B*** add: "year."

30 "the reign of"— ~ in **Spanish family**, MS **L**, **Printings**, **YS**.

31 MS **M** adds: "And similarly:."

32 "conquest" — MS **O**: "exile." MS **B** adds: "of the land, which is the exile of."

33 "Jehoiakim" — **Printings**: "Zedekiah."

34 "year" — ~ in MSS **G**, **N**, **W**, **M**, **R**, **HgT**, **YS**, **AgE**.

35 "of the reign of" — ~ in MS **M**, **Printings**, **YS**.

36 "as...says" — MS **N**: "And this is as...says"; MS **B**: "Does not the master say"; MS **O**: "and...says."

37 On this citation formula in the Babylonian Talmud see: Abraham Weiss, *Leqorot hit-havvut ha-bavli*, Publications of the Institute of Jewish Studies in Warsaw (Warsaw: Institute of Jewish Studies in Poland, 1929). The usage here is non-standard, by Weiss's definition, since the *baraita* has not yet been quoted in our passage. It is possible that the citation is from *TB ʿArakhin* 12a.

38 Ed. Ratner, p. 110; ed. Milikowsky, 394, 525. On the whole passage, see also *Pirqei derabbi eliʿezer*, Ch. 49 (transl. Friedlander, 391-5, and notes).

And[39] he came to Jerusalem "*in the seventh year*" (Jeremiah 52:28).

But in another verse it says: "[*And the king of Babylon took him* [*in the eighth year of his reign*]" (2 Kings 24:12).

What is the meaning of "*in the seventh year*" and what is the meaning of "*in the eighth year*"?

—"*In the eighth year*" of his reign, and "*in the seventh year*" from when he conquered Jehoiakim.

The contradictory scriptural passages in question describe the same event, the captivity of the young King Jehoiachin, who ruled only three months before Nebuchadnezzar had him exiled to Babylon along with his family and court and the spoils of Jerusalem.[40] *Seder ʿolam* resolves the contradiction by positing a dual use of the term "reign": In the one case it refers to the actual beginning of Nebuchadnezzar's rule, while in the other it refers to his reign over Judæa, which he subjugated in the second year after coming to power.[41]

The second difficulty hinted at by the *baraita* concerns two descriptions of the captivity of Zedekiah and the final destruction of Jerusalem. On the one hand both 2 Kings 25:8-9 and Jeremiah 52:12-3 state: "*Now in the fifth month, in the tenth day of the month, which was the* nineteenth *year of Nebuchadnezzar king of Babylon, came Nebuzaradan, captain of the guard, which served the king of Babylon, unto Jerusalem, and he burned the house of the Lord*, etc." However according to Jeremiah 52:29: "*In the* eighteenth *year of Nebuchadnezzar he carried away captive from Jerusalem*, etc."

Here again the Talmud appears to be offering an abbreviated allusion to a passage from *Seder ʿolam* (Chapter 27), which dealt with the same problem:[42]

---

39 See Milikowsky's apparatus.

40 Martin Noth, *The History of Israel*, translated by S. Goldman (London: Adam & Charles Black, 1958), 281-2.

41 For modern approaches to resolving the contradiction, see Noth, 281, n. 4; M. Cogan and H. Tadmor, ed., *II Kings*, The Anchor Bible (Garden City: Doubleday & Co. Inc., 1988), 311-3; John Bright, ed., *Jeremiah*, The Anchor Bible (Garden City: Doubleday & Co. Inc., 1988), 369.

42 Ed. Ratner, p. 121; ed. Milikowsky, 414-5, 534.

So it says:[43] "*...the nineteenth year...*," but in another place it states "*...the eighteenth year...*"

What is the meaning of "*eighteenth*" and what is the meaning of "*nineteenth*"?

—Rather, "*the nineteenth*" of his reign, and "*the eighteenth*" from when he conquered Jehoiakim.

The Talmud, or the source which it is using, appears to have combined these two separate *baraitot* from *Seder ʿolam*[44] into a single cryptic *baraita*, which it utilized in order to establish that eight years elapsed between the beginning of Nebuchadnezzar's empire and the captivity of Jehoiakim.

[11b] In the first year he conquered Nineveh. In the second he[45] conquered Jehoiakim.

The Talmud is again citing *Seder ʿolam* (end of Chapter 24)[46] in support of its claim that Jehoiakim was vanquished in Nebuchadnezzar's second year. The passage of *Seder ʿolam* reads as follows:

---

43 See Milikowsky's apparatus; cf. Ratner's note 7.

44 This is the view of Ratner, *ibid.* n. 7 and in his Introduction pp. 94-5. In the latter reference he calls our attention to the interesting passage in *TB ʿArakhin* 12a where the same *baraita* is cited. As distinct from our pericope in *Megillah*, where the Talmud entertains no doubts as to the proper interpretation of the *baraita*, the *ʿArakhin* passage goes through several objections before Rabina arrives at the correct explanation. This phenomenon is open to several possible interpretations: e.g., it might teach us that the *Megillah* passage derives from a later redactional stratum which was already familiar with the conclusions of the *ʿArakhin* passage; alternatively, it could indicate that the redactors of *Megillah* were familiar with the full contexts of *Seder ʿolam*, whereas those of *ʿArakhin* were not. It is likely however that the "ignorance" of the *ʿArakhin* pericope is feigned, a typical talmudic literary ploy designed to produce a suitably dialectical *sugya*. Note however that the **Spanish family** of witnesses, cited in our notes above to the talmudic text, incorporate some of the dialectics of the *ʿArakhin* passage into *Megillah.*

45 MS **B** and **AgE** add: "went up and." This is identical to the reading in the good manuscripts of *Seder ʿolam*; see Ratner 109 (n. 40); Milikowsky's apparatus (392).

46 Ed. Ratner, *ibid.*; Milikowsky, 392, 542. The preceding passage claims to relate a number of events that took place in the "beginning" of Jehoiakim's reign, based on the ascriptions of Jeremiah Chaps. 23-27. Note however the discrepancy between p. 108 and Jeremiah 25:1 (noted by Ratner, n. 28; no variant to this reading is cited by Milikowsky, 389-90); cf. Jeremiah 46:2.

> "*The word of the Lord which came to Jeremiah the prophet against the Gentiles; against Egypt, against the army of Pharaoh-necho king of Egypt, which was by the river Euphrates in Carchemish, which Nebuchadrezzar king of Babylon smote in the fourth year of Jehoiakim the son of Josiah king of Judah*" (Jeremiah 46:1-2).
>
> It was the first year of Nebuchadnezzar; that year he went up and conquered Nineveh. In the second he went up and conquered Jehoiakim.

This tradition does not appear to be based on any biblical source, nor is it historically accurate. The destruction of Nineveh was carried out by Nebuchadnezzar's father Nabopolassar in 612 B.C.E. together with the Median Cyaxares, seven years before Nebuchadnezzar's accession to the throne.[47] The chronology of Jehoiakim's submission to Babylonia is somewhat more problematic. Nebuchadnezzar did invade Philistia in 604, overrunning it by 603/2 and bringing Jehoiakim under Babylonian vassalage.[48] However the precise dating, and the nature of the transition from vassalage to subjugation, are not at all clear. According to the traditional commentators to the Talmud, *Seder ʿolam*'s certainty that the conquest came in Nebuchadnezzar's second year is derived from a midrashic exposition that appears at the beginning of Chapter 25:[49]

> "*In the third year of the reign of Jehoiakim king of Judah came Nebuchadnezzar king of Babylon unto Jerusalem and besieged it*" (Daniel 1:1).

---

47 John Bright, *A History of Israel*, 2nd ed. (Philadelphia: The Westminster Press, 1972), 314-5; M. Noth, *The History of Israel*, 270. Tobit 14:14, according to the Greek versions, relates how before Tobias died "he heard of the destruction of Nineveh, which Nebuchadnezzar and Ahasuerus had captured." Several scholars have emended the text to "Nabopolassar" and "Cyaxares"; see: F. Zimmermann, ed., *The Book of Tobit*, Dropsie College Edition: Jewish Apocryphal Literature (New York: Harper & Brothers for Dropsie College, Philadelphia, 1958), 123; D. C. Simpson, "The Book of Tobit," in *The Apocrypha and Pseudepigrapha of the Old Testament*, ed. R. H. Charles, I: Apocrypha (Oxford: The Clarendon Press, 1913), 241; Charles Torrey, "'Medes and Persians'," *JAOS* 66 (1 1946), 8.

48 Bright, *op. cit.*, 326; Noth, 280-1.

49 Ed. Ratner, 110; ed. Milikowsky, 394, 525; cited by the *ʿArukh* (Kohut, 2:279) and Rashi to the *Megillah* and *ʿArakhin* passages.

Is it possible to say such a thing? Did he not rule "*in the fourth year of Jehoiakim*" (Jeremiah 25:1)![50]

What then is the meaning of "*In the third year of the reign of Jehoiakim*"?

—Since his rebellion.

The *baraita* is claiming that the event being referred to in Daniel is not Nebuchadnezzar's first capture of Jerusalem, which did not take place until Jehoiakim's fifth year, but rather the siege of Jerusalem that occurred in the eleventh and final year of Jehoiakim's reign; i.e., in the third year of the rebellion which began in Jehoiakim's eighth year.[51] Jehoiakim's eleventh year is the seventh after the Babylonian occupation (which commenced, as we have seen, in his fourth year). Now the Talmud has already demonstrated that the seventh year of the conquest of Jerusalem is also designated the eighth year of Nebuchadnezzar's reign (with reference to the captivity of Jehoiachin, which occurred later that same year). From this we deduce that there is a one-year interval between Nebuchadnezzar's accession to power and his subjugation of Jerusalem; which is equivalent to saying that the occupation of Jerusalem took place in his second year.

The calculations thus far are summarized in the following chart.

---

[50] The date in Daniel is truly problematic; see the discussion in Hartmann's commentary (128-9).

[51] 2 Kings 24:1: "*In his days Nebuchadnezzar king of Babylon came up, and Jehoiakim became his servant three years; then he turned and rebelled against him.*"

From beginning of Jehoiakim's reign	From beginning of Nebuchadnezzar's reign	From Nebuchadnezzar's conquest of Jerusalem (Jehoiakim)	
3	1		Beginning of Nebuchadnezzar's reign, conquest of Nineveh
4	2	1	Nebuchadnezzar conquers Jehoiakim
7 (2 Kings 24:1)	5	4	Jehoiakim rebels against Nebuchadnezzar
10 (2 Kings 23:36)	8 (2 Kings 24:2)	7 (Jeremiah 52:28)	Death of Jehoiakim; 1st Captivity (Jehoiachin)
21	19 (2 Kings 25:8)	18 (Jeremiah 32:1)	2nd Captivity: (Zedekiah)

The Esther-Midrash continues:

[11b] And[52] [53] it is written: "*And it came to pass in the seven and thirtieth year of the captivity of Jehoiachin king of Judah, in the twelfth month, on the seven and twentieth of the month, that Evil-merodach king of Babylon in the year that he began to reign did lift*

---

[52] MSS **B*** and **O** add: "this is."

[53] "and" — MSS **N**, **B**, **O**, **M*** and **R**: "as."

> *up the head of Jehoiachin king of Judah and brought him forth out of prison*" (2 Kings 25:27).[54]
>
> Eight and thirty-seven make forty-five.

The calculation is a simple one, demonstrating that within forty five years of the rise of Nebuchadnezzar (which was eight years prior to the captivity of Jehoiachin), Evil-merodach was enjoying his first year on the throne.[55]

> [11b] The twenty-three of Evil-merodach are a tradition [*gemara*].[56]
> And his[57] own two make seventy.

As noted above, the chronological scheme shared by Daniel and the talmudic sources ignores the reigns of Neriglissar and Nabonidus,

---

54 Maharsha observes astutely that if the Talmud were concerned strictly with proving that Nebuchadnezzar ruled for forty-five years, it would have been sufficient to skip to this passage. Instead, following its normal associative patterns of presentation, it chose to resolve the various problems and contradictions presented by the intervening material.

55 Noth, 282: "Jehoiachin was probably brought to the royal court and treated with honour as part of an act of amnesty." In fact, Nebuchadnezzar's reign lasted no more than forty-three years (605/4-562), as stated explicitly by the Babylonian priest Berosus, cited in Josephus' *Against Apion* 1:146 [H. St. J. Thackeray, transl., *Josephus* Vol. 1, The Loeb Classical Library (Cambridge, Mass. and London: Harvard University Press and William Heineman Ltd., 1966), pp. 220-1]; *Jewish Antiquities* 10:219 [R. Marcus, transl., *Josephus* Vol. 6, The Loeb Classical Library (Cambridge, Mass. and London: Harvard University Press and William Heineman Ltd., 1958), pp. 278-9]. *Leviticus rabbah*, 20:1 (444) also has Nebuchadnezzar ruling for forty-five years, but see the critical apparatus and notes there, which mention a tradition that read "forty" (e.g., *Ecclesiastes rabbah*, 2:15:3; [so also in Ratner's citation of *Leviticus rabbah*, based on printed editions]); *Pesiqta derav kahana*, 26:1 [ed. Mandelbaum, 384 (and apparatus); transl. Braude and Kapstein, 393].

According to *Seder ʿolam* Chapter 28 (ed. Ratner, 125; ed. Milikowsky, 419-21, 536), the reinstatement of Jehoiachin took place within two days of Nebuchadnezzar's death, a tradition which is deduced midrashically from the contradictory dates given by 2 Kings 25:27 (twenty-seventh day of twelfth month) and Jeremiah 52:31 (twenty-fifth day). Cf. L. Ginzberg, *Legends*, 6:380, n. 134. Josephus *Antiquities* (10:229, pp. 284-5) also emphasizes that Evil-merodach released Jehoiachin immediately (εὐθύς).

56 "are a tradition" — ~ in MSS **B** and **Mf**, and filled in in **B***.

57 "his" — MSS **B*** and **O**: "Belshazzar's."

who ruled from 560 until 539 when Babylonia fell to Cyrus the Mede. Evil-merodach actually reigned for only two years (662-560).[58] Thus the total number of years between Nebuchadnezzar's death and the fall of Babylon was actually twenty-three. Nabonidus' son Belshazzar was never more than an interim co-regent for about eleven years (549-39) during his father's temporary absence from the capital.[59]

The above passage from the Talmud is essentially an Aramaic paraphrase of the Hebrew text of *Seder ʿolam* Chapter 28:[60]

> Nebuchadnezzar reigned for forty-five years, Evil-merodach his son for twenty-three, and Belshazzar his son for three years.

The Talmud's characterization of Evil-merodach's twenty-three-year reign as a "*gemara*" refers to the fact that, unlike those of Nebuchadnezzar and Belshazzar, its duration is not derived either directly or indirectly from scriptural evidence.[61] From our perspective, we can surmise simply that the number was necessary in order for the three reigns to total seventy, so that it would be possible to introduce the homiletical motif of Belshazzar's calculation of Jeremiah's

---

58 Thus in the excerpt from Berosus in Josephus' *Against Apion* 1:147, pp. 222-3. However in the *Antiquities* 10:231 (pp. 284-7), Josephus gives the length of his reign as eighteen years! See Marcus' notes to the passage, and Ginzberg, *Legends*, 6:430, n. 2.

59 See Noth, 299-300; Bright, 353-4, 360-1; M. J. Gruenthaner, "The Last King of Babylon," *CBQ* 11 (1949), 406-427; Hartmann's commentary on Daniel, 34-5, 50, 185-6.

60 Ed. Ratner, 126; ed. Milikowsky, 422, 537.

61 I emphasize this in contrast to Ratner's claim (p. 126, n. 15; Introduction, p. 28) that "*gemara*" is being employed here as a formula for the citation of *Seder ʿolam* itself. The "tradition" being cited is not the *Seder ʿolam*, but the source of the latter's information. On the usages of the expression "*gemara*" in the Babylonian Talmud (it does not appear in Palestinian sources), see Ch. Albeck, "Sof hora'ah vesiyyum hattalmud," in *Sinai sefer yovel*, ed. J. L. Maimon, 73-79 (Jerusalem: Mosad Harav Kook, 1958), 78, n. 11; *Idem*, *Introduction to the Talmud*, 4-7, where he adduces ample evidence that the term refers to received (as distinct from logically derived) tradition; E. Z. Melammed, *An Introduction to Talmudic Literature* (Jerusalem: Galor, 1973), 326-30.

prophecy. The Talmud prefers to deal with a fixed series of numbers that "happen" to add up to seventy.[62]

The Esther-Midrash now resumes the narrative thread, thereby setting Belshazzar's actions in Daniel Chapter 5 in a new perspective. The remarkable similarities between the descriptions of Belshazzar's and Ahasuerus' feasts do indeed invite the sort of midrashic parallelism that underlies our passage:[63]

> [11b] When he[64] saw that[65] seventy years[66] had elapsed and they had not been redeemed[67] he said:[68] Seeing as they have not been redeemed,[69] now[70] they will no longer be redeemed.
>
> He took out[71] the vessels of the Holy Temple and made use of them.
>
> And[72] this is what Daniel told him:[73] "*But thou hast lifted up thyself against the Lord of heaven; and have brought the vessels of his house*

---

[62] Cf. *Leqaḥ ṭov* to Esther [in: Salomon Buber, ed., *Sifre de-aggadeta al megillat ester* (Vilna: Romm, 1886)], p. 86: "There *remained* twenty-three years for the rule of Evil-merodach...." Ratner's reliance on this passage to prove his interpretation of *gemara* (see above note) is puzzling, since it seems to clearly support the opposite position. It should be noted that *Seder ʿolam* does not connect Belshazzar's feast with the calculation of the seventy years, but is concerned with placing Cyrus (whose reign began within the same year) at the end of that period.

[63] See L. A. Rosenthal, "Die Josephsgeschichte, mit den Büchern Ester und Daniel verglichen," *ZAW* 15 (1895), 278-84 [reprinted in: C. A. Moore, ed., *Studies in the Book of Esther*, The Library of Biblical Studies (New York: Ktav, 1982), 277-83]; Hartmann's commentary to Daniel, 187.

[64] "he" — MS M: "they."

[65] "he saw that" — ~ in MS **O**.

[66] "years" — ~ in MSS **O**, **M**, **EY**, **HgT¹**, **YS**, **AgE**.

[67] "When...redeemed" — ~ in **Printings**.

[68] MSS **R** and **Mf** add: "certainly"; MS **W** adds: "now"; MS **N** adds: "Now certainly."

[69] "Seeing...redeemed" — ~ in MS **Mf**.

[70] "now" — ~ in MSS **G**, **N**, **B**, **O**, **L**, **M** and **Mf**; **HgT²**, **Printings** and **YS** add: "certainly."

[71] **Spanish family** and MS **N** add: "and brought."

[72] "And" — ~ in MSS **L**, **M** and **Mf**, **Printings** and **YS**.

[73] "him" — MSS **O** and **R***, **EY**: "Belshazzar."

> *before thee, and thou, and thy lords, thy wives, and thy concubines, have drunk wine in them*" (Daniel 5:23).
>
> And it is written:[74] "*In that night was Belshazzar the king of the Chaldeans slain*[75] *and Darius the Median took the throne, being about three-score and two years old*" (Daniel 5:30-1).

The midrash has added relatively little to the explicit themes of Daniel: The king's brazen profanation of the sacred Temple vessels inspires a divine punishment, as the end of Belshazzar's reign and of Babylonian rule are announced through the "writing on the wall" and executed forthwith. The Biblical account, while emphasizing the connection to Nebuchadnezzar (5:2), does not dwell on the occasion for the feast, even as it does not provide a reason for Ahasuerus' banquet.[76] Such reasons are supplied by the midrash in its introduction of the calculation motif.[77]

The midrash has not yet explained the nature of Belshazzar's miscalculation. It now returns us to the court of Ahasuerus whose own feast, which is painted in colors very similar to those of Belshazzar's, is also ascribed to a celebration of the expiry of Jeremiah's seventy years.

---

74 "And...written" — ~ in MS **B**.

75 MSS **B***, **O**, **L**, **M**, **Mf**, **Printings** and **YS** add: "And it is written."

76 Some medieval Jewish sources (*Yosippon* Ch. 3, etc.) claim that the feast was in celebration of a military victory over the Medes and Persians; see Ginzberg, *Legends*, 4:343 and 6:430, n. 2; I. S. Lange and S. Schwartz, ed., *Midraš Daniel et Midraš Ezra* (Jerusalem: Mikitze Nirdamim, 1968), 51.

77 The author of Daniel was of course very familiar with Jeremiah's prophecy, whose exposition becomes the central topic of Ch. 9. However the whole point of that episode is to turn the seventy weeks into weeks of *years*, defining an era of 490 years that would conclude in the time of its author, an interpretation which was presumably intended to *replace* the simple seventy-year projection. See Hartmann's commentary to Daniel, 426-50. To judge from Ginzberg, *Legends*, 6:430, n. 3, our Esther-Midrash is the only rabbinic source which ascribes Belshazzar's feast to the expiration of the seventy years. This tradition is recorded by Jerome in his *Commentary to Daniel*; see Jay Braverman, *Jerome's Commentary on Daniel*, 79: "The Hebrews hand down a story of this sort: Belshazzar, thinking that God's promise had remained without effect until the seventieth year, by which Jeremiah had said that the captivity of the Jewish people would have to be ended ... and turning the occasion of the failed promise into a celebration, gave a great banquet, by way of scoffing at the expectation of the Jews and at the vessels of the Temple of God."

Remember that the entire preceding section about Belshazzar is being presented by the Esther-Midrash from the perspective of an extended indirect report of Ahasuerus' thoughts.

> [11b] He[78] said: He counted[79] and made an error;[80] I shall count[81] and not make an error.
>
> Is it written[82] "for the *reign* of Babylon?" "[83] *For Babylon*" is written:[84] to the captivity of Babylon![85]

---

78 "He" — **HgT¹**: "Belshazzar"; MS **W**: "Ahasuerus."

79 "counted" —Genizah fragment: "calculated."

80 "He said…error" — ~ in **AgE**.

81 "count" — MSS **O, L, Mf, HgT²**, **Printings** and **YS**: "calculate."

82 "It is written" — MS **N**: "What is '*for Babylon*?'"

83 MS **Mf, HgT¹** and **EY** add: "*accomplished.*"

84 MSS **B*** and **O, HgT¹** add: "(as it says:) '*That after seventy years be accomplished for Babylon.*' In the end."

85 MS **B*** adds: "In the end." MS **O** adds: "which is the captivity of Jehoiachin. In the end"; **EY** adds: "which is Jehoiachin."

> How many are missing?[86] [87] —Eight. Put in[88] eight[89] in their stead: One[90] of Belshazzar and (five)[91] [two][92] of Darius,[93] and three of Cyrus,[94] and[95] two of his own —make seventy.[96]

Ahasuerus has decided that Belshazzar began his count too early. Jeremiah's vague phrase "*for Babylon*" was not intended to refer to the beginning of Nebuchadnezzar's rule (i.e., the conquest of Nineveh), but to the Babylonian subjugation of Jehoiachin which took place, according to our calculations, in the eighth year of Nebuchadnezzar's reign. This pushes forward the expiry date by eight years, which the midrash fills in according to the chronology of Daniel and *Seder ʿolam*:

•One more year of Belshazzar, referring to Daniel 8:1: "*In the third year of the reign of king Belshazzar*." The understanding is that the calculation of the expiry of the seventy years had been in the second year.[97]

---

86 "How…missing" — Genizah fragment: "Take out."

87 "missing" — MS **Y*** and **AgE**: "left over."

88 "Put in" — MS **N**: "Tale out eight and" ; MSS **G**, **B***, **Mf** and Genizah fragment, **Spanish family** and **Ashkenazic family**: "Calculate and put in"; **AgE**: "less."

89 "eight" — ~ in **Printings**. MS **M** adds: "years."

90 **HgT¹** adds: "year."

91 "five" — ~ in **AgE**.

92 "five…Cyrus" — **G**, **W**, **Ashkenazic family**, **Mf**, **HgT²**: "five of Darius and Cyrus"; MSS **N**, **B**, **O**, **EY**, **HgT¹**, Genizah fragment; "two of Darius and three of Cyrus."

93 "One…[two]" — ~ in Genizah fragment. MS **M** adds: "the Mede."

94 MS **M** adds: "the First."

95 "and"— ~ in MS **N** and **AgE**. **HgT¹** adds: "One year of Belshazzar and two of Darius and three of Cyrus and two of Ahasuerus; calculate forty-five of Nebuchadnezzar and three of Evil-merodach."

96 MS **W** adds: "years." **HgT¹** adds: "He took out the vessels of the Holy Temple and made use of them.

97 Cf. Braverman, *Jerome's Commentary on Daniel*, 80, n. 5, who observes that the biblical text "makes no mention of the year of Belshazzar's reign when the feast took place. Seder Olam Rabbah explicitly states that it was in the third year, obviously based on tradition."

•The two years of "Darius the Mede"[98] are not enumerated explicitly in scripture.[99] Given that Cyrus (see below) ruled for at least three years, two years is the largest time–period that can be assigned him if we wish to keep our total within the seventy-year limit. A two-year reign (at least) is also ascribed to Cyrus in the following midrash from *Seder ʿolam* Ch. 28,[100] based on Jeremiah 51:46, part of a chapter which prophesies the downfall of Babylon at the hand of the Medes:

> ...You do not find another year for Media in scripture, other than this one alone. And thus did Jeremiah say to them: "*And lest your heart faint, and ye fear for the rumor that shall be heard in the land*" —This is of Belshazzar.
>
> "*A rumor shall both come one year*" —This is of Darius.
>
> "*And after that in another year shall come a rumor*" —"*And Babylon, the glory of kingdoms, the beauty of the Chaldees' excellency, shall be as when God overthrew Sodom and Gomorrah*" (Isaiah 13:19)...[101]
>
> "*And violence in the land, ruler against ruler*" — This is Cyrus the Persian.

---

98 As is well known the existence of such a king, mentioned only in Daniel, is not acknowledged by historians; see Hartmann's commentary to Daniel, 35-6, 50-2, 191, etc. An interesting attempt to reconstruct the origins of the tradition from within the logic of Jewish religious thinking may be found in Charles Torrey, "'Medes and Persians,'" *JAOS* 66 (1 1946), 1-15. It seems to be widely accepted that the necessity for a Median overthrower of the Babylonian empire was created by prophecies such as those of Isaiah 13:17 ff. and Jeremiah 51:11, 28:11, 28; which predict that it will be Media that will overthrow Babylonia (a belief which, as suggested by Torrey, was likely inspired by the Median victory against that earlier oppressive empire, Assyria).

99 As noted by Rashi. Daniel Chapters 9 and 11 are located "*in the first year of Darius.*" See the discussion of this question in: E. E. Urbach, "Koresh vehakhrazato beʿeinei ḥaza"l," *Molad* 157 (1961), 368-74 [*Idem., The World of the Sages: Collected Studies* (Jerusalem: The Magnes Press, 1988), 403-10.

100 Ed. Ratner 129; ed. Milikowsky 425, 538.

101 Rashi to Isaiah 13:19 (cited by Ratner): "Two punishments befell [Babylon] during two years: [1] Darius killed Belshazzar and ruled for one year; and [2] in the second year it was overturned from heaven like Sodom and Gomorrah, as we learned in *Seder ʿolam* ..." Cf. his commentary to Isaiah 21:9 and Qimḥi to 13:19.

•As regards Cyrus, though there is no biblical source that explicitly defines the length of his rule,[102] Daniel Chapter 10 is dated "*in the third year of Cyrus king of Persia.*" *Seder ʿolam* Chapter 29[103] states that "Cyrus reigned for three partial (מקוטעות) years."[104]

As in the case of Evil-merodach above, it is likely that the total of five years assigned to Darius and Cyrus was arrived at in order to achieve the desired total of seventy years in the third year of Ahasuerus' reign. The textual traditions are at variance over whether to treat the two reigns as a single unit of five years, or to divide it up into separate periods of two and three years apiece. This confusion likely reflects the dubious status of the midrashic support for Darius' two-year rule, whose source was the *Seder ʿolam*, in a passage which was not cited explicitly by the Talmud.

•The assertion that Ahasuerus (Xerxes) was the immediate successor of Cyrus is another invention (albeit a venerable one) of the traditional Jewish historiography,[105] found in *Seder ʿolam* Chapter 28:[106]

> "*Also I in the first year of Darius the Mede, even I, stood to confirm and to strengthen him. And now I will shew thee the truth. Behold, there shall stand up yet three kings in Persia...*" (Daniel 11:1-2).
>
> —This is: Cyrus and Ahasuerus and Darius who built the Temple.

---

102 Actually Cyrus ruled as emperor for ten years, from 539 (when he captured Babylon) until his death in 530, when he was succeeded by his son Cambyses. See Noth, 304; Bright, 362-4.

103 Ed. Ratner 132; ed. Milikowsky 431, 542.

104 As we shall note below, in the conclusion of our pericope the Talmud seems to favor a division of one and three years. A widespread midrashic tradition, apparently not utilized either in *Seder ʿolam* or in our current passage, treats Darius and Cyrus as virtual co-regents ruling by rotation; cf. Ginzberg, *Legends*, 4:344-9, 6:430-2.

105 The traditional ordering of kings does at any rate appear to be an old one. It is, for example, supposed in the arrangement of materials in Ezra 4-5, which passes from Cyrus (4:5) to Ahasuerus (4:6) to Darius (4:24 ff.). See J. M. Myers, ed., *Ezra. Nehemiah*, Vol. 14, The Anchor Bible (Garden City, N.Y.: Doubleday & Company, 1965), 34-5; Torrey, "'Medes and Persians,'" 1-3, 6-9; *Idem.*, *Ezra Studies*, reprint ed., The Library of Biblical Studies, ed. H. M. Orlinsky (New York: Ktav, 1970), 37-40, 140-2, etc.

The identification of the third year of Ahasuerus' reign as the date of the feast is of course explicitly spelled out in Esther 1:2. The equation of the occasion for this feast with that of Belshazzar's—the removal of the Temple vessels and the calculations that justified it—is the invention of the midrashic authors and ties in with the central thematic concerns of the midrash.

Our midrashic narrative now continues, applying to Ahasuerus the phraseology that was employed previously with respect to Belshazzar:

> [11b] When he[107] saw that[108] seventy years[109] had elapsed and[110] they had not been redeemed he said:[111] Since now[112] they have not been redeemed,[113] they will [114] no longer be redeemed.
>
> He took out[115] the vessels of the Holy Temple and made use of them.
>
> Satan came[116] and danced among them,[117] and he killed Vashti.[118]

...Continued from previous page

106 Ed. Ratner, 129; ed. Milikowsky, 426, 539.

107 "he" — **Printings** and **YS**: "they."

108 "he saw that" — ~ in MSS **G** and **M**.

109 "years" — ~ in MSS **G, O, M, Printings, EY, AgE**.

110 "seventy...and" — ~ in Genizah fragment.

111 MS **N** adds: "now certainly."

112 "now" — ~ in **Spanish family**.

113 "Since...redeemed"—MS **G**: "certainly"; MS **W**: "now"; MSS **N, B, Ashkenazic family, Mf, AgE**: "now certainly"; ~ in Genizah fragment.

114 **Spanish family** add: "now."

115 **Spanish family**, **AgE** and Genizah fragment add: "and brought."

116 "came" — in Aramaic in MSS **Y, L, HgT²**; all other witnesses word it in Hebrew.

117 Satan appears here in his function as executor of divine punishment; cf. E. Urbach, *The Sages*, 169-70. Similar images appear elsewhere in rabbinic literature; see e.g.: *TB Pesaḥim* 112b: "Do not stand in front of an ox that is coming up from the meadow because Satan is dancing between its horns"; *Numbers rabbah*, 20:11: "When a man goes to commit a sin Satan dances for him until he completes the transgression; once he has destroyed him he informs him..." In passages of this sort Satan is functioning

Continued on next page...

The parallelism between the actions and fates of Belshazzar and Ahasuerus would not be complete unless both suffered equivalent punishments for their desecrations of the sacred vessels. Working from the scriptural sources alone, Ahasuerus appears to live out his reign none the worse for his blasphemy. Our anonymous commentator tries to furnish the story with some appearance of divine justice through his assertion that the Vashti incident (which, as our midrash will say, would eventually be regretted by the sobered king) was intended to fulfill that purpose.[119]

> [11b] But did he not calculate correctly?
>
> — He[120] also erred, because he should have counted to "*the desolations of Jerusalem*" (Daniel 9:2).

The preceding computations were so convincing that the Talmud is initially unable to fault them. Why indeed did the redemption foretold by Jeremiah not come to pass by Ahasuerus' third year? The solution follows the lines of the previous passage: Just as Ahasuerus demonstrated above that Belshazzar had erred in beginning his count too early, so does the Talmud assert now that Ahasuerus himself should not have started counting from the captivity of Jehoiachin, but from the actual destruction of Jerusalem during the reign of Zedekiah, which we have dated to Nebuchadnezzar's nineteenth year. Daniel 9:2, upon which this revised interpretation of Jeremiah is based, is explicitly

...Continued from previous page

less as a theological being than as a casual metaphor for a human who has put himself in a dangerous situation.

118 The execution of Vashti is not spelled out in the biblical account; cf. Ginzberg, *Legends*, 4:378, 6:456-7, n. 42, and Chapter 6 below.

119 Midrashic literature supplies other ways in which Ahasuerus was punished for his sins (generally identified as his obstruction of the reconstruction of the Temple), notably through the diminution of his empire. See Ginzberg, *Legends*, 4:379, 6:457, nn. 47-8.

120 "He" — MS O: "They."

intended as an interpretation of Jeremiah's prediction.[121] This new date is eleven years later than our previous one.

> In the end[122] how many are missing?[123] —Eleven.
>
> And how many did he[124] reign? —Fourteen.

The chronology of the first fourteen years of Ahasuerus' reign is spelled out explicitly in Esther, and summarized in *Seder ʿolam* Chapter 29[125] in a passage which was evidently being used by the author of our midrash:

> "*And*[126] *in the reign of Ahasuerus, in the beginning of his reign they wrote an accusation against the inhabitants of Judah and Jerusalem*" (Ezra 4:6). "*Then ceased the work of the house of God which is in Jerusalem. So it ceased unto the second year of the reign of Darius king of Persia*" (4:24).
>
> "*In the third year of his reign, he made a feast*, etc." (Esther 1:3).
>
> For four years Esther remained hidden in Shushan the palace.[127] "*Esther was brought also unto the king's house in the tenth month, which is the month of Tevet, in the seventh year of his reign*" (Esther

---

121 See Hartmann's concise summary of the various biblical authors' (including Zechariah and Chronicles) understandings of Jeremiah's prophecy on pp. 246-7 of his commentary to Daniel.

122 "In the end" — **Ashkenazic family**: "And in the end." MS **N** adds: "you find"; MS **L** and **YS** add: "when you calculate"; MS **Mf** adds: "what do you find?"

123 "missing" — MS **Y***: "Alternate reading: left."

124 MS **R** adds: "also."

125 Ed. Ratner 132-5; ed. Milikowsky 431-2, 542-3.

126 The various additions mentioned in Ratner's n. 10 are not attested by the witnesses recorded in Milikowsky's apparatus.

127 This tradition is used in midrashic sources to exemplify Esther's modesty in trying (unlike her Gentile compatriots) to avoid being brought before the king. See for example *Panim aḥerim* B, 63-4 (which is evidently citing *Seder ʿolam*). The Second Targum to Esther 2:8 elaborates: "And when Mordecai heard that virgins were being sought, he took Esther and hid her... so that they would not take her, and he placed her in a room inside a room so that the royal messengers would not see her; however the Gentile girls, when the messengers would pass through, would dance and show off their beauty, etc." (See also **AgE**, 20). See Ginzberg, *Legends*, 4:389, 6:458, n. 55 (which does not cite *Seder ʿolam*). Ratner (n. 13) also refers us *Genesis rabbah*, 1:1 (p. 1, and note Albeck's reference to the Kalir).

2:8). And for all five[128] years Haman was amassing the spoils for Mordecai.[129]

"*In the first month, that is, the month Nisan, in the twelfth year of king Ahasuerus, they cast Pur*, etc." (Esther 3:7). On the thirteenth of Nisan[130] Haman wrote the letters "*to destroy, to kill , to cause to perish, all Jews*" (Esther 3:13).

[On the fifteenth of Nisan Esther came before the king].[131]

On the sixteenth of Nisan they hanged Haman on the gallows.[132]

On the twenty-third of Sivan Mordecai wrote letters to revoke Haman's letters.[133]

On the thirteenth of Adar[134] "*the Jews...slew and destroyed five hundred men*" (Esther 9:5-6), and they hanged Haman's ten sons (9:14) who "*wrote an accusation against the inhabitants of Judah and Jerusalem*" (Ezra 4:6).[135] On the thirteenth of Adar, "*on that day*[136] *the number of those that were slain in Shushan the palace was brought before the king*" (Esther 9:11).

At the same date in the next year: "*Then Esther the queen, the daughter of Abihail, and Mordecai the Jew, wrote with all authority, to confirm this second letter of Purim*" (9:29).

The points that are of direct relevance for our calculation are: (1) Haman's lot was cast in the twelfth year of Ahasuerus' reign. (2) The actual events occurred during the following (i.e., thirteenth) year.

---

128 See Milikowsky's apparatus; Ratner's n. 15.

129 The meaning is apparently that Haman was amassing a personal fortune, which would eventually be taken over by Mordecai; see our analysis of Proem #4 in Chapter 2 above.

130 According to Esther 3:12.

131 This line is missing from MS **N** (Antonin), which forms the basis of Milikowsky's edition; but is found in several other manuscripts cited in his critical apparatus. The date is not spelled out in the biblical text; see our analysis of *TB Megillah* 15a below. See Ginzberg, 4:423, 6:471-2, n. 142.

132 This follows from the tradition used in the previous note.

133 This is specified in Esther 8:9.

134 Esther 9:1.

135 See references in Ratner's n. 20; Ginzberg, 6:463, n. 95.

136 I.e., "*in the twelfth month...on the thirteenth day of the same*" (9:1).

(3) Esther's "second letter" is presumed to have been sent a year later;[137] giving us a minimum of fourteen years.

Now to resume the main thread of our discussion: We have successfully explained the error of Ahasuerus' calculations of why the redemption did not occur by the third year of his rule. This however raises a more serious difficulty: Even according to the latest revision of the starting date, which pushes it ahead by eleven years, the expiry of the seventy years should have occurred in the final year of Ahasuerus' reign. Does this not count as a refutation of Jeremiah's oracle? And thus does the Talmud object:

> [11b] In[138] his[139] fourteenth he ought to have built the Holy Temple.[140] So why is it written "*Then ceased the work of the house of God which is at Jerusalem. So it ceased unto the second year of the reign of Darius of Persia*" (Ezra 4:24)?
>
> Says Rava:[141] They were partial years.

Rava is apparently claiming that the number of years in our calculations was artificially inflated, due to the fact that when kings succeeded one another within a single year that year would be counted for both the outgoing and incoming monarchs.[142] This allows us to push the conclusion of the seventy years forward up to two years, into the reign of Darius "II" son of Ahasuerus, when the rebuilding of the Temple was actually completed.

---

137 So also in *Leqaḥ ṭov* 88: "And the Megillah was established in Ahasuerus' fourteenth year, as it says: '*to confirm this second letter of Purim*' —In the second year it gained wide acceptance among the entire nation." See also Rashi here and to Esther 9:29; sources cited by Ratner, 134, n. 26. Cf. Moore's commentary to Esther, 95: "Exactly when her letter was written is not stated; it could have been ten days or ten years after Mordecai's."

138 "In" —MSS **N**, **O**, **L**, **EY**: "And in."

139 "his" — ~ in MS **M**.

140 "Holy Temple" — **HgT**[2]: "*House of God*." The usage is taken from Ezra 4:24, cited below.

141 "Rava" — MS **Mf**: "Rabbah."

142 See Rashi.

Rava's dictum is based on a passage in *Seder ʿolam* Chapter 29:[143] "Cyrus reigned three[144] partial years," a phrase which is open to several interpretations.[145] However we choose to divide up the reigns, the text seems to be saying that the total years of Darius and Cyrus now add up to four, rather than five years as we had previously estimated.[146]

> [12a] This was also taught {in a *baraita*}: There was[147] one[148] year more to Babylon,[149] [150] Darius came up[151] and completed it.

This *baraita* also derives from *Seder ʿolam* (Chapter 28),[152] where it appears as part of Daniel's calculation that the seventy years

---

143 Ed. Ratner, 132; ed. Milikowsky 431, 542.

144 Cf. Ratner's n. 9; Milikowsky records no variants to the reading "three."

145 Rashi understands this to mean that Darius ruled one and Cyrus three years. He bases himself on *Seder ʿolam* Ch. 28 (Ratner 129): "You do not find a year of Media[n rule] in scripture, other than this one only," implying that Darius' reign was limited to one year, the second one overlapping Cyrus. Cyrus' third year is recorded explicitly (Daniel 10:1). If we accept the reading according to which the Talmud's original assumption was that Darius ruled two and Cyrus three years, then it is Darius' years that are being counted as "partial," as two rather than one. Hence Ratner observes (n. 9) that for the Talmud to make sense, *Seder ʿolam* should have read "four" instead of three.

146 Note that the traditional commentators are in disagreement about where to introduce the "partial years." Rashi places them between Darius the Mede and Cyrus (basing himself on *Seder ʿolam*'s reference to Cyrus' partial years) and between Nebuchadnezzar [Belshazzar? The reading in Rashi is problematic; see sources cited by Ratner] and Evil-merodach, with the conclusion of the seventy years not occurring until the completion of the Second Temple under Darius II. The "Rid" [Ditrani, Isaiah, *Tosefot rid*, reprint ed. (Jerusalem: 1974)] disputes this, arguing that if we take the language of *Seder ʿolam* literally, Darius was the one who *completed* the full seventy years, adding one year to the total, after Belshazzar had already ruled for a further year following his own calculation. Hence the two-year discrepancy must have already been introduced prior to the start of Belshazzar's reign, somewhere between Nebuchadnezzar, Evil-merodach and Belshazzar.

147 "was" — Thus in **AgE**; MSS **B** and **O**: "is"; ~ in other witnesses.

148 "one" —**G**, **O**, **M**, **EY**, **Printings**, **AgE**: "another."

149 "Babylon" — MSS **B** and **O**: "Belshazzar."

150 MSS **G**, **W**, **M**, **Mf**, **EY**, **HgT**, **Printings**, **AgE** add: "and."

151 "came up" — Only in MS **Y**; all other witnesses: "stood."

152 Ed. Ratner, 128-9; ed. Milikowsky, 425, 538.

expired in the first year of Darius the Mede. The Talmud is implicitly contrasting this tradition with our previous assumption that the period had already expired in Belshazzar's third year. This proves that a "partial" year had been counted sometime previous to this.[153]

Rava's[154] dictum raises some interesting questions about the relationship between the Talmud and *Seder ʿolam*. Why does he not simply cite the *baraita* as such instead of seemingly trying to pass it off as his own dictum. A number of possibilities, some more likely than others, suggest themselves:

•Rava was not familiar with *Seder ʿolam* and arrived at the same solution independently. —Highly unlikely in light of the generally close dependence of our passage on *Seder ʿolam*.[155]

•The word "partial" is not authentic to *Seder ʿolam*, but is a late scribal gloss based on the Rava's dictum in the Talmud.[156]

•Rava's statement was intended as a quotation from *Seder ʿolam*.

•Rava was intentionally going beyond the scope of *Seder ʿolam*, as if to say: *Seder ʿolam* is speaking only of Cyrus, but the rule should be applied [also, or instead] to other kings.

---

153 Cf. Maharsha.

154 It is possible that "Rava" is not to be taken here as a literal attribution, but merely as a hypothetical reference to the author of the pericope, all of which is an elaboration of Rava's original dictum: "What is {the meaning of} '*when the king Ahasuerus sat*?' —When his mind became settled" [See our remarks at the beginning of the present chapter]. The Talmud is then saying, in effect: "This is how Rava *would* have resolved the difficulty in conformity with his interpretation."

155 Pp. 19-68 of Ratner's Introduction consists of an investigation into this question. He concludes that *Seder ʿolam* was known to many, but not all, the Amoraim. On p. 65 there he mentions the explicit citation of the *baraita* as evidence of Rava's familiarity with *Seder ʿolam* [in spite of the fact that that quote is most likely from the "anonymous Talmud"], ignoring our problem of Rava's bringing the *baraita* in his own name. For an instructive attempt to deal with an analogous problem, see: Chaim Milikowsky, "*Seder ʿOlam* and the Tosefta," *Tarbiẓ* 49 (3-4 1980), 246-263; *Idem.*, *Seder Olam: A Rabbinic Chronography*, 1:12-24.

156 It is however found in all Ratner's texts, and in several medievals from Rashi onwards.

Daniel's Miscalculation

Our Midrash has already succeeded in making its basic point, of demonstrating that Ahasuerus' feast was occasioned by the king's conviction that the seventy years allotted for the redemption of Israel had elapsed and that he could now with impunity continue to obstruct the construction of the Temple and to profane its vessels. The midrash now appends some assorted comments on related themes, brought here either by virtue of thematic associations, or with a view to tying up "loose ends."

> [12a] Says Rava:[157] And[158] Daniel also[159] erred in this calculation.[160]
>
> As it is written: "*In the first year of his reign I Daniel understood by books the number of the years, whereof the word of the Lord came to Jeremiah the prophet, that he would accomplish seventy years in the desolation of Jerusalem*" (Daniel 9:2).
>
> Since he says "*I understood*[161]," this implies that he[162] erred.

It is not entirely clear how we are supposed to understand the exegetical basis of this comment. If we accept the reading of the principal textual tradition, according to which the midrash is rooted in the expression "בינתי" then we are presumably supposed to attach

---

[157] "Says Rava" — MSS **G**, **Mf**: "Says Rabbah"; ~ in **EY**.

[158] "And" — only in MS **Y**, **AgE** and **EY**.

[159] "also" — ~ in MS **O**.

[160] "this calculation" — MS **O** and **EY**: "that count."

[161] MSS **N**, **EY** add: "*by books*."

[162] MS **O** and **EY** add: "also."

significance to the morphology[163] or meaning[164] of the biblical word for "*I understood.*" Alternatively, the exegesis might be based on the choice of the ambiguous expression "ספרים," which can be rendered as either "books" or "numbers."[165] Nor does the Talmud spell out the precise content of Daniel's misunderstanding. Most commentators[166] agree with Rashi,[167] that Daniel expected the Temple to be rebuilt at the date indicated in the verse (Daniel 9:1) "*in the first year of Darius the son of Ahasuerus,*" which he computed to be the conclusion of seventy years from Nebuchadnezzar's subjugation of Jehoiakim; on reflection, however, Daniel realized that the starting point for the count should be the destruction of the First Temple, "*to the desolations of Jerusalem,*" as was deduced at the conclusion of the preceding talmudic discussions.[168]

---

[163] See Abba Bendavid, *Biblical Hebrew and Mishnaic Hebrew*, Vol. II, 481, who brings examples of "hollow" verbs of this sort being conjugated as regular ones in rabbinic Hebrew; cf. M. H. Segal, *A Grammar of Mishnaic Hebrew* (Oxford: Clarendon Press, 1927), 80. E. Kautzsch, ed., *Gesenius' Hebrew Grammar*, 203, observes that the form בינתי is in fact exceptional. Note carefully the comments of R. Samuel Masnouth in: I. S. Lange and S. Schwartz, ed., *Midraš Daniel et Midraš Ezra*, 80.

[164] I.e., understanding implies that something had hitherto been *not* understood or misunderstood.

[165] This is Rashi's interpretation here (possibly misunderstood by the translator of the Soncino English version, p. 67, n. 5), which is probably based on a different reading; and in his commentary to Daniel 9:2; though it hardly seems necessary to propose such an unlikely translation when the verse makes explicit mention immediately afterwards of "*the number of the years.*"

[166] E.g., Ibn Ezra: "All the *Ge'onim* are in unanimous agreement with the view of the ancients, who argued that Daniel erred in his calculation..."; *Leqaḥ ṭov*, 87 ("When Belshazzar was killed and Darius son of Ahasuerus the Mede succeeded him, Daniel began to wonder about the expiration of the seventy years..." So also in the *Meṣuddat david* commentary to Daniel *ad loc.*

[167] As noted by Maharsha, Rashi does not deal with this question in his commentary to our talmudic passage, but rather in his commentary to Daniel 9:2.

[168] Significant exceptions to the scholarly consensus include Judah Halevi (cited in Ibn Ezra's commentary; see the fascinating exchange between the two scholars, as recorded there), who seems to have difficulties accepting that a sage and prophet such as Daniel should have succumbed to such an error; and R. Isaiah Ditrani in *Tosefot rid*, who argues that the Talmud cannot be saying that Daniel initially computed from the

Continued on next page...

One is tempted to speculate why Rava goes out of his way here to ascribe to Daniel an error of this sort, when the comment does not appear to have been occasioned by any pressing textual difficulty in the scriptural passage. Two related possibilities that come to mind are:

•Rava's dictum is to be viewed within the context of a more general tendency among some rabbis to discourage messianic speculations and the demoralizing consequences that ensue when the expected hopes are not fulfilled.[169]

•Rava may be attempting to downgrade Daniel from the position of a true prophet, who speaks with oracular infallibility, to that of a righteous and wise man who is nonetheless subject to errors of human judgment. This issue (which is in evidence in such phenomena as the exclusion of Daniel from the "Prophets" section of the Bible)[170] should probably be regarded as a by-product of the more general controversies over the status of apocalyptic speculations about the "end of days."[171]

...Continued from previous page

subjugation of Jehoiakim ("*to Babylon*"), since that very verse in Daniel states explicitly that he knew that he was supposed to calculate from "*the desolations of Jerusalem*"; hence Ditrani prefers to interpret that the whole passage took place in the reign of Darius "II" (the Persian), that Daniel had begun his count from the destruction of the first Temple, and that the discrepancy consisted only of the two "partial" years mentioned previously by the Talmud. Ditrani does not appear to have read Rashi's comments on Daniel 9:2, or he would have noted that this realization (i.e., that the count should begin from Zedekiah's captivity) is perceived by the midrash as the *result* of Daniel's "understanding," not its premise. But cf. *Leqaḥ ṭov*, 88: "...there was one year missing to complete the seventy '*to the desolations of Jerusalem*,' so Darius the Great [i.e., the Persian!] arose and completed them."

169 For an overview of this issue in rabbinic literature see: E. Urbach, *The Sages*, especially 680-5, 1002-3. On 681, Urbach reviews the attitudes of some Babylonia *Amora'im* regarding the desirability of messianic speculation, but does not deal with Rava (however see *ibid*., p. 65).

170 See Di Lella's Introduction to the Anchor Bible commentary to Daniel, 25.

171 An interesting discussion of the question may be found in Ginzberg, *Legends of the Jews*, 6:413-4, n. 76, where he observes that this seems to be a point of contention between Babylonian and Palestinian sources: The latter, while agreeing that the *Book* of Daniel belongs among the Hagiographa, entertain no doubt that the *man* Daniel was a true prophet; the Babylonian Talmud, on the other hand, tends to deny Daniel prophetic status; as in *TB Megillah* 3a / *Sanhedrin* 94a [on this passage, see: E. Segal, "'The Goat of the Slaughterhouse...'— On the Evolution of a Variant Reading in the

Continued on next page...

Contradictions

Our discussion continues:

> [12a] At any rate, the verses do contradict one another! It[172] is written: "*that after seventy years be accomplished at Babylon I will visit you*" (Jeremiah 29:10); and it is written: "*that he would accomplish...in the desolations of Jerusalem*" (Daniel 9:1)!

In keeping with the premises with which we have been operating so far, there are two different sets of seventy-year calculations that are being referred to in the scriptures:

1) Jeremiah's count beginning from the captivity of Jehoiachin, which concludes at the end of the reign of Darius the Mede, and the beginning of that of Cyrus.

2) Daniel's count, which starts at the destruction of the Temple under Zedekiah, and concludes with the building of the Second Temple in the second year of Darius the Persian.

Note that the Talmud's objection seems to tacitly reject what has hitherto been its working assumption, that Daniel's calculation is an *interpretation* of Jeremiah's, not an alternative one.[173] The new interpretation is necessitated by the fact that the Bible itself (Ezra 1:1) identifies Cyrus' decree as the fulfillment of Jeremiah's prophecy.

The Talmud now proposes a solution to the contradiction:

> [12a] Says Rava:[174] Merely for "visiting," but not for redemption.[175]

...Continued from previous page

Babylonian Talmud" ; Ginzberg does not cite our passage in his discussion. See also: Braverman, *Jerome's Commentary on Daniel*, 48, n. 73, 60, n. 33; cf. E. E. Urbach, "Mattay paseqah ha–nevu'ah," *Tarbiẓ* 17 (1946), 6, n. 42 [reprinted in: Urbach, E. E., *The World of the Sages: Collected Studies* (Jerusalem: The Magnes Press, 1988), 9-12]; *Idem.*, *The Sages*, 651; Geza Vermes, "Josephus' Treatment of the Book of Daniel," *JJS* 42 (2 1991), 157-8, and n. 14.

172 "It" —MS **L** and **YS**: "For it."

173 The Talmud's inconsistency on this point seems to have inspired R. Isaiah Ditrani to apply all the references to Darius the Persian; see our discussion of his views above.

174 "Says Rava" — MS **L**: "And says Rava"; **AgE**: "Says R. Abba"; **EY**: ~.

175 "but...redemption" — Only in MSS **Y**, **R**, **HgT^2**, **AgE**; Others: ~.

And[176] this is what is written: "*Now in the first year of Cyrus king of Persia, that the word of the Lord by the mouth of Jeremiah might be fulfilled, the Lord stirred up the spirit of Cyrus king of Persia, that he made a proclamation throughout all his kingdom and put it also in writing, saying*" (Ezra 1:1); and it is written:[177] "*Thus saith Cyrus king of Persia, The Lord God of Heaven hath given me all the kingdoms of the earth; and he hath charged me to build him an house at Jerusalem, which is in Judah*" (1:2);[178] "*Who is there among you of all his people, his God be with him, and let him go up to Jerusalem, which is in Judah, and build the house of the Lord God of Israel, he is the God which is in Jerusalem*" (1:3).

Rava asserts that the decree of Cyrus was actually the fulfillment of Jeremiah's prophecy which foretold, not the full restoration of the Temple, but a more limited "visiting," which was accomplished when permission was granted for the return of the exiles. The "visiting"[179] is identified by the various commentators as: the stirring of Cyrus' spirit;[180] the return of the Jews to their homeland;[181] their release from servitude;[182] or the laying of the foundations for the Second Temple.[183]

"Cyrus His Anointed"

[12a] Rav Naḥman bar Rav Ḥisda[184] expounded:[185] What is it that is written "*Thus saith the Lord to his anointed, to Cyrus, whose right hand I have holden, to subdue nations before him...*" (Isaiah 45:1)?

---

176 "And" — ~ in MSS **B** and **R**, and added in emendations.

177 "and...written" — ~ in MSS **G**, **N**, **B**, **Printings**; MS **R**: "for it is written."

178 MSS **B***, **O**, **M**, **Mf**, **EY** add: "and it is written"; MS **R** adds: "for it is written."

179 There might be midrashic significance to the fact that the same root used to designate "visitation", "פקד," is employed in Ezra 1:2 to mean that God has "charged" him with the building of the Temple; the traditional commentators do not pick up on that possibility.

180 Qimḥi's commentary to Jeremiah 29:10.

181 Rashi to Ezra 1:1; *Meṣuddat david* to Jeremiah 29:10; Maharsha to the Talmud.

182 Ibn Ezra to Ezra 1:1.

183 Rashi to Ezra 1:1;

184 "Rav Ḥisda" — MS **P** and **EY**: "Isaac."

185 "expounded" — ~ in MS **M**.

> Is[186] Cyrus his[187] anointed?
>
> —Rather:[188] The Holy One said to the "anointed one" {Messiah}: I accuse you[189] with regard to Cyrus.[190] I said "*he shall build my* {*city*},[191] *and he shall let go*[192] *my captives*"[193] (Isaiah 45:13).
>
> And[194] he said: "*Who is there among you of all his people, his God be with him, and let him go up to Jerusalem*" (Ezra 1:3)!

This last passage is of course not an integral part of the preceding midrashic exposition, but a separate comment that is brought here because of its thematic resemblance to Ezra 1:2, which was quoted by Rava.

Rav Naḥman[195] objects to the fact that Isaiah refers to the Persian king as His "anointed one," a term which carries with it special associations in Jewish parlance, whether as the actual Messiah[196] or, at the least, as one who has been literally anointed with oil as part of the religious investiture rites of a priest or king.[197]

---

186 "Is"— **Spanish family**: "And is"; **Printings** and **AgE**: "And was."

187 "his" — found only in MS **Y**.

188 "Rather" — ~ in MSS **G**, **W**, **L**, **R** and **Mf**.

189 "you" — ~ in **Ashkenazic family**.

190 MS **M** adds: "king of Persia."

191 "city"— Emended according to biblical text; MSS **Y**, **G**, **O**, **W**, **L**, **R**, **HgT²**, **Printings**, **YS**, **AgE**, Genizah fragments: "house."

192 "let go" —MSS **Y** (before emendation), **G**, **O**, **W**, **R**, **P**, **EY**, **Printings**, **AgE**, Genizah fragment, **YS**: "gather."

It is clear from the nature and distribution of these variants that the principal textual tradition did not contain a direct quote from the biblical verse, merely a paraphrase using standard rabbinic phraseology. See Rashi.

193 "captives" —only in MS **Y**, **Printings** and **AgE**; all others: "captivity."

194 "And" — ~ in MS **R**.

195 He was a fourth-generation Babylonian; see Albeck, *Introduction to the Talmud*, 370-1.

196 For an overview of rabbinic Messianic concepts, see Urbach, *The Sages*, 649-90 and bibliographical references on 990, n. 2, and 1034-6.

197 This is the view of Rashi. On the various usages of the root "משח," see the standard dictionaries.

The solution makes use of a common midrashic device,[198] that of re-punctuating the verse so as to alter the relationships between its components. In the present instance, a separation is inserted between "*to his anointed*" and "*to Cyrus*," so that the second part of the verse is no longer taken as a modifier of the first, but as the *content* of God's message to the Messiah. The verse is now read as follows: "*Thus saith the Lord to his Messiah* [I am complaining to you] *about Cyrus, whose right hand I have holden, to subdue nations before him...*"[199] It is not really explained how or why God should be addressing the Messiah on this occasion. The impression is that the Messiah is, as it were, "waiting in the (celestial) wings" for certain events to occur before his coming, but is being obstructed by Cyrus' half-hearted execution of his orders. Our midrash criticizes Cyrus for not taking more decisive measures to ensure the rebuilding of the Temple.

Louis Ginzberg[200] has collected several instances of such negative assessments of Cyrus in the Babylonian Talmud. For example, in *TB Rosh hash-shanah* 3b-4a several different sages vie to adduce midrashic evidence to the effect that Cyrus disappointed his initial noble intentions. Ginzberg suggests that these criticisms should be regarded as a characteristically Babylonian phenomenon, which contrasts with the generally favorable judgment of the Persian ruler in Palestinian sources.[201] He attributes this difference to the different political situa-

---

[198] On the phenomenon, see I. Heinemann, *Darkhei ha-'aggadah*, 109-10; James Kugel, "Two Introductions to Midrash," 77-80.

[199] Note however Rashi's observation that the Masoretic cantillation separates "*to his anointed*" from "(*to*) [concerning] *Cyrus*," implying that the latter is not simply modifying the former (cf. Norzi's *Minḥat shai* to the verse). What the Talmud is doing here is applying to a scriptural text the method of חסורי מחסרא, which it employs so frequently in its interpretations of Tannaitic texts; see: J. N. Epstein, *Mavo' lenosaḥ ha-mishnah* (Jerusalem: Magnes Press, 1948), 595-672.

[200] *The Legends of the Jews* 6:433-4, n. 7.

[201] The above-mentioned pericope in *TB Rosh hash-shanah* 3b-4a provides good support for this view. It opens with a complementary remark by the Palestinian R. Abbahu, which is afterwards contrasted or modified with a long series of derogatory comments most of which are attributed to Babylonian sages. Nonetheless, Ginzberg also includes references to derogatory statements from Palestinian sources (e.g., *Song*

Continued on next page...

tions of the two Jewish communities: In the Land of Israel they looked to Persia as an ally in the struggle against Rome, whereas in Babylonia they felt the sting of Persian or Zoroastrian persecution.[202]

E. E. Urbach has challenged Ginzberg's view,[203] arguing that Palestinian sources also express negative evaluations of Cyrus and his proclamation.[204] For Urbach, it is precisely in Roman Palestine that we ought to seek the origins of this midrashic motif, as a reaction to Julian the Apostate's failed attempt to rebuild the Temple in Jerusalem.[205] Without any sympathy for Jews or Judaism, but acting out of a determination to restore the traditional values of pagan Rome and to demonstrate his disdain for Christianity, Julian's project ultimately failed. It would be natural, argues Urbach, that the rabbis would note the parallels between the two foreign monarchs and, in typical

...Continued from previous page

of Songs rabbah, 6:[11] in the name of R. Joḥanan; *Ecclesiastes rabbah*, 10:12; *Esther rabbah*, Proem 8).

202 See also: Samuel Krauss, *Paras veromi batalmud uvamidrashim* (Jerusalem: 1948).

203 E. E. Urbach, "Koresh vehakhrazato be'einei ḥaza"l," *Molad* 157 (1961), 377-74 [reprinted in: *The World of the Sages: Collected Studies* (Jerusalem: The Magnes Press, 1988), 407-10]. Urbach does not mention Ginzberg at all, but it is hard to understand that his remarks could have been intended as anything other than a refutation of Ginzberg's hypothesis. Urbach suggests as well that the later Jewish traditions may really preserve some authentic memories from the Persian era, including the anti-Cyrus propaganda of Ctesias.

204 His central proofs are from: (a) *TB Rosh hash-shanah* 3b, where the Palestinian R. Isaac refers to Cyrus' eventual moral decline; (b) R. Joḥanan's cynical assessment of Cyrus' motives in *Song of Songs rabbah*, 4:4. Those sources which blame the inferior status of the Second Temple on its foreign patron (e.g., *Pesiqta rabbati*, 160a) need not be perceived necessarily as *ad hominem* criticisms of Cyrus.

205 An event which has few other overt echoes in rabbinic literature; see S. Lieberman, "The Martyrs of Caesarea," *Annuaire de l'institut de philologie et d'histoire orientales et slaves* 7 (1939-44), 412-3; M. Avi-Yonah, *The Jews of Palestine: A Political History from the Bar Kokhba War to the Arab Conquest*, translated by M. Avi-Yonah (New York: Schocken Books, 1976), 193-8; Y, Geiger, "Ha-mered bimei gallus ufarshat binyan ha-bayit bimei yulianos," in *Eretz Israel from the Destruction of the Second Temple to the Muslim Conquest*, ed. Z. Baras, S. Safrai, Y. Tsafrir and M. Stern, 202-17, 1 (Jerusalem: Yad Yitzhaq Ben-Tzvi), 1982; Joshua Schwartz, "Gallus, Julian and Anti-Christian Polemic in Pesikta Rabbati," *Theologische Zeitschrift* 46 (1 1990), 1-19.

midrashic fashion, would read into Cyrus' actions the questionable motives that had guided Julian.[206] As was the case with Julian, so too with Cyrus, a project that was founded upon such impure motivations was doomed from the start to failure.

Concluding Remarks

The complex midrash to which the present chapter was devoted is, unlike much of the other material in the Esther-Midrash, a decidedly Babylonian creation with no substantial parallel outside the Babylonian Talmud. At its core stand[207] four dicta of the fourth-century Babylonian Amora Rava, which presumably constitute the earliest strata of the pericope:

1) Says Rava: What is {the meaning of} "*when the king Ahasuerus sat*?" —When his mind became settled.

2) Says Rava: They were partial years.

3) Says Rava: And Daniel also erred in this calculation.

4) [At any rate, the verses contradict one another!…] Says Rava: Merely for "visiting," but not for redemption.

While it is not inconceivable that these statements should have derived from separate and unrelated contexts,[208] the coincidences of their common attribution and the fact that they are not found elsewhere in the Babylonian Talmud makes it much more likely that they originated in an integrated midrashic interpretation.

---

[206] As described by Johanan Hans Levy, "Yulianus keisar uvinyan ha-bayit," in *Studies in Jewish Hellenism*, ed. J. Amir, 221-54, 2nd ed. (Jerusalem: Bialik Institute, 1969).

[207] I am ignoring for purposes of this summary the last two units, which are (as we have already stated) independent passages appended here through associative redaction. For an overview of the source-structure of the pericope see: A. Weiss, *Studies in the Literature of the Amoraim*, 282-3, where it is observed that the passage is made up of "long and short *derashot* by Rava to Esther 1:2-3… Rava's expositions have a distinctive character. Their point of departure is contradictions between verses, and their sole purpose seems to be to resolve these contradictions."

[208] We entertained above the possibility that in at least some of the cases the attribution might be fictitious or hypothetical.

The fundamental themes of the pericope lend themselves well to a homily on Esther; in particular, we should note the intertextual parallel that is drawn between Belshazzar's and Ahasuerus' feasts, and the resulting insights provided as to the reasons for Ahasuerus' banquet and the identity of the vessels that were displayed there, as well as the monarchs' agendas *vis à vis* the Temple (which connect conveniently to Ahasuerus' appearance in Ezra 4:6 in the role of the king who obstructs the Temple's reconstruction).

In the final analysis however, the greater part of the passage is not devoted to these provocative and fascinating thematic concerns, but rather to intricate and elaborate calculations of the respective chronologies of Jeremiah's "seventy year" prophecy. It is difficult to imagine how such intellectually demanding stuff could have been incorporated into a sermon directed to a congregation of non-mathematicians.

We might argue initially that the mathematical component of the passage—most of which is contained in the (presumably later) "anonymous Talmud" additions, and is in any case copied largely out of *Seder ʿolam*—did not occupy such a central position in the homily's original form. The facts however militate strongly against such a position: Three of Rava's four attributed dicta relate directly to the computational aspect of the pericope.[209] None of them make complete sense unless supported by the specific dates of the reigns and events in question. Even if we give the ancients credit (as we ought) for widespread familiarity with the Bible,[210] it stills strikes us as farfetched that the average congregant in a Babylonian synagogue would be expected to have mastered the intricacies of the *Seder ʿolam* chronology, or to be able to recalculate it on the spot.

---

209 Whereas the first merely serves to connect it to Esther 1:2, and relates only peripherally to the thematic content.

210 But note that the texts being referred to here are, almost without exception, *not* taken from passages that would constitute part of the normal synagogal lections.

Chapter Five

The Feast

"Persia and Media...Media and Persia"

[12a] It is written:[1] "*the power of Persia and Media, the nobles and princes of the provinces*" (Esther 1:3).

And it is written: "*...of the kings of Media and Persia*" (Esther 10:2).

—Says Rav Ḥisda:[2] They made a stipulation with one another: If the kings are from us then the eparchs[3] will be from you, and[4] if the eparchs are from us then the kings will be from you.[5]

---

1 "It is written" —Only in MS **Y** and **EY**; ~ in all other witnesses.

2 "Says Rav Ḥisda" —**Printings**: "Says Rava."

3 On the significance of this term see: J. Fürst, *Glossarium Graeco-Hebraeum* (Strasbourg: 1890-91), 72; Samuel Krauss, *Griechische und lateinische Lehnwörter im Talmud, Midrasch und Targum*, 231; Saul Lieberman, *Tosefta ki-fshuṭah*, Vol. 8 (New York: The Jewish Theological Seminary of America, 1973), 779-80, 890-1; I. Ziegler, *Die Königsgleichnisse des Midrasch beleuchtet durch die römische Kaiserzeit* (Breslau: Schlesische Verlags, 1903), 15; Kohut, *Aruch Completum* 1:239-40; Daniel Sperber, "On Roman Administrative Procedure," *Tarbiẓ* 46 (1977), 315-6 [reprinted in his *Essays on Greek and Latin in the Mishna, Talmud and Midrashic Literature* (Jerusalem: Makor, 1982), Hebrew Section 92-5]; M. Avi-Yonah, *The Jews of Palestine: A Political History from the Bar Kokhba War to the Arab Conquest*, translated by M. Avi-Yonah (New York: Schocken Books, 1976), 92 (but cf. 130, 132).

4 "and" —only in MSS **Y** and **R**; ~ in all other witnesses.

5 "If the kings...kings will be from you" —MSS **G**: "If the eparchs are from you then the kings will be from us; if the kings are from you then the eparchs will be from us"; MS **N**: "If kings are from you then kings are from us, {if} eparchs are from us then eparchs are from you" [!]; MSS **B**, **W**, **L**, **R**, **Mf**, **HgT²**, **Printings**, **AgE**: "If the kings are from us then the eparchs will be from you; if the kings are from you then the eparchs will be from us"; MS **O**, **EY**, Geniza fragment: "If the kings are from you then the eparchs will be from us; if the kings are from us then the eparchs will be from you"; MS **M**, **HgT¹**: "(If the)[~ in **HgT¹**] kings are from you then the eparchs are from us, and if the eparchs are from you then the kings are from us"; **YS**: "If the eparchs are from us then the kings are from you; if the kings are from us then the

Continued on next page...

The textual stimulus to this comment is the inconsistent orders of the words "Persia" and "Media" in two different verses in Esther.[6] The midrash presumes that the ordering of items, like everything else in the

...Continued from previous page

eparchs are from you"; MS **P**: "If the kings are from them [!] then the eparchs are from you, if the kings are from ȳōū then the eparchs are from ȳōū."

There undoubtedly exists some connection between this pericope and the passage in *TB ʿAvodah zarah* 8b:

> ...For when Rav Dimi arrived he said: The Romans fought thirty-two battles against the Greeks but were unable to vanquish them until they decided to collaborate with Israel. They agreed to the following conditions: If the kings are from us, then the eparchs are from you; if the kings are from you, then the eparchs are from us...

I am however unable to determine which passage is borrowing from which.

[6] Rashi explains the objection differently, noting that the word "Media" appears in the first verse next to "*the nobles*," implying that the nobles, not the kings, were Median; but in the latter verse it appears next to "*the kings*," implying that the kings, not the nobles, were Medians. Possibly, Rashi did not see the shift in order as sufficient grounds for the objection. His explanation does however supply a more specific textual basis for the Talmud's solution; i.e., the introduction of the distinction between kings and eparchs. Maharsha however prefers to see the problem as lying only in the relative ordering, not the juxtapositions of the words. Rabbi Arieh b. Asher, in his *Ṭurei even* commentary, objects to Rashi's explanation, noting that the word "*nobles*" does not appear in the citation in the printed Talmuds; this of course is not a serious difficulty in light of the common scribal tendency for abbreviated quotations, and the fact that several witnesses do have longer quotations; see Strashun's glosses to *Esther rabbah*, 1.3:18. Cf. the *Ga'on* of Vilna's suggestion (cited by the *ʿAnaf Yosef* here and in his commentary to *Esther rabbah ibid.*) that with respect to royal chronicles it makes sense to speak first of Media since their empire (according to Jewish reckoning) preceded that of the Persians. See the detailed discussion on this point in Azulai's *Petaḥ ʿeinayim*.

Bible, is significant, usually as an indication of the relative importance of the items;[7] hence any variation in the order demands an explanation.[8]

A similar explanation is brought in *Esther rabbah*, 3:18:

> ...Sometimes Media is given precedence over Persia, and sometimes Persia is given precedence over Media. When the government is held by Media, Persia is subordinate to it; when the government is held by Persia, Media is subordinate to it.

Other than explaining the stylistic inconsistency, it is not immediately obvious what homiletical or ideological point the midrash might be trying to make.[9] A more careful study, however, reveals that it is presenting a widespread view in Jewish historiography that, following the overthrow of Belshazzar, the Babylonian empire was divided up between Persia and Media, as foretold in "the writing on the wall": "*PERES*; *Thy kingdom is divided, and given to the Medes and Persians*" (Daniel 5:28).[10] Since Daniel (5:31) and the *Seder ʿolam* traditions

---

[7] The point may be more than a literary one. Presumably the Babylonian rabbis were familiar with the rigid hierarchical stratification that typified the centralized administration of the later Parthian and Sasanian eras; see: A. Perikhanian, "Iranian Society and Law," 627--80; and V. G. Lukonin, "Political, Social and Administrative Institutions: Taxes and Trade," 681-746 (especially 698-712), in *The Cambridge History of Iran*, ed. E. Yarshater, 3 (2) (Cambridge etc.: Cambridge University Press, 1983); Richard N. Frye, *The Heritage of Persia*, 2nd ed., History of Civilisation (London: Weidenfeld and Nicolson, 1965), 51-5, 191-212, 229-33.

[8] I. Heinemann, *Darkhei ha-'aggadah*, 99: "...Since Scripture reflects reality in all its particulars, it follows that the *order* of the utterances should also reflect the order of the things themselves... However in several instances the order comes to indicate the *importance* of the items... the order of the words also demonstrates the honor which the speakers or the text accord to the things." Cf. the opening passage in the *Mekhilta* [*Bo'* 1; ed. Horovitz-Rabin, p. 1-2, ed. Lauterbach, 2-3], which enumerates several examples of the principle that a single exception to a usual order serves as an indication that all the items in the list are of equal importance [See also *Tosefta Keritut* 4:15; *Genesis rabbah* 1:15 (13-4) *Leviticus rabbah* 36:1 (835-7); and other parallels cited by the Theodor and Margulies]. A different approach to this phenomenon in biblical literature may be found in: A. Bendavid, *Biblical Hebrew and Mishnaic Hebrew*, Vol. 1, 50-1.

[9] See Ginzberg, *Legends*, 4:367, 6:452, n. 7.

[10] The inconsistency in the depiction of the two empires' ruling simultaneously as well as successively is also implicit in Daniel 8:3: "...*I...saw...a ram which had two horns;*

Continued on next page...

examined in our previous chapter go on to describe *successive* rules of Darius the Mede,[11] and afterwards Cyrus the Persian, it is understandable why the midrashic sources should take it upon themselves to demonstrate that there was some sort of coordination or rotation agreement between the two nations. This is consistent with the references in Daniel to "*the law of the Medes and Persians*" (Daniel 6:8,12) and to the "*chronicles of the kings of Media and Persia*" mentioned in Esther.

C. C. Torrey[12] has argued that the picture of a cooperative rotation of monarchies between the Medes and the Persians formed an integral part of the historical picture of this era as developed in later Second-Commonwealth Judaism. Spurred on by a typological faith in Media as the destroyer of Babylon,[13] the Jewish writers were faced with the historical fact that Babylon had actually fallen to Cyrus the Persian. The later Jewish historians played down Cyrus' role in the event, and ascribed it primarily to the "Darius the Mede"[14] of Daniel. The many references to the "*law of the Medes and the Persians*" in

...Continued from previous page

and the two horns were high; but one was higher than the other, and the higher came up last"; which is explained in 8:20 "...*The ram which thou sawest having two horns are the kings of Media and Persia.*" Note Hartmann's commentary thereto (234).

11 See previous chapter. Urbach, "Koresh vehakhrazato be'einei ḥaza"l," 370/405, speculates that underlying Daniel's "Darius the Mede" is the historical figure of Gobryas, originally a Babylonian vassal, who led the conquest of Babylon which was completed by Cyrus, as recounted by Xenophon and Herodotus, and was Cyrus' son-in-law. Gobryas' biography thus matches several of the details that were added to the Daniel account by the aggadic traditions.

12 Charles Torrey, "'Medes and Persians,'" *JAOS* 66 (1 1946), 1-15. Torrey's reconstruction was countered by H. L. Ginsberg, *Studies in Daniel*, Vol. 14, Texts and Studies of the Jewish Theological Seminary of America (New York: Jewish Theological Seminary, 1948), 52, n. 56. See also Paton, 127-8.

13 This was based on the precedent of Media having destroyed Israel's other great enemy, Assyria. This inspired the Hebrew prophets to prophesy that Media would also free them from the yoke of Babylon (Isaiah 13:17; Jeremiah 51:11, 28); see Torrey, 6-7.

14 Torrey seems to have taken the phrase "*received the kingdom*," as did the midrashic sources cited below, as implying that the throne was given to Darius, through a voluntary act or agreement (with the Persians), not simply taken by force

Daniel (6:9, 13, 16), Esther and other works, and especially the change in order of the two nations between Esther 1:3, 1:14 and 1:19, point (in Torrey's view) to "the existence of a real coalition, of a formal administrative union" under an alternating headship, between the kings of the two empires.

While Torrey's elaborate theory cannot be equated in all respects with that of the midrashic rabbis, it nonetheless makes a useful and instructive point of comparison. Both Torrey and the rabbis were trying to recreate a harmonistic retelling of the Median and early Persian periods, as they emerge from, and only from, the totality of information contained in the Bible, with special emphasis on Daniel, Esther and Ezra. Torrey[15] does not demonstrate familiarity with our midrashic passages (though he is aware of some equivalent traditions in *Seder ʿolam* and the Targums to Esther), nor is he committed to the hermeneutical methods or principles that underlie them—and yet he ends up reading the evidence in a manner that is, in its essential respects, identical with the conclusions of our texts in the Esther-Midrash and *Esther rabbah*.

The notion of a cooperative partnership between Cyrus and Darius does actually appear in rabbinic retellings of the events of the time. The following example, from *Panim aḥerim* B[16] is built upon many of the same biblical passages used by Torrey in creating his historiographical reconstruction:

> Says Rav: On that night when Belshazzar was assassinated, and they placed Darius on the throne, when the candelabrum fell and crushed Belshazzar's brain—Cyrus and Darius were reclining there. Darius said to Cyrus: Arise and take the throne, for you are worthy to rule,[17]

---

15 Torrey's use of apocryphal materials (1 Esdras and Tobit) does not substantially change the picture that he paints.

16 Ed. S. Buber, 60-1.

17 Probably based on *Song of Songs rabbah*, 3:3/4: "'*Arise, ye princes*' (Isaiah 21:5) —This refers to Cyrus and Darius; '*anoint the shield*' —They received the kingdom. [Darius] said to [Cyrus]: You rule first. [Cyrus] said to [Darius]: Did not Daniel interpret: '*PERES*; *Thy kingdom is divided, and given to the Medes and Persians*'? First to

Continued on next page...

since Daniel used to say to you that you would seize the throne; because Cyrus was still in the service[18] of Nebuchadnezzar, and Daniel would greet him every day, until Cyrus said to Daniel: You have caused me discomfort. Why are you greeting me, for if the king hears of it he will kill you. He said to him: The Holy One will one day grant you dominion; for Isaiah has already prophesied concerning you that you are destined to reign, and that you will give your son permission to build the Temple, for thus does it say: "*Thus saith the Lord to his anointed, to Cyrus*, etc."

For this reason, Darius said to Cyrus: Arise and seize your throne. Cyrus said to him: Did not Daniel say: "*PERES*; *Thy kingdom is divided, and given to the Medes and Persians*" (Daniel 5:28)![19] After Media takes the throne, Persia will rule subsequently. And Darius was a Median, and Cyrus a Persian; as it says: "*And Darius the Median took the kingdom*" (Daniel 5:31).

And some say that his father was a Median and his mother was Persian...[20]

...Continued from previous page

Media and subsequently to Persia; hence: You will rule first." Cf. *Genesis rabbah*, 63:14 (p. 699, and Theodor's comments); Urbach, "Koresh vehakhrazato be'einei ḥaza"l," 370/405.

18 Following Ginzberg's identification of אפיקין as "*officium*" (*Legends*, 6:431); cf. Buber's n. 56.

19 Urbach, *op. cit.*, 371/406, compares this dialogue with the passage in Josephus, *Antiquities* 11:3-6 (pp. 6:3-4-7), according to which Cyrus makes an explicit appeal to Isaiah 45:1 to justify his claim to the throne.

20 See Ginzberg, *Legends*, 4:344-5. Similar harmonistic traditions (though without explicit reference to a rotation agreement) underlie Josephus' account of the fall of Babylon in *Antiquities* 10:248-9 (trans. Marcus, 6:294-7): "And not long afterwards both he [Belshazzar] and the city were captured when Cyrus, the king of Persia, marched against it... Now Darius who with his relative Cyrus put an end to the Babylonian sovereignty..." As noted by Marcus (295, n. *d*), Josephus seems to be doing his best to satisfy both the Greek traditions, which identify Cyrus as the conqueror of Babylon, and Daniel's reference to "Darius the Mede" as accomplishing this task (See also *Antiquities* 10:272, pp. 6:308-9). The *Yosippon* (Ch. 3) relates how Darius and his son-on-law Darius joined forces in a rebellion [a detail derived from Josephus; it does not appear in the midrashic accounts. See: Geza Vermes, "Josephus' Treatment of the Book of Daniel," *JJS* 42 (2 1991), 157-8, 163], though Belshazzar was actually beheaded by one of his own eunuchs who brought Darius and Cyrus the Babylonian monarch's severed head. According to this account, the kingdom was then divided by lot between the two victors (cf. Torrey, "Medes and Persians," 10). It should be noted that, however we may choose to assess the evidence from the rabbinic traditions, it ap-

Continued on next page...

This determination to uphold simultaneously both the predictions of a *division* of Babylon between Media and Persia, and the description of *successive reigns* of a Mede and a Persian, appears to underlie all the above attempts to posit an orderly rotation of Median and Persian rulers, a rotation whose existence is presupposed by our own passage in the Esther-Midrash.

"*His Excellent Majesty*"

> [12a] "*When he shewed the riches of his glorious kingdom and the honor of his excellent majesty many days, even an hundred and fourscore days*" (Esther 1:4).

...Continued from previous page

pears quite likely that the author of the *Yosippon* did identify Darius the Mede with Gobryas, as suggested by Urbach (see above). Note that the tradition preserved in MS Jerusalem 8° 41280 and other texts derived from R. Gershom's exemplar records that Darius was killed in an ambush during the battle over Babylon, "Then the princes of Media appointed Cyrus to reign over them ...and from that day onwards the kingdom of Media and Persia became one." However, according to D. Flusser this is an interpolation added to fill in a lacuna in the *vorlage* [see: D. Flusser, ed. *Josippon: The Original Version; MS Jerusalem 8° 41280 and Supplements*, Texts and Studies for Students "Kuntresim" Project, Vol. 49, 1978 (The Zalman Shazar Center: Jerusalem), 5]. It is however intriguing to speculate about where the scribe received this tradition [see D. Flusser, ed. *The Josippon* (*Joseph Gorionides*), 1979-81 (Mosad Bialik: Jerusalem)]. The original reading of the *Yosippon* is confirmed by the Chronicle of R. Eleazar b. R. Asher (the so-called "Yerahmeel Chronicle"; see Flusser, 1978, pp. 6, 295). See also R. Samuel Masnuth's Midrash to Daniel, 56-7; Ginzberg, 6:430. *Song of Songs rabbah*, 3:3/4 seems to have combined the two traditions such that, as in the *Yosippon*, Belshazzar's beheading is an "inside job," but, in common with the other traditions, the overthrow was carried out (albeit unwittingly) by Cyrus and Darius themselves —This narrative twist was accomplished by turning Cyrus and Darius into Belshazzar's gatekeepers. Cf. *Midrash on Psalms*, 75:3 (ed. Buber 338 [and notes]; transl. Braude 2:10). On this passage, see: E. E. Urbach, "Koresh vehakhrazato be'einei ḥaza"l," 369-70 [404-5].

> Says R. Yose[21] bar Ḥanina:[22 23] This teaches you[24 25] that he clothed himself in the priestly garments and sat down.[26 27]
>
> It is written here: "{*the riches of his glorious kingdom and the honor of his excellent*} *majesty* {*many days, even an hundred and fourscore days*}."
>
> And it is written there: "{*And thou shalt make holy garments for Aaron thy brother*} *for glory and for majesty*" (Exodus 28:2).

This passage is clear and straightforward as regards both its hermeneutic structure and its thematic point. Its proof is based upon a standard *gezerah shavah* built around the use of the word תפארת, "majesty" or "glory,"[28] in our verse and in Exodus 28, where the same term is used to describe the priestly vestments.[29] The thematic message is an extension of the idea that was so central to the previous chapter, and which will pervade much of the Esther-Midrash, namely that Ahasuerus' feast, like Belshazzar's before it, was convened in order to

---

21 "R. Yose" —MS **O**: "Rav Joseph"; MS **R** and **YS**: "Mar Zuṭi." No Amora named "mar Zuṭi bar Ḥanina" is listed in Albeck's *Introduction to the Talmuds*. On R. Yose bar Ḥanina see: J. S. Zuri, *Rabbi yose bar ḥanina mikkisrin* (Jerusalem: 1926).

22 "bar Ḥanina" — ~ in MS **L**, and added in emendation.

23 "Says R. Yose bar Ḥanina"— ~ in MS **P** and Genizah fragment.

24 "you" —only in MS **Y**; all other witnesses: ~.

25 "This teaches you" — ~ in Genizah fragment.

26 "and sat down" — ~ in MS **M** and **Printings**; **EY**: "he wrapped himself and stood up"; MSS **G**, **B**, **W** add: "upon them."

27 "This teaches...down" —Genizah fragment: "{ }says: It was priestly garments that he wore." This unique reading makes a lot more sense than the awkward alternative found in all the other witnesses (including two other Genizah fragments); and can be explained quite easily as a copyist's error from לבש to וישב. The variants and omissions in the various witnesses reflect the difficulties in understanding the majority reading.

28 Maharsha observes that the midrash does not appear to be based on the word כבוד ("glory," "honor"), which also appears in both verses.

29 See also Paton, 135.

make blasphemous use of the vessels of the Jerusalem Temple,[30] as a sign that the time for redemption had expired and Ahasuerus could now obstruct the rebuilding of the Temple without fear of divine interference.[31]

An identical passage is included in *Esther rabbah*, 2:1:[32]

> R. Levi[33] says: He showed them the garments of the High Priesthood.
>
> It states here: "*his excellent majesty*" and it states elsewhere: "*And thou shalt make holy garments for Aaron thy brother for glory and for majesty.*"
>
> Just as the "majesty" mentioned there refers to the garments of the High Priesthood, so does the "majesty" mentioned here refer to the garments of the High Priesthood.[34]

It should be remarked that in *Esther rabbah* the king's action is limited to "showing" the priestly garments; it does not state explicitly,

---

30 A similar midrash could presumably have been fashioned around the similarities with Daniel 5:2-4; however the latter passage is formulated in Aramaic, which would have blunted the force of the *gezerah shavah*. The poignancy of the pagan king dressing himself in the priestly robes, with all their associations of national and religious glory, would at any rate not have been equaled by any generic reference to unspecified vessels (compare, e.g., the emotional effect of the scene in George Lucas' "Raiders of the Lost Ark" in which a Nazi dons those same robes).

31 See the *Yefeh ʿanaf* commentary to *Esther rabbah*, 2:1.

32 Cf. Jacob Neusner, *The Midrashic Compilations of the Sixth and Seventh Centuries: An Introduction to the Rhetorical, Logical and Topical Program*, Vol. 2, 32.

33 A third-generation Palestinian Amora, known primarily as an aggadist; see Albeck, *Introduction to the Talmud*, 256-7. R. Yose bar Ḥaninah, to whom the Babylonian tradition is attributed, lived during the second Amoraic generation (Albeck, 185-6).

34 The Second Targum to Esther identifies the vessels at the banquet with those of the Temple, but makes no specific reference to the priestly garments. The First Targum takes a completely different approach, alluding to a lost treasure of Cyrus uncovered by Ahasuerus. Similarly, the preceding section of the *Esther rabbah* pericope to Esther 1:4, which speaks of "six treasures" but not of the Temple vessels, is alluded to in *Exodus rabbah*, 9:7 (ed. Shinan, 213) and in *Panim aḥerim* B, but no specific reference is made to the tradition about the priestly garments (see Shinan's notes).

as does the Babylonian version, that he actually donned them, though the wording does not rule out that possibility.

As is the case with most *gezerah shavah*s, whether in halakhic or aggadic contexts, the proof should not be taken too seriously.[35] The word "תפארת" and its cognates are found in many different contexts in the Hebrew Bible,[36] a fact which could have stimulated comparisons and associations with such varied themes as the House of David (e.g., Zechariah 12:7), the righteous (e.g., Proverbs 28:12), the Temple (e.g., Isaiah 63:15 or 64:10), Jerusalem (e.g., Isaiah 52:1), and others.

The Second Feast

[12a] "[37] [38] [39]*And when these days were expired, the king made* [*a feast unto all the people that were present in Shushan the palace* {*both unto great and small*}, *seven days, in the court of the garden of the king's palace*]" (Esther 1:5).

Rav and Samuel—

One says: He was a clever king,[40] and one says: He was a stupid king.[41]

---

[35] Heinemann, *Darkhei ha-'aggadah*, 122-3 makes some perceptive observations on the philological and fanciful aspects of the *gezerah shavah*. While the mode may have come into use as a legitimate lexicographic tool [S. Federbush, *Bintivot ha-talmud*, 2nd ed. (Jerusalem: Mossad Harav Kook, 1983), 118-45], it came to be used mechanically, basing proofs on incidental similarities of wording. Hence the rabbis appreciated that even in halakhic contexts the *gezerah shavah* could not be used as a true exegetical mode; see *TP Pesaḥim* Ch. 6:1 (33a); J. N. Epstein, *Prolegomena ad Litteras Tannaiticas* (Tel Aviv and Jerusalem: The Magnes Press and Dvir, 1957), 510-12; M. Elon, *Jewish Law: History, Sources, Principles*, 243-6, 295-8; S. K. Mirsky, "Maḥtzavtan shel tzurot ha-piyyuṭ," *Yedi'ot ha-makhon leḥeqer ha-shirah ha-'ivrit birushalayim* 7 (1958), 1-129.

[36] See S. Mandelkern, *Veteris Testamenti Concordantiæ*, 940.

[37] MS **R** adds: "And it is written."

[38] MSS **N, L, M, W, Spanish family**, Genizah fragment add: "'...*many days, even an hundred and fourscore days* '" (Esther 1:4).

[39] MSS **B*, W, Spanish family** add: "And it is written."

[40] "a clever king" —MSS **N, O, P, HgT**, Genizah fragment, **AgE**: "clever."

[41] "a stupid king" —MSS **N, O, P, EY, HgT**, Genizah fragments: "stupid."

The[42] one who says he was a clever king[43]—He acted well in that he called together those who were[44] distant at the beginning, because[45] the inhabitants of his own[46] city were subject to him;[47] whenever he wanted[48] he could win them over.[49]

And the one who[50] says he was stupid[51] —He[52] ought to have called [53] together the inhabitants of his own town[54] at the beginning, so that if those[55] rebelled[56] against him, then these would stand[57] by him.[58][59]

---

42 "The one" —MSS **O**, **P**, **EY** and **AgE**: "According to the."

43 "a clever king" —MSS **N**, **O**, **P**, **EY**, **HgT**, Genizah fragments: "clever."

44 "those who were" —**Printings** and **AgE**: "he who was."

45 "because" —only in MSS **Y**, **P** and Genizah fragment; MS **G, EY**: "and"; MS **N**: "he thought"; ~ in all other witnesses.

46 "his own"—MS **O**: "the."

47 "were subject to him" — ~ in **Printings**.

48 **Spanish family** adds: "them."

49 "win them over" —**Spanish family**: "call them together."

50 "the one who" —**Pesaro printing**: "One."

51 "stupid" —MSS **G**, **B**, **W**, **L**, **R**, **Mf** and Genizah fragment: "a stupid king." MS **N** has an indecipherable three-word addition at this point.

52 "He" —**HgT**: "Because he."

53 "to have called" —MS **R**, **AgE** and Genizah fragment: "to call."

54 "He ought...town" —MS **O**: "It was the inhabitants of the town that he ought to have called."

55 "those" —**AgE**: "one of them."

56 "rebelled" —MSS **N**, **B**, **W**, **M**, **R**, Genizah fragments: "would rebel."

57 **Spanish family** and Genizah fragment add: "and be."

58 "him" —MS **N**: "them."

59 Genizah fragment (TS FI (2) 67) has a different reading for the entire preceding passage: "'*And when these days were expired*' —Rav and Samuel: One says he was a stupid king because he ought to have called together the inhabitants of his own city first, so that if the distant ones would rebel against him, these would stand beside him. And one says he was a clever king, because he called together the distant ones in the beginning, because he could honor the inhabitants of his own city whenever he wanted." While the uniqueness of the reading lies primarily in the abbreviated *arrangement* of the material (the fragment is from an aggadic anthology, not a full text of the Talmud), note that the last phrase differs substantially in its *content* from the re-

Continued on next page...

The textual witnesses are inconsistent as to which biblical text is being cited at the beginning of this passage,[60] a fact which gives rise to some confusion about where precisely we are expected to look for the textual stimulus for the talmudic comments. It would appear that, unlike the previous interpretations in our midrash, the present one is not focused on any particular word or phrase, but on the actual events described in the narrative: After entertaining the dignitaries from the outlying provinces for one hundred and eighty days, Ahasuerus now convenes a second feast for the "locals," the inhabitants of his capital Shushan. Rav and Samuel debate the political wisdom of this arrangement. Why should he entertain the "strangers" first, and only afterwards the "natives?"[61] The whole discussion has a whimsical character to it; the rabbis seem to be approaching the story as a model of political wisdom (or folly, as the case may be), not as a source of religious or moral instruction.

The underlying issue of this disagreement seems to be the question of how much of a hold Ahasuerus had at the time of the banquet, whether by force or by actual loyalty, over the natives of Shushan. Thus the view that praises him for turning his attention first to the distant provinces supposes that the king has no problems on the home-front; whereas the author of the opposing view assumes that

...Continued from previous page

maining witnesses. The Genizah text does not seem to be worried (as are the other texts) about appeasing dissatisfied citizens, but rather with an apparently unselfish bestowing of honors upon them.

60 Following my policy in presenting variant readings, I have not copied all the different ranges in the verse citation. I will merely mention in general that most witnesses from the **Spanish** and **Ashkenazic families** and others begin their quotation from the end of verse 4. The intention was apparently to begin immediately from where the previous pericope had left off, without meaning to suggest that the midrash was actually based on that text.

61 Cf. *Panim aḥerim* B (58, and see Buber's n. 35) and Second Targum to Esther 1:5: "With the completion of the days in which he had made feasts for all the provinces, he said: I shall [now] make a feast for the inhabitants of my own place."

Ahasuerus maintains only flimsy control over the locals, whose allegiance ought to be ascertained before turning to the provinces.[62]

The debate over whether Ahasuerus was a clever or stupid monarch is a recurring one in our midrash,[63] though it does not seem to have a parallel in *Esther rabbah* or other early Palestinian sources.

Why Were They Deserving of Extinction?

> [12a] His disciples[64] asked Rabbi Simeon ben Yoḥai: Why were the "enemies of" Israel[65] in[66] that generation[67] deserving of extinction?
>
> He said to them: You tell me.[68]
>
> They said to him:[69] [70] Because they benefited from the feast of that wicked man.

---

62 Maharsha suggests such an interpretation in his allusion to the tradition that the feast was convened to mark the successful squelching of a rebellion (Sources for this tradition are listed by Ginzberg, *Legends*, 6:452, n. 7). C. Moore, in his commentary to Esther 1:2 (pp. 5, 12) cites several scholars who propose a similar explanation, referring to Xerxes' putting down of uprisings in Egypt and Babylon. See our remarks at the beginning of the previous chapter.

63 R. Jacob Reischer observes in his *ʿIyyun yaʿaqov* commentary to **EY** that the positions taken in the current passage would presumably correspond with those delineated above 11a, about whether the king came to power on his own merits or through bribery. We should make note of the fact that the debate in that pericope is over whether a comment of Rav's should be interpreted in a laudatory or derogatory manner. The possibility suggests itself that the midrash's subsequent doubts in other passages over whether laudatory or pejorative interpretations should be attributed to Rav [and hence, by extension, the opposing positions would be those of Rav's usual debating partner, Samuel] might have arisen originally from the ambiguities of that passage.

64 "His disciples" — ~ in MS **M**.

65 **YS** adds: "who were."

66 "Israel in" — ~ in MS **O**, **HgT**.

67 "in that generation" — ~ in MSS **G**, **B** (and filled in in **B***), **M** (and filled in in **M***), **P**.

68 "me" —only in MSS **G**, **N**, **O**, **W**, **EY**; ~ in other witnesses.

69 "They said to him" — ~ in MS **B** (and added in **B***).

70 "to him" — ~ in MS **N**.

As it is written: "*unto all the people that were present in Shushan the palace* etc." (Esther 1:4). And "*people*" refers to none other than Israel, as it is written:[71] "*this people have I formed for myself*" (Isaiah 43:21).[72]

He said to them:[73] If that is so, then let those in[74] Shushan be killed, {but} let those of the whole[75] world not be killed.

They said to him: You tell us.[76]

He said to them: Because they bowed down to the image.[77]

They said to him:[78] And is there partiality in the matter? [79]

He said to them: They acted only inwardly.[80] So also the Holy One only acted towards them[81] inwardly.

---

71 "is written" —**AgE**: "says."

72 "as it is written: '*unto...*'...'*...myself*'" —only in MS **Y** and **AgE**; ~ in all other witnesses.

73 "He said to them"— ~ in MS **P** and **Printings**.

74 "in" —**Spanish family**: "of."

75 "whole" — ~ in MSS **G**, **N**, **O**, **W**, **HgT²**.

76 "us" — ~ in MSS **M**, **Mf**, **Printings** and Genizah fragments.

77 **Spanish family** and Genizah fragment add: "of Babylon"; **HgT²** adds: "of Nebuchadnezzar."

78 **AgE** adds: "Let him learn from you."

79 "matter" —MS **R**: "(Torah)[matter]."

Cf. the use of the phrase in *TB Yevamot* 79a. Reischer in the *ʿIyyun yaʿaqov* to **EY** here cites sources that ascribe some measure of partiality to God. *Exodus rabbah*, 14:3 (263) [=*Tanḥuma Va'era*, 14; *Seder eliyahu rabbah*, (7) 8 (42-3); cf. other versions listed in Shinan's notes to *Exodus rabbah*] contains the remarkable passage: "Blessed be the name of the Holy One, before whom there is no partiality, and he penetrates hearts and examines the kidneys..." The passage goes on to tell that the Israelites were secretly punished during the plague of darkness for not choosing to leave Egypt."

80 "I.e., they only did so out of fear of death, as stated explicitly in Daniel [3:6,11], and had no intention of actually worshipping the idol" (Maharsha).

81 "towards them" — ~ in MSS **G**, **O**, **W**, **P** and **HgT**.

And this is exactly[82] as it is written:[83] "*For he doth not afflict willingly nor grieve the children of men*" (Lamentations 3:33).

This *baraita*[84] is presented as a second pericope[85] to Esther 1:5, connecting to the topic of Ahasuerus' second feast, to which the general

---

[82] "And...exactly" — ~ in Genizah fragment.

[83] "is written" —**AgE**: "says."

[84] The content and style testify that what we have before us is a *baraita* in spite of the fact that the Talmud does not employ any of the normal citation formulae. This fact might be explainable on the grounds that the source did not reach the Babylonian redactors *via* "normal" channels, but as part of a (Palestinian) midrashic text (see below). The identification of R. Simeon with his Patronymic is typical of midrashic works emanating from the "school of R. Ishmael"; see: E. Z. Melammed, *An Introduction to Talmudic Literature*, 172.

[85] S. Abramson has noted (orally) that it is a standard redactional procedure in the Babylonian Talmud to place Palestinian pericopes after Babylonian material, even where this conflicts with the chronological order.

The passage in which Esther 1:4 is explicitly cited is found only in the Yemenite texts (see notes to text); i.e., it probably entered MS **Y** from *Aggadat Esther*, and is not an original reading of the Talmud [on the phenomenon, see: E. Segal, "The Textual Traditions of Ms. Columbia University to TB Megillah," 41-69], nor is the proof really necessary, since the Jews can be assumed to be included among "*all the people*, etc. The addition is probably taken from *Abba gorion*, 32 (to Esther 4:1, and alluded to in *Panim aḥerim* A, 47, to Esther 3:14), where it forms part of a dictum of R. Isaac Nappaḥa: "It was with an elaborate slander [or plot] that Haman attacked Israel, as it says: '*And when these days were expired...*' And '*people*' refers to none other than Israel, as it is written: '*They shall call the people unto the mountain...*' (Deuteronomy 33:19). Said Haman to Ahasuerus: Their God despises licentiousness; so procure for them harlots and prepare them a feast, and decree that they attend and eat and drink as they wish... and so that they will not be able to argue in their defense that they were brought against their will..." (A virtually identical passage is found in *Esther rabbah*, 7:19 [not part of the original midrash, see Zunz-Albeck, *Ha-derashot beyisra'el*, 128, 402], but there the second proof-text is neither Isaiah 43:21 nor Deuteronomy 33:19, but Deuteronomy 33:29!). See also the "Homily for Purim" in *Pesiqta ḥadeta*, included in Jellinek's *Bet-ha-Midrasch*, 6:55-6. The citation from Esther by itself is found in other midrashim on Esther (see below); the interpretation of Isaiah 43:21 is found in *Mekhilta Shirata*, 9 (ed. Lauterbach 2:69; ed. Horovitz-Rabin, 145); *Mekhilta derabbi shimʿon ben Yoḥai* (ed. Epstein-Melammed, 78, 98). On the narrative motifs see Ginzberg, *Legends*, 4:415, 6:467-8, n. 122.

population was invited. For the rabbis, it is understood that "*all the people*" included Jews[86] as well.[87]

The radical departure of this discussion from its scriptural source stands out in clear relief when we compare it with the material from the Book of Esther which it should be interpreting. The midrash makes two major assumptions that are not found in the scriptural account: (1) That God himself had an interest in promoting Haman's unrealized plot, which was intended as a punishment of sorts; and (2) that the Jews had done something to deserve that fate. In Esther itself, there is no apparent indication that the Jews had done anything to bring upon themselves divine wrath; Haman's plot is depicted as the unprovoked (or at least, unjustified) attack of a malicious villain, and the Jews as innocent and passive victims. Other than the basic hero-villain contrast, there is little moral or religious substance to the plot. Ultimately, not only did the Jews not *deserve* extinction,[88] but it is not clear that God had ever really *planned* such a fate for them.[89]

---

[86] The expression "enemies of Israel" is a classic instance of rabbinic euphemism, founded on the premise that direct *verbal* association of extinction with Israel would somehow evoke such a phenomenon *in fact*. See I. Heinemann, *Darkhei ha-'aggadah*, 94, 169-70; Saul Lieberman, *Hellenism in Jewish Palestine: Studies in the Literary Transmission, Beliefs and Manners of Palestine in the 1st Century B.C.E.-4th Century C.E.* (New York: The Jewish Theological Seminary of America, 1962), 28-37; E. Z. Melamed, "Euphemism and Scribal Circumlocutions in Talmudic Literature," in *Benjamin De Vries Memorial Volume*, ed. E. Z. Melamed (Jerusalem: Tel Aviv University, 1968), 119-48.

[87] It is likely that the midrash is implying an unstated and unfavorable contrast with the behavior of Daniel and his companions in Daniel 1:8-16.

[88] Cf. *Genesis rabbah*, 76:1 (897); *Pesiqta derav kahana*, 19:5 (ed. Mandelbaum, 307; transl. Braude-Kapstein, 327): "R. Berakhiah and R. Ḥalabo in the name of R. Samuel bar Naḥman [in the name of R. Jonathan]: Israel were deserving of annihilation in the days of Haman had it not been for the fact that they had linked their fate with that of that old man [Jacob]. They said: Even as our patriarch Jacob was frightened [of Esau, Genesis 32:8], in spite of God's assurances, all the more so us!" The *Pesiqta derav kahana* concludes: "This is why the prophet chides them and says to them: '*And forgetest the Lord thy maker*, etc.' (Isaiah 51:13)..." According to this tradition the crime of the Jews of that generation was that they had despaired of their redemption, as is spelled out explicitly in the wording of the *Pesiqta rabbati* 33 (ed. Friedmann, 151b; transl. W. G. Braude, *Pesikta Rabbati*, Yale Judaica Series (New Haven and London: Yale

Continued on next page...

In the comparison between the explicit meaning of the text and the reading that underlies the exchange between R. Simeon and his disciples, we may discern an essential difference between the homiletical and the exegetical uses of scripture. The preacher's message will often be concerned with the improvement of his congregation. In the framework of a Scripture-based discourse such a message can be conveniently composed by equating whatever shortcomings the preacher has diagnosed in his own community with those of the biblical figures being described in the current lection. In the present instance, one can surmise that R. Simeon ben Yoḥai felt that his contemporary Jews were not sufficiently uncompromising in their opposition to Roman paganism and too ready to tolerate social intercourse with Judæa's idolatrous conquerors.[90] These shortcomings were projected back onto the Jews of the Babylonian and Persian empires.[91]

A similar discussion is recorded in *Song of Songs rabbah*, 7:8 and in *Lamentations rabbah*, 3:33,[92] in an Amoraic passage that deals

...Continued from previous page

University Press, 1968), 638-9): "'*And forgetest the Lord thy maker*'—Scripture is speaking of the tribulations of Haman, when they became afraid [temporarily] and despaired of the redemption."

89 This is not a simple instance of מידה כנגד מידה (See Heinemann, *Darkhei ha-'aggadah*, 63-5), where the nature of the sin is deduced from its punishment, since ultimately there is no punishment here, nor is there any indication that Haman was acting as an instrument of God's will.

90 On R. Simeon's unbending opposition to Rome see Avi-Yonah, *The Jews of Palestine*, 65 (and other passages listed in Index *s.v.* R. Simeon b. Yohai); Urbach, *The Sages*, 675. *ʿAnaf yosef* to **EY** attempts to interpret our passage in light of R. Simeon's biography.

91 The Babylonian sources, while accepting this approach in its general outlines, seem to have singled out less drastic transgressions than those mentioned by the *baraita*, such as laxity in the study and observance of the Torah; see the Concluding Remarks to Chapter 2. However cf. *Pirqei derabbi eliʿezer* beginning of Ch. 49 (transl. Friedlander, 388).

92 Ed. Buber, 34.

with the alleged eradication of the "inclination" towards idolatry during the era of the Second Temple.[93]

> ...If so, then why did Israel become endangered in the days of Haman?
>
> The rabbis and R. Simeon ben Yoḥai: The rabbis say: Because Israel worshipped idols, and R. Simeon said: Because they ate food cooked by gentiles.
>
> They said to him: But is it not true that only the residents of Shushan the palace partook of the feast, as it is written: "*And when these days were expired...*"!
>
> They said to him: But are not all Israel guarantors for one another, as it is written "*And they shall fall each upon his brother*" (Leviticus 25:37): Each for the sin of his brother...
>
> He said to them: If it is according to your view, then you have condemned all of Israel to extermination, as it is written: "*He that sacrificeth unto any god, save unto the Lord only, he shall be utterly destroyed*" (Exodus 22:20).
>
> They said to him: Nonetheless, they did not worship it with (all)[94] their heart, as it says: "*For he doth not afflict willingly.*" Even so, he will "*grieve the children of men.*" He set over them a most obdurate man to test them; namely Nebuchadnezzar,[95] who arose and aggrieved their wound.
>
> Rabbi Berakhiah in the name of R. Levi: ...In Babylon they acted in their heart but they did not act in their mouth, as it says: "*For he doth not afflict...*"...

In spite of the obvious similarities between the traditions, we ought not overlook the significant differences:

---

93 On this motif, see Ginzberg, *Legends*, 4:359, 6:449, n. 57; E. E. Urbach, "Hilekhot 'avodah zarah veha-metzi'ut ha-arkhi'ologit veha-historit ba-me'ah ha-sheniyyah uva-me'ah ha-shelishit," *Eretz-Yisra'el* 5 (1958), 195 [*The World of the Sages: Collected Studies* (Jerusalem: The Magnes Press, 1988), 131].

94 ~ in *Lamentations rabbah.*

95 Luria notes that "Haman" would have fit the context better.

•The Babylonian version speaks of a discussion between master and disciples,[96] in which R. Simeon's view is obviously meant to carry greater weight, while *Song of Songs rabbah* depicts a discussion between two disputants of equal authority.[97]

•The actual positions are reversed:[98] In the Esther-Midrash it is R. Simeon who speaks of the people bowing to the idol,[99] whereas in *Song of Songs rabbah* it is the Rabbis.[100]

---

[96] For a concise bibliography on master-disciple relations in rabbinic literature see: Steven D. Fraade, *From Tradition To Commentary: Torah and Its Interpretation in the Midrash Sifre to Deuteronomy*, SUNY Series in Judaica: Hermeneutics, Mysticism, and Religion, ed. R. Goldenberg, M. Fishbane, A. Green (Albany: State University of New York Press, 1991), 229-30. See also the discussion of Rabbi M. Schiff (cited in the *Ge'on ya'aqov* to **EY**).

[97] To be precise, the "rabbis" should be more authoritative than the individual opinion of R. Simeon, insofar as such considerations are relevant in non-halakhic discourse.

[98] As observed by the *'Anaf yosef* to **EY**.

[99] According to Rashi the reference is to Daniel Ch. 3. As explained by Maharsha, if we read 3:12 precisely it implies that Daniel's three companions were the only ones who refused to bow to Nebuchadnezzar's idol. Presumably the rest of the Jews were not so staunch [though if we follow that reasoning consistently Daniel himself would be implicated; cf. Ibn Ezra to Daniel 3:12; see also the *'Anaf yosef* to **EY**, who proposes a reading of Daniel that would not implicate the rest of the Jews. Similarly, Maharsha observes that the same reasoning could be applied to the account in Esther 3:2 that only Mordecai refused to bow before Haman, which implies that the other Jews did bow]. On Jewish compliance with Nebuchadnezzar's orders see *TB Sanhedrin* 93a; Ginzberg, *Legends*, 4:330; 6:419, n. 92; *Panim aḥerim* A, 47-8: "[The patriarchs] said before him: Master of the Universe, for what reason? He said to them: Because they did not sanctify my name in the days of the wicked Nebuchadnezzar, treating me as one unable to save them... [The heavenly entourage] said: It is clear and manifest before you that they did this only out of fear. Immediately the Holy One was overcome with compassion over Israel." Though Rashi's explanation is supported unanimously by the Palestinian midrashim, some of the commentators give consideration to the possibility that in the Babylonian pericope the reference is to the worship of Haman who, according to midrashic tradition, proclaimed himself a god. Maharsha and R. Josiah Pinto ("Rif" to **EY**) argue (not altogether convincingly) that had that been the case, the decree would probably not have affected Jews outside Shushan. Pinto raises the question that, if the punishment had been incurred in Nebuchadnezzar's days, then why should God have delayed so long in exacting retribution? Other midrashic sources have no difficulty in stretching even farther the period between crime and punishment; e.g., *Genesis rabbah*, 67:4 (758), according to which

Continued on next page...

•In *Song of Songs rabbah* the midrash's initial assumption is merely that the Jews were "endangered," and only when discussing the implications of the "idolatry" accusation is it suggested (rhetorically) that they *deserved* to be destroyed. The Babylonian version, on the other hand, *begins* with the premise that they were "deserving of extinction," even though this understanding is effectively rejected in the conclusion.

•In the Babylonian Esther-Midrash the argument that the Jews outside Shushan should have been exempted from the decree is considered sufficient to do away with the "partaking in the feast" explanation.[101] In *Song of Songs rabbah rabbah*, it is countered.

Taken together, there does not seem to be any fundamental ideological or exegetical disagreement[102] that would account for all the dif-

...Continued from previous page

the persecutions of Haman were a delayed punishment for Jacob's stealing of the birthright from Esau (who was the progenitor of Amalek).

[100] Cf. *Abba gorion* (ed. Buber, 9; see also *Leqaḥ ṭov*, 90): "When the Jews observed the Temple vessels there, they did not wish to recline with them, so he prepared for them a separate feast... Said R. Ḥanina bar Pappa: This [probably, the reference to (only) "*the people that were present*, etc.," which implies that others were absent] teaches that when the great men of the generation heard this they fled... Said R. Simeon b. Yoḥai: We learn from this [from the fact that "all the people" of Shushan participated in the feast?] that they ate food cooked by gentiles *against their will*" (On the significance of the last three words see our citation from *Abba gorion* 32 and *Esther rabbah* 7:19 in the notes above). See also the First Targum to Esther 1:5; Ginzberg, *Legends*, 4:370, 6:454, n. 17. On the prohibitions related to gentile foodstuffs see *TB ʿAvodah zarah* 36b, *Shabbat* 17b; Melammed, *An Introduction to Talmudic Literature*, 31; see the entry בישולי גוים in: S. J. Zevin, ed., *Talmudic Encyclopedia*, Vol. 4 (Jerusalem: Talmudic Encyclopedia Institute, 1984), 657-75.

[101] Note also that while the Palestinian sources treat the Jews' participation in the banquet as primarily a dietary infraction, the Babylonian Esther-Midrash is less clear about where the transgression lay. In light of the previous pericopes, which emphasize the blasphemous use of sacred vessels and the implied despair of redemption, the Jews' attendance at the feast would have graver religious implications. This theme is developed perceptively by R. Josiah Pinto. See also Ibn Ezra's (first) commentary to Esther 2:19, and B. Walfish, "The Two Commentaries of Abraham Ibn Ezra on the Book of Esther," 336.

[102] E. g., it is hardly likely that the Babylonian rabbis could have rejected the widely held view that "all Israel are guarantors for one another."

ferences between the two traditions, most of which must probably be attributed to incidental variations in the transmission. At best, we might speculate that some of the distinctive aspects of the Babylonian version may have resulted from the redactors' wish to show their preference for the "idolatry" explanation,[103] as against the "gentile food" explanation, which they may have been considered too trivial to account for the gravity of the consequences.[104]

"The Court of the Garden..."

[12a] "*...In the court of the garden of the king's palace*" (Esther 1:5).

Rav and Samuel:

One says: Him who was worthy of the court, to the court;[105] and[106] him who was worthy[107] of the garden, to the garden; and[108] him who was worthy of the palace, to the palace.[109]

---

103 The larger pericope in *Song of Songs rabbah* is built around traditions about the eradication of idolatry in the generation of Mordecai and Esther, and the assertion that "most of that generation were righteous." There is nothing in the Babylonian materials that suggests that they held such a premise.

104 R. Josiah Pinto: "How is it possible that for the sin of partaking of Ahasuerus' feast they should incur a punishment of death and destruction, when the consumption of carrion does not carry with it the penalty of *karet*? How could all this dread have been incurred by the transgression of a single prohibition?" (See also the *ʿIyyun yaʿaqov* commentary to **EY**.) This of course might have been precisely the point being made by the proponents of that view: Even the transgression of a relatively unimportant decree of rabbinic [see *Talmudic Encyclopedia* 4:657] origin (and one whose observance may have been lax in the preacher's community) is capable of bringing the Jewish people to the brink of destruction.

105 "Him who...to the court" — ~ in **Pesaro printing** and **YS**.

106 "and" —Only in MSS **Y**, **N**, **B**, **AgE** and Genizah fragment; ~ in all other witnesses.

107 "and him who was worthy" — ~ in Genizah fragment.

108 "and" —Only in MSS **Y**, **N**, **O**, **AgE** and Genizah fragment (apparently); ~ in all other witnesses.

109 "court, to the court...to the palace" —MS **R**: "palace, to the palace; him who was worthy of the court, to the court; him who was worthy of the garden, to the garden."

> And one says: He seated them in[110] the court and it did not contain them. He seated them[111] in the garden and it did not contain them.[112] Until[113] he brought them into[114] the palace.[115][116][117]
>
> In a *baraita*[118] it taught:[119] He seated them in[120] the court,[121] and opened[122] two entrances, one to the garden and one to the palace.

As with much of the material in our midrash, this passage also begins with an undefined dispute between Rav and Samuel. It is followed here by a third interpretation ascribed to a *baraita.*

The various midrashic comments all seem to be responding to a confusion in the biblical account, which speaks of three different types of location without specifying the differences or precise relationships that exist between them:[123] A courtyard, a garden and something called

---

110 "in" —MSS **G**, **W**, **M**, **R**: "to."

111 "He seated them" — ~ in MSS **G**, **B***, **W**, **P**, **Printings**, Genizah fragment and **YS**.

112 "He seated them in the garden ...contain them" — ~ in **EY** and **HgT^2**. Genizah fragment adds: "In the pa{...} contain them."

113 "Until" —Genizah fragment: "And."

114 "brought them into" —MS **M**, **YS**, Genizah fragment: "seated them in."

115 "palace" —Genizah fragment: "houses."

116 **Printings** and Genizah fragment add: "and it contained them."

117 "And one says...into the palace" — ~ in MS **B**, and added in **B***.

118 "*baraita* [*matnita*]" —Genizah fragment: "mishnah [*matnitin*]."

119 On the form see: J. N. Epstein, "Zur babylonisch-aramäischen Lexikographie," in *Festschrift Adolf Schwartz* (Berlin and Vienna: 1917), 321, n. 3 [and in Hebrew translation in: *Studies in Talmudic Literature and Semitic Languages*, translated by Z. Epstein (Jerusalem: Magnes Press, 1983), 36]; *Idem.*, *Mavo' lenosaḥ ha-mishnah*, 1296; *Idem.*, *A Grammar of Babylonian Aramaic* (Jerusalem and Tel-Aviv: Magnes Press and Dvir, 1960), 95; Ch. Albeck, *Meḥqarim bivrayta vetosefta veyaḥasan lattalmud*, 12, 48-53.

120 "seated them in" —Genizah fragment: "brought them into."

121 Genizah fragment adds: "and seated them there."

122 All other witnesses add: "for them."

123 See Maharsha. The comments of R. Judah, R. Nehemiah and R. Phineas in *Esther rabbah* 2:6 reflects a similar confusion about the relationship between the three units,

Continued on next page...

a *bitan* whose precise definition is not entirely clear.[124] The simple meaning of the verse implies that there is a structure called a *bitan*, which has an attached garden, and that in that garden is a courtyard, in which the king's banquet took place. Thus, the courtyard is the focus of the action, and the other terms are merely modifiers that define *which* courtyard. The midrashic interpretations read the verse differently, as if it speaks of three different places, each of which was used separately as a venue for the feast.[125]

Each of these three interpretations accounts in a different manner for the mention of all three locations:

1) The first interpretation states that guests were assigned to a place appropriate to their social standing. Presumably the palace or pavilion (*bitan*) represents the highest status and the courtyard the lowest. The idea behind this explanation seems to be influenced by the

...Continued from previous page

understanding that both the court and the garden (not just the court *of* the garden) were in use.

124 The three are also mentioned together in Esther 7:7-8. For a detailed discussion of the significance of the biblical term see: A. Leo Oppenheim, "On Royal Gardens in Mesopotamia," *JNES* 24 (1965), 328-33 [reprinted in C. A. Moore's *Studies in the Book of Esther*, 350-5]. The First Targum to Esther 1:5 discerns only *two* places, the court and the "inner garden," reading *bitan* as a modifier ("inside") of "garden" (thus also Ibn Ezra; see also Oppenheim, *op. cit.*). This also seems to be similar to the understanding of the Second Targum, which speaks of a "secret (גנזא) court planted with trees bearing fruit and spices." The wording is clearly related to the tradition found in *Abba gorion*, 10, and *Panim aḥerim* B, 58, but note carefully the variant readings cited by Buber on 10, n. 147, from which it is impossible to deduce how that midrash understood *bitan*. R. David Luria's commentary to *Pirqei derabbi eli‘ezer*, Ch. 49 (n. 45) tries to discern an exegesis of our passage in the paraphrase of that midrash, but I find his argument unconvincing (though it is accepted by Friedlander, 392, n. 11). See Ginzberg, *Legends*, 4:370-1, 6:454, n. 20.

125 On this type of midrashic interpretation, which disconnects the elements of a sentence in order to re-order them, see Heinemann, *Darkhei ha-'aggadah*, 108-10. See also M. Beer, *The Babylonian Amoraim*, 111, n. 27: "It would appear that their views reflect the actual gardens of the wealthy in their own days." Valuable information (with illustrations) on the construction of palaces during Sasanian times is collected in: Dorothy Shepherd, "Sasanian Art," in *The Cambridge History of Iran*, ed. Ehsan Yarshater, 1055-1112, 3 (2) (Cambridge, etc.: Cambridge University Press, 1983), 1055-76.

baraita below, in which the "*beds of gold and silver*" (in verse 6) are given a similar rationale.[126]

2) The second interpretation states that the three locales were mentioned in the order in which they were filled. Initially, the king placed them in the "inferior" courtyard, but as the crowd became too numerous they had to direct guests to the *bitan* itself.[127]

3) The *baraita* takes a different view, one more in keeping with the simple meaning of the verse:[128] The actual placement of the guests was in the courtyard, but from it there was access to the palace and garden.

As with much of the midrashic treatment of Ahasuerus' feast, there does not appear to be much of an attempt here to elicit ideological or religious teachings from the story. Aside from the immediate exegetical interest in explaining and clarifying the details of the scriptural account, the overwhelming impression is that the rabbis were caught up in the extravagance and grandeur of the biblical description, and were employing the tools of midrashic hermeneutics in order to magnify the sumptuousness and general perfection of the event.[129] The assumption that, irrespective of our evaluations of the king himself, the

---

126 The *Tosafot* to that passage are aware of the similarity, and use it as the basis for an objection; see our discussion below. Cf. the discussion of this question in Azulai's *Petaḥ ʿeinayim*.

127 An argument could be made in preference of the reverse order: In such an extravagant affair, the king would initially invite the celebrants to the best places, and only because of the overflow would he have to resort to the lesser ones. This would fit well with the *logical* order of the terms, but the Talmud seems to have chosen to mechanically follow the literal or physical order. The *Mattenot kehunnah* to *Esther rabbah* 2:6 uses this distinction to explain the dispute between R. Judah and R. Nehemiah there as to whether the court or the garden was the innermost structure.

128 As recognized by Reischer in the *ʿIyyun yaʿaqov*. However the verse itself does not suggest direct access from the courtyard to the *bitan*.

129 *Pirqei derabbi eliʿezer*, Ch. 49 suggests that by exaggerating his wealth, the midrash is strengthening the identification of Ahasuerus with Daniel's fourth king of Persia, who "*shall be far richer than they all...*" (Daniel 11:2). However I do not see any convincing indication that this was the principal concern of our midrashic sources.

royal banquet is to serve as an model of the ideal feast, is one that seems to govern almost all of the midrashic interpretations of the event.

"Ḥur, Karpas and Tekhelet..."

[12a] *"Ḥur, karpas and tekhelet [White, green, and blue* (hangings)...].

What is "*ḥur*" ["*white*"]?

Rav[130] says: "many holes" [131] [*ḥorei ḥorei*].[132]

And Samuel[133] says: He spread out for them[134] fine white wool.[135]

The Hebrew word *ḥur* listed among the hangings that ornamented Ahasuerus' feast is a *hapax legomenon* in the Bible.[136] The dispute between Rav and Samuel reflects the two most likely etymologies:

1) From the root חר, meaning "hole" or "cavity."[137]

2) From the root חור, meaning "white."[138]

While the precise meaning of the word is not certain, most modern commentators favor the translation "white,"[139] as attributed

---

[130] **Spanish family** adds: "and Samuel: One says."

[131] "many holes"—MS **N**: "very white" [*ḥivarei ḥivarei*].

[132] =filigreed?

[133] "Samuel" —**Spanish family**: "one."

[134] MS **W** and Genizah fragment add: "garments of."

[135] Genizah fragment adds: "which are worn by free men." The phrase is found in the *ʿArukh* (ed. Kohut, 3:482, cited by Maharsha) as an "alternative explanation" (פ"א).

[136] I.e., it appears only in Esther, in the present verse and in the description of Mordecai's royal garb in 8:15.

[137] See: F. Brown, S. R. Driver and C. A. Briggs, *The New Brown-Driver-Briggs-Gesenius Hebrew and English Lexicon* (Lafayette: Associated Publishers and Authors, Inc., 1980) [=*BDB*], 301, 359; R. Jacob Emden's glosses.

[138] *BDB*, 301.

[139] Thus in Ibn Ezra, First Targum to Esther (who regards it as a color [גון]), and in all the standard English translations. Cf. *BDB*, 301; P. Haupt, "Critical Notes on Esther," *American Journal of Semitic Languages and Literature* 24 (1907-8), 97-186

Continued on next page...

here to Samuel.[140] Rav's rendering, while generally taken to reflect the translation "holes,"[141] is not really much more explicit than the verse itself.[142]

The concern of both Rav and Samuel appears to be for philological exegesis of a rare and difficult word, without any particular homiletical intention. Both interpretations are etymologically reasonable, and may reflect some knowledge of the *realia* of royal luxury in Persia.

[12a] "...*Karpas*...['green']" —

Says R. Yose bar Ḥanina:[143] Mattresses [*karim*] of stripes [*passim*].

This interpretation also appears to be a simple attempt at philology, but much less convincing than the previous one. There is a

...Continued from previous page

[reprinted in C. Moore's *Studies in the Book of Esther*, 9]; Paton, 145; C. Moore's commentary to Esther, 1, 7.

140 The assumption appears to be that a color of an undefined fabric is of wool. A similar assumption governs all rabbinic discussions regarding *tekhelet* dye (e.g., Mishnah *Kila'im* 9:1, *TB Yevamot* 4b). *Esther rabbah* cites the rendering of Aquila "ειρίνεον" (woolen) (see also Zunz-Albeck, 266, n. 99). The same word for "fine wool" (מילא) is employed by the First Targum to render *ḥur* in Esther 8:15 (The Second Targum combines several elaborate traditions). The Septuagint versions [H. B. Swete, *Esther*, Vol. 2, The Old Testament in Greek (Cambridge: Cambridge University Press, 1905)] read βυσσίνος ("fine white linen"), whereas the Syriac (brought by Paton) has "wool."

141 Thus in R. Nathan b. Jehiel's *ʿArukh* [ed. Kohut, 3:482]: "perforated curtains"; Rashi: "The work of the beds was composed of holes"; Jastrow, 439, etc.

142 A third derivation is suggested in the reading of the *ʿArukh* and Genizah text cited in the apparatus, according to which the verse is referring to the garb of "free men." Etymologies from the root חרר, ["free"; see *BDB*, 359] are found in various rabbinic sources, such as *Esther rabbah*, 2:7 (in the name of R. Isaac). The interpretations seem to be rooted in the mores of the Roman empire, where the toga (especially the *toga virilis)*, the distinctive public garb of the (usually upper-class) Roman citizen, was fashioned of white woolen cloth, and a purple [=*tekhelet*?] stripe woven into the garment functioned as the distinctive mark of public officials. See: H. T. Peck, ed., *Harper's Dictionary of Classical Literature and Antiquities* (New York: Cooper Square Publishers, 1965), 64, 1590. See also *Aruch Completum* 5:145-6.

143 "Yose bar Ḥanina" —MS **P**: "Asi."

virtual consensus among lexicographers that the term *karpas* as it appears in Esther should be translated as "cotton" or "flax."[144] While it is not entirely certain how we are to precisely understand R. Yose's *notarikon*,[145] it clearly does not speak of either flax-linen or of cotton.[146] Moreover, the fact that derivatives of *karpas* were still in use in several languages that would have been known to R. Yose[147] suggests that he had in mind not merely a translation, but an additional layer of meaning that would add some concrete detail to the description. I am unable to discern any homiletical message that might be implied in the detail.

> [12a] "{*Fastened with cords of fine linen and purple to silver rings and pillars of marble*}: *the beds were of gold and silver*" (Esther 1:6).

---

[144] See Paton, 144, who writes that the word originated in Sanskrit and was introduced with few changes into Persian, Aramaic, Greek and Latin; Haupt, "Critical Notes," 105/8; Moore's commentary to Esther, 1, 7.

[145] On this type of *notarikon* (not an acrostic, but "the dismembering of words into individual letters") see Heinemann, *Darkhei ha-'aggadah*, 105; 235, n. 25.

[146] On *kar* as a mattress for reclining the whole body see sources cited by Kohut, *Aruch Completum*, 4:309-10. *Pas* has been rendered variously as "stripes" (e.g., Jastrow, 1190) or "colored stuffs" (Paton, 144). Cf. *Genesis rabbah* 84:5 (p. 1010); see: E. Ben-Yehudah, *Thesaurus Totius Hebraicæ et Veteris et Recentioris*, Complete International Centennial ed. (New York and London: Thomas Yoseloff, 1960), 6:5011. R. Jacob Emden understands *pas* as "silk."

[147] Thus, the Greek and Syriac versions use cognate words; similarly, Aquila, cited in *Esther rabbah* 2:7, renders καρπάσινον. As a resident of the Hellenized city of Caesarea, R. Yose could be expected to be familiar with the Greek and/or Latin ("*carbasus*") forms of the word; see Saul Liebermann, *The Talmud of Caesarea: Jerushalmi Tractate Neziqin*, Supplement to Tarbiẓ, 2:4, (Jerusalem: 1931), 9, 13-8, 99-100.

> It was taught [148]{in a *baraita*}: R. Judah says:[149] Him who was worthy of gold, to a gold[150] one; and[151] him who was worthy of[152] silver, to silver.[153]
>
> Said[154] R. Nehemiah:[155] If it is so, then you are[156] casting[157] envy into the feast.
>
> Rather:[158] They were of silver and their legs were of gold.[159]

The textual basis for this discussion is a perceived imprecision in the verse: It refers to both silver and gold beds, without offering any explanation of how the two were differentiated. The midrash tends to feel uncomfortable with such arbitrary or undefined details as the lack of explicit criteria for the distribution of the gold and silver couches.[160] However, it seems more likely that, while ostensibly concerned with the

---

148 "It was taught" — ~ in **AgE**.

149 "R. Judah says" —MSS **G, O, W, EY**: "Said R. Judah"; ~ in MS **P**.

150 "gold, to a gold" —only in MSS **Y**, **M** and **AgE**; all other witnesses: "silver, to a silver."

151 "and" —only in MSS **Y**, **N**, **AgE** and Genizah fragment; ~ in all others.

152 "and him...of" — ~ in MS **M**, **HgT²**, **Printings**, **YS**, Genizah fragment.

153 "silver, to silver" —only in MSS **Y**, **M** and **AgE**; all other witnesses: "gold, to gold."

154 "Said" —only in MSS **Y**, **G**, **B**, **M**, **YS**; all other witnesses: "Said to him."

155 "Nehemiah" —MSS **L** and **Mf**: "Neḥuniah."

156 "If it...are" —MSS **O**, **P**, **HgT¹**: "And are you not."

157 MS **L** adds: "a matter of."

158 "Rather" — ~ in MS **Mf**. MS **N** adds: "Even."

159 Maharsha raises (and rejects) the possibility that the idea of silver legs was somehow suggested by the reference to גלילי כסף above. He notes correctly that it would have made more sense to fashion the beds of gold and the legs of silver (cf. *ʿAnaf yosef* to **EY**). The First Targum to Esther 1:6 has "beds whose poles were of gold and legs were of silver," which does not agree entirely with either the Bavli or *Esther rabbah* (see below). See *Pirqei derabbi eliʿezer*, Ch. 49 (transl. Friedlander, 392); Ginzberg, *Legends of the Jews*, 4:371, 6:454, n. 20; Prudence Harper, "Sasanian Silver," in *The Cambridge History of Iran*, ed. Ehsan Yarshater, 1113-29, 3 (2) (Cambridge, etc.: Cambridge University Press, 1983).

160 On the underlying premises of such exegesis see Heinemann, *Darkhei ha-'aggadah*, 21-6, 96-100.

seating (or reclining) arrangements at Ahasuerus' feast, the disagreement between Rabbis Judah and Nehemiah[161] really revolves around two different models of perfection. R. Judah proposes a model of justice in which each person is assigned a station appropriate to him/herself,[162] while R. Nehemiah prefers a model wherein the attainment of harmony and elimination of conflict are the foremost ideals.[163] As we have had occasion to observe previously with respect to several other midrashic elaborations of the banquet account, the current interpretation presupposes that the feast should be viewed as a paradigm of an ideal celebration.[164]

---

161 The dispute is found in similar formulation in *Esther rabbah*, 2:8. R. Judah's position is almost identical with the Babylonian version except that "hatred" appears instead of "envy" (though the Hebrew words קנאה and שנאה differ by only one letter). The continuation differs in some interesting ways from the *TB* version: "...Rather, they were of silver, but they were plated with gold. And R. Taḥlifa bar bar Ḥanah says: They were of gold, but they were fastened with silver fastenings. And Samuel says: the outer frame was of gold and the inner was of silver" [on the last phrase, see J. N. Epstein, *The Gaonic Commentary on the Order Toharot*, 131; Kohut, *Aruch Completum*, 3:380-1]. The *Tosafot* note that R. Nehemiah's objection could have been directed as well at the opinion of Rav or Samuel above, that placement in the court, garden or palace was according to status. See Reischer's *ʿIyyun yaʿaqov* to **EY**; H. D. Azulai, *Petaḥ ʿeinayim* (Livorno: 1790).

162 See Rashi.

163 Although the attribution is to a Palestinian Tanna, the notion that the feast should be striving to avoid all disharmony or contention seems to fit in well with the Persian religious feasts, as described by Mary Boyce, "Iranian Festivals," in *The Cambridge History of Iran*, ed. Ehsan Yarshater, 3 (2), 793-4. Note particularly the following citation (p. 793) from Ferdowsi's *Shah-nama*, describing the Mihrigan feast: "All men began to tread the path of God, abstaining from contention and observing a feast inaugurated royally... He banished then all grief and labour from the minds of men" [from A. G. Warner and E. Warner, ed., *Shah-nama*, Trubner's Oriental Series (London: 1905-25), 1:175; 1:62-3]. See also the similar characterization of the gahambar feast (Boyce, 796; see also 800-1): "and if the gahambar feast in his neighbourhood were held at the house of an enemy, still he must go, for these seasons were above all the time for reconciliation and furthering of brotherly love, as well as piety."

164 The assumption is more explicit here than in the others; for example, it cannot be read as a glorification merely of the king's wealth (see above). A similar sentiment about envy is expressed by R. Yose bar Zebida in *TB Berakhot* 33b and *Megillah* 25a, where the Mishnah's (*Berakhot* 5:3; *Megillah* 4:9) disqualification of the liturgical for-

Continued on next page...

"...Bahaṭ and Shesh..."

[12a] "...*Upon a pavement of red* [bahaṭ] *and blue ...marble*" (Esther 1:6).[165]

Says R. Yose bar Ḥanina:[166] Stones that glisten [*a̲banim mitḥoṭeṭot*] on their owners.[167]

And similarly, it says: "*the stones of a crown, lifted up as an ensign* [mitnosesot] *upon his land*" (Zechariah 9:16).

This brief lexicographical discussion presents us with some curious difficulties which obstruct our comprehension at the most fundamental level. As with some of the other midrashic comments in the present section, this midrash attempts to explain one of the many rare words that were employed by the biblical author in his depiction of Ahasuerus' banquet. The word in question, בהט, is one that has challenged modern lexicographers as well.[168] Rabbi Yose bar Ḥanina employs a far-fetched notarikon-style interpretation, based on a phrase which uses the same consonants as *bahaṭ*— if we allow for the fact that a *Ḥ* has been substituted for the *H*![169] Thus, ***bahaṭ*** ← *'a̲banim*

...Continued from previous page

mula "Your mercies extend unto a bird's nest" is ascribed to the fact that "he is introducing jealousy within the order of Creation" [and cf. *Genesis rabbah* 12:8 (p. 106), =*Leviticus rabbah*, 9:9 (189)]. On the passage, see: E. Segal, "Justice, Mercy and a Bird's Nest," *JJS* 42 (2 1991), 180-1. Note the ironic wording in *Esther rabbah*: "...you are introducing hatred into the feast of that wicked man!" implying that Ahasuerus' personal wickedness need not stop us from an idealized view of his feast! Cf. *TB Shabbat* 89a, *Megillah* 7a; *Soṭah* 2b, *Giṭṭin* 7a.

165 **Spanish family** adds: "What is '*bahaṭ*'?"

166 "Yose bar Ḥanina" —**Printings**: "Asi."

167 **MS P** and **EY** add: "And some say: Stones that dazzle the eyes in their place."

168 Werner Dommerhausen, *Die Estherrolle: Stil und Ziel einer alttestamentlichen Schrift*, Stuttgarten Biblische Monographen, ed. J. Hospecker and W. Pesch (Stuttgart: Katholisches Bibelwerk, 1968), 146 (cited in Moore's commentary to Esther, 7) surmises that this may have been an intentional choice by the author designed to produce an exotic effect. See Paton, 145; Ben-Yehudah, 1:469. The suggested translations have included alabaster (most likely), porphyry, emerald, crystal and more.

169 R. Gershom (cited by *ʿArukh*) derives *mitḥoṭeṭot* from הטה ("incline"?), which he relates to offering, possibly in the sense that the subjects would offer the jewels in

Continued on next page...

mitḥoṭeṭot.[170] Such interpretations are acceptable according to the norms of aggadic hermeneutics.

More puzzling is the inclusion of an additional proof-text from Zechariah, whose connection to the preceding comments is not explained. This verse does contain a mention of jewels, using the same word "*ab̲nei*," but this does not strike us as an adequate justification for its inclusion here. There is a morphological rather than a lexicographical resemblance between the words *mitḥoṭeṭot* and *mitnosesot*, but this would not normally be considered an acceptable midrashic link between verses, especially when we consider that *mitnosesot* does not connect in any obvious way to the starting point of the whole discussion, *bahaṭ*.[171]

There is some room for speculation that our passage preserves a fragmentary remnant of what was originally a longer homiletical midrash, which concluded with a contrast between the jewels of

...Continued from previous page

tribute [Kohut understands that the owners lean towards the gems]. MS **P** reads "מתהפתות."

170 Note that this is the same R. Yose b. Ḥanina to whom was ascribed the similar-type etymology of *karpas* above; see our remarks there. According to M. Garsiel, *Biblical Names*, this sort of non-rigorous permutation of root consonants was an accepted convention of biblical word-plays. The *ʿArukh* (Kohut, 3:366-7) explains the word as referring to taking pleasure or enjoyment. See notes 2 and 3 to Ben-Yehudah, 2:1509, which cite the various commentators and conclude: "The derivation and meaning are unknown... From all these explanations it seems that none of them possessed a tradition about its meaning, and that none of these interpretations is sufficient or satisfactory."

171 The need to accommodate both roots probably underlies R. Ḥananel's fanciful explanation (also cited by the *ʿArukh*), according to which the jewels caused their owners *to sin* (*maḥṭi'ot*) against the crown (in handling objects too wonderful for commoners), and hence to flee (*nasim*) from the king. This explanation bears some similarity to that of Rashi, who uses *ḤṬṬ* in its normal sense of "dig," and therefore explains that the owners must "dig up" money to pay for such valuable gems; accordingly the acquisition of such valuables constitutes a "trial" (*nisayon*")! (Rashi does not allude to this interpretation in his commentaries to either Esther or Zechariah, though he does translate "להתנוסס" in Psalms 60:6 in the sense of "trial," apparently taking his cue from the Targum.) Some commentators and translators have proposed reading the word in Zechariah as related to *NṢṢ*, "gleam or shimmer"; see Kohut.

Ahasuerus' pavement and the brilliance of the Jews in messianic times. No such midrash is however found in any known collection.[172]

> [12a] "...*And white* [dar] *and black marble*" (Esther 1:6).
>
> Rav says: Rows upon rows [*darei darei*].
>
> And Samuel says: There is a precious[173] stone in the maritime cities, and its name is "Dura." He laid it down[174] in the middle of[175] the feast and it provided[176] them[177] with light as at noon [*kaṣṣahorayim*].[178]
>
> "...*and white* [dar] *and black marble* [*vesoḥaret*]."

---

172 *Esther rabbah*, 2:9 contains a similar passage, but also without any homiletical thrust: "R. Nisa of Caesarea says: {This refers (?)} to a jewel that is beloved of its master." Note that, according to the version we have cited it is by no means certain (in spite of the claims of Radal, *Yefeh ʿanaf* and Maharzu to the contrary) that R. Nisa's dictum refers to *bahaṭ* at all: It lacks the verbal word play (using the word *ahuvah* instead of *mitḥoṭeṭot*), and is attached to a comment of R. Joḥanan that is undoubtedly explaining "ודר וסחרת"; the *Mattenot kehunnah* and *Mishnat derabbi eliʿezer* (of R. Eliezer of Pinchov) both attach the R. Nisa's comment to "שש." This situation raises the possibility that the Bavli may also have mistakenly and artificially applied the dictum to the wrong phrase.

173 "a precious" —MS **Mf** and Genizah fragment: "a."

174 "laid it down" —Only in MS **Y** and **Spanish family**; all others: "placed it." **Spanish family** adds: "for them."

175 "the middle of" — ~ in **Spanish family** and **AgE**.

176 "provided" —MS **Y*** and **AgE**: "would provide."

177 "them" — ~ in MS **N**.

178 "as at noon" —Only in MSS **Y**, **G**, **B**, **L***, **W**, **AgE***; MS **R**: "at noon"; ~ in all other witnesses.

{A *baraita*} of the School[179] of Rabbi Ishmael[180] taught:[181] That he proclaimed liberty [*deror*][182] for all owners of merchandise [*seḥorah*].[183]

There is some confusion in the arrangement of the biblical lemmas in the textual witnesses,[184] but the internal logic of the exegetical word-plays indicates that the verbal connections to the verse are as follows:

1) Rav's statement is clearly tied to *dar*.[185]

2) Samuel is probably explaining both *dar* and *soḥaret*, but the picture is confused by textual considerations. Although the *dar* / *dura* connection is obvious it seems likely that there is also an intended word-play between *soḥaret* and "*seʿudah vehe'irah*," with *ʿayin* and *ḥet* treated as interchangeable, as is common in various Aramaic and Hebrew dialects.[186]

---

179 "of the school" —Genizah fragment: "The words."

180 MS **P** adds: "Said R. Ishmael."

181 "taught" —MS **M**: "says."

182 "'...*and white*...' ...liberty" ~ in MS **Mf**.

183 "merchandise" —MSS **Y***, **R**, **Mf**: "a feast [*seʿudah*]." **HgT** adds: "because he removed their tariffs."

184 The Yemenite texts **Y** and **AgE** attach Rav and Samuel's explanations to "*vedar*," and introduce a new lemma before the *baraita* (*vesoḥaret* in **Y**, *vedar vesoḥaret* in **AgE**). All the other witnesses have only a single lemma (*vedar vesoḥaret*) at the very beginning of the passage, a situation which might reflect the strong influence of Rashi's interpretation as described below.

185 *Contra* Rashi, who (for the sake of symmetry) wants to have all the explanations account for both *dar* and *soḥaret*. He discerns an implied allusion to *soḥaret* as well, in the sense of "around"; i.e., the rows were arranged in a circle. Rashi is probably being influenced in this instance by the phraseology of the First Targum, which speaks of "decorated ropes encompassing them all around (*ḥazur ḥazur*)."

186 See e.g. *TP Berakhot* 2:3 (4d); J. N. Epstein, *A Grammar of Babylonian Aramaic*, 17-8; *Idem.*, *Studies in Talmudic Literature and Semitic Languages*, translated by Z. Epstein (Jerusalem: Magnes Press, 1983), 177; *Idem.*, *Mavo' lenosaḥ ha- mishnah*, 8-12. The alternative Yemenite reading of " והיתה מאירה " may have been intended to provide an extra consonantal H (rather than the ʿ) in order to make the pun work as follows: *seʿudah vehayetah me'irah*.

The minority of texts that add "like at noon" [*kaṣṣahorayim*] at the end of Samuel's dictum are of course positing a different (or additional) word-play to *vesoḥaret*, substituting a *Ṣ* for *S* as well as *H* for *Ḥ*.[187] The scarcity of this reading in the various textual witnesses[188] argues strongly for its not being original, especially when we consider that it had been read and explained by Rashi, whose readings exerted a powerful influence on the manuscript traditions![189]

3) The *baraita* of the School of Rabbi Ishmael[190] clearly contains puns on both *dar* and *soḥaret*.[191]

As to the actual meanings of the phrases, some are clearer than others.

---

[187] See Maharsha and Strashun.

[188] It is also missing in a Genizah fragment.

[189] Note that two of the witnesses read the word only in marginal emendations, a likely indication of how it entered the other texts as well. Several of the texts that do include it are of the Ashkenazic type that routinely incorporate Rashi's readings. The otherwise consistent testimony of the "Yemenite family" is here compromised by the fact that **AgE** (as recorded by Buber) has the word only in a gloss, not in the body of the MSS.

We should make it clear that Rashi does seem to have had the word in the MSS before him and that there are no grounds for thinking that he himself introduced it as an emendation. Not only does he not employ the normal formulas for emendation (*hakhi garesinan*), but he ultimately does not even feel comfortable basing the midrash on the word as found, but rather on the supposed equivalent "*sihara*" (="moonlight") [On this apparent confusion between sunlight and moonlight, see below]! It may be significant that in his biblical commentary to Esther, Rashi makes no mention of the Talmud's interpretation, stating simply that the verse refers to various gems.

[190] See Ch. Albeck, *Meḥqarim bivraita uvetosefta*, 43 ff., 45.

[191] However the minority reading of *se'udah* raises the question: Allowing that *'ayin* is being read as *ḥet* as before, it is less than satisfying, even by midrashic standards, to equate *R* and *D*. The reading thus seems so unreasonable, in spite of its distribution over various discrete textual families, as to almost recommend it as a *lectio difficilior*. I nonetheless do not feel that it could be authentic, and it probably owes its origin, if not to the roving eye of a copyist, then to a student who (more concerned with the content than with the word-plays) was troubled by the apparent irrelevance of the reference to merchandise in the context of a feast.

All commentators concur that Rav is referring to rows, i.e., to the orderly arrangement of the jewels in the pavement.[192]

Samuel's interpretation of *dar* agrees with the general view of lexicographers which identifies it with the pearl,[193] as in Syriac and Arabic. The identification is also found elsewhere in midrashic literature.[194]

The etymological identification accounts for only part of Samuel's comment. The second element constitutes an aggadic embellishment according to which the jewel had a wondrous property to illuminate the hall with non-reflected light. We have tried to indicate above how this tradition may have been derived from a rather far-fetched play on the sounds of the consonants. However, traditions about self-illuminating gems appear elsewhere in rabbinic texts, as well as in unexpected corners of ancient literature. The phenomenon has been well documented in a fascinating study by Daniel Sperber[195] which indeed sheds much light on our subject.

Sperber notes firstly that a similar tradition is related concerning Noah's ark, as in the following passage from *Genesis rabbah*, 31:1:[196]

---

192 See Rashi; *Aruch Completum*, 3:136; Jastrow, 322. Since Rav's interpretation makes no explicit reference to jewels, he might conceivably be referring to rows of mosaic stones, or even to the arrangement of the couches.

193 Or mother-of-pearl; see *BDB*, 204; Paton, 143-4; Moore's commentary, 7; Kohut, 3:136; Daniel Sperber, "Gilgulei avanim," in *Studies in Rabbinic Literature, Bible and Jewish History*, ed. Y. D. Gilat, Ch. Levine and Z. M. Rabinowitz, 261-7 (Ramat-Gan: Bar-Ilan University Press, 1982), 261, n. 2.

194 *Esther rabbah*, 2:9: "Says R. Huna: There is a place where they call the pearl *durah*" [the word *margalit* is employed throughout that passage in the various dicta that are cited with reference to our verse]; *TP Sanhedrin* 10:1: "There they refer to the pearl as *dura*" [following the Genizah text of Louis Ginzberg, *Yerushalmi Fragments from the Genizah*, Vol. 1, Texts and Studies of the Jewish Theological Seminary of America (New York: The Jewish Theological Seminary of America, 1909), 262]; see Sperber, *ibid.* On the dual use of *margalit* in rabbinic texts as both "pearl" (in Babylonia) and as (generic) "jewel" (in Palestine) see Sperber, 265, n. 25.

195 See reference above.

196 Ed. Theodor-Albeck, 283. Parallels cited in notes include *TB Sanhedrin* 108b, *Pirqei derabbi eliʿezer* Ch. 23 (ed. Friedlander, 166-7). See also Targum Ps. Jonathan

Continued on next page...

> "*A window* [ṣohar] *shalt thou make to the ark...*" (Genesis 6:16).
>
> ...R. Levi says: A jewel [*margalit*].
>
> R. Phineas in the name of R. Levi: For the full twelve months in which Noah was in the ark he did not require the light of the sun by day, nor the light of the moon by night. Instead, he had a jewel which he would hang. When it dimmed he would know that it was day-time, and when it gleamed he would know that it was night-time.[197]

A similar legend speaks of such a luminous jewel which supplied light for Jonah in the belly of the fish.[198]

It appears possible that Samuel's dictum may also have been formulated originally in connection with the Noah story, or that at least the phraseology of shining "as at noon" was taken from there,

...Continued from previous page

to Genesis 6:16 (where the jewel is called a יוהרא); *TP Pesaḥim* 1:1 (27b); Ginzberg, *Legends*, 1:162, 5:18, 41; Sperber, 262, n. 8.

197 Cf. the version in *Pirqei derabbi eli'ezer*, where the jewel is compared to "a lamp which illuminates in its splendor." The citation in **YS** 53 [D. I. Heimann, I. Lehrer and I. Shiloni, ed., *Yalquṭ shim'oni lerabbenu shim'on hadarshan*, Vol. 1 (Jerusalem: Mosad Harav Kook, 1973-), 178 (and notes); see also **YS** 57, p. 192, citing *Midrash avkir*] reads, instead of "in its splendor" (בגבורתו): "and like the sun which illuminates at noon." Similarly in *TB Sanhedrin* 108b: "He affixed jewels so that they might give off light as at noon" [but cf. the reading of MS **P**, cited in *Diqduqé soferim*, n. ב]. The reference to "noon" (בצהרים) would appear to be required in order to create a verbal midrashic connection with *ṣohar* [Sperber, 261-2, n. 3, accepts the **YS** reading of *Pirqei derabbi eli'ezer* as original]. It is also probable that an allusion to such a tradition in Genesis underlies the reading in *Megillah* which also makes reference to noon. This is hinted at in Strashun's comments.

198 Sperber, 262, citing: *Midrasch Jona* (*Bet ha-Midrasch,* ed. Jellinek, 1:98); *Pirqei derabbi eli'ezer*, Ch. 10 (ed. Friedlander, 69-70); *Tanḥuma Vayyiqra*, 8 (which also relates that "it shone for Jonah as the sun which shines in its splendor at noon" (citing Psalms 97:11); Ginzberg, *Legends*, 4:249; 6:350, n. 31. See also *Exodus rabbah*, 1:17, where the name "(Je)zohar" (צחר) in 1 Chronicles 4:7, identified by the midrash as Miriam, is interpreted as meaning that "her countenance was like noon." See Shinan's notes, p. 67.

where "כצהרים" provides a better word-play on "צהר" than on "סוחרת."[199]

Sperber[200] notes that a fifth-century Chinese account of the eastern Roman Empire tells of the "moonshine pearl" that is capable of shining by night, a report which is confirmed by other Chinese writers in the eighth century. These sources dovetail with a motif found in the early Roman writers Pliny,[201] Lucian[202] and Aelian[203] about a jewel that shines at night with (according to Pliny) the light of the moon.[204]

Sperber observes[205] that while all the Greek and Latin sources make reference to an assortment of luminous jewels, it is only in the rabbinic traditions, which emanate from the same period, that the gem

---

199 However cf. Paton's suggestion (p. 146) that *soḥaret* might be related to the root *shaḥor*, "black" or "dark."

200 262-4.

201 D. E. Eichholz, ed., *Pliny Natural History*, Vol. 10. The Loeb Classical Library (London and Cambridge, Mass.: William Heineman Ltd. and Harvard University Press, 1962), 37:48 (pp. 272-3): "A similarly bright colourless stone is the 'astrion,' or 'little star'… It has inside it at the centre a star shining brightly like the full moon [huic intus a centro stella lucet fulgore pleno lunae]…" Pliny lived in the first-century (C.E.).

202 "*De Dea Syria* [The Goddesse of Surrye]" in: A. M. Harmon, ed., *Lucian*, Vol. 4, The Loeb Classical Library (Cambridge, Mass. and London: Harvard University Press and William Heineman Ltd., 1953), 32 (pp. 386-7): "[The statue of Venus in Hierapolis] carries on her head a stone called 'Lamp' (λυχνίς) which derives its name from its actions. That stone shines in the night with great clarity and serves all the temple with light, exactly as if it were from lamps. In the day its shining is dim, but it has a fiery tinge." Lucian lived in second-century Samosta (Mesopotamia).

203 A. F. Scholfield, ed., *Aelian On the Characteristics of Animals*, Vol. 2, The Loeb Classical Library (Cambridge, Mass. and London: Harvard University Press and William Heineman Ltd., 1959), 8:22. See Sperber, 264-5, n. 23. Aelian lived in the 2nd-3rd-centuries.

204 This suggests an intriguing comparison to Rashi's introduction of the same image (סידרא), in contradiction to the texts of the Talmud.

205 P. 265.

in question is identified as the pearl (*durra*).[206] However it is the pearl that is singled out in the Chinese versions of the story! On the basis of this data, Sperber concludes as follows:

> It therefore appears likely that the tradition regarding various stones which shine at night first became known in the Roman world during the first centuries B.C.E. in the eastern sector of the empire, from Italy to the East (Pliny, Aelian) to Syria and the banks of the Euphrates (Lucian). During that period this tradition reached the Jews, in both their western habitation in Palestine and in the eastern diaspora of Babylonia (Samuel), except that in the Jewish sources these luminous gems are identified with the pearl (*durra*). Reports of these glimmering pearls were transmitted by merchants—presumably from eastern Persia—to China at the end of the fifth century. It was these reports which gave rise to the Chinese tradition that in Ta-t'sin[207] are found pearls—chu—which shine and glimmer at night.

The final explanation, attributed to the *baraita* of the School of Rabbi Ishmael,[208] offers a completely non-literal interpretation of the verse,[209] according to which it has nothing whatsoever to do with the physical trappings of the banquet hall. We have had previous encounters with the rabbis' concerns for taxes and tariffs,[210] which we

---

206 This of course fits in very nicely with the Samuel's association of the gems with "maritime cities" (*kerakkei hayyam*). The same phraseology is found in the First Targum to this verse.

207 The eastern portion of the Roman empire, comprising southern Syria and Palestine (Sperber, 262, n. 13).

208 Albeck, *Introduction to the Talmud*, 40-3 (and n. 54), is skeptical about the Tannaitic attributions of these *baraitot*, especially the aggadic ones: "We conclude therefore that the *baraitot* of the Tanna of the School of R. Ishmael... have the status of Amoraic *baraitot* and are not treated as full-fledged *baraitot*" (p. 43).

209 Cf. Josephus, *Antiquities*, 11:189 (6:1, ed. Marcus, 6:404-5): "He also sent throughout the country and proclaimed to the people that they might give up their work and rest..." Though Marcus notes that "This sentence is an addition to Scripture," it appears more precisely to be transferred from 2:18 ("and he made a release to the provinces"), though it is not evident why Josephus should have done so. The detail is not included in its expected place in *Antiquities* 11:203 (6:2; pp. 410-11).

210 On trade in Parthian and Sasanian Persia see: V. G. Lukonin, "Political, Social and Administrative Institutions: Taxes and Trade," in *The Cambridge History of Iran*, ed.

Continued on next page...

treated as a normal reading-in of a common contemporary problem. We should note in the present instance that the difficult word *soḥaret*[211] virtually cries out for some such etymological interpretation, and that this is the only explanation in our pericope that does not demand some tampering with radical consonants. This interpretation fits into the general pattern of the midrash, discerning as it does a further way in which the feast was an ideal one and the undiluted pleasure of the guests was assured.

Repeating with the Vessels

[12a] "*And they gave them drink in vessels of gold, the vessels* [kelim] *being diverse* [shonim] *one from another*" (Esther 1:7).[212]

It should say[213] "*meshunnim*"!

...Continued from previous page

E. Yarshater, 3 (2), 738-46 [see especially 740-1, where he speaks "of the interminable payments of dues that had to be made at every frontier crossed and every city entered, the state monopoly on the sale of certain goods." See also: J. Newman, *Commercial Life of the Jews in Babylonia Between the Years 200 and 500 C.E.* (London: n. d.). M. Beer, *The Babylonian Amoraim*, 225-7, deals with the widespread scholarly view that the Jewish "clergy" enjoyed a general exemption from Persian customs duties, a view which is based largely on the precedents related in *TB Bava meṣiʿa* 65a and 167a (see also *TB ʿAvodah zarah* 4a); see the literature he cites on 225, n. 13; on 227, n. 18, he cites our passage in connection with the issue; M. Beer, "Lish'elat shiḥruram shel amora'ei bavel mittashlum missim umekhes," *Tarbiẓ* 33 (1964), 248-58. Cf. Boyce, "Iranian Festivals," 793: " ...and when the people rejoiced at the remission of taxes by Bahram Gor [There follows a citation from the *Shah-nama*, ed. Warner, 7:11; 7:2121:] 'They all flocked to the Fire-fanes, to the halls / Where New Year's Day and Sada feast were kept.'"

211 For modern attempts to explain the word see: Paton, 146; Haupt, "Critical Notes on Esther," 106/10; Moore's commentary, 1 and 7. Most commentators understand it as a kind of stone.

212 MSS **G**, **N**, **B**, **W**, **P** and Genizah fragment add: "'*Diverse* [shonim]!?'"

213 "say" —**Pesaro printing**: "have said."

Says Rav:[214] [215]A divine voice came out and said:[216] [217] Others[218] perished [*kalu*] because of my vessels [*kelai*], and you are doing the same [*shonin*][219] with them!

The hermeneutical basis of this midrash rests on its interpretation of two words from the verse:

a) The form "*shonim*" ("diverse")— The midrash expects the rabbinic Hebrew form "*meshunnim.*"[220]

---

[214] "Rav" —only in MS **Y**; MSS **G, W, L, R, P, Mf, Printings, AgE**: "Rava"; MSS **N, B*, Spanish family, YS**: "Rabbah."

[215] "Said Rav" — ~ in MSS **B** (and added in **B***) and **M**.

[216] MSS **G, N, EY, W, Ashkenazic family, AgE** add: "to them"; MSS **B*, O, P** and **HgT** add: "to him."

[217] **Spanish family** adds: "Wicked man!"

[218] "Others" —Only in MSS **Y, O, HgT¹, P, AgE** and Genizah fragment; other witnesses: "first ones" [There may be an implied pun on *shonim* and *rishonim*].

[219] MS **P** and **EY** add: "and drinking."

[220] On this midrashic mode see Heinemann, *Darkhei ha-'aggadah*, 116-7. According to A. Bendavid, *Biblical Hebrew and Mishnaic Hebrew*, Vol. 1, 125-6, the *piʿel* became the form in which the sense of "differing" is expressed after the *qal* had been assigned to the sense of "teaching" under the influence of Aramaic (which differentiates between the roots שנא and תנא). See also p. 130 there. The form *meshunneh* does not occur at all in the Bible. On rabbinic Hebrew's general preference for *piʿel* constructions see: Henoch Yalon, *Studies in the Hebrew Language* (Jerusalem: Bialik Institute, 1971), 110-11; Z. Ben-Ḥayyim, "Mesoret ha-shomeronim veziqqatah limsoret ha-lashon shel megillot yam ha-melaḥ velilshon ḥaza"l," *Leshonenu* 22 (1958), 246-51; Ben-Yehudah, 6977 and 7809-11; *BDB*, 1038-9; Jastrow, 1605.

Esther rabbah, 2:11, while not objecting to the *shonim* form, expounds the word in the same way as in our talmudic pericope: "R. Samuel bar [Rav] Naḥman says: ...and they repeat the mischief"; the passage also contains several additional hermeneutical variations on the word. Thus, the king's vessels were put to shame, as if transformed (*mishtanot*) into lead, by those of the Temple, a phenomenon which is compared to a matron whose face is "transformed" by envy at the sight of a prettier servant girl [so too in *Abba gorion*, 10-11; *Pirqei derabbi eliʿezer*, Ch. 49 (ed. Friedlander, 393); cf. Targums to 1:7]. According to R. Taḥlifa bar Ḥama, the delicate (or fragile) work was subject to quick transformation (the phrase is difficult; see Luria, *Mattenot kehunnah*). It is possible that there is an additional word-play on the word *shennishtamesh*, "that [Belshazzar/Ahasuerus] made use of [the vessels]." *Abba gorion*, 10-11, *Panim aḥerim* B, 59, and Second Targum also interpret that the provi-

Continued on next page...

b) *Kelim*, "vessels," is midrashically read as if from the homonymous verbal root meaning "perish" or "expire."[221]

In Rav's homiletical reinterpretation the phrase is removed from its context and treated as if it were a quotation[222] in which God (through the medium of the *bat qol*)[223] makes his own "editorial" evaluation of the situation. The content of the message presupposes the midrashic interpretations which we have examined above (found already in *Seder ʿolam*), according to which Ahasuerus is repeating the mistakes of Belshazzar[224] in making use of the Temple vessels at the banquet. In this instance though, unlike that of Belshazzar, there is no real indication, even in the midrashic version of the story, that Ahasuerus ever "perished" on account of this act.[225]

...Continued from previous page

sions were so extravagant that no cup was used twice (לא היה שונה ושותה בו). See Ginzberg, *Legends*, 4:371, 6:454, nn. 21-2.

Henoch Yalon, *Studies in the Hebrew Language*, 151-4, discusses an alternative usage of the root *ShN'* in rabbinic Hebrew, in the sense of "wildness" or "deviation from norms," citing our passage as an example and justifying the interpretation on the basis of the comparison with the carousing at Belshazzar's feast. Without questioning the validity of Yalon's basic claim regarding the existence of such a usage, his interpretation of the present passage seems unnecessary and unpersuasive.

221 Maharsha observes correctly that the interpretation is based on the doubling of the word *kelim* in the Hebrew idiom; hence one refers to the actual (Temple) vessels, and the other to the king's supposed doom. In *Esther rabbah*, 2:11, the duplication is expounded differently (see *Yefeh ʿanaf*), as implying a comparison between Ahasuerus' vessels and those of Elam or the Temple. The midrash there also plays on the "perishing" meaning of *KLY* ("vessels which cause to perish," *kelim mekhallim*), and echoes the same *idea* as Rav's in the paraphrase "What is it that caused Belshazzar's 'egg' to be uprooted from the world?..." (but cf. *Mattenot kehunnah*).

222 On this kind of exposition, see Heinemann, *Darkhei ha-'aggadah*, 131-6. Note particularly his discussion on 136 about the extent to which such interpretations were intended to overrule the plain meaning of the text.

223 On the *bat qol* see: E. E. Urbach, "Halakhah unevu'ah," *Tarbiẓ* 18 (1947), 1-27 [included in his *The World of the Sages: Collected Studies*, 21-47], Appendix; Saul Lieberman, *Hellenism in Jewish Palestine*, Appendix A.

224 See Rashi.

225 Maharsha is sensitive to this difficulty, and explains (following the talmudic passage above) that Ahasuerus' punishment was realized in his hasty execution of Vashti.

In general the brief explanation achieves a fine balance between the use of text-centered hermeneutical methods (mostly word-plays) and a thematic statement that reinforces the fundamental historical perspective which has defined the midrashic reading the Esther story. The midrash has been particularly effective is the way it has introduced God into the narrative, assuring us that he is indeed at work behind the scenes, acting to ensure that historical justice will ultimately be meted out. The importance of this divine assurance transcends the immediate requirements of the story line,[226] and is intended to provide reassurance to the congregation that their own oppressions and exiles will similarly be righted in the end.

"*Wine in Abundance*"

> [12a] "*And royal wine in abundance* [rav], *according to the state of the king*" (Esther 1:7).
>
> Says[227] Rav:[228] This teaches that they[229] gave each and every one to drink wine that was older than himself.[230]
>
> How is this? —Whoever was forty years of age, they would give him to drink wine[231] that was fifty years old. For this reason it says: "*rav*" [great, old], because the wine was older than those who were drinking it.[232]

---

[226] Though it is especially necessary in Esther, precisely because God is not mentioned explicitly in that book; see: Eliezer Segal, "Human Anger and Divine Intervention in Esther," *Prooftexts* 9 (1989), 247-56.

[227] "Says" — ~ in **Pesaro printing**.

[228] "Rav" —**EY**: "Rava"; ~ in **Venice printing**.

[229] "they" —only in MSS **Y** and **L**; all other witnesses: "he."

[230] MSS **L**, **M**, **EY**, **Mf**, **Printings**, **YS**, **AgE*** add: "in years." This addition was felt to be necessary because without a modifier the Hebrew word for "older" can mean simply "bigger."

[231] "wine" — ~ in **AgE** (but added in emendation).

[232] "How is this...drinking it"—Only in MS **Y** and **AgE**; **HgT²** adds: "And Samuel says: This teaches that to each and every one they gave to drink wine that was older than himself in years"; **YS**: "If there was a person {who was old}, they would say to him: How old are you? He would say to them: I am forty years of age. He would give

Continued on next page...

This simple comment continues the midrashic pattern of embellishing the opulence and general perfection of the feast. Rav is here stimulated by the dual meaning of the Hebrew word "*rav*" used to describe the royal wine. In its contextual sense, it refers to the abundant quantities of the beverage that were made available to the guests.[233] The midrash latches on to a secondary meaning of the word, meaning "old,"[234] implying that the wine was older than the drinkers.[235]

The same explanation, in a more explicit formulation, is brought anonymously in *Panim aḥerim* B[236] and in the Second Targum, and was incorporated as an explanatory addition into some texts of the Talmud.[237]

...Continued from previous page

him to drink wine that was fifty years old. For this reason it says: 'rav *according to the state of the king*' —*Abba gorion*"; ~ in all other witnesses.

233 Maharsha: "If the simple sense were intended, it should have used the {more common and unambiguous} word '*harbeh.*'"

234 This usage is attested in the Bible. See e.g. Genesis 25:23 (which contrasts רב and צעיר), Job 32:9 (where רבים parallels זקנים). See Ben-Yehudah, 7:6343; *BDB*, 913. In Aramaic (see *TB Sukkah* 5b), the root *RBY* is commonly used to indicate youth or adolescence (cf. commentators to Genesis 21:20); see Kohut, 7:239 ff. Rabbinic Hebrew, like Biblical Hebrew, maintains a morphological distinction between the otherwise combined roots *RBY* and *RBB*; on the phenomenon see: Gideon Haneman, "Uniformization and Differentiation in the History of Two Hebrew Verbs," in *Archive of the New Dictionary of Rabbinic Literature*, ed. M. Z. Kaddari, 2 (Ramat-Gan: New Dictionary of Rabbinic Literature Project, Bar-Ilan University, 1974), 24-30 [reprinted in: Moshe Bar-Asher, ed., *Qovetz ma'amarim bil'shon ḥaza"l*, Vol. 2 (Jerusalem: [Akademon], 1980), 8-14].

235 See Heinemann, *Darkhei ha-'aggadah*, 126.

236 Ed. Buber, 59.

237 See critical notes to text above. It is likely that **AgE** is not citing the *Panim aḥerim* passage as part of its talmudic text, but as an additional source (as does the **YS**). Such incursions of material from **AgE** (many of them from *Panim aḥerim*) into MS **Y** are common; see E. Segal, "The Textual Traditions of Ms. Columbia University to TB Megillah," 45, n. 6.

"According to the Law"

[12a] "*And the drinking was according to the law; none did compel*" (Esther 1:8).

What is "*according to the law*"?[238]

—Says Rav Ḥanin[239] [240] in the name of R. Meir:[241] Like the law of the Torah:[242] How is it with the law of the Torah —there is more eating than drinking;[243] So too, as regards the feast of that wicked man,[244] [245] there was more eating than drinking.[246]

This comment, like some of the previous ones, builds upon a shift that took place in the meaning of a word between the biblical and rabbinic idioms. The word *dat*, "law," entered the Hebrew lexicon from the Persian, and it is used in the books of Esther, Ezra and Daniel

---

238 "What...law"— ~ in MSS **B** and **P**, and added in **B***.

239 "Rav Ḥanin"—[Reading slightly unclear]; MSS **B**, **R**: "R. Ḥanin"; MSS **O**, **M**: "Rav Ḥanan"; **Pesaro printing**: "Rabbi Ḥakhin"; MS **Mf**, **Venice printing**, **YS**, Genizah fragment: "Rabbi Ḥanan"; **EY**: "Rav ʿAnan"; MS **N**: "R. Joḥanan"; MS **L**: "R. Ḥanina"; **AgE** (Buber): "R. Ḥana"; **AgE** (MS Oxford): "R. Hagai."

240 "Says Rav Ḥanin" — ~ in MS **W**; MS **G**: "It teaches {in a *baraita*}."

The reading of MS **G** probably reflects an original text of "Says R. Ḥana" [חנא → תנא], as we find in **AgE**, listed above. The wish to regard the dictum as a *baraita* would of course be consistent with the appearance of R. Meir's name; though R. Joḥanan frequently cites dicta (treated by the Talmud as Amoraic) in the names of *Tanna'im* of various generations; see Albeck, *Introduction to the Talmud*, 68-9, 184.

241 "in...Meir" — ~ in MSS **P** and **L**.

242 **YS** adds: "A bullock and three tenths of fine meal for the consumption of the altar, and a wine offering of half a *hin*."

243 MS **W** adds: "as it is written: '*And their drink offerings shall be half an hin of wine unto a bullock, and the third part of an hin unto a ram, and a fourth part of an hin unto a lamb*" (Numbers 28:14).

244 "that wicked man" —MSS **B**, **R**, **AgE**: "Ahasuerus"; MS **L**: "the wicked Ahasuerus."

245 "as regards...wicked man" —MS **N**: "here."

246 "So too...drinking" — ~ in **YS**.

primarily[247] to indicate royal decrees.[248] In rabbinic texts *dat* generally appears in contexts connected with Jewish religious law.[249] R. Ḥanin therefore reads into the description of the drinking procedures an implied comparison with Jewish law.[250] The basis of the comparison is not spelled out at all in the Talmud, but there appears to be agreement among most of the commentators that the analogy is to the sacrificial procedures, in which the animal sacrifices[251] or their accompanying meal offerings[252] are of larger quantities than the wine libations.[253] This interpretation is an odd one when we consider that not a single food is mentioned in the entire description of the feast,[254] and that the

---

247 In Ezra 7:14, Daniel 6:6; 7:12. 21. 25. 26 the term is used with reference to the law of God; Cf. Deuteronomy 35:2, where there is doubt whether אשדת should be read as one or two words. See also A. Bendavid, *Biblical Hebrew and Mishnaic Hebrew*, 1:65.

248 See Paton, 146-7; Haupt, 13/109; *BDB*, 206; Moore's commentary, 7-8; Ben-Yehudah, 2:1011-3; Kohut, 3:169.

249 The word does not occur with frequency in talmudic texts. It generally appears in a small number of fixed phrases, such as "the law of Moses (and Israel)" or "the law of a Jewish woman" [e.g., *Mishnah Ketubbot* 7:6; *Tosefta Ketubbot* 7:6-7; these expressions may be derived from documentary formulas, which often reflect the ancient usages of Persian "Reichsaramaïsch")]; or המרת דת ["apostasy" in *TB Pesaḥim* 96a, *Sukkah* 56b, *Yevamot* 71a, etc.]. See however *Genesis rabbah*, 18:5 (p. 166): "...This implies that intercourse for Noahides acquires, as distinct from Jewish law (שלא כדת). Cf. *TP Qiddushin* 1:1 (58b-c).

250 Heinemann, *Darkhei ha-'aggadah*, 113-6, brings many examples of instances where midrashic interpretations are built upon biblical words that have become technical terms in talmudic usage. Cf. First Targum, which substitutes the more common rabbinic equivalent "כהלכתא."

251 According to R. Ḥananel.

252 According to Rashi; see also the gloss in **YS** cited above.

253 An exception is the *Ga'on* of Vilna (cited in the *'Eṣ yosef* and in Rabbi Z. H. Chajes' glosses), who explains the dictum in terms of *Mishnah Avot* 6:4 "This is the way of Torah: You shall eat bread with salt and you shall drink a *mesurah* of water, etc." (cf. Ezekiel, 4: 10-11).

254 The relationship between drinking and eating also forms the basis of anonymous comments in *Esther rabbah*, 2:13 and *Abba gorion*, 11 (see Buber's n. 160):

Continued on next page...

very Hebrew word for the feast, "משתה" is derived from the root for drinking.[255]

In light of the above considerations we may suggest the following reconstruction of the thought processes that gave rise to the midrash: The darshan seems to have initially focused on the phrase "the drinking was according to the [royal or Persian] *dat*," which, for him, invited a comparison with "drinking according to *Jewish dat*."[256] The concept of a distinctive Torah approach to drinking translated itself (if we accept the standard interpretations) into an insight into the respective proportions of food to drink used in the sacrifices. Most likely, the homilist's primary interest was in uncovering a rationale for elements of the sacrificial cult, and not in what this told us about Ahasuerus' banquet.[257]

How this interpretation is to be applied to the Esther is never really spelled out. The most that can be said about the pericope in its present form and context is that it can to be read together with the other passages in our midrash which seek to emphasize the perfection

...Continued from previous page

"...According to the law of each locale. There is a place where they prefer to eat and afterwards to drink; and there is a place where they drink, and afterwards eat."

255 See Maharsha (and *ʿEṣ yosef*): "...It was because eating was not mentioned at all, but only the '*mishteh,*' so that you should not imagine that it was devoted primarily to drinking —for that reason it was written 'according to the *dat*' of the Torah, where eating is more plentiful than drinking. It was merely that the generic term for a feast happens to be '*mishteh.*' R. Josiah Pinto ("Rif" to EY) also remarks that the midrash runs counter to the plain sense of the verse. He explains that the midrash is responding to an internal contradiction between this phrase and the subsequent denial of any compulsion at the banquet (cf. *ʿIyyun yaʿaqov*). This difficulty is one that has been noted by modern exegetes; see Moore's commentary.

256 Other midrashic interpretations to this verse base themselves on the understanding that there are varying drinking practices among different nations; see *Abba gorion*, 11; *Esther rabbah*, 2:13; etc.

257 J. Preuss, *Biblical and Talmudic Medicine*, 575, suggests that the issue is essentially one of healthy dietary habits.

of the royal banquet.[258] However the final product is less than satisfying, as regards both its exegesis and its homiletical message.

It is very tempting to posit an original in which the exegesis took the form of a contrast, rather than an analogy: Thus, unlike the *dat* of the Persians who drink more than they eat, the Torah teaches us to moderate our drinking, always imbibing less than we eat."[259] It is even possible that the comment was originally devised in order to be incorporated into a sermon on the evils of drunkenness and the virtues of temperance.[260]

[12a] "...*none did compel*" (Esther 1:8).

---

[258] But cf. *TB Niddah* 24b, cited by *Tosafot* (see also the *Tosafot* in *Niddah*), where Abba Saul observes that such a diet is injurious to the bones.

[259] Other midrashim are actually built upon such contrasts; see e.g., the sources listed by Ginzberg, *Legends*, 4:374, 6:455, n. 31, in which the religious piety that characterizes a Jewish feast is contrasted sharply with the rowdiness at Ahasuerus' feast (as our Esther-Midrash itself observes on the next page).

[260] The most elaborate rabbinic homily on this theme is found in *Leviticus rabbah*, 12 (ed. Margulies, 243-68). The passage includes a section (par. 1, p. 254-5) which interprets the Vashti incident as an object lesson in the follies of drunkenness: "...Thus did wine drive a wedge of death between Ahasuerus and Queen Vashti, as it says: '*On the seventh day, when the heart of the king was merry with wine ...*' (Esther 1:10)." The whole *Leviticus rabbah* passage was copied into *Esther rabbah* 5:1 and rearranged so that the Ahasuerus segment can constitute its climax. See Margulies' notes 343 and 254; Neusner to *Esther rabbah*, 126. He comments on the passage again in his *From Literature to Theology in Formative Judaism: Three Preliminary Studies*, 93-6. While it is not clear from his sketchy treatment here how the widespread phenomenon of wholesale copying between midrashic collections can be harmonized with his conviction that each of these collections represents a consistent and cogent authorial position, he includes a study of this question in his *The Midrashic Compilations of the Sixth and Seventh Centuries*, 2:61-67. In the latter discussion Neusner presents a radically modified version of the original thesis, recognizing that the final redactors made use of existing literary units, a recognition which returns us to the conventional source-critical methodologies employed by mainstream midrashic scholarship that he so vehemently and vocally rejects. See also the similar arguments in his *Making the Classics in Judaism: The Three Stages of Literary Formation*, Brown Judaic Studies, ed. J. Neusner et al. (Atlanta: Scholars Press, 1990); *Idem.*, *The Peripatetic Saying: The Problem of the Thrice-Told Tale in Talmudic Literature*, Brown Judaic Studies, ed. J. Neusner *et al.* (Chico: Scholars Press, 1985); Eliezer Segal, "Human Anger and Divine Intervention in Esther," 252, n. 1; cf. Ginzberg, *Legends*, 4:374.

> Says Rava:[261] This teaches that to each and every one they[262] gave to drink[263] wine from[264] his own country.

This passage continues the midrash's pattern of describing the feast in idealized terms,[265] emphasizing not only the magnificence and variety of the menu, but also the painstaking detail that had been applied to its planning, in order to create an affair of exemplary harmony and appropriateness.

The exegetical logic of the explanation is relatively loose:[266] The verse spoke of aspects of the drinking that were left to the guests' discretion, a generalization that was left open to different interpretations.[267] Rava has selected one possibility, though the choice

---

261 "Says Rava" —**HgT²**: "Says R. Joḥanan"; MSS **L** and **M**: "Says Rav"; **Printings**: "Says R. Eleazar"; ~ in MSS **G**, **W**, **Mf** (and added in emendation), **YS**.

262 "they" —Thus in MSS **Y**, **N**, **L**, **AgE**; all others: "he."

263 MSS **L**, **M**, **Mf** and Genizah fragment add: "of."

264 "from" —Thus in MSS **Y**, **W**, **R**, **AgE**; all others: "of."

265 Rashi, continuing the exegesis of the previous passage, explains that the consideration was not only for the pleasure of the participants, but also in order to minimize the likelihood of intoxication.

266 Cf. R. Josiah Pinto: "We should explain why it ignored the plain sense, i.e. that no one was compelled to drink against their will..." He goes on to explain that Rava was responding to a contradiction with the previous passage, which implies that constraints were after all placed on the drinking (i.e., they could not drink more than they ate), hence a different understanding is required, namely that the freedom from compulsion referred to the kinds, not the quantities, of the beverages. The feeling that there is a discrepancy between the two clauses of the verse is shared by some modern commentaries; e.g., Paton, 141-2; and may underlie the different text of the Septuagint (preferred by Moore; see below).

267 The Septuagint, which speaks of drinking "*not* according to the established law," (οὐ κατὰ προκείμενον νόμον) implies that ordinarily people could be forced to drink. This interpretation is stated explicitly by Josephus (*Antiquities*, 11:188 [6.1], ed. Marcus, 6:404-5): "The king also commanded his servants not to force them to drink by bringing them wine continually, as is the custom among the Persians, but to permit each of the banqueters to use his own judgment in satisfying his desires." See Ginzberg, 6:454-5, n. 23; Moore's commentary, 1, 7-8; Haupt's "Critical Notes," 106/10.

of this particular explanation does not seem to hinge on a hermeneutical consideration (e.g., word-play or *gezerah shavah*).[268]

> [12a] "*For so the king had appointed to all the officers of his house, that they should do according to every man's pleasure* [literally: *the pleasure of a man and a man*" (Esther 1:8).
>
> Says Rava:[269] That they should do according to the pleasure of Mordecai and Haman.
>
> Mordecai— as it is written: "*there was a Jewish man whose name was Mordecai*" (Esther 2:5); Haman[270]—, as it is written: "*the hostile man and inimical man is this wicked Haman*" (Esther 7:6).[271]

The hermeneutical method employed by this midrash is relatively straightforward. It builds upon the Hebrew phraseology which indicates that the king had commanded to cater to the pleasure (or: will, desire) of all the participants, an idea which is expressed in a phrase that translates literally as "the pleasure of a man and a man."[272] Rava reads

---

268 The Palestinian midrashic collections generally interpret the phrase in terms of the alleged Persian custom of forcing guests to imbibe from a huge cup (a dangerous action which could be avoided only by means of a bribe to the butler), a practice which was waived on this occasion. See *Abba gorion*, 11; *Panim aḥerim* B, 59; Second Targum; *Esther rabbah*. The last-named source offers some additional possibilities: that they need not drink unmixed wine [אנפקא, see *TB Giṭṭin* 69b; Kohut, 1:153, and Geiger's reservations in S. Krauss, ed., *Additamenta ad Librum Aruch Completum*]; or that Jews were not compelled to partake of libation wine ("יין נסך"), in keeping with the view that they could participate in the feast without violating dietary restrictions). See also: H. J. Pollock, ed., *Sefer ʿaqedat yisḥaq ... rabbi yisḥaq ʿaramah ...*, reprint ed., Vol. 6 ([Israel]: n. d.), to Esther 1:8.

269 "Says Rava" —**AgE**: "Says R. Abba"; ~ in MSS **G**, **W**, **Mf** and **Spanish family**.

270 "Haman" —**HgT²** : "the wicked Haman."

271 "Mordecai—as it is written ... Haman—as it is written ... '...*Haman*'" —MS **N** reverses the order of the clauses.

272 In biblical Hebrew syntax, such expressions are of course normal ways for expressing the sense of "each" or "every"; see Gesenius-Kautzsch, 395-6 (par. 123), 447-9 (par. 139). Halakhic midrashim of the school of R. Akivah treat such doublings as "expansions" (רבויין; e.g., *Sifra Emor* 4:18). These forms are not however employed in Mishnaic Hebrew [see: M. H. Segal, *A Grammar of Mishnaic Hebrew*, 208-11 (pars. 434-9); A. Bendavid, *Biblical Hebrew and Mishnaic Hebrew*, 2:472-3], and

Continued on next page...

this in a narrowly literal manner, as indicating two specific men, Mordecai and Haman, and shows that each of these figures is referred to elsewhere as a man (איש). The method is of course that of a *gezerah shavah*, and it carries with it the implication that the word "man" is to be read in our passage as if it were an abbreviated citation for the respective proof-texts.[273]

However we may understand the exegetical basis of Rava's comment, it is much more difficult to account for its *meaning*: In what respect can Ahasuerus' feast be said to involve a fulfillment of the wishes of Mordecai and Haman, figures who have not yet made their entrance onto the stage of our narrative?

As applied to Mordecai, this question can be provided with a reasonable answer in terms of the structure of the plot. It is the royal banquet, and (according to the midrashic version) the excessive drinking to which it gave rise, that would result in the deposing of Vashti, making it possible for Esther to be chosen queen, a development which is of course necessary for the favorable resolution of the story.[274]

...Continued from previous page

hence we are justified in regarding our passage (at least secondarily) as an additional instance of exegesis based on changes which occurred in the language between the biblical and rabbinic dialects.

273 Heinemann, *Darkhei ha-'aggadah*, 122-4, deals with several variations on the aggadic *gezerah shavah* mode that resemble the usage in our passage. The one that seems most pertinent is that (#4) wherein "phrases are treated as citations" —i.e., as intertextual allusions. See the instructive examples that he adduces there.

Using the same method, it would have been possible to produce a variety of alternative interpretations; e.g., an identification with "*The Lord is a* man *of war*" (Exodus 15:3) would yield a midrash in which the pleasure of God was being satisfied in the events of the king's banquet.

274 See E. Segal, "Human Anger and Divine Intervention in Esther," 248-9. This consideration is, so far as I am aware, not raised by any of the Jewish commentators [cf. Moore, 13: "from a literary point of view, Vashti *had* to be deposed, else how could the Jewish Esther have ascended the throne and saved her people?"]. This is likely to be because, according to the midrashic retelling, the feast serves other functions, related to the fate of the Temple vessels and the punishment of Nebuchadnezzar and Belshazzar through Vashti.

When applied to Haman, however, the question becomes much more troublesome. Neither the unelaborated details of the biblical account nor the major midrashic embellishments seem to furnish any persuasive reasons as to how the feast would have worked to Haman's advantage. Quite the contrary, we would expect that precisely those considerations which worked in Mordecai's favor would automatically be operating to the detriment of his enemy. At best we might suggest that Rava's remarks are meant to be understood in light of the view (voiced above) that the Jews had brought the danger upon themselves through their participation in the feast.[275] This interpretation however sounds forced and unpersuasive.

The perplexities presented by this text have inspired a number of different attempts on behalf of the traditional commentators to make sense of Rava's statement, none of them very convincingly.[276]

It is probable that Rava's explanation is a truncated version of the more elaborate homily that occurs in *Esther rabbah* 2:14 and in several

---

275 Such an interpretation is proposed in R. Moses Alsheikh's commentary to Esther, and in the *Ge'on ya'aqov* to **EY**.

276 Rashi writes that Mordecai and Haman were butlers at the feast. The implication would seem to be that the king's order was not, as the plain sense of the verse would have it, to satisfy the tastes of the guests, but rather those of the servants [Rashi is apparently identifying the two antagonists with the "*officers of his house*" mentioned above in the verse. Maharsha finds this unwarranted departure from the text incomprehensible; the *'Anaf yosef* recognizes that Rashi has departed from the *peshaṭ*, but tries to justifies it]. Not only is the assumption that the two were employed in that capacity lacking any corroboration in known midrashic traditions [Ginzberg includes this detail in his account of the feast in *Legends*, 4:370, however the only source that he cites for it (in 6:454, n. 18) appears to be our passage! (The reference to *Pirqei derabbi eli'ezer* does not seem to relate to this detail)], but it does not seem to have any point to it (note that the interpretation does not figure in Rashi's commentary to the verse in Esther). R. Josiah Pinto explains that Rava is referring to the absence of coercion at the feast: From Mordecai's perspective this was regarded as desirable, in order to prevent the Jews from transgressing; however from Haman's perspective it would be preferable for the Jews to sin by choice, rather than under coercion (cf. the *Ge'on ya'aqov* cited above). An elaborate variation on this basic interpretation is cited from the *Iyyei hayyam* in the *'Anaf yosef* to **EY**. In the Maharsha's simpler version, Mordecai was pleased in not being coerced into partaking, while Haman (representing gentiles as a group) took pleasure in the availability of the delicacies.

other Palestinian sources,[277] in which God regards Ahasuerus' notion that he is capable of satisfying the preferences of all his guests as a blasphemous display of royal *hubris*:

> The Holy One said to him:[278] I myself am unable to satisfy all my creatures, and yet you propose "*to do according to every man's pleasure*"![279]
>
> In the normal course of the world, when two individuals wish to marry the same woman, can she be married to both of them? Rather, it must be either one or the other!
>
> Similarly, when two ships are approaching the harbor, and one requires a northerly wind and the other requires a southerly wind, Can the single wind drive both craft simultaneously? —Rather, it must favor either the one or the other!
>
> Tomorrow, two individuals will approach you in law, "*a Jewish man*" and "*the hostile man and inimical man.*" Can you indeed satisfy both of them? —Rather, you will elevate the one and crucify the other!...[280]

Read in the light of this midrash, Rava's statement makes perfect homiletical sense. It represents not the sage's own admiring assessment of Ahasuerus' feast, but part of an ironic reconstruction of what the king mistakenly *thought* he was capable of doing. In the end, as the midrash spells out explicitly, it was Mordecai's pleasure that was realized, and not Haman's. In direct contrast to the midrash that

---

277 *Abba gorion*, 12 (there are some differences in wording and arrangement of the material, but none are substantial; see Buber's notes). Cf. the First Targum to Esther: "to do according to the pleasure of the Israelite man, and according to the pleasure of the man of every people and tongue." See also Maharsha.

278 *Abba gorion* adds: "Wicked one!"

279 *Yefeh ʿanaf* suggests that the use of the phrase "man and man" in the Hebrew, rather than a mere "everyone," was perceived as implying that even opposites would be satisfied.

280 It is interesting how the phraseology hearkens back to the story of Joseph and the dreams of the butler and chief baker in Genesis 40. Intertextual allusions to the Joseph story have of course been noted by many modern biblical scholars, as well as by the midrashic rabbis; see Segal, "Human Anger and Divine Intervention in Esther," 250-1, 245, nn. 19 and 20.

actually lies before us in the Babylonian Talmud, the entire thrust of the passage is to demonstrate the folly of Ahasuerus' self-delusion.[281]

If we accept the premise that the more original version of the midrash is the one preserved in the Palestinian midrashic texts, then how are we to account for the fundamental changes that were introduced into the Babylonian version? It would seem that we have before us a further instance of a phenomenon that is already familiar to us from other passages which we have analyzed: The Babylonian redactors were interested only in the *hermeneutical* content of the sources, not in their homiletical dimensions. In the present instance, this fact finds expression in the Talmud's exclusive focus on the exegetical mechanics of the "*man and man*" wording in the verse. In the original Palestinian midrash, by contrast, what was central was the theological statement that was implicit in God's berating of Ahasuerus,[282] and the sense of dramatic irony which it added to the plot, as it provided a divine assurance at the outset of the story that the culmination will favor Mordecai and his people. All of this is of course entirely absent in the Babylonian tradition of Rava's dictum.

The homiletical thrust of the Palestinian midrash is given further confirmation in its dramatic continuation:[283]

---

281 I am surprised that this interpretation, which seems to be the only acceptable one of the pericope, is not suggested (to the best of my knowledge) by any of the traditional commentators, in spite of the fact that they can be presumed to have been familiar with the *Esther rabbah* parallel. This can be partially attributed to the authority of Rashi, who set the parameters for much of the discussion. The only commentator who seems to hint at such a possibility is the *Ge'on yaʿaqov* to **EY**, who is probably echoing the words of the midrash in his comment: "It is a matter of wonder how this wicked man could have given equal pleasure in his feast to both Mordecai and Haman!" He does not however follow up this idea.

282 I. e., that mortals can never aspire to all the things that God can do, and that even God is subject to certain logical and moral limitations.

283 Parallel material (incorporated into a different context, on Song of Songs 4:16: "*Awake, O north wind; and come, thou south*, etc.") is contained in *Song of Songs rabbah*, 4:31, *Leviticus rabbah*, 9:6 (183-5) and *Numbers rabbah*, 13:2.

> R. Huna in the name of R. Benjamin ben Levi[284] says: Because in this world, at the time when the northerly wind is blowing the southerly wind cannot blow, and at the time when the southerly wind is blowing the northerly wind cannot blow.
>
> However in future times, at the ingathering of the exiles, the Holy One has said: "I shall bring a north-westerly wind[285], which will be made up of two winds. This is what is written: "*I will say to the north, Give up; and to the south, Keep not back: bring my sons from far, my daughters from the ends of the earth*" (Isaiah 43:6).
>
> Who is it who can accommodate to the pleasures of those who fear him? —It is the Holy One,[286] about whom it is written: "*Thou openest thine hand, and satisfiest the desire of every living thing*" (Psalms 145:16).

Esther rabbah, unlike the Babylonian Esther-Midrash, has incorporated the interpretation of Esther 1:8 into a literary homily, with a suitable conclusion culminating in a "messianic peroration."[287] The Babylonian redactors, interested only in the exegetical elements of the

---

[284] In *Song of Songs rabbah*: "R. Joshua b. R. Benjamin bar Levi." In *Leviticus rabbah*: "R. Yose in the name of R. Benjamin bar Levi." Cf. B. Z. Bacher, *Aggadat amora'ei ẹretz yisra'el* (Tel-Aviv: 1930), 3:666. See Albeck, *Introduction to the Talmud*, 321.

[285] (ἀργέστης?) See Jastrow, 115; Samuel Krauss, *Griechische und lateinische Lehnwörter im Talmud, Midrasch und Targum*, 127; J. Fürst, "Noten zu Midrasch Wajikra rabba," in *Der Midrasch Wajikra Rabba*, ed. A. Wünsche, 268-98, 26 (Leipzig: Otto Schulze, 1884), 272. Kohut, 1:272, somewhat fancifully derives the sense from the fact that the word appears in various Greek writers (Homer, Hesychius, Aristotle) as referring to winds from different directions; hence it is being used by the rabbis to indicate a multi-directional wind. Of the major talmudic lexicographers, the only one to express a preference for the alternate reading ἀγρέστης ("wild and fast wind") is Jacob Levy, *Wörterbuch über die Talmudim und Midraschim*, reprint ed., Vol. 1 (Darmstadt: Wissenschaftliche Buchgesellschaft, 1963), 26 (cf. Kohut, *ibid.*).

[286] The contradiction between this assertion and God's own admission above that "I myself am unable to satisfy all my creatures" was noted by the *Yefeh ʿanaf* to *Esther rabbah*. He resolves the problem reasonably by noting that there is a difference between the fundamentally contradictory demands of the righteous and the wicked, and the legitimate requests of the righteous, which God will strive to satisfy.

[287] *Song of Songs rabbah*, *Leviticus rabbah* and *Numbers rabbah* all omit the Psalms reference, producing a more appropriate conclusion.

passage, saw no need for such literary niceties. The resulting product is a flat, pointless comment which (if our interpretation is correct) was taken by subsequent students to be saying the opposite of what its original authors had intended.

Concluding Remarks

The material discussed in the present chapter has consisted largely of brief exegetical comments attached to individual words and phrases of Esther 1:3-8. While demonstrating an impressive range of hermeneutical methods,[288] there did not seem to be much that was original or unusual in this area. Most of the textual phenomena upon which the exegetical comments were based were noted by other rabbinic collections as well, though usually treated in a somewhat different manner.

Thematically, the present section continued to develop the central motifs that were introduced in the previous sections, especially the placing of the Esther story into the context of the larger history of the eras between the two Temples, as reconstructed by the *Seder ʿolam* under the influence of the stories in Daniel. Accordingly, in this episode as well it was the fate of the Temple that became the central concern of the midrash. Ahasuerus' feast was interpreted in light of Belshazzar's, as a blasphemous act of defiance in which the sacred vessels were profaned and the king donned the ceremonial vestments of the High Priest. Most of these themes were accepted universally in the aggadic rewriting of the Esther narrative, and were shared by Babylonian and Palestinian sources alike.

In stark contrast to the intense vilification of Ahasuerus as the opponent of the Temple's reconstruction we encountered a more sympathetic attitude towards the king which found expression in the estimations of the royal feast. The attitude was revealed to some extent

---

288 Notably: redundancies, puns (often taking the form of "*notarikon*s") and *gezerah shavah.* While these hermeneutical tools are the basic stuff of all aggadic midrash, they are particularly prominent in our passage because of the concentration of unusual words and *hapax legomena* in the biblical text.

in the recurring debates about whether he was a silly or wise king, a question which was posed in a surprisingly neutral way, without linking it to moral or religious judgments. More remarkable however were those instances wherein we discerned an approach that viewed the feast as an ideal one, in which every detail was arranged in the most perfect possible manner. To some extent this attitude is merely an elaboration on the mood created by the biblical portrayal. The opulence that dominates the scriptural descriptions was expanded by the rabbinic preachers into supernatural or legendary dimensions.[289] It is nonetheless worthy of note that the same rabbinic texts which are so vehement in their determination to transform Ahasuerus into an arch-villain are enthusiastic in their admiration for the king's feast. This admiration is directed not merely at the magnificence of the physical facilities and victuals, but extends as well to the wisdom and fairness that are read into many of the details,[290] which become the focus for competing ideals of justice and harmony. The interest of the rabbis in these details seems to be more esthetic than religious.

A new narrative theme which is introduced in this section (it was presupposed in some of the proems) has it that the Jews were, at least in part, responsible for the threat to which they were subjected. The discussions on this point raised new considerations in the midrashic evaluation of the plot: What are the ritual, ideological and national implications of the Jews' participation in Ahasuerus' banquet?

Aside from the recurring disputes between Rav and Samuel, there is nothing distinctive in the distribution of the attributed dicta:[291] The sources that comprise this section contain a representative sampling

---

[289] E. g., the miraculous *durra* pearl.

[290] E. g., the assignment of rooms and couches and the concern for release from customs duties.

[291] A. Weiss, *Studies in the Literature of the Amoraim*, 283-4: "Among the sages cited the most prominent are Rav and Samuel and Rava. Rav and Samuel seem to dominate the first part [Weiss treats as one unit the material covered here in Chapters 5 and 6—E.S.], supplying five exegetical dicta…which enter the realm of exegesis and explanatory midrash.

of Tannaitic and Amoraic, Palestinian and Babylonian sources.[292] On the whole, the comparison with similar traditions in Palestinian collections discloses no similarity whatsoever in the attributions, a fact which should caution us against attaching too much weight to the names that accompany the statements.

The Palestinian parallels to this section also took the form of brief exegetical comments rather than developed homiletical units. This is not surprising, since the verses in question are not found at the beginning of a lectionary division, where the bulk of the homiletical creativity tends to be concentrated. Nonetheless we did discern at least one additional instance (the final pericope) where the Babylonian redaction seems to have altered what had originally been a successful literary homily by treating the homiletical "eisegesis" as if it were nothing more than exegesis.

---

[292] Cf. Weiss: "The material derives from assorted sages, and includes *baraitot* and dicta of Amoraim from Babylonia and Palestine, though they have been arranged to follow the order of the verses. As regards its content, it contains simple literal interpretation of the scriptural text, explanatory midrash, and also plain [i.e., homiletical—E.S.] midrash."

Chapter Six

Vashti

"The Royal House"

[12a] *"Also Vashti the queen made a feast for the women in the royal house which belonged to king Ahasuerus"* (Esther 1:9).

"The women's house" is what it should have said!

—Says R. Abba bar Kahana:[1] Both[2] of them had sinful intentions.

Says Rav Pappa:[3] This is what people say: He with gourds and[4] his wife[5] [12b] with pumpkins.

The passage takes its initial cue from an apparent violation of social convention or narrative logic: If Vashti were holding a separate banquet,[6] would we not expect it to be held in the women's quarters,[7]

---

1 "bar Kahana" — ~ in **Printings**.

2 "Both" —MSS **G**, **L**, **M**, **Spanish family** and Genizah fragment: "This teaches that both."

3 "Says Rav Pappa" —MSS **L** and **M**: "Says Rava"; ~ in **Spanish family**, **Printings** and **AgE** (Buber; it is found in **AgE** MS Oxford).

4 "and" — ~ in MS **B** (and added in emendation) and **HgT**[1].

5 "his wife" —MS **N**: "she"; MS **P**: "his sister" [a corruption of ואיתתיה to ואחתיה].

6 Cf. Moore's commentary, 13: "Women could be present at Persian meals..., but Queen Vashti chose to have a separate party for the women..." Similarly, Paton, 143: "A separate feast for the women was not demanded by Persian custom." See also *ibid.*, 149-50.

7 A בית הנשים is mentioned elsewhere in Esther (1:20; 2:9,11, 13,14). This fact likely inspired the Talmud's current objection. On the women's quarters of the Sasanian courts see V. G. Lukonin, "Political, Social and Administrative Institutions: Taxes and Trade," in *The Cambridge History of Iran*, ed. E. Yarshater, 3 (2), 712-3.

Continued on next page...

rather than in the regular palace where the king's feast was being held? R. Abba bar Kahana therefore sees the scriptural phraseology not as a description of the physical venue of the event,[8] but as a way of drawing a comparison between the characters of the king and the queen.[9] In the present instance it seems unlikely that Ahasuerus is being accused of any specific act of licentiousness, but rather that Vashti is displaying an immodest forwardness that was considered inappropriate to her sex.

The vilification of Vashti, while it finds no apparent justification in the details of the biblical account, should not surprise us as a midrashic motif. Not only is there a general reluctance among the rabbis to acknowledge the righteousness of heathens,[10] but in the particular instance of Vashti we have already noted on several occasions how her fate was identified with that of her ancestors Nebuchadnezzar and Belshazzar. From a midrashic perspective, the very fact that she is

...Continued from previous page

Note that in Josephus' paraphrase of the episode Vashti *does* hold the banquet in her own palace (ἐν τοῖς βασιλέοις) [Antiquities 11:190 (6:1; ed. Marcus, 6:402-7)].

[8] Alternatively (as proposed by Maharsha), the point is that she did actually hold her affair in the open areas of the palace, where the women would be visible and accessible to the men. The implication is the same.

[9] Several other midrashic collections make note of this detail in the biblical story. *Esther rabbah*, 3:10 understand the reference to royal quarters as referring to the spaciousness of the halls or to their decorativeness (also in *Abba gorion*, 13), which were required for a variety of reasons, and (according to one possibility) the reference is to the fact that the women could be held as hostages in the event of an uprising by one of their spouses (so too in MS Cambridge of *Abba gorion*; see Buber's n. 188). Most similar in its treatment of the biblical text is *Panim aḥerim* B, 59-60: "Why did she make it in the royal palace? From here you can learn that women want to know everything. She took them into the king's sleeping quarters, and she told them 'this is the king's dining hall; this is where he eats, this is where he drinks, this is where he sleeps.' An alternate explanation: As soon as the women realized that they were making use of the Temple vessels, they refused to eat with them." A version of this tradition is incorporated into the Second Targum.

[10] Heinemann, *Darkhei ha-'aggadah*, 48, notes that the midrashic antipathy to the pagan nations is a natural response to the latter's ideological and political oppression of the Jewish people. "The aggadah even adds to the wickedness of the biblical villains; even individuals whom scripture does not describe in a negative light, such as Lot's wife, the Pharaoh of the Joseph story... and also Vashti are condemned..."

punished at the conclusion of the episode provides evidence that she was a sinner.

The proverb of Rav Pappa[11] is susceptible to several interpretations. Minimally it has the sense of such English sayings as "What's sauce for the goose is sauce for the gander," or "six of one and half a dozen of the other."[12] That is to say, the king and the queen were acting out of equally licentious motives. The traditional commentators[13] have sought elaborate meanings that are more specific to the context.[14]

---

[11] See variant readings listed in notes to text. Rav Pappa, a fifth-generation Babylonian Amora, was a student of Rava (see Albeck, *Introduction to the Talmud*, 417-8). The Talmud already notes the tendency to confuse the traditions of the master and the disciple (see sources listed by Albeck, 417). Rav Pappa had a particular propensity for citing popular proverbs ("as people say"), a factor which may be used to either strengthen or challenge the attribution to him here (e.g., it might be argued that scribes would tend to attribute to him even those proverbs which he had not brought). See the list of Rav Pappa's proverbs in *Aruch Completum*, 1:160-2

[12] Paton, 143: "The man reads and his wife holds the light."

[13] The principal explanations cited in the traditional literature include:

•Rashi: "'He with *qare*'—i.e., large gourds; 'and his wife with *buṣine*' —i.e., small gourds. This is to say that both of them are committing adultery with the very same species.

Rashi's opinion that both terms refer to the same species, with the only difference being one of size, is consistent with his explanation of *TB Sukkah* 56b [=*Ketubbot* 83b; *Temurah* 9a]: "Says Abaye: a *buṣina* is better than a *qara*," which he interprets as: "...I will give you a small unpicked gourd. If you choose to leave it until it grows into a *qara...*" R. Jacob Tam in the *Tosafot* [discussed in Ibn Ḥabib's commentary to **EY** *Megillah*] objects to this interpretation, arguing on the basis of several talmudic passages which distinguish between the two (assuming that *qara* is the same as *delaʿat*); cf. R. Ḥananel to the passage.

•*Arukh* of R. Nathan b. Jehiel [Ed. Kohut, 7:183; cited also in Ibn Ḥabib's commentary to **EY**]: "If the male is unable to find a woman with whom to commit an indiscretion, he bores a small hole in a gourd with which to fornicate. Similarly, if a woman cannot find a male, she makes a phallus out of a squash with which to fornicate."

•R. Samson of Sens [Cited from *Tosefot Sens* in: Responsa of R. Moses Mintz [*She'elot uteshuvot r. moshe mintz*, reprint ed. (Tel-Aviv: 1969), 110] (and from there in *ʿEṣ yosef* to **EY**)]: "'He with a *qara*' —which is covered with large leaves. 'And his wife with a *boṣina*' —whose leaves are too small to cover it. This means that her

Continued on next page...

"The Seventh Day"

[12b] *"On the seventh day, when the heart of the king was merry with wine"* (Esther 1:10).

And[15] until the seventh day[16] was his[17] heart not merry[18] with wine?![19]

—Rather, [20] says Rava:[21] *"The seventh*[22] *day"*[23] was the sabbath.[24]

...Continued from previous page

whoring is displayed more publicly than his." See also Preuss, J., *Biblical and Talmudic Medicine*, 489.

14 Some discussion of the botanical identifications is called for here. The Aramaic בוציניא is used to render the word הקשאים in Numbers 11:5. Yehuda Feliks, *Mixed Sowing Breeding and Grafting: Kil'ayim I-II, Mishna, Tosephta and Jerusalem Talmud, a Study of the Halachic Topics and Their Botanical-Agricultural Background*, Bar-Ilan University Series of Research Monographs in Memory of...Pinkhos Churgin (Tel Aviv: Dvir, 1967), 51, identifies the *qish-shu* with the "cucumis melo," which was grown in assorted types and shapes. See I. Löw, *Die Flora der Juden* (Vienna and Leipzig: 1928), 1:533, 3:352; *Idem., Aramäische Pflanzennanen* (Leipzig: 1881), 66, 331; S. Krauss, ed., *Additamenta ad Librum Aruch Completum*, 99-100 (notes by B. Geiger).

According to Feliks, (*op. cit.* 67), the talmudic קרא is the calabash gourd (lagenaria vulgaris), see illustration on p. 69.

15 "And" —MSS **G** (apparently, before emendation), **N**, **R**: "Rather." Genizah fragment: "<...> was his heart not merry with wine."

16 "day" — ~ in MS **R**.

17 "his" —MS **L**: "the king's."

18 "was his heart was not merry" —in MSS **Y, O, P, W, EY** and Genizah fragment the phrase is formulated in Aramaic; the other witnesses have it in Hebrew.

19 "with wine" —MSS **Y**, **W**, **Printings**, Genizah fragment word this in Aramaic; the other witnesses in Hebrew; ~ in MS **B**.

20 "Rather"—Found only in MSS **Y**, **B**, and (apparently) Genizah fragment; ~ in all other witnesses.

21 "Rava" —MS **N**: "Rabbah"; MS **R** and **YS**: "R. Abba."

22 "seventh" — ~ in MS **M**.

23 "*day*" — ~ in MSS **B** and **L** (and maybe Genizah fragment).

24 MS [**W**], **EY**, **Printings** add: "When Israel eat and drink, they commence with words of Torah and ["and" — ~ in **EY**; **Printings** add: "words of"] praises. However the nations of the world, when they eat and drink only begin with words of frivolity. And thus was it at the feast of that wicked one; those would say 'Median

Continued on next page...

This teaches that the wicked Vashti would bring the daughters of Israel and strip them naked, and make them do work on the sabbath.[25]

For this reason it was decreed upon her[26] that she be slaughtered[27] naked on the sabbath.[28] [29] [30]

And this is what is written: "*After these things, when the wrath of king Ahasuerus was appeased, he remembered Vashti, and what she had done, and what was decreed against her*" (Esther 2:1). —As she had done, so was it decreed against her.[31]

This midrash combines a number of separate exegetical traditions, each one of which was probably derived from a specific textual stimulus. In some cases, interpretations are assumed though their sources are not stated explicitly in our text. We will review the elements one-by-one:

•The significance of the "seventh day" leads Rava to the conclusion that the incident occurred not (or at least: not only)[32] on the

...Continued from previous page

women are beautiful' and those would say 'Persian women are beautiful.' Ahasuerus said to them: 'The vessel which I use is neither Median nor Persian, but rather Chaldean. Do you wish to behold her?' They said to him: 'Yes, but provided that she be naked.' Because in the measure that a person gives out, so do they measure out to him" (MS **W** adds: "All this was missing from the copy"); **YS** adds: "Israel, when they eat and drink, occupy themselves with Scripture, with Mishnah, with Talmud, with aggadot. However the nations of the world, when they eat and drink, they mention sexual matters. These began saying 'the Persian women are beautiful,' and those saying 'the Median women are beautiful.' Ahasuerus, who was a fool, said 'there is none as beautiful as Queen Vashti. And you cannot say that this is because she wears royal garments and ornaments herself.' They said to him: 'If that is so...'"

25 MS **M** and **YS** add: "day."

26 "upon her" — ~ in MS **L**.

27 "slaughtered" —MSS **G W** (before emendation): "burned"; MS **R**: "stripped."

28 "on the sabbath" —MS **R**: "on the sabbath day"; ~ in **HgT^2**.

29 "naked on the sabbath" —**Spanish family**: "on the sabbath naked."

30 "For this reason... sabbath" — ~ in **Printings**.

31 "As she...against her" — ~ in MSS **W**, **P** and **YS**.

32 The argument is actually couched in stronger terms: If we are dealing with the seventh day of the feast, and if the king's order arose from his being merry with wine, then it is difficult to explain why the Vashti incident did not arise earlier, since the king

Continued on next page...

seventh day of the *feast*, but also on the seventh day of the *week*, the Jewish sabbath.[33] Since the main point of the plot at this stage is to describe Vashti's fall, it follows that there is some special connection between that fall and the sabbath. Using the familiar assumption that not only does the punishment invariably fit the crime,[34] but that the crime can even be deduced from the punishment, Rava infers that Vashti had sinned in a manner related to the sabbath. Since as a gentile she cannot be accountable for her own "violations" of the sabbath restrictions, we are forced to conclude that her sin had involved forcing Jews to work on sabbath.

•A similar correlation is taken to exist between Vashti's being forced to display her nakedness (seen as part of her punishment) and an inferred association with nakedness as part of her crime. This detail is easily grafted on to the previous story about her working her Jewish servants on the sabbath.

The deduction is however flawed by the absence of an important link in the reasoning. The detail of Vashti's being commanded to appear

...Continued from previous page

and his companions had presumably been just as drunk and just as merry since the feast's beginning. *Ergo*, there must have been some special (divinely ordained) narrative symmetry in the selection of the seventh day for the provocation. See also Alsheikh's commentary to Esther 1:9: "He was not drunk." Cf. Alkabetz's *Manot hal-levi*, who feels that the Talmud's objection is not really resolved. The *ʿEṣ yosef* also expresses discomfort with the logic of the objection, since ultimately it is not the king's merriment that is connected with the sabbath. His difficulty does not however seem warranted, since the king's merriment is merely being perceived as a necessary prelude to Vashti's fall. His solution, that the "king" here is an allusion to God, is also far-fetched, though supported by other midrashic passages (e.g., *Abba gorion*, 14 and parallels).

33 The identification of the seventh day with the sabbath is also ascribed to R, Joshua b. Levi in *Esther rabbah*, 3:11, without drawing any thematic or narrative conclusions. The *Mattenot kehunnah* commentary there suggests that the interpretation might stem from the use of the definite article, implying the *well known* seventh day.

34 See Mishnah *Soṭah* 1:7; *Tosefta Soṭah* Ch. 3-4 (ed. Lieberman, 158-76; *Tosefta Ki-fshuṭah*, 636, and sources cited in notes); E. Urbach, *The Sages*, 371-3, 437-9; and our discussion below. The *ʿIyyun yaʿaqov* commentary notes that while the sabbath and nakedness themes do constitute an appropriate retribution, the death penalty itself (as perceived by the midrash) is not warranted by her crime as related in our passage!

naked is not stated explicitly in the biblical text of Esther, and the Talmud does not bring, either here or elsewhere in the midrash, any grounds for such an addition to the plot. However our story, as well as some other midrashic comments below, assume that to have been the case.

The source for the "nakedness" tradition is undoubtedly Esther 1:11,[35] a verse which is not expounded at all in the Babylonian Esther-Midrash:[36] "*To bring Vashti the queen before the king with the crown royal, to show the people and the princes her beauty, for she was fair to look on.*" According to the midrashic manner of reading such expressions, Vashti is understood to be wearing *only* the crown.[37]

---

[35] See *Abba gorion*, 14-5: "'*To bring...with the royal crown*' —Says R. Abba: That she should have nothing on her except the crown, but rather naked" (Buber, n. 209, correctly observes that there is a conflation of two textual traditions). So too in the First Targum. *Esther rabbah*, 3:13: "R. Phineas and R. Ḥama bar Goria in the name of Rav: She wished to come in with even a G-string (צלצול) like a whore, but they did not allow her. He said to them: Naked! She said: I shall go in without the crown. They will say: she is a slave-girl..." See also Ginzberg, *Legends of the Jews*, 4:374-5, 6:455:31 and 34.

[36] Note the variant readings cited above, in which several witnesses incorporate the story of how this peculiar demand came to be made, as recorded in *Abba gorion*, 13 (in the name of R. Abbahu) [the slightly different version contained in **YS** accords with *Panim aḥerim* B, 60; yet a third variation on the same idea is found in *Esther rabbah*, 3:13, in the name of R. Aibu (cited by Maharsha)]. The scribes involved were obviously troubled by the fact that the detail was not accounted for in the existing talmudic text. Nevertheless, the passage in question does not really supply an exegetical basis for the detail, but already presumes that it was so. Maharsha astutely reconstructs the hermeneutical logic that underlies the insertion: "There was no reason to mention that it was on the seventh day, other than to state that it was on the sabbath, which is called the 'seventh day,' that *his* heart was merry with wine —in contrast to the *Jews*, whose hearts were *not* merry with wine. Rather, after they have eaten and drunk they begin with words of Torah, etc." The *Yefeh ʿanaf* to *Esther rabbah*, 3:13 observes simply that the alleged debate of the princes serves to fill in a gap in the unfolding of narrative, by explaining how the idea arose of exhibiting the queen.

[37] This Jewish exegetical tradition is persistent enough to be considered (though not adopted) by several modern non-traditional commentators; see Paton, 148; Moore, 13. Several (e.g., Moore, *ibid.*, Ginzberg, *Legends*, 6:455, n. 31) refer to the similar story recounted by Herodotus (1:8-13) of how the Lydian ruler Candaules, proud of his wife's beauty, arranged for the servant Gyges to behold her naked.

The tradition that Vashti compelled Jewish girls to work naked on the sabbath is not found in any of the Palestinian midrashic collections.[38] It is however recorded in the Targum to Esther 1:11, with sufficient additional detail (e.g., the nature of the work that they did) so as to make it unlikely that the Targum is merely copying from the Babylonian Talmud:

> [12b] And the king ordered these seven princes to bring out Vashti the queen naked, on account of her having forced the daughters of Israel to work naked carding[39] wool and flax[40] on the sabbath day; and for this reason it was decreed upon her that she be brought naked with only the royal crown upon her head, by virtue of the merit of when her father's father Nebuchadnezzar dressed Daniel in crimson...

•The citation from Esther 2:1 as evidence that Vashti's fate was a fair retribution for her misdeeds is interpreted as a simple "*heqesh*"; i.e. the two juxtaposed expressions are taken to explain each other. In the present instance, this is understood to mean that "*what was*

---

38 The sole exception is the late *Pirqei derabbi eli'ezer*, Ch. 49 (transl. Friedlander, p. 394 [The passage in question is missing from some later printings, but was interpreted by R. David Luria]. This version accords with the Talmudic account, without the additional details supplied by the Targum). While some of the Palestinian midrashim do ascribe Vashti's punishment to moral or religious sins, rather than mere disobedience to the king, the sins in question are her opposition to the rebuilding of the Temple (e.g., *Abba gorion*, 18; *Panim aḥerim* B, 61), or (by extension) her descent from Nebuchadnezzar and Belshazzar (*Panim aḥerim, ibid.*) [Note how the two motifs are combined in *Esther rabbah*, 5:2 (to Esther 2:1): "And why did this befall her? Because she would not allow Ahasuerus to give his permission to the building of the Temple; saying: What my ancestors have destroyed you wish to build!"].

39 See Kohut, *Aruch Completum*, 5:365-6; Krauss, *Additamenta* etc., 282 [citing his *Talmudische Archäologie* (Leipzig: 1910-2), 1:532; see also his *Qadmoniyyot ha-talmud* (Berlin, Vienna, Tel-Aviv: 1924-45)]; A. S. Herschberg, "Ḥayei ha-tarbut beyisra'el bitequfat ha-mishnah veha-talmud: ḥeleq a, ha-ṣemer veha-pishtah bimei ha-talmud," *Ha-qedem* 3 (St. Petersburg 1912), 7-29.

40 Maharsha notes these apparently superfluous details, and suggests that "perhaps he is thereby indicating her wickedness, because carding is particularly painful to naked people." On the differences between the processes of carding wool and scutching flax (which have halakhic consequences), see Abraham Goldberg, *Commentary to the Mishnah Shabbat* (Jerusalem: The Jewish Theological Seminary of America, 1976), 146.

decreed[41] *against her*" was the same as "*what she had done.*"[42] We should note that, in spite of the fact that this bit of exegesis fits neatly into the current exposition,[43] it is essentially redundant, since the correlation of crime of punishment is already an established and unquestioned midrashic (and theological) principle.[44]

"*But the Queen Vashti Refused*"

> [12b] "*But the queen Vashti refused to come at the king's commandment by his chamberlains*, etc." (Esther 1:12).
>
> Seeing that she was a wanton[45]—as the master says: Both of them had sinful intentions— for what reason[46] did she not come?

---

[41] R. David Luria to *Pirqei derabbi eli'ezer* Ch. 49 (nn. 70, 72) notes that the passive form of the verb suggested to the homilist that the reference was not to Ahasuerus' command, but to a divine decree.

[42] Maharsha: "If we were to interpret it only according to its plain sense, that he recalled her [cf. Rashi to Esther 2:1: "'*He remembered...*' her beauty, and was saddened"; similarly in Ibn Ezra] and regretted killing her in his rage, there would have been no need to say '*what she had done*,' but only '*what was decreed against her*'; i.e., that her execution had saddened him. It is for this reason that they expounded '*what she had done*' as referring to her enslavement of the Jewish maidens, and accordingly was the decree issued against her." The *'Iyyun ya'aqov* observes that according to the plain sense Vashti had not, strictly speaking, "*done*" anything, her crime against the king being one of omission and disobedience.

[43] Compare the Talmud's treatment of the verse with the more contextual understanding of *Leviticus rabbah*, 12:1 (p. 254) [= *Esther rabbah*, 5:1; cf. transl. Neusner, 126]: "...He wished to have her brought in naked, but she refused. For this reason he became incensed against her and had her executed. After killing her he began to wonder about it [see Margulies' note]. This is what is written: '*After these things...*'" See also *Esther rabbah* 5:2 (dictum of R. Aibu).

[44] Heinemann, *Darkhei ha-'aggadah*, 64-70 traces the development of the expression "*middah keneged middah*" (measure for measure) from the original "by the standard which a person measures, will he\she ultimately be measured" (cf. Matthew 7:2). Heinemann deals with several examples of mathematical proportionality between actions and their respective rewards or punishments. He notes (67-8) how the assumption that there is a qualitative equivalence between deed and punishment underlies several biblical passages, but was elaborated considerably by the rabbis. Of particular importance is his distinction between instances of "*talio*" and "moral analogy."

[45] "she was a wanton" —**AgE**: "it was to her liking."

[46] "for what reason" —**Spanish family** and **AgE**: "why."

Says R. Yose bar Ḥanina: This teaches that leprosy sprouted on her forehead.[47]

In a *baraita* it teaches: Gabriel came and made her a tail.

So much did the Holy One do to her with his wiles because she did not give leave to Ahasuerus[48] for the Temple to be built. She said to him: That which my forefathers have destroyed you wish to build!

And furthermore: In order not to leave her[49] "*name and remnant*" (Isaiah 14:22).[50]

The Talmud's objection is not directed towards a specific feature of the text, but to an apparent inconsistency in the plot as embellished by the midrash. Having taken such pains to vilify Vashti and paint her as a sluttish and immoral creature, how are we to account for the fact that she does not in the end agree to exhibit herself before the royal guests? This would appear to be an act of modesty and propriety. The two answers that the Talmud produces both state that she had been stricken with a humiliating blemish, leprosy or the "tail."

It is not obvious why these particular blemishes were chosen. Rashi tries to show that they were inspired by *gezerah shavah* associations with other scriptural passages.[51] As regards the leprosy, the

---

47 "forehead" —Only in MSS **Y** and **R**; ~ in all other witnesses.

48 **AgE** adds: "to give permission."

49 "her" —**AgE**: "Nebuchadnezzar."

50 "So much did…'…*remnant*'" —Only in MS **Y** and **AgE**; **HgT**: "Her maidservants said to her: Mistress, you have grown a tail!"; ~ in all others.

51 Rashi's derivations of the both explanations are offered with such certainty that he seems to be citing them from a midrashic source of some sort, though the reference to the "Yerushalmi" in the printed Rashi and *Tosafot* is possibly a scribal error, as argued by Ginzberg, *Legends of the Jews*, 6:455-6, n. 35 and literature cited there; the reference to the Yerushalmi is lacking in the quotation of the Ravan [S. Ehrenreich, ed., *Sefer even ha'ezer*, reprint ed. (Jerusalem: 1975), 175b]. I have failed to locate it in any known rabbinic text. See the glosses of Z. H. Chajes to our passage, where he includes a penetrating discussion of the phenomenon. It is possible that we have before us an instance of citation from the "*Sefer yerushalmi*" which was current among early Ashkenazic scholars and included assorted additions from various sources; see V. Aptowitzer, *Introductio at Sefer Rabiah* (Jerusalem: Mekize Nirdamim, 1938), 275-7; subsequent studies on the "*Sefer yerushalmi*" are listed by E. E. Urbach, *The*

Continued on next page...

reference to "*what was decreed* [nigzar] *against her*" (Esther 2:1) was paired with the account of King Uzziah of Judah: "*And Uzziah the king was a leper unto the day of his death, and dwelt in a several house, being a leper; for he was cut off* [nigzar] *from the house of the Lord*" (2 Chronicles 26:21).[52] The "tail" interpretation, according to Rashi, was deduced by analogy to 1 Samuel 9:24: "*And the cook took up the shoulder, and that which was upon it, and set it before Saul*, etc." "*That which was upon it*" is designated in Hebrew as the *ʿaleha*, using the same word that in Esther 2:1 means "(decreed) *against her.*" R. Joḥanan in *TB ʿAvodah zarah* 25b[53] identifies the *ʿaleha* of 1 Samuel with the *'aliyah*, the fat-tail of the sheep. Hence the extension of the identification of Vashti's "decree" with the growth of a tail.

Rashi's explanation, though ingenious, does not seem warranted by the actual wording of the passage. It is entirely likely that R. Yose bar Ḥanina and the author of the *baraita* had simple chosen two examples of bodily afflictions that would be likely to cause humiliation, especially to a naked woman.[54] In the case of the "leprosy" interpretation there are of course additional associations,[55] since venerable Jewish tradition regards this plague as a punishment for

...Continued from previous page

Tosaphists: Their History, Writings and Methods, fourth enlarged ed. (Jerusalem: Bialik Institute, 1980), 712, n. 69. Cf. *Leviticus rabbah*, 17:3 (p. 376, and parallels noted by Margulies).

52 The association with this story undoubtedly underlies the texts that locate the leprosy on Vashti's *forehead*, just as the Bible relates concerning Uzziah that "*the leprosy even rose up in his forehead*" (2 Chronicles 26:19). Note how the Talmud's פרחה echoes the scriptural זרחה (rose up).

53 Also in *TP Megillah* 1:14 (72c).

54 Ibn Ezra states (in his second commentary) that the detail is to be understood metaphorically, as a way of indicating that Vashti had become as repulsive as a beast to Ahasuerus; see B. Walfish, "The Two Commentaries of Abraham Ibn Ezra on the Book of Esther," 340.

55 Some insights into the image of leprosy in aggadic literature are contained in: Y. Frankel, "The Image of Rabbi Joshua ben Levi in the Stories of the Babylonian Talmud," in *Sixth World Congress of Jewish Studies in Jerusalem*, edited by Avigdor Shinan, World Union of Jewish Studies, 1977, 414-5 (especially n. 39). See also Preuss, *Biblical and Talmudic Medicine*, 337.

various sins, principally that of slander.[56] It is accordingly possible that R. Yose saw leprosy as the fitting punishment for Vashti's lobbying the king to postpone the rebuilding of the Temple. The significance of the tradition about Gabriel giving her a "tail"[57] is not as clear-cut. The commentators are not in agreement about what precisely is being referred to. A persistent tradition reads this tail as a euphemism for a penis,[58] while others[59] insist that the text means what it says. In either

---

[56] See E. L. Segal, "Law as Allegory? An Unnoticed Device in Talmudic Narrative," *Prooftexts* 8 (2 1988), 249.

[57] Gabriel makes frequent appearances in the midrash to execute God's various interferences in the narrative; see Ginzberg, *Legends*, 5:4-5, n. 8 (and the dozens of references in 7:172-4 [Index]); A. Marmorstein, "Anges et Hommes dans l'Agada," *REJ* 84 (1927); E. Urbach, *The Sages*, 142-5, and bibliography on 1018-9; Braverman, *Jerome's Commentary on Daniel*, 95-6, n. 5; Shinan's notes to *Shemot rabbah*, 75 [In the stories about the young Moses "he is given the role of a savior from dangers"]. See also Ibn Adret, in the passage referred to below.

[58] This idea seems to be presupposed in the insistence of R. Nathan b. Jeḥiel [*ʿArukh*, ed. Kohut, 3:304. There appears to be no justification for Kohut's suspicion that this is an interpolation to the *ʿArukh*—more likely, it was censored out of some witnesses, as it was from later printings of the Talmud, because of its *risqué* subject matter] that "anything which is superfluous, which is a different size from that which is next to it, and which differs in its nature from what is normal, is designated 'tail'... It is manifestly evident that it is not referring to an actual tail." R. Nathan completed the *ʿArukh* in 1102 in Italy [See Urbach, *The Tosaphists*, 691]; a similar assumption underlies the interpretation of R. Solomon Ibn Adret to the talmudic Aggadot, composed in Barcelona in the 13th century [J. Perles, "Perushei aggadot larashba," In *R. Salomo ben Abraham ben Adereth*, 24-56, Breslau: 1863; the section is copied by Ibn Ḥabib in his commentary to the **EY**], who writes that "in all places, both in Scripture and in the words of the Sages, the term 'head' is used as an equivalent for the important end of anything, and the 'tail' designates its inferior end... and by extension the term is borrowed in order to designate any human limb which is superfluous, like a scab [!]...." In Ginzberg's *Legends*, 6:456, n. 35, the interpretation is formulated in explicit Latin: "*Venit Gabriel et fecit ei membrum virile*" [though it is not clear whether the Latinization was the work of Ginzberg himself or of his translator Henrietta Szold].

[59] This explanation seems to be implied in Rashi's *gezerah shavah* from the *aliyah* of the sheep. Maharsha takes issue with the *ʿArukh*'s interpretation, arguing: "I have no idea what could have compelled him to adopt such an interpretation. Why should we not state that he made her a literal tail like a beast? In a similar vein we say [*TB ʿEruvin* 18a; the *ʿEṣ yosef* in **EY** there cites Adret's interpretation (see above) to show that here too the word was not intended literally] that Adam was created with a tail, with

Continued on next page...

case we have a graphic (and comical) image that serves to contradict—according to the one interpretation—the queen's humanity,[60] and—according to the other interpretation—her femininity, including the very ideal of female beauty for which Vashti was prided by Ahasuerus and which initially gave rise to his command to exhibit her before his guests.

The interpolated passage found in the Yemenite texts of MS Columbia and *Aggadat esther*[61] offers two reasons for Vashti's downfall here: her opposition to the building of the Temple, and her descent from Nebuchadnezzar and Belshazzar. It is interesting to note that neither of these explanations is the one proposed by the Babylonian Esther-Midrash here, namely that she was herself a morally promiscuous person. While the idea that Vashti is acting out the divine retribution to Babylonia is one that was underscored quite strongly in the Proems above, her personal role in obstructing the Jewish redemption is not indicated in the Talmud.[62] The traditions about her

...Continued from previous page

which Eve was fashioned." See also Arieh b. Asher, *Ṭurei Even* to our passage. J. Preuss, *Biblical and Talmudic Medicine*, 58, also adduces several rabbinic sources [principally *TB ʿEruvin* 18a, *Genesis rabbah*, 14:[10] (134)] according to which the absence of a tail is considered a mark which distinguishes humans from beasts.

60 See Maharsha, cited above.

61 Yet again the addition derives from *Panim aḥerim* B (ed. Buber, 60-1). Buber calls our attention to the similar words of the First Targum to 1:1: "the construction of the Temple had been postponed...on account of the advice of the sinful Vashti the daughter of Evil-merodach the son of Nebuchadnezzar, and because she had not permitted the building of the Temple, therefore it was decreed upon her to be killed naked..." Similarly in *Abba gorion*, 17 (the first reason only); see Ginzberg, *Legends*, 4:379, 6:457, n. 48.

62 Josephus, *Antiquities*, 11:190 (6:1; ed. Marcus, 406-7) regards Vashti's decision as praiseworthy and in keeping with the "laws of the Persians, which forbid their women to be seen by strangers" [cf. Paton, 149-50; Moore's commentary, 13]. The majority of rabbinic elaborations of this episode seem to favor Vashti's stance at the expense of the king's foolishness (e.g., the following passage in the Babylonian Esther-Midrash and the parallels cited in our analysis below). See Ginzberg, *Legends*, 6:456, nn. 35-6.

disfigurement appear to be unique to the Esther-Midrash, with no parallels in the Palestinian collections.[63]

"Very Wroth"

> [12b] *"Therefore the king was very wroth, and his anger burned in him"* (Esther 1:12).
>
> What[64] did she send him[65] that he[66] was so[67] fired up?
>
> —Rather,[68] says Rava:[69] Thus[70] did she send[71] to him:[72] You are the[73] son of Father's stable-keeper! *"He drank wine before the thousand"* (Daniel 5:1) and was not satisfied.[74] Yet[75] that man became drunk with his wine immediately.
>
> At once: *"and his anger burned in him."*

This comment fills in the flow of narrative events by inserting a fictitious dialogue between the accounts of Vashti's disobedience and the king's reaction, where the biblical author has remained tantalizingly

---

63 In Rashi's commentary to Esther 1:12 he presents the talmudic explanation introduced by "Our Rabbis said," apparently as a way of distancing himself from the tradition.

64 "What"—MSS **L**, **M** and **Printings**: "why?"

65 "did she send him" —Only in MS **Y**, **HgT**, **AgE** and Genizah fragment; ~ in all other witnesses.

66 "he" —MSS **N**, **B**, **L**, **M**, **Mf**, **HgT**, **YS**: "his anger."

67 MSS **G**, **N**, **B**, **O**, **P**, **R**, **W**, **Mf**, **L**, **EY**, **HgT**, **YS** add: "increasingly."

68 "Rather" —Only in MS **Y** and **AgE**. [אלא (which frequently appears in oriental MSS as אילא or אולא) is a graphic variant on "(ו)אזלא" found in most other witnesses.]

69 "Rava" —MSS **P**, **R**, **YS**: "Rabbah."

70 "Thus" —Only in MSS **Y**, **O**, **AgE**; ~ in all other witnesses.

71 "Rather...to him" —MS **G**: "She sent."

72 "to him: — ~ in MSS **M**, **Mf**, Genizah fragment. MS **B** adds: "saying"; **HgT** adds: "thus."

73 "You are the" —Only in MS **Y** and **AgE**; ~ in all other witnesses.

74 "and was not satisfied" — ~ in MS **P** and **YS**.

75 "yet [lit.: "and"]" — ~ in MSS **N** and **M**; MS **R**: "for."

silent. The content of the exchange does not seem to be based on any obvious clues from the biblical text, though the traditional commentators have made some interesting attempts to explain the midrash as a response to textual stimuli.[76] Rava attempts to reconstruct what sort of thing Vashti would have been likely to say under such circumstances.[77] In the present instance, as we shall note below, some of the specific "facts" that are alluded to by Vashti have not yet been spelled out in our midrash.

Several midrashic collections contain similar reconstructions of Vashti's alleged berating of Ahasuerus. An examination of these parallels offers us some insights into the possible origins and development of Rava's comment.

Thus, in the Palestinian midrashim the passage is introduced as follows: "She sent to him speaking words that touched his heart." The style implies that "words (דברים) that touched his heart" is somehow derived from the wording of the verse. According to Maharzu to *Esther rabbah* 3:14, the exegesis is based on a midrashic reading of the phrase "at the king's commandment" (דבר המלך) as if it meant: "with her own words to the king," or "about the king" (referring to her royal ancestry).[78] This is consistent with a well known midrashic propensity

---

[76] Maharsha tries to pin it on the redundancy of the verse's employing two phrases to indicate the king's anger, implying that there was an additional incitement beside the material described so far. He also suggests that the mention of the anger burning *in him* was taken to mean that he was enraged at something that related to his person; i.e., a personal insult. A somewhat similar explanation is proposed by the *Ga'on* of Vilna (cited in *ʿEṣ yosef* to **EY**). The *Yefeh ʿanaf* to *Esther rabbah* (see below) discerns in the wording "*the* ***queen*** *Vashti*" a hint that she was appealing to her royal descent. *Mishnat rabbi eliʿezer* there finds further confirmation to this approach in the reversal of the normal word order (which usually speaks of "*Vashti the queen*"; cf. Alsheikh's commentary to Esther 1:12). None of the above explanations should be ruled entirely out of hand, however none strikes me as being as likely as the one based on דבר, cited below.

[77] See Heinemann, *Darkhei ha-'aggadah*, 13, 23-4.

[78] Although the midrashic tradition seems to be unanimous in tracing Vashti's descent to Nebuchadnezzar, there is disagreement as to whether her father was Belshazzar or

Continued on next page...

to treat the vague biblical Hebrew term דבר (thing, matter) in undefined contexts (e.g., in phrases like "after these things," etc.) as if it were saying "after these words," providing the homilist with a pretext for introducing a fictitious conversation.[79]

Most of the Palestinian midrashim which comment on Vashti's refusal contain some version of the "stable-keeper"[80] accusation, but they add other arguments as well.[81] The "stable-keeper" clause itself is

...Continued from previous page

Evil-merodach. In particular, the Targums identify her as the daughter of Evil-merodach, the Second Targum being inconsistent on this point since it also contains the quote from Daniel 5:1, referring to Belshazzar. See Buber's n. 224 to *Abba gorion*, 15 [in which he cites the conflicting textual evidence for *Abba gorion*, and proposes that the "Evil-merodach" tradition is in all cases a secondary development]. See also *Pirqei derabbi eli‘ezer*, end of Ch. 49 (transl. Friedlander, 394); Ginzberg, *Legends*, 6:455, n. 31.

79 See e.g., *Genesis rabbah*, 44:5, p. 428 (to Genesis 15:1); *ibid.*, 55:1, p. 587 (to Genesis 22:1), and many more instances in the literature. In several instances the exegesis is founded on the Aramaic root which carries the sense of "lead" or "guide"; thus a passage like our current one could have been read as "on account of the words which led him on" Cf. the many midrashim on the root נגד (in the form הגיד: relate, tell) which read it as if from the Aramaic root meaning "pull," thereby producing allusions to דברים שמושכין את הלב "words which draw the heart" (see *TB Shabbat* 87a); e.g., the explanations of Genesis 9:22 in *Genesis rabbah*, 36:5 (339), and of Genesis 15:21 interpreted in a similar manner below, *TB Megillah* 16b. Alternatively, there may be a play on the word על in its Aramaic sense of "enter" or "penetrate," understood as "words that penetrated to the heart."

80 Whereas out Babylonian text uses the Persian-based "Ahuriar" [See Kohut, 1:43; Krauss, *Additamenta*, 12 (note by B. Geiger)], the Palestinian texts prefer the Latin "comes stabili [or: stabuli]" (Greek: κόμης στάβλου; see Kohut, 7:123; Buber's notes to *Abba gorion*, 16). A variation of this line is also found in the Second Targum to Esther 1:12 (see Paton, 149; Sperber, *The Bible in Aramaic*, 4a:182), without explicit mention of the "stable-keeper."

81 These include the following: (1) "If they regard me as beautiful, then they might murder me in order to possess me; but if they should find me ugly it will be counted to your disgrace" (*Esther rabbah*, 3:14; *Abba gorion*, 15; Second Targum). (2) "My ancestral laws (i.e., those of Nebuchadnezzar, as instanced in Daniel 3:21) would never have allowed a death sentence to be executed upon a naked victim" (*Esther rabbah*, *ibid.*; *Abba gorion*, 16). In *Esther rabbah* and *Abba gorion* (see Buber's comments, p. 15, n. 222), we can discern the redactional combination of the various separate traditions, as each is followed by the refrain: "She hinted to him, but he did not catch the

Continued on next page...

expanded in the other texts, though in different ways.[82] This situation suggests that our Babylonian text preserves the original shorter version, which was subsequently elaborated by the Palestinian homilists.

The idea that Ahasuerus was not of royal lineage was alluded to in the preceding discussion on Esther 1:1,[83] where the view was put forth that he had purchased the throne for himself. There is however no source, other than the present one and its Palestinian parallels, that would furnish a basis for Ahasuerus' apprenticing as a stable-keeper for

...Continued from previous page

hint; she pricked him, but he did not feel the prick." In the Second Targum the story is structured so that each of her replies is sent back to a separate delegation.

82 In *Esther rabbah*, 3:14 the segment reads: "She sent to him saying: You were the stable-keeper of my father's house, and you were accustomed to procure for yourself naked whores. Now that you have acceded to the throne you have not reformed your despicable ways." In *Abba gorion*, 15-6 [as well as in *Panim aḥerim* B, 60 (to Esther 1:10)], the theme is expanded in a different way: "She sent to him: O you fool, your mind has been destroyed by your wine! Know that I am the granddaughter of Nebuchadnezzar [in *Panim aḥerim* B: daughter of Belshazzar son of Nebuchadnezzar], before whom kings and princes would let themselves be trampled [in *Panim aḥerim* B: act as clowns; this reading is preferred by Ginzberg, *Legends*, 6:456, n. 36, because it fits the subsequent allusion to Habakkuk 1:10: "*...the princes shall be a scorn* (משחק; lit.: play) *unto them, they shall deride* (ישחק) *every strong hold*"] whereas that man was but the stable-keeper of my father's house, and a runner before his chariot!" The passage from Habakkuk is part of the prophet's description of the grandeur of the Chaldeans, making it an appropriate text to be applied to Nebuchadnezzar.

83 See our remarks to that passage on 11a (where reference is made to the similar assumption underlying Proems #1 and #11). It is noteworthy that in that passage the Talmud entertains doubts whether Rava's original statement ("that he reigned by himself") was to be understood as a compliment or an insult. If we take the attributions seriously, then that doubt might be resolved by the present dictum of Rava's in which the tradition is used to the king's discredit. Rabbinic sources make Ahasuerus the son of Darius (*Abba gorion*, 4, *Panim aḥerim* B, 61) or Cyrus the Persian (Second Targum to 1:1, 2); see Ginzberg, *Legends*, 6:451, n. 4.

the Babylonian monarchs.[84] We may perhaps assume that this was a standard example of the least respected function in a royal court.[85]

"*...Which Knew the Times*"

> [12b] "*And the king said to the wise men, which knew the times*" (Esther 1:13).
>
> Who are "*the wise men*"? —The rabbis.
>
> "*Who knew the times*"[86] —Who know how to intercalate years and to determine months.

This comment is founded on the shift in meaning that transpired in the meaning of "*ḥakham*" (wise man) between the biblical period, when it would refer generically to all forms of wisdom, and the rabbinic era, when it came to refer to the rabbinic sage, expert in the wisdom of the Torah.[87] Following naturally from this premise is the

---

[84] It is conceivable that the sounds of "*ba'arah bo*" (burned in him) suggested those of "*bar ahuriareh*" (stable-keeper). This could not however hold true of the Palestinian sources which use Latin or Greek equivalents that do not permit such word-plays. Might this justify a conclusion that this comment originated in Babylonia, and was later transposed to Palestine?

[85] The Latin title was somewhat more prestigious than is suggested in my translation. The *comes sacri stabuli* was considered a rank of nobility, if not a very exalted one, in the later Empire, as indicated in the Codes of Justinian (12:11:1) [S. P. Scott, ed., *The Civil Law*, AMS ed., Vol. 15: The Code of Justinian (Cincinnati: The Central Trust Company, 1973), 250] and Theodosius (6.13) [Clyde Pharr, ed., *The Theodosian Code*, Vol. 1. The Corpus of Roman Law (Princeton: Princeton University Press, 1952), 130]. These sources deal with the status of a *comes stabuli* who retires without further rise in rank. For further discussion see: G. Wissowa, ed., *Paulys Real-Encyclopädie der Classischen Alterumswissenschaft*, Vol. 8:4 (Stuttgart: J. B. Metzlerscher Verlag, 1901), 678. For rabbinic sources on the status of the royal *comes*, see Ziegler, *Die Königsgleichnisse des Midrasch*, 32, 114, 160-3.

[86] "The rabbis. '*Who knew the times*'" —MS **M**: "'*who knew the times*'? —the rabbis." MS **N** adds: "The rabbis."

[87] The course of this development is delineated by Heinemann, *Darkhei ha-'aggadah*, 115-6 (and sources cited on 240, nn. 102-3). He notes that traces of the equation Torah=wisdom are already to be found in later biblical works, as well as in the Apocryphal books of Ben Sira and Baruch. See also David Halivni, ed., *A Commentary on the Palestinian Talmud by Louis Ginzberg*, Vol. 4. Texts and Studies of the Jewish Theological Seminary of America (New York: The Jewish Theological

Continued on next page...

conclusion that the knowledge of "times"[88] mentioned in the verse refers to *halakhic* times;[89] i.e., the complex regulations that govern the determining of the Hebrew calendar.[90] Such an interpretation is rendered possible by the common midrashic assumptions that the models of rabbinic religious and communal leadership that existed in their own time had been in force throughout the biblical era, and that the great prophets and kings of Israelite history had in fact led the lives

...Continued from previous page

Seminary of America, 1961), 19-31; Urbach, *The Sages*, 198. *Ḥakhamim* is of course the normal designation for (unidentified) rabbis in Tannaitic texts. Maharsha notes that although the term "wise men" is employed frequently in the Bible in contexts where it is obviously referring even to gentiles (e.g., Exodus 7:11), the designation "*who knew the times*" evokes the phraseology of 1 Chronicles 12:32 (see below). Maharsha also suggests that the fact that it is Memucan who ultimately renders the judgment shows that the rabbis had withdrawn from the case.

88 Modern commentators have had perceptible difficulties in figuring out the significance of this particular detail in the biblical story, and several have suggested emending the Masoretic test (usually from העתים to הדתים "laws" [This might very well have been the plural form; see Ibn Ezra's commentary to Esther 1:8, and Barry Walfish, "The Two Commentaries of Abraham Ibn Ezra on the Book of Esther," 333]. See Moore's commentary, 9; Paton, 151-2.

89 In spite of the ingenious explanations of the traditional commentators (see *ʿIyyun yaʿaqov* and *ʿAnaf yosef* to **EY**, Alkabetz, etc.) the midrash, in singling-out the rabbis' calendrical expertise, does not seem to be ascribing to it any specific relevance to the question of Vashti's behavior.

90 The extraordinary wisdom that was required for dealing with this abstruse subject was mentioned in talmudic sources; e.g., the frequent references to סוד העיבור . Note in particular *TB Shabbat* 75a: "Says Rabbi Samuel bar Naḥmani: Says R. Jonathan: Whence do we know that a person is commanded to calculate seasons and constellations? —Because it says '*for this is your wisdom and your understanding in the sight of the nations*' (Deuteronomy 4:6); what is the wisdom and understanding which are in the sight of the nations? —Conclude that this refers to the calculation of seasons and constellations." *Rosh hash-shanah* 20b, *Ketubbot* 111a and other sources listed by Kohut, *Aruch Completum*, 6:22. On the historical significance of the intercalations see Gedaliahu Alon, *The Jews in their Land in the Talmudic Age*, Vol. 1, translated by Gershon Levi (Jerusalem: The Magnes Press, 1980), 201-2, 237-48.

of talmudic rabbis.[91] This identification leads naturally to the subsequent discussion among the distraught sages.

Similar identifications are found elsewhere in rabbinic literature. In most of the parallels it is spelled out clearly that the interpretation is based on the association with 1 Chronicles 12:32,[92] which speaks of the children of Issachar in David's time as "*men that had understanding of the times*," a phrase that was interpreted with reference to rabbinic scholarship.[93] A fine example is the following excerpt from *Esther rabbah* (4:1):

> Who were they?
>
> —Says R. Simon:[94] This is the tribe of Issachar, as it is written: "*and of the children of Issachar, which were men that had understanding of the times, to know what Israel ought to do...*"
>
> R. Tanḥuma says: For times.[95]

---

[91] This sort of literary anachronism, often involving the injection of the values of Torah-study and halakhic observance into the scriptural narratives, is described at length by Heinemann, *Darkhei ha-'aggadah*, 35-9, who draws parallels to other literatures and homiletical norms.

[92] See also *Genesis rabbah*, 72:5 (p. 842) and parallels cited in the critical apparatus; *Abba gorion*, 16. Similarly, in the First Targum: "...to the wise men the children of Issachar, who were wise in the knowledge of the times and seasons in the book of the Law, and in the calculation (וחושבנא) of the world." The last phrase might refer to the calculations of the seventy years, but more likely it is identical to the καιρός of the midrashim (see below).

[93] E.g., *TB Yoma* 26a; Ginzberg, *Legends*, 5:368, n. 389 and especially n. 391, which contains a detailed discussion on the origins of this (apparently post-Tannaitic) tradition, which may have originated as a piece of pro-Tiberian propaganda [On this phenomenon in general see Stuart S. Miller, "Intercity Relations in Roman Palestine: The Case of Sepphoris and Tiberias," *AJS Review* 12 (1 1987), 1-24.]

[94] I.e., R. Simeon b. Pazi, the third-generation Palestinian sage; see Albeck, *Introduction to the Talmud*, 258-61.

[95] καιρός. See Kohut, 7:208, and Krauss' note in *Additamenta*, 374-5; cf. *Genesis rabbah*, 72:5 (842) and Albeck's notes; *Pesiqta derav kahana*, 1:8 (ed. Mandelbaum, 13; transl. Braude-Kapstein, 18). The reference seems to be to the pinpointing of (astrologically?) opportune moments. This of course would constitute a very different interpretation that the halakhic expertise that is referred to in the other explanation.

R. Yose bar Qaṣri[96] says: For intercalations...[There follows a pericope on 1 Chronicles 12:32, on the theme of Issachar's prowess as leaders of the sanhedrin].

That wicked man said to them: Since I decreed that Vashti should come before me naked and she did not do so—what should be her judgment?...

It is certain that the connection to the 1 Chronicles verse underlies the Babylonian midrash as well, though it has been omitted for some reason.

Having defined the participants in the next scene as the rabbis of the time, the Esther-Midrash continues its reconstruction of the consultation between them and Ahasuerus:

[12b] "*What shall we do unto the queen Vashti according to the law, because she hath not performed the commandment of the king...*" (Esther 1:15).

He says to them:[97] Pronounce judgment upon her[98] for me.[99] [100]

They say:[101] How shall we act?

---

[96] See Albeck, *Introduction to the Talmud*, 168; Theodor's notes to *Genesis rabbah* 14:1 (126).

[97] "to them" —in MSS **N**, **M**, **P** and **YS** the wording is in Hebrew; all other witnesses formulate it in Aramaic.

[98] "Pronounce...her" — ~ in MS **P** (there is a blank space left in the MS).

[99] "for me"— ~ in MS **B** (before emendation).

[100] "me" —**HgT²**: "him."

[101] "say" —MSS **W**, **R**, **YS**, **HgT²**: "said."

MS **Y** (only)	MS **B** (with variants from other witnesses)
If we should tell him "Leave her be," that would be contemptuous of the throne.	Shall we say[102] to him: "Kill her"?[103] Tomorrow his wine will dissipate,[104] [he[105] will remember][106] [107] and he will demand her[108] from us.[109]
If we should tell him "Kill her," tomorrow he will sober up from his wine and recall her, and he will demand her from us.	Shall we[110] say to him: "Leave[111] her be"? We[112] will be showing contempt for the throne.[113]

It[114] is better that we remove ourselves from it.[115]

---

102 "Shall we say" —thus in **Spanish family** only; all other witnesses: "If we should say."

103 "'Kill her?'" —**Spanish family**: "["that"—**EY**] he should kill her."

104 "his wine will dissipate" —MSS **G**, **M**, **EY**, **AgE**: "his wine will sober up"; MSS **O**, **P**, **HgT**, **YS**: "his wine will release him"; MS **W**: "when his wine awakens"; MS **L**: "when his wine awakens from him"; MS **R**: "his wine awakens"; **Printings**: "his wine ceases"; Genizah fragment: "<...> his wine awakens"; MS **Mf**: "it will dissipate from its master."

105 "he"—MSS **G**, **N**, **W**, **M**, **R**, **P**, **Mf**, **EY**, **YS**, **AgE**, Genizah fragment: "and he."

106 MSS **W**, **L**, **M**, **Mf**, **EY**, **HgT**, **YS**, **AgE**, Genizah fragment add: "her."

107 "he will remember" — ~ in MSS **B** (before emendation), **O** and **Printings**.

108 "her" —MS **R**: "him" (!).

109 "from us" — ~ in MSS **O** and **P**.

110 "Shall we" —Only in **Spanish family**; all other witnesses: "if we."

111 "'Leave...'" —MSS **L**, **P**, **EY**: "[that—MS **L**] he should leave...."

112 "We" —MSS **G**, **L**, **Mf**, **AgE**: "He will say that we."

113 "We will...throne" —**Spanish family** (including [**B**]) and Genizah fragment: "Now he will say [to us —[**B**]]: You have no concern for contempt for the throne."

114 "It" —**Spanish family**: "Rather, it."

115 "from it" — ~ in MSS **G**, **B**, **O**, **P**, **EY**, **HgT**[1], **Ashkenazic family**.

They said to him:[116] Since the day when the Temple was destroyed and we were exiled from our land, counsel has been removed from us and we do not know how to adjudicate capital cases.

Rather,[117] go to Ammon and Moab who know how to adjudicate,[118] because they sit[119] like wine[120] upon its lees.[121]

And[122] they spoke to him[123] with good reason:[124] [125] [126] "*Moab hath been at ease from his youth, and he hath settled on his lees, and hath not been emptied from vessel to vessel, neither hath he gone into captivity: therefore his taste remained in him, and his scent is not changed*" (Jeremiah 48:11).[127]

"*And the next unto him was Carshena, Shethar, Admatha, Tarshish, Meres, Marsena, and Memucan*" (Esther 1:14).

This fictitious conversational exchange attempts to explain the transition from the initial midrashic supposition that Ahasuerus had addressed his question to the Jewish sages, to the explicit biblical identification of the seven non-Jewish wise men who were ultimately consulted by the king.

A similar tradition is preserved in *Esther rabbah*, 4:1:[128]

---

116 "to him" (in Hebrew)—MSS **G**, **B** and **Ashkenazic family**: (in Aramaic); ~ in MS **W**.

117 "Rather" —MS **Mf**: "They said to him"; ~ in **Printings** and Genizah fragment.

118 "who know...adjudicate" —Only in MS **Y** and **AgE**; ~ in all other witnesses.

119 MSS **G**, **B**, **W**, **M**, **HgT²**, **Printings** and **YS** add: "in their places"; MSS **L**, **R**, **Mf**, **EY** add: "on their places."

120 MSS **B**, **W**, **M** and **Printings** add: "that sits."

121 **EY** adds: "and its taste has not dissipated."

122 "and" — ~ in MS **L** (before emendation)

123 "him" —MS **B**: "you(!). [Yes]."

124 All witnesses except MS **Y** add: "as it is written" [MS **R**: "as it says"].

125 "And they spoke...reason" —**YS**: "for its reason (?). And they say to you. (?)"

126 "Who know...reason" —Genizah fragment: And this is what is written."

127 **Spanish family**, MSS **M**, **Mf** and **Printings** add: "Immediately:."

128 A version of the tradition is also found in the First Targum to Esther 1:13-4, but is missing from the other Palestinian compendia.

That wicked one said to them: Seeing that I have decreed that Vashti should come before me naked and she did not do so, what should be her fate?

They said to him: Your Majesty! While we were still in our own land we used to consult the *urim ve-tummim*. But now we are removed from there.

And they recited before him the following verse: "*Moab hath been at ease from his youth*, etc."

He said to them: "Are there any of them here?"

They said to him: From those who are next to them.[129]

This is what it says: "*And the next unto him was Carshena*, etc."

"*The righteous is delivered out of trouble, and the wicked cometh in his stead*" (Proverbs 11:8).

"*The righteous is delivered out of trouble*" —these are the tribe of Issachar.

"*And the wicked cometh in his stead*" —these are the seven princes of Persia and Media.

An alternative interpretation: [The midrash proceeds to fashion three alternative contrasts based on similar verses from Proverbs].

These Babylonian and Palestinian traditions serve to complement each other, each filling in information that is missing in the other. The *Esther rabbah* version is not as explicit about the considerations which

---

[129] The meaning is obscure. The verse explicitly identifies the seven as Persians and Medians, who were not neighbors of Ammon or Moab. Note also the objection of the *Tosafot* to *TB*, that according to talmudic tradition Ammon had been scattered by Sennacherib, a historical assumption which has important halakhic implications. R. Jacob Tam's suggestion that the word "Ammon" be deleted was not adopted in any of the known textual witnesses. A reasonable solution to the problem is proposed by Maharzu to *Esther rabbah*, who argues that we should not put too fine a point on the names Ammon and Moab, but that these were merely chosen as proverbial examples of nations that had not suffered exile. He also suggests that the scriptural phraseology "*which sat the first in the kingdom*" suggested to the homilist that they had been inhabiting ("*sat*") their respective lands from the earliest times ("*the first*") without interruption.

moved the rabbis[130] to withdraw themselves from the judgment, though it is clear that they are presupposing the midrashic conclusion of the episode, according to which the sobered king had his counselors executed for their efforts.[131] It is not unlikely that the midrashic portrayals of the deliberations of the rabbis were meant to reflect the perceptions of delicate vulnerability that accompanied the minority status of the contemporary Jewish communities and their leaderships.

Aside from what they have in common, there are also some interesting differences between the two traditions with respect to the wording of the sages' reply to Ahasuerus. *Esther rabbah* places in the rabbis' mouths arguments which (at least by rabbinic assumptions) would reflect the reality of its historical context at the transition between the First and Second Temple eras.[132] The Babylonian version, on the other hand, makes reference to circumstances that are usually associated with the closing years of the Second Commonwealth, namely the loss of the authority to adjudicate capital cases in Jewish courts.[133]

---

[130] As noted above, the Babylonian version speaks generically of "rabbis," whereas the Palestinian traditions all go out of their way to identify the protagonists here with the tribe of Issachar, as suggested by the *gezerah shavah.*

[131] This tradition is not stated explicitly in the Babylonian sources. It is however found in the Palestinian sources; e.g., *Abba gorion*, 17-8 [with an almost identical account in *Panim aḥerim* B, 61 and First Targum to Esther 2:1]: "'*After these things, when the wrath of king Ahasuerus was appeased*' (Esther 2:1) —When he sobered up from his wine he sought her. They said to him: It was you who executed her. ...He said to them: ...I did not act properly. Who was it that advised me to have her killed? They said: The seven princes of Persia and Media. Immediately he had them killed, and therefore they are not mentioned again. And some say that they had advised him to cancel the construction of the Temple, and for that reason it was decreed that they should die." See Ginzberg, *Legends*, 4:380, 6:457-8, n. 52.

[132] On the *urim vetummim* see Exodus 29:30, Numbers 27:21, etc. They are enumerated among the five things which existed in the First Temple, but not the Second. On the rabbinic traditions regarding their use, see sources cited by Ginzberg, *Legends*, 6:442, n. 36; S. J. Zevin, ed., *Talmudic Encyclopedia*, Second Revised ed., Vol. 1 (Jerusalem: Talmudic Encyclopedia Institute, 1978), 391-7 (especially section #5).

[133] See *TP Sanhedrin* Ch. 1 (18a): "More than forty years before the Temple was destroyed, the authority over capital punishment was taken away from Israel." [See also *ibid.*, Ch. 7 (24b); cf. *TB ʿAvodah zarah* 8b.] On the historical background see Alon,

Continued on next page...

The hermeneutical deductions which gave rise to this elaborate retelling of the biblical story emanate ultimately from the fact that the biblical narrator uses three different terms to designate the king's counselors: "*the wise men which knew the times*" identified above as the Jewish sages; "*the seven princes of Persia and Media*"; and (in 2:2) "*the king's servants that ministered unto him.*"[134] This inconsistency inspired a basic narrative schema according to which Ahasuerus initially approached the rabbis, who for some reason did not provide him with his answer. Thereupon he turned to the seven princes, who were ultimately replaced by the ministering servants. It is not too great a step from here to the conclusion that the princes were done away with for their troubles, and that it was through their anticipation of such a fate that the perspicacious rabbis had withdrawn themselves from the deliberations. The Bavli's detailed reconstruction of the rabbis' reasoning, though it succeeds nicely in delineating their motives, does not add substantially to the basic framework of the midrashic account, and should probably be regarded as a secondary elaboration of an already existent foundation.

While the above reconstruction provides an adequate explanation of the development of the tradition, the *Esther rabbah* parallel confronts us with some additional indications of the literary context against which such a tradition might have developed. As we have seen,

...Continued from previous page

The Jews in Their Land in the Talmudic Age, 1:207-11; some earlier literature is surveyed by Jacob Mann, "Seqirah hisṭorit 'al dinei nefashot bazzeman hazzeh," *Ha-ṣofeh leḥokhmat yisra'el* 10, 11 (1926-7), 200-8; 192 [=*The Collected Articles of Jacob Mann*, Vol. 1 (Gedera: M. Shalom Ltd., 1971), 254-63]. While it is of course possible—even likely—that an analogous situation prevailed following the Babylonian conquest as well, there can be little room for doubt that the midrash's frame of reference is the situation under the Romans. It should however be noted that the loss of judicial autonomy under Roman rule was not associated with exile (a phenomenon whose relevance to that historical context is questionable) nor, for that matter, with the destruction of the Temple.

134 Note the citations from *Abba gorion* and *Panim aḥerim* B above. The former seems to rely on the negative evidence, that the seven princes do not reappear in the story; whereas the latter adds explicitly that their place is taken by "*the king's servants that ministered unto him.*"

the Palestinian version of the story concludes with a series of comments in which the Jewish sages and the Persian counselors are respectively identified with the Righteous\Wise and Wicked\Fool of Proverbs.[135] Such linking of the narrative protagonists with the prototypes of Wisdom literature is of course one of the hallmarks of the proem structure.[136] This fact sparks suspicions that the idea of building an interpretation around the contrast between the Jewish rabbis and the heathen wise men may have been originally inspired by the homiletical need to fashion proems to Esther 2:1 and its midrashically implied allusion to Ahasuerus awakening from his stupor and executing his advisers.[137]

"And the Next to Him..."

> [12b] "[138]*And the next unto him was Carshena, Shethar, Admatha, Tarshish, Meres, Marsena, and Memucan*" (Esther 1:14).

---

[135] The verses expounded (and their respective contrasts) are as follows: Proverbs 11:8 (righteous\wicked); 11:9 (hypocrite\just); 14:16 (wise\fool); 22:3 (prudent\simple). On this passage see Jacob Neusner, *From Literature to Theology in Formative Judaism: Three Preliminary Studies*, 90-1, whose remarks concerning the single-minded character of the assorted "*davar aḥer*" expositions takes no notice of the literary considerations that might be involved; e.g., that the structure might have been dictated by the proem form, and by a later redactor's determination to assemble a broad assortment of synagogue homilies, etc.

[136] See the "Concluding Remarks" to Chapter Two above.

[137] This supposition does involve several difficulties: For one thing, the passage does *not* appear as a proem in *Esther rabbah*, 5:1, where a proem is inserted, but one that was transposed secondarily from *Leviticus rabbah*, 12. At any rate it is questionable whether there is justification for speaking of proems for individual sections and chapters of Esther, which (unlike the Pentateuch) would have been read in a single unit, rather than being divided into smaller lections. We are therefore probably speaking, at the most, of "literary" proems, originating in the later editorial needs of the redactor of the midrashic compendia, as distinct from "homiletical" proems that orally introduced the lections in the synagogue. This would be true of other "proems" in *Esther rabbah*, such as 3:1 (to Esther 1:9), which can be explained as artificial transpositions of material that had originated elsewhere.

[138] MSS **M**, **R**, **Mf**, **Spanish family** and **Printings** add: "Immediately."

Says R. Levi: This entire[139] verse was stated with reference to the sacrifices.[140]

"Carshena"[141]—The Ministering Angels said before the Holy One: Master of the Universe! Did the nations of the world[142] offer before you[143] fat lambs [*kar*][144] of the first year [*shanah*],[145] as[146] Israel offered before you?[147]

"Shethar"[148]—Did they offer before you[149] turtle-doves [*turim*],[150] or[151] young pigeons?[152]

---

139 "entire"—Only in MS **Y**, **AgE** and **Spanish family**; ~ in all other witnesses.

140 MS **P** adds: "of Israel."

141 "'Carshena'"— ~ in MSS **B** (before emendation), **L**, **R**, **Mf** and Genizah fragment.

142 "the nations of the world"—**Printings**: "they."

143 "before you"— ~ in MSS **B**, **L**, **Mf**, **AgE**.

144 "fat lambs" —MSS **L**, **Mf**, **EY**, **HgT1**, **AgE**, **YS**: "bullocks" (*parim*); MS **R**: "rams."

145 "fat lambs of the first year"—MS **P**: "young bullocks" [פרים בני בקר]. MS **Mf** adds: "before you."

146 "as"—Only in MS **Y**; all other witnesses read: "in the way that."

147 "offered before you"—MS **M**: "did in the wilderness."

148 "'Shethar'"— ~ in MS **B** (before emendation) and Genizah fragment.

149 "before you"— ~ in MS **L** and Genizah fragment.

150 "turtledoves"—MSS **L**, **Mf**, **Spanish family**, **Printings**: "two turtledoves" [שתי תרים].

151 MSS **W**, **Mf** and **P** add: "two."

152 **AgE** adds: "in the way that Israel offered before you."

"Admatha"[153]—Did they[154] erect before you[155] an altar of earth [*adamah*],[156] as it is written:[157] "*An altar of earth thou shalt make unto me*"[158] (Exodus 20:24)?

"Tarshish"[159]—Did they serve before you[160] in priestly vestments,[161] regarding which[162] it is written:[163] "*a beryl* [tarshish], *and an onyx, and a jasper*"[164] (Exodus 28:20; 39:13).

"Meres"[165]—Did they stir before you[166] in the blood?[167] [168]

"Marsena"[169]—Did they stir before you[170] in the meal offerings?[171]

---

153 "'Admatha'"— ~ in MS **B** (before emendation) and **M**.

154 "they"—**EY**: "the nations of the world."

155 "before you"— ~ in MSS **G, B, L, M, R, YS**.

156 "earth"—MS **N**: "stones." MSS **G, B, L, R, YS** add: "before you."

157 "as it is written"—MSS [**B**], **O, HgT**: "as it says."

158 "as it is written: '...*unto me*'"— ~ in MSS **G, B** (before emendation), **W**, **Ashkenazic family**; MS **P**: "'*thou shalt make unto me*'" [=homoioteleuton].

159 "'Tarshish'"— ~ in MS **B** (before emendation) and Genizah fragment.

160 "before you"— ~ in MSS **G, Ashkenazic family**.

161 MSS **B, G** and **W** add: "before you." MS **M** adds: "in the way that Israel did."

162 "regarding which" —Only in MSS **Y, G, Mf, Printings, YS**; all other witnesses read: "as."

163 "regarding...written"— ~ in **AgE**.

164 "regarding...'...*jasper*'"— ~ in MS **M**.

165 "'Meres'"— ~ in MS **B** (before emendation) and Genizah fragment.

166 "before you"— ~ in MSS **G, O, B, R, W, L, Mf, Printings, YS**, Genizah fragment; MS **B**: "with their hands"; MS **O**: "בדים?"

167 "in the blood"—MS **R**: "'Meres'" [probably a graphic confusion between בדם and מרס].

168 MS **W** and printings add: "before you."

169 "'Marsena'"— ~ in Genizah fragment.

170 "before you"— ~ in MSS **G, W, Mf, Z, Ashkenazic family, Printings**.

171 **Printings** add: "before you."

> "Memucan"—Did they prepare [*hekhinu*] before you[172] the table of[173] the shewbread.[174]

This ingenious homily[175] takes its initial cue from the wording of Esther 1:14: "*And the next unto him*, etc." The unvocalized Hebrew והקרב[176] also lends itself to such readings as "*vehiqriv*" or "*vehaqrev*" (he offered; to offer), the most common terms employed to designate sacrificial offerings.[177] The exegesis was probably inspired as well by the biblical author's unusual precision in detailing the names of the king's princely counselors, figures who are peripheral to the plot and who do not reappear in the subsequent narrative.[178] To the midrashic

---

172 "before you"— ~ in MSS **G**, **B**, **Mf**, **Ashkenazic family**, **Printings**, Genizah fragment.

173 "of"—MSS **G**, **L**, **Z**, **YS**: "and"; MSS **O** and **P**: "on" (!); MS **R**: "with"

174 "of the shewbread"— ~ in **Printings**.

175 Heinemann, *Darkhei ha-'aggadah*, 112, cites our passage as an exceptional midrashic instance of the kind of allegorical etymology more commonly associated with Alexandrian exegesis. The word "allegorical" also figures in the characterization of Ginzberg, *Legends*, 6:456, n. 40. Maharsha attempts to identify the selection of these particular rituals as well as to demonstrate their centrality and appropriateness to the narrative context. The homily cited in the *Ḥiddushei ge'onim* commentary to **EY** takes the diametrically opposite position, arguing that the selection and order or the sacrificial items appear to be arbitrary.

176 Cf. Haupt, 109\13; Paton, 154.

177 Rashi: "This is a reference to sacrificial offerings. The Ministering Angels made mention before the Holy One of the sacrifices which used to be offered to him by the Jews, so that he should exact vengeance upon Vashti and Esther would come to reign in her place." Maharsha adds that Rashi's interpretation is supported by the syntactical inconsistency; i.e., the use of a singular participle when a plural would be expected if it were modifying the "seven princes"; cf. Paton, 152-3. Maharzu to *Esther rabbah*, 4:2, suggests that underlying the interpretation is the midrashic rule that references to "the king" in Esther are to be applied to God.

178 On these names, and their relation to Esther 1:10, see: Haupt, 110\14; Werner Dommerhausen, *Die Estherrolle: Stil und Ziel einer alttestamentlichen Schrift*, Stuttgarten Biblische Monographen, ed. J. Hospecker and W. Pesch (Stuttgart: Katholisches Bibelwerk, 1968), 146, who takes a symbolist approach remarkably similar to that of our midrash; H. S. Gehman, "Notes on the Persian Words in the Book of Esther," *JBL* 43 (1924), 324-5 [in Moore: 238-9]. Jaques Duchesne-

Continued on next page...

mind the only justification for the inclusion of such inconsequential detail would be if the names held a deeper significance. The natural method for eliciting such significance is through word-plays which evoke verbal associations. If we bear in mind how central to the midrashic version of Esther are the concerns for the rebuilding of the Temple and Ahasuerus' profanation of the sacred vessels, it is not surprising that the theme of the sacrificial service would have suggested itself to our homilist. Indeed, several of the names (particularly: Admatha, Tarshish, Meres, Marsena) evoke such associations without excessive forcing of the text.[179]

As explained so far, this midrash demands that we remove this section of verse 14, with its glimpse into the world of the Ministering

...Continued from previous page

Guillemin, "Les Noms des Eunuques d'Assuérus," *Muséon* 66 (1953), 105-8 [in Moore's *Studies*, 273-6]; Moore's commentary, 8-10.

179 The connections to some of the other words are less obvious. E.g., *kar* does not appear in the sacrificial regulations of the Pentateuch (the single occurrence is in the poetic blessings of Deuteronomy 32:24), though it is undoubtedly part of the biblical lexicon (see dictionaries [e.g., Ben-Yehuda 3:2506-7] and concordances [e.g., Mandelkern, 598-9]). Hence the widespread, but textually indefensible, substitution of the more familiar and graphically similar "*parim*" (bullocks) in many witnesses. The allusion is most likely to the daily Tamid offerings, as enjoined in Exodus 29:38, Numbers 28:3, etc. By contrast, *MRS* does not occur at all in biblical Hebrew (it does have a cognate in Arabic), but is found frequently in rabbinic Hebrew denoting the stirring of sacrificial blood to prevent its clotting (e.g., Mishnah *Pesaḥim* 5:3; Mishnah *Yoma* 4:3; Ben-Yehuda, 4:338-9). I am not aware of the word being used in connection with the meal offerings; cf. First Targum, which appears to skip over the Marsena reference. It is interesting that the first explanation of *Esther rabbah*, 4:2, which does not follow the allegorical interpretation of the names, nonetheless has Marsena as the individual responsible for mixing or sifting the king's flour. On Tarshish, cf. Aharon Mirsky, ed., *Yosse ben Yosse: Poems* (Jerusalem: Bialik Institute, 1977), 187, and notes to l. 103. The verb הכן does not appear in the Bible (to the best of my knowledge) in connection with the shewbread. *Esther rabbah*, *ibid.*, cites Ezra 3:3, with reference to the altar (see Strashun's gloss and *Yefeh ʿanaf*). There are several other appropriate verses which might have been quoted in our context; e.g., 1 Kings 6:19 (the sanctuary), Zephaniah 1:7 (sacrifices), 1 Chronicles 22:14, 29:3, *et al.* (the Temple), and many more.

Angels,[180] from the earthly narrative into which it is embedded. This raises certain questions with respect to its connection to the preceding passage in our midrash, which is built upon the assumption that the seven princes were actual persons,[181] and to the subsequent comment, which identifies Memucan with Haman. It would be easiest to simply posit that the interpretations reflect differing approaches which were not intended to be harmonized.[182] Nevertheless we may note that the talmudic sources already show signs of a determination to accept simultaneously both the approaches. This tendency is most pronounced in the First Targum, which inserts a clause in order to bridge between the reference to the Jewish sages in verse 13 and the sacrificial symbolism of verse 14. According to this version, it is the tribe of Issachar, not the angels, who make mention of the sacrificial acts:[183]

> And the children of Issachar declined to adjudicate that case; however they prayed before the Lord, and thus did they say: Master of the

---

180 See W. Bacher and M. Schwab, "Vocabulaire de l'Angelologie," *MGWJ* 42 (1898), 25-258, 570-2.

181 Most of the rabbinic comments to the passage see the names as those of actual persons, though nonetheless subject to etymological exposition. Thus, *Esther rabbah*, 4:2 regards the names as indicative of their functions in the royal court; *Abba gorion*, 16-7, *Panim aḥerim* B, 31, and the Second Targum (=Sperber, 182) interpret them as references to their national origins.

182 *Esther rabbah*, 4:2, similarly juxtaposes an explanation of the names that is virtually identical to our Babylonian midrash (also attributed to the Ministering Angels) to one which views the names as those of actual people. R. David Luria inserts a ד"א ("alternative interpretation") before the second interpretation. A subsequent interpretation in *Esther rabbah, ibid.* gives a symbolic reading according to which the names allude to the punishments which God will inflict upon Babylon [expounding Isaiah 14:21, part of a chapter which is central to the historical perspective of the midrashic retelling of Esther, and which precedes the verse that formed the basis of Proem #1 of our midrash]. See Ginzberg, *Legends*, 4:377, 6:456, nn. 39-40. Neusner, *From Literature to Theology in Formative Judaism: Three Preliminary Studies*, 93-4, is forced to recognize that these interpretations are mutually contradictory, but nonetheless insists on characterizing them as "distinct, and yet complementary" [though, by his own admission, hardly interdependent]. The points of common ground which he discerns are so general as to be trivial.

183 Maharsha cites the Targum and briefly compares it with the talmudic version.

> Universe! Confuse their feast, and recall the righteous ones who offered before you in the Temple... Then the king turned and proceeded to ask counsel from his princes who were next to him, and these were their names...

The author or compiler of this text was evidently determined to have it both ways, with the princes functioning both as characters and as symbols. If we prefer to adopt only one interpretation, we would have to isolate the beginning of verse 14 from its end, such that "*the seven princes*, etc." is not summarizing the preceding list of names, but is resuming the story-line directly from verse 13. This solution would not however solve the problem of Memucan being explicitly identified by our midrash as Haman.[184]

Memucan Is Haman

> "*What shall we do to the queen Vashti according to the law*" (Esther 1:15).
>
> The king began to say to them: What do you say should be done?[185]
>
> And of them all, none but Memucan replied, as it says: "*And Memucan answered*" (Esther 1:16).[186]

This comment, found only in the Yemenite texts, is interpolated from *Panim Aḥerim* B[187] where it introduces a comment similar to that which follows in the Babylonian Esther-Midrash.

The Esther-Midrash now continues, explicating the next verse:

> [12b] "*And Memucan answered, before the king and the princes, Vashti the queen hath not done wrong to the king only*" (Esther 1:16).

---

184 See our comments above on the reading of the First Targum. It is not impossible that the compiler was applying the "shewbread" tradition to Marsena, thereby leaving "Memucan" free to be identified with Haman.

185 "should be done" —**AgE**: "that I should do." This is the reading in *Panim aḥerim* B (see below).

186 "'*What...*' ...answered"—Only in MS **Y** and **AgE**; ~ in all other witnesses.

187 Ed. Buber, 61.

> It teaches{in a *baraita*}: Memucan is Haman.[188] And why is his name called Memucan? —Because he was designated [*mukhan*][189] for misfortune.

This comment derives from the midrashic rule of "retreat from anonymity,"[190] which assumes that Scripture would not have taken the trouble to introduce and identify minor and ephemeral characters unless these individuals were actually the same as better-known figures who, for some reason, are being referred to by other names.[191] In the present instance, "Memucan" is taken to be a designation for Haman, [192] under the assumption that he was preordained[193] or fated for misfortune or punishment.[194] Whether this means that he was[195] predestined to a life of evil, or that his own wicked ways were assured

---

188 "Memucan is Haman"—**HgT¹**: "Haman is Memucan."

189 "*mukhan*"—MSS **G**, **P**, **HgT¹**: "*memukhan*." We note below that some commentators base the exegesis on the *ketib* "מומכן."

190 The phrase is taken from Heinemann, *Darkhei ha-'aggadah*, 13, 21, etc. The description of this midrashic assumption is found on pp. 28-31. See also Joseph Heinemann, *Aggadah and its Development*, 57.

191 On the assumption that one name is real and the other a descriptive epithet, see our remarks at the beginning of Chapter Three.

192 This view is shared by the First Targum to Esther (which adds the detail of his Agagite lineage, apparently to explain his inclusion in the list of princes). Maharsha's attempt to link the Haman-Memucan equation to an exposition of the initial letters of words in Psalms 22:21 is farfetched. The identification is mentioned by Ibn Ezra in his second commentary here; see B. Walfish, "The Two Commentaries of Abraham Ibn Ezra on the Book of Esther," 337.

193 For similar instances of biblical personages who are depicted as "preordained" (מותקן) to their respective roles, see *Genesis rabbah*, 30:6 [pp. 274-5], *Esther rabbah*, 6:3, and parallels; the pericope is discussed in: E. L. Segal, "'The Same from Beginning to End'—On the Development of a Midrashic Homily," 158-65.

194 The ambiguity of the rabbinic "פורענות," which can denote either retribution, misfortune or generic evil, is a common a common source of difficulty in interpreting midrashic sources. Note e.g. the use in Sifre Numbers 91 (ed. Horovitz, p. 92), where פורענות appears as the equivalent of רעה ("*wretchedness*") in a paraphrase of Numbers 11:15 [The instance is noted by A. Bendavid, *Biblical Hebrew and Mishnaic Hebrew*, 1:334, 363].

195 Presumably, as the heir to Amalek.

of bringing upon him an appropriate retribution, is not clarified by the midrash.[196]

Not all rabbinic traditions accept the identification of Memucan with Haman. Other opinions, accepting the need to provide some identification, claim that it is Daniel;[197] others apparently see no necessity at all for linking Memucan with other biblical personages.[198]

---

196 Cf. Maharsha who treats of the possibilities that (a) he was ordained to be punished by hanging; (b) he would bring misfortune upon others (Vashti, the Jews, etc.). The *ʿEṣ yosef* to **EY** is overly literal-minded in raising the question of why Haman is not called Memucan in other appropriate passages as well.

197 Thus in the Second Targum to Esther 1:15 and *Panim aḥerim* B, 61 [in the previous verse there he is identified as being "from Jerusalem." This detail is also mentioned in *Abba gorion*, 17, without any explicit mention of Daniel]. The Targum and *Panim aḥerim* add a variation on the "designated" etymology, namely that Daniel had been preordained to be the vehicle of Vashti's execution. This interpretation would presumably tie in with Samuel's dictum in *Esther rabbah*, 4:3 that these same princes had served in the court of Belshazzar [Radal, Maharzu and *Yefeh ʿanaf* explain that this was derived from the epithet (Esther 1:14) "*which sat the* first *in the kingdom*"]. The identification of Memucan with Daniel is also cited in the name of a "midrash" by the *Tosafot*, who add that his advice to have Vashti executed was occasioned by his own inability to govern his overbearing wife. The only early source that resembles the Tosafot's "midrash" is the Second Targum to Esther 1:16: "and Memucan had married a Persian woman who was wealthier than himself, and she would agree to speak to him only in her own tongue. So Memucan said to himself that he would seek a pretext to compel all women to give honor to their husbands." See Ginzberg, *Legends*, 4:377-8, 6:457, n. 43. It should however be noted that, although the Second Targum does state previously that Memucan was Daniel, it seems more likely that the tradition about Memucan's wife is a distinct unit, which takes the position that Memucan was a gentile prince [in that entire passage he is referred to without exception as Memucan, never as Daniel], deducing the story of his unfortunate marriage from the (otherwise irrelevant) particulars of the royal decree in Esther 1:17 and 20.

Pirqei derabbi eliʿezer contains the following remarkable passage (end of Ch. 49; transl. Friedlander, 394):

> R. Zechariah says: Merit is transmitted through the meritorious. Through Daniel, who was Memucan [the last phrase is missing in Friedlander's MS; see the discussion in his note 7] the kingdom was transferred to Esther. Because he said to the king: Do not cry, for all that you have done to Vashti you have done in accordance with the Torah, and whoever observes (the precepts of) the Torah, the Holy

Continued on next page...

A Commoner Jumps to the Front

[12b] Says R. Abba bar[199] Kahana:[200] From this {you learn} that a commoner jumps to the front.

Our midrash presumes that the order in which the names[201] are enumerated reflects their relative importance.[202] Hence the fact that

...Continued from previous page

One establishes their kingdom; for such is it written in the Torah: "*and he shall rule over thee*" (Genesis 3:16).

This last snippet of male chauvinism, which assigns a death penalty for spousal [as distinct from royal] disobedience, has no parallel in classical rabbinic literature, and may have some bearing on identifying the work's provenance.

On Daniel's being designated as the instrument for Babylonia's fall, cf. *Genesis rabbah*, 99:2 (p. 1237) and *Tanḥuma*, *Vayḥi*, 14 (ed. Buber, 13, p. 219), based on Daniel 7:4. None of these sources mention any specific association with Vashti. In fact, the only sources cited by Ginzberg (*Legends*, 6:457, nn. 44-5) for a "personal antipathy" (*ibid.*, 4:378) between Daniel and Vashti are from medieval Yemenite anthologies. Note in particular **AgE**, p. 15: "...And why is [Daniel] referred to as Memucan? —Some say that he invoked upon her the Divine Name until she became blemished, for thus it is written: '*and Mumcan* [Thus in the *ketib*; expounded from the word "*mum*" (blemish); cf. *Leqaḥ ṭov*, 93, where the *ketib* is expounded as proof that he had been pre-ordained for misfortune] *answered*.'" On the character of Yemenite midrashic traditions see: Liebermann, Saul, *Yemenite Midrashim*, second ed. (Jerusalem: Wahrmann, 1970).

198 This would appear to be true of *Esther rabbah*, 4:6, which makes no reference to Haman, though several of the insulting comments towards the end of the pericope (including allusions to his wife) may reflect such an identification. A similar passage is found in *Abba gorion*, 17. Ginzberg paraphrases these passages in *Legends*, 4:394 with "Haman" as the subject, but remarks in 6:463, n. 97, that "These sources do not state explicitly the identity of Memucan and Haman, but they seem to presuppose it." In general (see previous notes) one can assume that several of the midrashic comments which in their present contexts appear to be speaking of Haman or Daniel were originally about an "actual" Memucan.

199 "R. Abba bar"—**Printings** and **AgE**: "Rav"; (thus in **AgE** ed. Buber; the words are found in MS Oxford).

200 "bar Kahana"— ~ in MS **Mf**.

201 The comment assumes that they are names of people, in contradistinction to the previous exegesis. See our observations above. That the least of the company should be allowed to speak first is however the recommended procedure in a Jewish sanhedrin trying a capital case, in order to prevent the junior judges from being influenced by their superiors (see Mishnah *Sanhedrin* 4:8), a point which is taken up by R. Jacob Reischer in his *ʿIyyun yaʿaqov* to **EY**. He does not seem aware that precisely this

Continued on next page...

Memucan, the lowliest of the company,[203] is the only one of the group to volunteer an answer is regarded as a sign of his effrontery.[204] The remark about the commoner jumping to the front has the ring of a popular proverb.[205]

There is no necessary connection or dependence between R. Abba bar Kahana's comment and the identification of Memucan as Haman.

"Every Man Should Bear Rule in His Own House"

[12b] "...*That every man should bear rule in his own house...*" (Esther 1:22).

...Continued from previous page

question is raised in *TP Sanhedrin* 4:8 (22b) and *Esther rabbah*, 4:6, where our verse is cited in a debate (between R. Joḥanan and Resh Laqish) about whether gentile courts followed the Jewish procedures; see *Mattenot kehunnah* to *Esther rabbah*. Rabbi M. Margalit in the *Mar'eh happanim* commentary to the *TP* passage observes that the premise there contradicts that of our midrash. The Second Targum to Esther 1:16 states clearly that Memucan (=Daniel) was following accepted court practice in speaking first. See Ginzberg, *Legends*, 6:456, n. 42.

202 On the importance attached by midrashic exegesis to the ordering of items in scripture see Heinemann, *Darkhei ha-'aggadah*, 99, 108.

Virtually identical phraseology is employed in *Esther rabbah*, 4:6. In *Panim aḥerim* B the deduction is made without the proverb. In *Abba gorion*, 17, the observation is contained in the question: "What did Memucan see that he jumped to offer counsel?"

203 On the ἰδώτης, see Kohut, 3:183-4; Ziegler, *Die Königsgleichnisse des Midrasch*, 2

204 Thus Rashi, *Mattenot kehunnah* and *Yefeh ʿanaf* to *Esther rabbah*, 4:6, etc. In *Panim aḥerim* B, 61: "...He was the last of them, and yet he responded first." The *ʿIyyun yaʿaqov* connects this comment to traditions (?) about Haman's tree being prepared since the days of Creation.

205 Thus Ginzberg, *Legends*, 4:394: "the popular adage." I have not been able to find a proverb, whether from ancient or subsequent literatures, that conveys precisely the same sense. Pope's "Fools rush in where angels fear to tread" is hardly appropriate, nor is Bernard Malamud's *Idiot's First* (a play on "women and children first"). Cf. Matthew 19:30 *et al.*

> Says Rava:[206] Were it not for the first letters, there would not have survived from the "enemies of Israel" any who would remain or escape.[207]
>
> What did he send to them?[208] —"...*That every man should bear rule in his own house*..."[209] [210] This is obvious![211] [212] [213] Even[214] a bald man in his own home is like a captain!

The general sense of this comment is quite clear: The fact that Ahasuerus had to issue an edict proclaiming so obvious a principle as the husband's authority in the home served to call into question the king's intelligence and credibility. This episode would eventually be turned to the Jews' advantage, when the population did not hasten to obey the edict calling for the annihilation of the Jews.[215] Interestingly, this confident expression of unchallenged patriarchal supremacy appears to be unique to the Babylonian Talmud, having no equivalent in the Palestinian midrashim to Esther. It might reflect a typically oriental family structure not shared by the Jews of Palestine. The interpretation also strengthens the impression, implicit in the biblical narrative itself,

---

206 "Rava"—MSS **G**, **W**, **Ashkenazic family**: "R. Abba bar Kahana"; MS **B**, **YS**: "R. Abba"; **AgE**: "Rav"; MS **P**: "Rabbah."

207 The phrase is taken from Joshua 8:22; Jeremiah 42:17; 44:14; Lamentations 2:22.

208 "What...them?"—MSS **G**, **W**, **EY**, **HgT**[2]: "They say: What is it that he sends [corrupted in **EY** to "permitted" (דשדר → דשרי)] to us?"; MS **B**: "What is written in the first letters?"; MSS **O**, **P**, **HgT**[1]: "What is written in them?"; MS **M**: "They said: What did he send to them?"; MS **R**, **YS**: "He sent to them"; MS **Mf**: "They said: What is that which he is sending?"; **Printings**: "They say: "What is this that he sends [**Pesaro**: "permits"] to us?"

209 MSS **G**, **W**, **L**, **HgT**[2] add: "They say"; MS **Mf**, **YS** and Genizah fragment add: "They said"; MS **R** adds: "What did he say?"

210 MS **B** adds: "Why does he have to say this?"

211 "This is obvious"— ~ in MS **M** and Genizah fragment.

212 "'...*That every*...'...obvious"— ~ in **AgE**.

213 MSS **B**, **P**, **EY** add: "for."

214 "Even"— ~ in MSS **G**, **B** and **W**.

215 Rashi: "They would have hurried to murder them in obedience to the royal command of the middle letters [i.e., those of Esther 3:13-5], without waiting for the appointed date." See *ʿIyyun yaʿaqov*.

that the groundwork is being laid—even before the introduction of Haman's plot—for the fending off of the threat to the Jews.[216]

Similarly, the general sense of the cited proverb is easily understood: The lowliest of men wields absolute authority over his own household.[217] The precise meanings of the words are however obscure and the subject of disagreements among the commentators and lexicographers.[218]

---

216 It is not apparent whether the king's stupidity is being portrayed here as part of the divine guidance that directs the events in the story. See E. Segal, "Human Anger and Divine Intervention in Esther"; *ʿIyyun yaʿaqov*: "...This implies that it was God's hand in order to save the Jews."

217 The sentiment is of course implicit in the biblical text itself (1:22). An analogous adage in Hebrew is adduced in *Avot derabbi natan* A:28 [Solomon Schechter, ed., *Aboth de Rabbi Nathan*, newly corrected ed. (New York: Feldheim, 1967), 85], in the name of R. Simeon b. Gamaliel: "Whoever imposes peace in his household is considered by Scripture as if he had imposed peace on each and every one in Israel; and whoever imposes envy and dissension in Israel is counted as if he had imposed envy and dissension in Israel. For each and every one is a king in his own house, as it says: '*that every man should bear rule in his own house*.'" [The reading of the printed editions in *Genesis rabbah*, 12:10 "There is no place where a person is not in charge of his household" is not borne out by any of the reliable manuscripts; cf. Theodor-Albeck, 108, to l. 3 ff.] The point is similar (though much more explicitly "gender-specific") to that found in sayings such as Publilius Syrius' "Gallus in suo sterguilinio plurimum potest"; for a sampling of variations on that theme in the proverbs of other cultures, see: Walter K. Kelly, *A Collection of the Proverbs of All Nations* (Andover: Warren F. Draper, 1879), 34-6.

218 Hebrew or Aramaic *Qaraḥa* normally refers to a bald person. Rashi here chooses to render the word as "גרדן," "weaver" or "wool-dresser"; so too in J. Levy's *Wörterbuch über die Talmudim und Midraschim*, 4:102: "Weber." Kohut, *Aruch Completum*, 7:192, proposes a Persian derivation meaning "stupid," a theory which is rejected unceremoniously by B. Geiger, *Additamenta*, 374. Maharsha also expresses his amazement at Rashi's curious translation and cites several passages in which baldness is treated as an insult or liability (e.g. *TB Bekhorot* 58a).

The rare word (see also *TB Shabbat* 94a) פרדשכא (פרכשא in MS Y, פרדכשא in other witnesses) raises even more serious questions. In spite of attempts to assign it a Greek [e.g., the derivation from παρατάχις, "police," "soldier," proposed by J. Perles, *Etymologische Studien* (Breslau: 1871), 132; accepted by Jastrow, 1215-6, but not attested in standard Greek dictionaries] or Latin origin [see Benjamin Mussafia's gloss to the *Arukh*, ed. Kohut, 6:412, identifying it with "produx" (also not attested in this sense in the standard Latin dictionaries], the

Continued on next page...

Concluding Remarks

The treatment of Vashti's rebellion in the Babylonian Esther Midrash, though it is composed of several (usually) brief individual comments, demonstrates a remarkable measure of exegetical consistency[219] on a number of points. The most important of these is

...Continued from previous page

transliterations assumed by these etymologies are, to say the least, unlikely. Ultimately, the word has a decidedly Persian feel to it, a fact which prompted most lexicographers to look for a Persian derivation. Kohut, 6:412, equates it with the late Persian *pardaχtan* [basing himself on I. A. Vullers, *Lexicon Persico-Latinum Etymologicum*, reprint ed., Vol. 2 (Graz: Akademische Druck-U. Verlagsanstalt, 1962)], meaning "to complete work," which he fancifully connects with a high official. The word in question is actually a verb denoting "be done with, freed of," or "accomplish," [see D. N. MacKenzie, *A Concise Pahlavi Dictionary* (London, New York and Toronto: Oxford University Press, 1971), 64-5] none of which senses have any meaningful relevance to our context. H. Fleischer, in his "Nachträge" to J. Levy's *Wörterbuch über die Talmudim und Midraschim*, 4:102 (Fleischer's comments are on 4:228) also points to a Persian root *bar-shuda(k)* meaning "to rise" or "to raise" [cf. MacKenzie, 1], but he too cannot indicate a nominal use of the root. Perles, *Etymologische Studien*, 132 [the proposal is seconded by S. Krauss, "Notes and Corrections" to *Aruch Completum* vol. 8, 68] tries to link it to *shah*, or *padshah*, "king." [cf. W. Bacher, *Die Agada der babylonischen Amoräer*, 125]. Distinguished Iranologist B. Geiger, in his contributions to Krauss' *Additamenta* to the *Aruch Completum*, 336, rejects all these theories as untenable, hesitantly preferring an etymology based on the Syriac דחשא, "constable" or "footman" with the Persian prefix *fra* or *par*, indicating a rank above that of the דחשא.

Geiger's rejection of Perles' explanation is based largely on its inappropriateness to the *TB Shabbat* context. It is not at all obvious however that it is the same word which appears in both pericopes, and in light of the textual evidence here, with the superior MS **Y** reading פרכשא , it does not seem unreasonable to propose a trivial emendation producing פדכשא, *padiχsha(y)*, "ruler; powerful, authoritative, authorized," rendered by the Aramaic ideogram *ShLYṬ'* [thus according to MacKenzie, 63]. This meaning is certainly more appropriate to the context of our passage, in which an extreme contrast between lowest and highest social ranks is expected, than an allusion to an intermediary functionary. And, once we have allowed ourselves to emend *R*s for *D*s, may we also suggest with much greater hesitancy that *qaraḥa* might be changed to *qadaḥa*, which might derive from Pahlavi *kadagig*, "domestic servant" (MacKenzie, 48). The contrast that would thereby be produced between the lowly servant and the mighty ruler would aptly convey the point of the adage.

219 The selection of midrashic interpretations in this section does not however appear to have been proposed with a view to presenting an internally consistent retelling of the story, since the redactors appear to have had no qualms about leaving in mutually con-

Continued on next page...

the uncompromising determination of the rabbis to depict her as a wicked and immoral villain,[220] in spite of the fact that the biblical facts taken by themselves would be susceptible to a favorable evaluation.[221] In this Vashti may be contrasted with Ahasuerus himself, whose deeds and personality, though usually painted in malevolent or ludicrous colors, nevertheless elicited sympathy or admiration from at least some of the Jewish sages who attempted to discern elements of political shrewdness and social grace in the arrangements of the magnificent banquet. The reasons for the differences in the treatments of the two monarchs can probably be accounted for not so much by exegetical factors, but by the respective roles which they filled as historical and eschatological archetypes. Vashti, as was emphasized already in the Proems, is the last remnant of the royal house of Babylonia[222] and it is through her that Nebuchadnezzar, the arch-fiend who destroyed God's Holy Temple, will finally receive his delayed (if vicarious) retribution[223]—though, to be sure, she deserves punishment for her own sins as well. For Jews in talmudic times[224] this enmity would be transferred as well to the latter-day cohorts of Nebuchadnezzar, the Romans who had laid waste the second Temple and whose punishment had yet to be exacted. By contrast, Ahasuerus was the heir of Media and Persia,[225] "friendly" conquerors who had put an end to Babylonian

...Continued from previous page

tradictory traditions; e.g., the name "Memucan" is given both a symbolic and a narrative interpretation.

220 This involves not only sexual licentiousness, but also the blasphemy of forcing Jewish maidens to desecrate the sabbath.

221 In light of her alleged sexual immorality, the midrash has to make a special effort to account for her declining an opportunity for immodest exhibitionism.

222 We are reminded of this detail when Vashti taunts Ahasuerus for having been her father's stable-keeper.

223 Historical justice thus requires that Vashti be killed for her disobedience, a detail which is not spelled out in the biblical account.

224 Who are vicariously represented in ancient Shushan by the anachronistic rabbis of the Sanhedrin who maintain a constant and effective presence in the background of the events.

hegemony and set in motion the Return to Zion. During the Talmudic era Jews, especially those of subjugated Palestine, would look hopefully to Persia as a potential ally and the only military power with a realistic hope of overthrowing the Roman yoke.[226]

The individual comments[227] about Vashti thus coalesce into a complex but consistent picture which goes far beyond her function in the biblical story, where her role is primarily to make room for Esther. In the midrash Vashti herself has become a central character, a fiend not only by virtue of her own immoralities and religious outrages, but primarily as the last remnant of the wicked dynasty of Nebuchadnezzar. For these reasons she will face a fittingly humiliating

...Continued from previous page

225 See Samuel Krauss, *Paras veromi batalmud uvamidrashim*; Salo W. Baron, *A Social and Religious History of the Jews*, second revised ed., Vol. 2 (New York and London: Columbia University Press, 1962), 95-6; Gedaliah Alon, *The Jews in their Land in the Talmudic Age*, Vol. 1, 14-6.

226 An analogous phenomenon might be discernible in the midrashic descriptions of Ishmael and Esau. Both these figures, as depicted in Genesis, are morally and religiously ambivalent. The rabbinic tradition reflects some of this ambivalence in its retelling of the life of Ishmael [e.g., Ginzberg, *Legends*, 1:265-9], whose descendants did not play a particularly central role in Jewish affairs [but cf. Baron, *ibid.*, 92]; however Esau, who arguably had a much stronger claim to sympathetic treatment, seing how he eventually forgave Jacob for tricking him out of his blessing, is nevertheless condemned and "slandered" almost without exception, by virtue of the fact that later generations had come to regard him as the embodiment of the Roman evil [Much material in this spirit is collected by Ginzberg, 1:316 ff.].

227 A. Weiss, *Studies in the Literature of the Amoraim*, 284, remarks that the section is dominated primarily by Rava's dicta, with other tannaitic and amoraic material being included through secondary association. Looking at the material examined in Chapters 5 and 6 of our study as a single unit, he concludes that the pericope originated in a brief explanatory midrash by Rav and Samuel, which was subsequently expanded by Rava. According to Weiss (290-1), this pattern characterizes the Esther-Midrash as a whole, with Rava's expositions being much more elaborate than those of Rav and Samuel, which he was utilizing (and may have redacted in a preliminary manner) along with some of the other traditions from the earlier strata. While Weiss' observations are generally valid as regards the Babylonian components of the midrash, they do not give full credit to the Palestinian materials which occupy such a central place, suggesting that the Babylonian rabbis were expanding a midrash that had already undergone a decisive organization (perhaps including the Rav and Samuel traditions) in the Land of Israel.

end, ordered to publicly degrade herself, given an embarrassing disfigurement. The rabbinic principle of "measure for measure" is made to operate with great effectiveness.

Bibliography

Abramson, Shraga, ed. *Tractate 'Abodah Zarah of the Babylonian Talmud, Ms. Jewish Theological Seminary of America.* New York: The Jewish Theological Seminary of America, 1957.

Albeck, Ch., ed. *Midrash bereshit rabbati.* Jerusalem: 1940.

---------"Sof hora'ah vesiyyum ha-talmud." In *Sinai sefer yovel*, ed. J. L. Maimon. 73-79. Jerusalem: Mossad Harav Kook, 1958.

---------*Einleitung und Register zum Bereschit Rabba.* Second Printing ed., Vol. 1: Einleitung. Veröffentlichen der Akademie für die Wissenschaft des Judentums, Jerusalem: Wahrmann, 1965.

---------*Introduction to the Talmud, Babli and Yerushalmi.* Tel-Aviv: Dvir, 1969.

---------*Meḥqarim bivrayta vetosefta veyaḥasan lattalmud.* 2nd ed., Jerusalem: Mossad Harav Kook, 1969.

Alkabetz, Solomon. *Manot hallevi.* reprint ed., Jerusalem: 1983.

Alon, G. *Toledot ha-yehudim be'eretz yisra'el bitqufat ha-mishnah veha-talmud.* fourth ed., Vol. 2. [Israel]: Hakibutz Hameuchad, 1975.

---------*The Jews in their Land in the Talmudic Age.* Vol. 1. Translated by Gershon Levi. Jerusalem: The Magnes Press, 1980.

Aptowitzer, V. *Introductio at Sefer Rabiah.* Jerusalem: Mekize Nirdamim, 1938.

Arieh b. Asher. *Ṭurei Even.* Vol. Megillah. Vilna: 1836.

Avi-Yonah, M. *The Jews of Palestine: A Political History from the Bar Kokhba War to the Arab Conquest.* Translated by M. Avi-Yonah. New York: Schocken Books, 1976.

Azulai, H. D. *Petaḥ fiEinayim.* Livorno: 1790.

Bacher, B. Z. (W.) *Aggadat amora'ei eretz yisra'el.* Tel-Aviv: 1930.

---------*Die Agada der palästinensichen Amoräer.* Vol. 1. Strassburg: 1892-99.

---------"Talmud." In *The Jewish Encyclopedia*, ed. I. Singet et al. 1-27. 12. New York and London: Funk and Wagnalls, 1907.

---------*Die Agada der babylonischen Amoräer.* Frankfurt a/M: 1913.

---------*Die Proömien der alten jüdischen Homilie.* Leipzig: 1913.

---------*Tradition und Tradenten.* Leipzig: 1914.

Bacher, W. and M. Schwab. "Vocabulaire de l'Angelogie." MGWJ 42 (1898): 25-258, 570-2.

Bar-Asher, Moshe, ed. *Qovetz ma'amarim bil'shon ḥaza"l.* Vol. 2. Jerusalem: [Akademon], 1980.

Baron, Salo W. *A Social and Religious History of the Jews.* second revised ed., Vol. 2. New York and London: Columbia University Press, 1962.

Barth, Lewis M. "Literary Imagination and the Rabbinic Sermon: Some Observations." In *Seventh World Congress of Jewish Studies in Jerusalem*, edited by D. Krone, World Union of Jewish Studies, 29–35, Year.

Basser, Herbert. *Midrashic Interpretations of the Song of Moses.* Vol. 2. American University Studes: Series 7, Theology and Religion, New York, Frankfort on the Main, Berne: Peter Lang, 1984.

---------"Pesher Hadavar: The Truth of the Matter." Revue de Qumran 13 (1988): 389-8.

Beer, Moshe "Lish'elat shiḥruram shel amora'ei bavel mittashlum missim umekhes." Tarbiẓ 33 (1964): 248-58.

---------*The Babylonian Amoraim: Aspects of Economic Life*. Ramat-Gan: Bar-Ilan University Press, 1974.

Ben-Ḥayyim, Z. "Mesoret ha-shomeronim veziqqatah limsoret ha-lashon shel megillot yam ha-melaḥ velilshon ḥaza"l." Leshonenu 22 (1958): 223-45.

Ben-Yehudah, E. *Thesaurus Totius Hebraicæ et Veteris et recentioris*. Complete International Centennial ed., New York and London: Thomas Yoseloff, 1960.

Bendavid, A. *Biblical Hebrew and Mishnaic Hebrew*. revised expanded ed., Vol. 1. Tel-Aviv: Dvir, 1967.

---------*Biblical Hebrew and Mishnaic Hebrew*. Vol. II. Tel-Aviv: Dvir, 1971.

Bietenhard, Hans, ed. *Der Tannaitische Midrasch Sifre Deuteronomium*. Berlin, New York: Peter Lang, 1984.

Bloch, P. "Studien zur Aggadah." MGWJ 34-5 (1885-6): 34:166-84, 210-24, 257-69, 385-404; 35:165-87, 389-405.

Boyarin, Daniel. "Rhetoric and Interpretation: The Case of the Nimshal." Prooftexts 5 (1985): 269-76.

---------*Intertextuality and the Reading of Midrash*. Indiana Studies in Biblical Literature, Bloomington: Indiana University Press, 1990.

---------"The Song of Songs: Lock or Key? Intertextuality, Allegory and Midrash." In *The Book and the Text: The Bible and Literary Theory*, ed. Regina M. Schwartz. 214–30. Oxford: Basil Blackwell, 1990.

Boyce, Mary. "Iranian Festivals." In *The Cambridge History of Iran*, ed. Ehsan Yarshater. 792-815. 3 (2). Cambridge, etc.: Cambridge University Press, 1983.

Braude, W. G., ed. *Pesikta Rabbati*. Yale Judaica Series. New Haven and London: Yale University Press, 1968.

--------- ed. *The Midrash on Psalms*. 3rd ed., Yale Judaica Series. New Haven: Yale University Press, 1976.

Braude, W. G. and I. J. Kapstein. *Pesiḳta de-Rab Kahana*. Philadelphia: Jewish Publication Society of America, 1975.

Braverman, Jay. *Jerome's Commentary on Daniel: A Study of Comparative Jewish and Christian Interpretations of the Hebrew Bible*. Vol. 7. The Catholic Biblical Quarterly Monograph Series, ed. B. Vawter et al. Washington: The Catholic Biblical Association of America, 1978.

Bregman, Marc. "Past and Present in Midrashic Literature." Hebrew Annual Review 2 (1978): 45–59.

---------"Circular Proems and Proems Beginning with the Formula '*Zo hi shene'emra beruaḥ haq-qodesh*'." In *Studies in Aggadah, Targum and Jewish Liturgy in Memory of Joseph Heinemann*, ed. J. Petuchowski and E. Fleischer. 34-51 (Hebrew section). Jerusalem: The Magnes Press, Hebrew Union College Press, 1981.

---------"The Triennial Hafṭarot and the Perorations of the Midrashic Homilies." JJS 32 (1981): 74-84.

---------"Early Sources and Traditions in the Tanḥuma–Yelammedenu Midrashim." Tarbiẓ 60 (1991): 269-74.

Bright, John. *A History of Israel*. 2nd ed., Philadelphia: The Westminster Press, 1972.

---------ed. *Jeremiah*. The Anchor Bible. Garden City: Doubleday & Co. Inc., 1988.

Brown, F., S. R. Driver, and C. A. Briggs. *The New Brown-Driver-Briggs-Gesenius Hebrew and English Lexicon.* Lafayette: Associated Publishers and Authors, Inc., 1980.

Brüll, N. "Die Entstehungsgeschichte des babylonischen Talmuds als Schriftwerkes." Jahrbücher für jüdische Geschichte und Literatur 2 (1876): 1-123.

Bruns, Gerald L. "Midrash and Allegory: The Beginnings of Scriptural Interpretation." In *The Literary Guide to the Bible*, ed. Robert Alter and Frank Kermode. 625-46. Cambridge, Mass.: The Belknap Press of Harvard University Press, 1987.

---------"The Hermeneutics of Midrash." In *The Book and the Text: The Bible and Literary Theory*, ed. Regina M. Schwartz. 189–213. Oxford: Basil Blackwell, 1990.

Buber, Solomon, ed. *Midrash Tanḥuma.* Vilna: 1885.

--------- ed. *Sifre de-aggadeta al megillat ester.* Vilna: Romm, 1886.

---------ed. *Midrash tehillim.* Vilna: 1891.

--------- ed. *Midrash mishlei.* Vilna: 1893.

--------- ed. *Midrash Zuṭa.* Berlin: 1894.

---------ed. *Midrasch Echa Rabbati.* Wilna: Wittwe & Gebrüder Romm, 1899.

---------ed. *Midrash sekhel tov by R. Menahem b. Solomon.* Berlin: 1900-01.

--------- ed. *Aggadat Bereshit.* Cracow: Fischer, 1902.

--------- ed. *Midrash zuṭa 'al shir ha-shirim rut eikhah veqohelet.* Vilna: 1925.

Chajes, Z. P., ed. *Perush masekhet mashqin lerabbi shelomo ben hayyatom.* 2nd ed., Jerusalem: 1910.

Cogan, M. and H. Tadmor, ed. *II Kings.* The Anchor Bible. Garden City: Doubleday & Co. Inc., 1988.

Dan, Joseph. *The Hebrew Story in the Middle Ages.* Sifriyyat Keter, Jerusalem: Keter, 1974.

Daube, David. "Rabbinic Methods of Interpretation and Hellenistic Rhetoric." HUCA 22 (1949): 239–65.

De-Vries, B. "Ha-sugim ha-sifrutiyyim shel ha-'aggadah." In *Meḥqarim besifrut ha-talmud*, ed. E. Z. Melammed. 290-9. Jerusalem: Mossad Harav Kook, 1968.

--------- "Ofyah ha-sifruti shel ha-'aggadah." In *Meḥqarim besifrut ha-talmud*, ed. E. Z. Melammed. 284–9. Jerusalem: Mossad Harav Kook, 1968.

Ditrani, Isaiah. *Tosefot rid.* reprint ed., Jerusalem: 1974.

Dommerhausen, Werner. *Die Estherrolle: Stil und Ziel einer altestamentlichen Schrift.* Stuttgarten Biblische Monographen, ed. J. Hospecker and W. Pesch. Stuttgart: Katholisches Bibelwerk, 1968.

Duchesne-Guillemin, Jacques. "Les Noms des Eunuques d'Assuérus." Muséon 66 (1953): 105-8.

Dunsky, Samson, ed. *Midrash rabbah: Esther.* Montreal: Northern Printing and Lithographing Company, 1962.

---------ed. *Midrash shir ha-shirim: midrash ḥazita.* Jerusalem and Tel Aviv: Dvir, 1980.

Ehrenreich, S., ed. *Sefer even ha'ezer, hu' sefer ra'avan.* reprint ed., Jerusalem: 1975.

Eichholz, D. E., ed. *Pliny Natural History.* Vol. 10. The Loeb Classical Library. London and Cambridge (Mass.): William Heinemann Ltd. and Harvard University Press, 1962.

Einhorn, Ze'ev Wolf. "Maharzu." In *Midrash Rabbah*, Vilna: Rom, 1878.

Eisenstein, J. D., ed. *Ozar Midrashim: Bibliotheca Midraschica.* Reprint ed., [Israel]: 1969.

Elon, M. *Jewish Law: History, Sources, Principles.* Jerusalem: The Magnes Press, 1973.

Enelow, H. G., ed. *The Mishnah of R. Eliezer; or the Midrash of Thirty-Two Hermeneutical Rules.* New York: Bloch, 1933.

Epstein, J. N. "Zur babylonisch-aramäischen Lexikographie." In *Festschrift Adolf Schwartz*, 317-27. Berlin and Vienna: 1917.

---------*Mavo' lenosaḥ ha-mishnah.* Jerusalem: Magnes Press, 1948.

---------*Prolegomena ad Litteras Tannaiticas.* Tel Aviv and Jerusalem: The Magnes Press and Dvir, 1957.

---------*A Grammar of Babylonian Aramaic.* Jerusalem and Tel-Aviv: Magnes Press and Dvir, 1960.

---------*Introduction to Amoraitic Literature.* ed. E. Z. Melamed. Tel Aviv and Jerusalem: Dvir and Magnes Press, 1962.

---------ed. *The Gaonic Commentary on the Order Toharot Attributed to rav Hay Gaon.* Jerusalem and Tel-Aviv: Dvir and Magnes Press, 1982.

---------*Studies in Talmudic Literature and Semitic Languages.* Translated by Z. Epstein. Jerusalem: Magnes Press, 1983.

Epstein, J. N. and E. Z. Melamed, ed. *Mekhilta d'rabbi šimfion b. jochai.* Jerusalem: Mekize Nirdamim, 1955.

Esh, S. *(הק(בה Der Heilige <Er sei gepriesen>.* Leiden: 1957.

Faur, Jose. *Golden Doves with Silver Dots: Semiotics and Textuality in Rabbinic Tradition.* Bloomington: Indiana University Press, 1986.

Federbush, S. *Bintivot ha-talmud.* 2nd ed., Jerusalem: Mossad Garav Kook, 1983.

Feldblum, Meyer S. "Prof. Abraham Weiss: His Approach and Contribution to Talmudic Scholarship." In *The Abraham Weiss Jubilee Volume*, ed. S. Belkin et al. 7-80. New York: Shulsinger Bros., 1964.

---------*Dikduke Sopherim Tractate Gittin.* New York: Horeb, Yeshiva University, 1966.

Feliks, Yehuda. *Mixed Sowing Breeding and Grafting: Kil'ayim I-II, Mishna, Tosephta and Jerusalem Talmud, a Study of the Halachic Topics and Their Botanical-Agricultural Background.* Bar-Ilan University Series of Research Monographs in Memory of...Pinkhos Churgin, Tel Aviv: Dvir, 1967.

Fillipowsky, Z., ed. *Yuhasin (Hashalem) by R. Abraham Zakut.* Frankfort a/M: 1925.

Finkelstein, Louis, ed. *Siphre ad Deuteronomium.* Corpus Tannaiticum. Berlin: Abteilung Verlag, 1939.

---------*Ha-perushim ve-'anshei keneset ha-gedolah.* New York: Jewish Theological Seminary of America, 1950.

Flusser, David, ed. *Josippon: The Original Version; MS Jerusalem 8º 41280 and Supplements.* Vol. 49. Texts and Studies for Students "Kuntresim" Project. Jerusalem: The Zalman Shazar Center, 1978.

---------"Mishlei yeshu veha-meshalim besifrut ḥaza"l." In *Jewish Sources in Early Christianity: Studies and Essays*, ed. H. Safrai. 150-209. 2nd ed., Vol. Tel-Aviv: Sifriyyat Po'alim, 1979.

---------ed. *The Josippon (Joseph Gorionides).* Vol. 1. Jerusalem: Mosad Bialik, 1979-81.

Fox, Harry. "The Circular Proem Composition: Terminology and Antecedents." PAAJR 49 (1982): 1-33.

Fraade, Steven D. "Interpreting Midrash 1: Midrash and the History of Judaism." Prooftexts 7 (1987): 179-94.

---------"Interpreting Midrash 2: Midrash and Its Literary Contexts." Prooftexts 7 (1987): 284–300.

---------*From Tradition To Commentary: Torah and Its Interpretation in the Midrash Sifre to Deuteronomy*. SUNY Series in Judaica: Hermeneutics, Mysticism, and Religion, ed. R. Goldenberg M. Fishbane A. Green. Albany: State University of New York Press, 1991.

Fraenkel, Jonah. "Hermeneutical Questions in the Study of the Aggadic Narrative." Tarbiz 47 (1977-8): 139–172.

---------*Darkhei ha-aggadah veha-midrash*. Yad Ha-Talmud, ed. E. E. Urbach. Givatayim: Massadah, 1991.

---------"The Image of Rabbi Joshua ben Levi in the Stories of the Babylonian Talmud." In *Sixth World Congress of Jewish Studies in Jerusalem*, edited by Avigdor Shinan, World Union of Jewish Studies, 403-17, Year.

Freedman, H. and Maurice Simon. *The Midrash*. Vol. 9. London: Soncino Press, 1939.

Friedlander, G., ed. *Pirke de rabbi eliezer*. 4th ed., New York: Sepher-Hermon Press, 1981.

Friedman, Shamma. "A Critical Study of *Yevamot X* with a Methodological Introduction." In *Texts and Studies, Analecta Judaica*, ed. H. Z. Dimitrovsky. 275-442. 1. New York: The Jewish Theological Seminary of America, 1977.

---------"Some Structural Patterns of Talmudic *Sugiot*." In *Sixth World Congress of Jewish Studies in Jerusalem*, edited by A. Shinan, World Union of Jewish Studies, 389-402, Year.

Friedmann, [L.] M., ed. *Bavli masekhet makkot*. Vienna: 1858.

---------ed. *Seder Eliahu rabba und Seder Elidahu zuta (Tanna d'be Eliahu)*. Vienna: Achiasaf, 1902.

---------ed. *Pesikta rabbati*. Vienna: 1880.

Frye, Richard N. *The Heritage of Persia*. 2nd ed., History of Civilisation, London: Weidenfeld and Nicolson, 1965.

Fuerst, W. J., ed. *The Books of Ruth, Esther, Ecclesiastes, the Song of Songs, Lamentations: The Five Scrolls*. The Cambridge Bible Commentary. Cambridge, London, New York, Melbourne: Cambridge University Press, 1975.

Fürst, J. "Noten zu Midrasch Wajikra rabba." In *Der Midrasch Wajikra Rabba*, ed. A. Wünsche. 268-98. 26. Leipzig: Otto Schulze, 1884.

---------*Glossarium Graeco-Hebraeum*. Strassbourg: 1890-91.

Gadamer, Hans-Georg. *Truth and Meaning*. Translated by G. Barden and J. Cumming. New York: Crossroad Publishing, 1986.

Gafni, Isaiah. "Ha-yetzirah ha-ruh\anit-sifrutit." In *Eretz Israel: from the Destruction of the Second Temple to the Muslim Conquest*, ed. Tz. Baras, S.Safrai, Y. Tzafrir, and M. Stern. 473-94. 1. Jerusalem: Yad Yitzhaq ben-Tzvi, 1982.

---------*The Jews in Babylonia in the Talmudic Era: A Social and Cultural History*. Monographs in Jewish History, ed. A. Grossman et al. Jerusalem: Zalman Shazar Center, 1990.

Garsiel, Moshe. *Biblical Names: A Literary Study of Midrashic Derivations and Puns.* Translated by P. Hackett. Ramat Gan: Bar-Ilan University Press, 1991.

Gaster, M., ed. *The Mafiaseh Book.* Philadelphia: Jewish Publication Society of America, 1934.

---------ed. *The Exempla of the Rabbis.* 2nd ed., 1988.

Gehman, H. S. "Notes on the Persian Words in the Book of Esther." JBL 43 (1924): 321-8.

Geiger, Y. "Ha-mered bimei gallus ufarshat binyan ha-bayit bimei yulianos." In *Eretz Israel from the Destruction of the Second Temple to the Muslim Conquest*, ed. Z. Baras, S. Safrai, Y. Tsafrir, and M. Stern. 202-17. 1. Jerusalem: Yad Yitzhaq Ben-Tzvi, 1982.

Ginsberg, H. L. *Studies in Daniel.* Vol. 14. Texts and Studies of the Jewish Theological Seminary of America, New York: Jewish Theological Seminary, 1948.

Ginzberg, Louis. *Yerushalmi Fragments from the Genizah.* Vol. 1. Texts and Studies of the Jewish Theological Seminary of America, New York: The Jewish Theological Seminary of America, 1909.

---------Louis. *The Legends of the Jews.* Translated by H. Szold. Philadelphia: Jewish Publication Society of America, 1909-39.

---------Louis. "Die Haggada bei den Kirkenvätern, V." In *Abhandlungen zur Erinnerung an Hirsch Perez Chajes*, ed. A. Z. Schwarz and V. Aptowitzer. 22-50. Vienna: The Alexander Kohut Memorial Foundation, 1933.

---------Louis. "Jewish Folklore: East and West." In *On Jewish Law and Lore*, 61-76. Philadelphia: Jewish Publication Society of America, 1955.

Goldberg, Abraham. "review of B. Mandelbaum's edition of *pesiqta derab kahana*." Kiryat Sefer 43 (1967-8): 69-79.

---------*Commentary to the Mishnah Shabbat.* Jerusalem: The Jewish Theological Seminary of America, 1976.

---------ed. *Collected Talmudic Scientific Writings of Hyman Klein.* Jerusalem: Akademon, 1979.

Goldschmidt, L., ed. *The Babylonian Talmud Seder Nezikin Codex Hambourg 165 (19).* reprint of Berlin 1914 ed., Jerusalem: Makor, 1969.

Goodblatt, David. *Rabbinic Instruction in Sasanian Babylonia.* Studies in Judaism in Late Antiquity, ed. Jacob Neusner. Leiden: Brill, 1975.

Green, William Scott. "Romancing the Tome: Rabbinic Hermeneutics and the Theory of Literature." Semeia 40 (1987): 147–68.

Grossfeld, B., ed. *The First Targum to Esther: According to MS Paris Hebrew 110 of the Bibliotheque Nationale.* New York: Sepher-Hermon Press, 1983.

Gruenthaner, M. J. "The Last King of Babylon." CBQ 11 (1949): 406-427.

Grünhut, E., ed. *Midrash al yit-hallal.* Vol. 2. Sefer ha-liqquṭim. Jerusalem: 1898-1902.

Grünhut, E. and J. Ch. Wertheimer, ed. *Midrash shir hashirim.* 2nd ed., Jerusalem: Ktav Yad Vasefer Institute, 1981.

Halivni, David, ed. *A Commentary on the Palestinian Talmud by Louis Ginzberg.* Vol. 4. Texts and Studies of the Jewish Theological Seminary of America. New York: The Jewish Theological Seminary of America, 1961.

Halperin, Jehiel. *Seder hadorot.* Jerusalem: Reprint: 1956.

Halperin, Raphael. *Atlas 'Ets-Ḥayyim.* Vol. 4. Tel-Aviv: 1980.

Hammer, R., ed. *Sifre: The Tannaitic Commentary on the Book of Deuteronomy*. Vol. 24. Yale Judaica Series. New Haven: Yale University Press, 1986.

Handelman, Susan. *The Slayers of Moses: The Emergence of Rabbinic Interpretation in Modern Literary Theory*. Albany: State University of New York Press, 1982.

Handelman, Susan. "Fragments of the Rock: Contemporary Literary Theory and the Study of Rabbinic Texts—A Response to David Stern." Prooftexts 5 (1985): 75-103.

---------"'Everything is in it': Rabbinic Interpretation and Modern Literary Theory." Judaism 35 (4 1986): 429–40.

Haneman, Gideon. "Uniformization and Differentiation in the History of Two Hebrew Verbs." In *Archive of the New Dictionary of Rabbinic Literature*, ed. M. Z. Kaddari. 24-30. 2. Ramat-Gan: New Dictionary of Rabbinic Literature Project, Bar-Ilan University, 1974.

Harmon, A. M., ed. *Lucian*. Vol. 4. The Loeb Classical Library. Cambridge, Mass. and London: Harvard University Press and William Heinemann Ltd., 1953.

Harper, Prudence. "Sasanian Silver." In *The Cambridge History of Iran*, ed. Ehsan Yarshater. 1113-29. 3 (2). Cambridge etc.: Cambridge University Press, 1983.

Hartmann, Geoffrey and Sanford Budick, ed. *Midrash and Literature*. New Haven and London: Yale University Press, 1986.

Hartmann, L. F. and A. De Lella, ed. *The Book of Daniel*. Vol. 23. The Anchor Bible. Garden City, New York: Doubleday & Company, 1978.

Haupt, P. "Critical Notes on Esther." American Journal of Semitic Languages and Literature 24 (1907-8): 97-186.

Havelock, Eric A. *Preface to Plato*. Cambridge, MA: Belknap Press of Harvard University Press, 1963.

Heimann, D., I. Lehrer, and I. Shiloni, ed. *Yalquṭ shimfioni lerabbenu shimfion hadarshan*. Vol. 1. Jerusalem: Mosad Harav Kook, 1973-.

Heinemann, Isaac. *Darkhei ha'aggadah*. Jerusalem and Tel-Aviv: Magnes and Masadah, 1970.

Heinemann, Joseph. *Derashot betzibbur bitequfat ha-talmud*. Dorot, Jerusalem: Mosad Bialik, 1971.

---------"Omanut haqqompozitziyyah bemidrash vayyiqra rabbah." Hasifrut 2 (1971): 150-160.

--------- "The Proem in the Aggadic Midrashim: A Form-Critical Study." Scripta Hierosolymitana 22 (1971): 100-22.

---------"Profile of a Midrash: The Art of Composition in Leviticus Rabbah." JAAR 39 (1971): 141-150.

---------*Aggadah and its Development*. Sifriyyat Keter 4: Hagut vehalakhah, ed. Joseph Dan. Jerusalem: Keter, 1974.

---------*Literature of the Synagogue*. Library of Jewish Studies, ed. Neal Kozodoy. New York: Behrman House, 1975.

---------"The Nature of Aggadah." In *Midrash and Literature*, ed. Geoffrey Hartman and Sanford Budick. New Haven: Yale University Press, 1986.

Herner, S. *Syntax der Zahlwörter im Alten Testamentum*. Lund: 1893.

Herr, M. D. "*Hashilton haromi besifrut hatanna'im*." Ph. D., Hebrew University, 1970.

Herschberg, A. S. "Ḥayei ha-tarbut beyisra'el bitequfat ha-mishnah veha-talmud: ḥeleq a, ha-tzemer veha-pishtah bimei ha-talmud." Ha-qedem 3 (St. Petersberg 1912): 7-29.

Hoffmann, D., ed. *Midrasch Tannaïm zum Deuteronomium.* Berlin: Itzkowski, 1909.

Horovitz, H. S. and I. A. Rabin, ed. *Mechilta d'rabbi ismael.* 2nd ed., Jerusalem: Wahrmann, 1970.

Horowitz, H. M., ed. *Beit fieqed ha'aggadot.* Vol. 2. Frankfort a\M: Slobotsky, 1881-4.

Hyman, Aaron. *Toledot tanna'im we'amora'im.* Reprint ed., Jerusalem: 1964.

Hyman, Aaron and Arthur Hyman. *Torah hakethubah vehamessurah.* Second revised edition ed., Tel Aviv: Dvir, 1979.

Issachar Ber ben Naftali hakohen. "Mattenot kehunnah." In *Midrash rabbah,* Vilna: Rom, 1878.

Jaffe, Samuel. "Yefe fiAnaf." In *Midrash Rabbah,* Vilna: Rom, 1878.

Jaffee, Martin S. "The 'Midrashic' Proem: Towards the Description of Rabbinic Exegesis." In *Approaches to Ancient Judaism,* ed. William Scott Green. 95–112. 4: Studies in Liturgy, Exegesis, and Talmudic Narrative. Chico: Scholars Press, 1983.

Jellinek, Adolph, ed. *Bet ha-Midrasch.* Jerusalem: Wahrmann, Reprint:1967.

Kadushin, Max. *Organic Thinking.* New York: The Jewish Theological Seminary of America, 1938.

Kadushin, Max. *The Rabbinic Mind.* New York: The Jewish Theological Seminary of America, 1952.

Kasher, Menahem. *Torah shelemah.* Jerusalem: 1927-81.

Kasher, Menahem M. and Jacob B. Mandelbaum, ed. *Sarei ha-elef.* Vol. 1. Jerusalem: Beit Torah Shelemah, 1978.

Kautzsch, E., ed. *Gesenius' Hebrew Grammar.* Second English ed., Oxford: Clarendon Press, 1976.

Kelly, Walter K. *A Collection of the Proverbs of All Nations.* Andover: Warren F. Draper, 1879.

Klein, Hyman. "Gemara and Sebara." JQR 38 (1 1947): 67-91.

Kohut, Alexander. *Aruch Completum.* Vienna-New York: 1878-92.

---------"Les Fêtes Persanes et Babyloniennes Mentionées dans les Talmuds de Babylone et de Jerusalem." REJ 24 (1892): 256-71.

Kraeling, C. H. *The Rand-McNally Bible Atlas.* 2nd ed., New York: Rand McNally, 1962.

Krauss, Samuel. *Griechische und lateinische Lehnwörter im Talmud, Midrasch und Targum.* Berlin: 1899.

---------*Das Leben Jesu nach jüdischen Quellen.* Berlin: 1902.

---------*Talmudische Archäologie.* Leipzig: 1910-2.

---------*Qadmoniyyot ha-talmud.* Berlin, Vienna, Tel-Aviv: 1924-45.

Krauss, Samuel. *Paras veromi batalmud uvamidrashim.* Jerusalem: 1948.

---------ed. *Additamenta ad Librum Aruch Completum.* Reprint ed., Jerusalem: Makor, 1969.

Kugel, James. "Two Introductions to Midrash." In *Midrash and Literature,* ed. Geoffrey H. Hartman and Sanford Budick. 77-103. New Haven: Yale University Press, 1986.

Kutscher, E. Y. "Some Problems of the Lexicography of Mishnaic Hebrew and its Comparison with Biblical Hebrew." In *Archive of the Dictionary of Rabbinical Literature Volume*, ed. E. Y. Kutscher. 29-82. 1. Ramat-Gan: New Dictionary of Rabbinical Literature Project, 1972.

---------*The Language and Linguistic Background of the Isaiah Scroll (I Q Isa^{a})*. English ed., Vol. 6. Studies on the Texts of the Desert of Judah, ed. J. Van der Ploeg. Leiden: E. J. Brill, 1974.

---------"Leshon ḥaza"l." In *Sefer Hanokh Yalon*, 246-80. Jerusalem: 1963.

Lange, I. S. and S. Schwartz, ed. *Midraš Daniel et Midraš Ezra*. Jerusalem: Mikitze Nirdamim, 1968.

Lauterbach, Jacob Z., ed. *Mekilta de-rabbi ishmael*. paper ed., Jewish Classics. Philadelphia: Jewish Publication Society of America, 1961.

Lerner, Mayer. *Anlage und Quellen des Bereschit Rabba*. Berlin: 1882.

Levy, Jacob. *Neuhebräisches und chaldäisches Wörterbuch über die Targumim und Midrashim*. Leipzig: 1876-89.

---------*Wörterbuch über die Talmudim und Midraschim*. reprint ed., Vol. 1. Darmstadt: Wissenschaftliche Buchgesellschaft, 1963.

Levy, Johanan Hans. "Yulianus keisar uvinyan ha-bayit." In *Studies in Jewish Hellenism*, ed. J. Amir. 221-54. 2nd ed., Vol. Jerusalem: Bialik Institute, 1969.

Lewin, B. M., ed. *Otzar Hageonim*. Haifa and Jerusalem: 1928-43.

Lieberman, Saul. "The Martyrs of Caesarea." Annuaire de l'institut de philologie et d'histoire orientales et slaves 7 (1939-44): 395-446.

---------"Roman Legal Institutions in Early Rabbinics and in the Acta Martyrum." JQR 35 (1944-45): 1-57.

---------*Hellenism in Jewish Palestine: Studies in the Literary Transmission, Beliefs and Manners of Palestine in the 1st Century B.C.E.-4th Century C.E.* New York: The Jewish Theological Seminary of America, 1962.

---------ed. *The Tosefta*. Vol. 2. New York: Jewish Theological Seminary of America, 1962-.

---------"Interpretations in Mishna." Tarbiẓ 40 (1 1970): 9-17.

---------*Tosefta ki-fshuṭah*. Vol. 8. New Tork: The Jewish Theological Seminary of America, 1973.

---------*The Talmud of Caesarea: Jerushalmi Tractate Neziqin*. Vol. 2. Supplement to Tarbiẓ, Jerusalem: 1931.

---------*Yemenite Midrashim*. second ed., Jerusalem: Wahrmann, 1970.

Liss, Abraham, ed. *The Babylonian Talmud with Variant Readings...: Tractate Sotah*. Vol. 1. Jerusalem: Institute for the Complete Israeli Talmud, 1977.

Loewe, Raphael. "The 'Plain' Meaning of Scripture in Early Jewish Exegesis." In *Papers of the Institute of Jewish Studies, London*, ed. J. G. Weiss. 140-185. 1. Jerusalem: Magnes Press, 1989.

Löw, I. *Aramäische Pflanzennanen*. Leipzig: 1881.

---------*Die Flora der Juden*. Vienna and Leipzig: 1928.

Lukonin, V. G. "Political, Social and Administrative Institutions: Taxes and Trade." In *The Cambridge History of Iran*, ed. E. Yarshater. 681-746. 3 (2). Cambridge etc.: Cambridge University Press, 1983.

MacKenzie, D. N. *A Concise Pahlavi Dictionary*. London, New York and Toronto: Oxford University Press, 1971.

Maimon, Judah Leib, ed. *Yihusei tanna'im ve'amora'im me'et rabbi yehudah berabbi kalonimos mishpeira*. Jerusalem: Mosad Harav Kook, 1963.

Maimonides, Moses (attributed). *Commentary to Esther*. Livorno: 1800.

Malter, Henry, ed. *The Treatise Tafianit of the Babylonian Talmud*. Vol. 1. Publications of the American Academy for Jewish Research. New York: American Academy for Jewish Research, 1930.

Mandelbaum, Bernard, ed. *Pesikta de Rav Kahana*. New York: The Jewish Theological Seminary of America, 1962.

Mandelkern, S. *Veteris Testamenti Concordantiæ*. Leipzig: Veit et Comp., 1896.

Mann, Jacob. "Seqirah hisṭorit 'al dinei nefashot ba-zeman ha-zeh." Ha-tẓofeh leḥokhmat yisra'el 10, 11 (1926-7): 200-8; 192.

---------*The Collected Articles of Jacob Mann*. Vol. 1. Gedera: M. Shalom Ltd., 1971.

Mantel, H. "The Nature of the Great Synagogue (Knesset ha-Gedolah)." In *Fourth World Congress of Jewish Studies in Jerusalem*, edited by S. Shaked and Y. Shenkman, World Union of Jewish Studies, 81-88, Year.

---------*Anshei keneset ha-gedolah*. 1983.

Margulies, Mordecai, ed. *Midrash haggadol on the Pentateuch: Exodus*. Jerusalem: Mosad Harav Kook, 1956.

---------ed. *Midrash haggadol on the Pentateuch: Genesis*. Jerusalem: Mosad Haraw Kook, 1967.

---------ed. *Midrash wayyikra rabbah*. Jerusalem: Wahrmann, 1972.

Marmorstein, A. "Anges et Hommes dans l'Agada." REJ 84 (1927):

Maybaum, Sigmund. "Die ältesten Phasen in der Entwickelung der jüdischen Predigt." Lehranstalt für die Wissenschaft des Judentums 19 (1903):

Melamed, E. Z. "Euphemism and Scribal Circumlocutions in Tamudic Literature." In *Benjamin De Vries Memorial Volume*, ed. E. Z. Melamed. Jerusalem: Tel Aviv University, 1968.

---------*An Introduction to Talmudic Literature*. Jerusalem: Galor, 1973.

Milikowsky, Chaim. "*Seder fiOlam* and the Tosefta." Tarbiẓ 49 (3-4 1980): 246-263.

---------"Seder Olam: A Rabbinic Chronology." Ph. D., Yale University, 1981.

Miller, Stuart S. "Intercity Relations in Roman Palestine: The Case of Sepphoris and Tiberias." AJS Review 12 (1 1987): 1-24.

Mintz, Judah and Meir b. Isaac Katznellenbogen. *She'elot uteshuvot r' mahar'i mintz umahara"m padua*. Cracow: 1882.

Mintz, Moses. *She'elot uteshuvot r. moshe mintz*. reprint ed., Tel-Aviv: 1969.

Mirsky, Aharon, ed. *Yosse ben Yosse: Poems*. Jerusalem: Bialik Institute, 1977.

Mirsky, S. K. "Maḥtzavtan shel tzurot ha-piyyuṭ." Yedi'ot ha-makhon leḥeqer ha-shirah ha-'ivrit birushalayim 7 (1958): 1-129.

---------ed. *Sheeltot de rab ahai gaon*. Jerusalem: Sura Research and Publication Foundation. Mosad Harav Kook, 1959-77.

Moore, Carey A., ed. *Esther*. The Anchor Bible. Garden City: Doubleday, 1971.

---------ed. *Studies in the Book of Esther*. The Library of Biblical Studies. New York: Ktav, 1982.

Moran, B. "Lefiarikhatah shel masekhet megillah." Ph. D., Bar-Ilan University, 1971.

Myers, Jacob M., ed. *Ezra, Nehemiah*. Anchor Bible. Garden City, N.Y.: Doubleday, 1965.

Neusner, Jacob. *A History of the Jews in Babylonia*. 2nd ed., Leiden: E. J. Brill, 1965-1970.

---------*The Peripatetic Saying: The Problem of the Thrice-Told Tale in Talmudic Literature*. Brown Judaic Studies, ed. J. Neusner et al. Chico: Scholars Press, 1985.

---------*The Oral Torah: The Sacred Books of Judaism*. San Fransisco: Harper and Row, 1986.

---------ed. *Sifre to Deuteronomy: An Analytical Translation*. Atlanta: Scholars Press, 1987.

---------*Esther Rabbah I: An Analytical Translation*. Vol. I. Brown Judaic Studies, Atlanta: Scholars Press, 1989.

---------*From Literature to Theology in Formative Judaism: Three Preliminary Studies*. Vol. 199. Brown Judaic Studies, ed. Jacob Neusner et al. Atlanta: Scholars Press, 1989.

---------*The Midrashic Compilations of the Sixth and Seventh Centuries: An Introduction to the Rhetorical, Logical and Topical Program*. Vol. 2. Brown Judaic Studies, ed. J. Neusner et al. Atlanta: Scholars Press, 1989.

---------*Translating the Classics of Judaism In Theory and Practice*. Vol. 176. Brown Judaic Studies, ed. J. Neusner. Atlanta: Scholars Press, 1989.

---------ed. *The Literature of Formative Judaism: Controversies on the Literature of Formative Judaism*. Vol. 13. Origins of Judaism. New York and London: Garland, 1990.

---------*Making the Classics in Judaism: The Three Stages of Literary Formation*. Brown Judaic Studies, ed. J. Neusner et al. Atlanta: Scholars Press, 1990.

---------ed. *Origins of Judaism*. Vol. 13. New York and London: Garland, 1990.

---------"Mr. Sanders' Pharisees and Mine: A Response to E. P. Sanders, *Jewish Law from Jesus to the Mishnah*." Scottish Journal of Theology 44 (1991): 73-95.

Newman, J. *Commercial Life of the Jews in Babylonia Between the Years 200 and 500 C.E.* London: n. d.

Noth, Martin. *The History of Israel*. Translated by S. Godman. London: Adam & Charles Black, 1958.

Noy, Dov. "Mishlei ha-melakhim shel rabbi shimfion ben yoḥai." Maḥanayim (La"g bafiomer 1961): 81-73.

Ong, Walter J. *Orality and Literacy: The Technologizing of the Word*. New Accents, ed. Terence Hawkes. London and New York: Methuen, 1982.

Oppenheim, A. Leo. "On Royal Gardens in Mesopotamia." JNES 24 (1965): 328-33.

Paton, L. B. *A Critical and Exegetical Commentary on the Book of Esther*. International Critical Commentary, ed. S. R. Driver, A. Plummer, and C. A. Briggs. Edinburgh: T & T Clark, 1964.

Peck, H. T., ed. *Harper's Dictionary of Classical Literature and Antiquities*. New York: Cooper Square Publishers, 1965.

Perikhanian, A. "Iranian Society and Law." In *The Cambridge History of Iran*, ed. E. Yarshater. 627--80. 3 (2). Cambridge etc.: Cambridge University Press, 1983.

Perles, J. "Perushei aggadot larashba." In *R. Salomo ben Abraham ben Adereth*, 24-56. Breslau: 1863.

---------*Etymologische Studien*. Breslau: 1871.

Pharr, Clyde, ed. *The Theodosian Code*. Vol. 1. The Corpus of Roman Law. Princeton: Princeton University Press, 1952.

Pines, S., ed. *The Guide of the Perplexed*. Chicago: University of Chicago Press, 1963.

Pollock, H. J., ed. *Sefer fiaqedat yisḥaq … rabbi yisḥaq fiaramah* …. reprint ed., Vol. 6. [Israel]: n. d.

Preuss, J. *Julius Preuss' Biblical and Talmudic Medicine.* 2nd ed., Translated by Fred Rosner. New York: Hebrew Publishing Company, 1978.

Rabbinowicz, R. N. N. *Diqduqé Soferim, Variæ Lectiones in Mishnam et in Talmud Babylonicum.* reprint ed., New York: M.P. Press, 1976.

Rabinovitz, Zvi Meir, ed. *The Liturgical Poems of Rabbi Yannai According to the Triennial Cycle of the Pentateuch and the Holidays: Critical Edition with Introduction and Commentary.* Jerusalem: Mosad Bialik and Tel-Aviv University, 1985-7.

---------ed. *Midrash haggadol on the Pentateuch: Numbers.* Jerusalem: Mosad Harav Kook, 1973.

Rabinowitz, Z. W. *Shafiare torath babel: Notes and Comments on the Babylonian Talmud.* ed. E. Z. Melamed. Jerusalem: The Jewish Theological Seminary of America, 1961.

Rappoport, S. J. *Toledot rabbi elfiazar ha-kalir.* reprint ed., Warsaw: Tevunah, 1913.

Ratner, B., ed. *Midrash seder olam.* S.K. Mirsky ed., New York: Moznaim, 1988.

Rosenblatt, S. *The Interpretation of the Bible in the Mishnah.* Baltimore: 1935.

Rosenthal, E. S. "Leshonot soferim." In *Yovel shai: sefer hayyovel leSha"Y Agnon,* 293-324. Ramat-Gan: 1958.

Rosenthal, E. S. and S. Lieberman, ed. *Yerushalmi Neziqin.* Texts and Studies in Rabbinic Lierature. Jerusalem: Israel Academy of Sciences and Humanities: Section of Humanities; The Institute for Advanced Studies, The Hebrew University of Jerusalem; The American Academy for Jewish Research, 1983.

Rosenthal, L. A. "Die Josephsgeschichte, mit den Büchern Ester und Daniel verglichen." ZAW 15 (1895): 278-84.

Rostovtzeff, M. *The Social and Economic History of the Roman Empire.* 2nd ed., Oxford: Clarendon Press, 1957.

Roth, Cecil. "Ecclesiasticus in the Synagogue Service." JBL 71 (3 1952): 171-8.

Sanders, E. P. *Jewish Law from Jesus to the Mishnah: Five Studies.* London and Philadelphia: SCM Press and Trinity Press International, 1990.

Sarason, R. S. "Toward a New Agendum for the Study of Rabbinic Midrashic Literature." In *Studies in Aggadah, Targum and Jewish Liturgy in Memory of Joseph Heinemann,* ed. J. Petuchowski and E. Fleischer. 55-73. Jerusalem and Cincinnati: The Magnes Press and Hebrew Union College Press, 1981.

Schäfer, Peter. "Research into Rabbinic Literature: An Attempt to Define the Status Quaestionis." JJS 37 (1986): 139–52.

Schechter, Solomon, ed. *Aboth de Rabi Nathan.* newly corrected ed., New York: Feldheim, 1967.

Schiffer, Ira J. "The Men of the Great Assembly." In *Persons and Institutions in Early Rabbinic Judaism,* ed. William Scott Green. 237-83. 3. Missoula: Scholars Press for Brown University, 1977.

Scholfield, A. F., ed. *Aelian On the Characteristics of Animals.* Vol. 2. The Loeb Classical Library. Cambridge, Mass. and London: Harvard University Press and William Heinemann Ltd., 1959.

Schwartz, Joshua. "Gallus, Julian and Anti-Christian Polemic in Pesikta Rabbati." Theologische Zeitschrift 46 (1 1990): 1-19.

Scott, S. P., ed. *The Civil Law*. AMS ed., Vol. 15: The Code of Justinian. Cincinnati: The Central Trust Company, 1973.

Segal, Eliezer. “"The Goat of the Slaughterhouse..."— On the Evolution of a Variant Reading in the Babylonian Talmud.” Tarbiẓ 49 (1-2 1979-80): 43-51.

---------“The Textual Traditions of Tractate Megillah in the Babylonian Talmud.” Ph. D., Hebrew University of Jerusalem, 1981.

---------“The Textual Traditions of Ms. Columbia University to TB Megillah.” Tarbiẓ 53 (1 1983): 41-69.

---------“The *Petiḥta* (Proem) in Babylonia.” Tarbiẓ 54 (2 1985): 177-204.

---------“Human Anger and Divine Intervention in Esther.” Prooftexts 9 (1989): 247-56.

---------*Case Citation in the Babylonian Talmud: The Evidence of Tractate Neziqin*. Vol. 1. Brown Judaic Studies, ed. E.S. Frerichs. Atlanta: Scholars Press, 1990.

--------- “Justice, Mercy and a Bird's Nest.” JJS 42 (2 1991): 176-95.

---------“Midrash and Literature: Some Medieval Views.” Prooftexts 11 (1991): 57–65.

---------“"The Same from Beginning to End" — On the Development of a MIdrashic Homily.” JJS 32 (2 1981): 158-65.

---------“Law as Allegory? An Unnoticed Device in Talmudic Narrative.” Prooftexts 8 (2 1988): 245-56.

Segal, M. H. *A Grammar of Mishnaic Hebrew*. Oxford: Clarendon Press, 1927.

Shepherd, Dorothy. “Sasanian Art.” In *The Cambridge History of Iran*, ed. Ehsan Yarshater. 1055-1112. 3 (2). Cambridge etc.: Cambridge University Press, 1983.

Shinan, Avigdor. “The Sins of Nadab and Abihu in Rabbinic Literature.” Tarbiẓ 48 (3-4 1979): 201-14.

---------“Letorat hapetihta.” Jerusalem Studies in Hebrew Literature 1 (1981):

---------“The Opening Section of Midrash Exodus Rabbah.” In *Studies in Aggadah, Targum and Jewish Liturgy in Memory of Joseph Heinemann*, ed. Jacob J. Petuchowski and Eztra Fleischer. 175-83 [Hebrew section]. Jerusalem: Magnes Press and Hebrew Union Colege Press, 1981.

---------“Sifrut ha-’aggadah bein higud fial peh umasoret ketuvah.” Jerusalem Studies in Jewish Folkore 1 (1981): 44-60.

---------ed. *Likkutei Tarbiz 4: The Aggadic Literature—A Reader*. Maslul Series: Studies Textbook Publishing Projects. Jerusalem: The Magnes Press, 1983.

---------ed. *Midrash Shemot Rabbah Chapters I-XIV*. Jerusalem and Tel-Aviv: Dvir, 1984.

Shneurson, S., ed. *Ḥemdah genuzah*. Jerusalem: 1903.

Silberman, Lou H. “Towards a Rhetoric of Midrash: A Preliminary Account.” In *The Biblical Mosaic*, ed. R. Polzin and E. Rothman. 15-26. Philadelphia and Chico: Fortress Press and Scholars Press, 1982.

Simon, M., ed. *The Tractate Megillah*. Vol. 2:4. The Soncino Talmud. London: Soncino Press, 1948.

Simpson, D. C. “The Book of Tobit.” In *The Apocrypha and Pseudepigrapha of the Old Testament*, ed. R. H. Charles. I: Apocrypha. Oxford: The Clarendon Press, 1913.

Sokoloff, Michael, ed. *The Geniza Fragments of Bereshit Rabba.* Texts and Studies in Rabbinic Literature. Jerusalem: Israel Academy of Sciences and Humanities, 1982.

Sperber, A., ed. *The Bible in Aramaic.* Vol. IV A. Leiden: E. J. Brill, 1968.

Sperber, Daniel. "On Roman Administrative Procedure." Tarbiẓ 46 (1977): 315-6.

---------*Roman Palestine 200–400: The Land.* Bar-Ilan Studies in Near Eastern Languages and Culture, Ramat-Gan: Bar–Ilan University, 1978.

---------*Essays on Greek and Latin in the Mishna, Talmud and Midrashic Literature.* Jerusalem: Makor, 1982.

---------"Gilgulei avanim." In *Studies in Rabbinic Literature, Bible and Jewish History*, ed. Y. D. Gilat, Ch. Levine, and Z. M. Rabinowitz. 261-7. Ramat-Gan: Bar-Ilan University Press, 1982.

Stein, E. "Die homiletische Peroratio im Midrasch." HUCA 8-9 (1931-2): 353ff.

Steinsaltz, A., ed. *Midrash ha-gadol fial ḥamishah humshei torah sefer vayyiqra.* Jerusalem: Mosad Harav Kook, 1975.

Stern, David. "Rhetoric and Midrash: The Case of the Mashal." Prooftexts 1 (1981): 261–91.

---------"Moses-cide: Midrash and Contemporary Literary Criticism." Prooftexts 4 (1984): 193-213.

---------"David Stern Responds." Prooftexts 5 (1985): 276–80.

---------"The Function of the Parable in Rabbinic Literature." Jerusalem Studies in Hebrew Literature 7 (1985): 90–102.

---------"Literary Criticism or Literary Homilies? Susan Handelman and the Contemporary Study of Midrash." Prooftexts 5 (1985): 96–103.

---------"Midrash and the Language of Exegesis: A Study of Vayikra Rabbah, Chapter 1." In *Midrash and Literature*, ed. Geoffrey H. Hartman and Sanford Budick. 105–24. New Haven: Yale University Press, 1986.

---------"Midrash and Indeterminacy." Critical Inquiry 15 (1988): 132-61.

Swete, H. B. *Esther.* Vol. 2. The Old Testament in Greek, Cambridge: Cambridge University Press, 1905.

Thackeray, H. St. J., ed. *Josephus: Against Apion.* Vol. 1. The Loeb Classical Library. Cambridge, Mass. and London: Harvard University Press and William Heinemann Ltd., 1966.

Theodor, J. "Zur Komposition der agadischen Homilien." MGWJ 28-30 (1879-81): 28:97–113, 164–75, 271–78, 337–50, 408–18, 455–62; 29:19–23; 30:500-510.

Theodor, J. and Ch. Albeck, ed. *Midrasch Bereschit Rabbah.* Berlin: 1903-36.

Torrey, Charles. ""Medes and Persians"." JAOS 66 (1 1946): 1-15.

---------*Ezra Studies.* reprint ed., The Library of Biblical Studies, ed. H. M. Orlinsky. New York: Ktav, 1970.

Urbach, E. *The Sages: Their Concepts and Beliefs.* Translated by I. Abrahams. Cambridge, Mass. and London, England: Harvard University Press, 1987.

---------"When Did Prophecy Cease?" Tarbiẓ 17 (1946): 1-11.

---------"Halakha and Prophecy." Tarbiẓ 18 (1947): 1-27.

--------- "Hilekhot 'avodah zarah veha-metzi'ut ha-arkhi'ologit veha-historit ba-me'ah ha-sheniyyah uva-me'ah ha-shelishit." Eretz-Yisra'el 5 (1958): 189-205.

--------- "Koresh vehakhrazato be'einei ḥaza"l." Molad 157 (1961): 368-74.

---------*The Tosaphists: Their History, Writings and Methods*. fourth enlarged ed., Jerusalem: Bialik Institute, 1980.

---------*The World of the Sages: Collected Studies*. Jerusalem: The Magnes Press, 1988.

Vermes, Geza. "Josephus' Treatment of the Book of Daniel." JJS 42 (2 1991): 149-66.

Vullers, I. A. *Lexicon Persico-Latinum Etymologicum*. reprint ed., Vol. 2. Graz: Akademische Druck-U. Verlagsanstalt, 1962.

Walfish, Barry. "The Two Commentaries of Abraham Ibn Ezra on the Book of Esther." JQR 79 (4 1989): 323-43.

Warner, A. G. and E. Warner, ed. *Shah-nama*. Trubner's Oriental Series. London: 1905-25.

Weiss, Abraham. *Leqorot hit-havvut ha-bavli*. reprint: Jerusalem, 1970 ed., Publications of the Institute of Jewish Studies in Warsaw, Warsaw: Institute of Jewish Studies in Poland, 1929.

---------*fiAl hayetzirah hasifrutit shel ha'amora'im*. New York: 1962.

---------*Studies in the Literature of the Amoraim*. New York: 1962.

Weiss, I. H. *Dor dor vedoreshav [Zur Geschichte der jüdischen Tradition]*. Vienna-Pressburg: 1891-1871.

Wilman, S., ed. *Tosefot ha-rosh ha-shalem*. Tel-Aviv: 1971.

Wissowa, G., ed. *Paulys Real-Encyclopädie der Classischen Alterumswissenschaft*. Vol. 8:4. Stuttgart: J. B. Metzlerscher Verlag, 1901.

Yalon, Henoch. *Studies in the Hebrew Language*. Jerusalem: Bialik Institute, 1971.

Zevin, S. J., ed. *Talmudic Encyclopedia*. Second Revised ed., Vol. 1. Jerusalem: Talmudic Encyclopedia Institute, 1978.

---------ed. *Talmudic Encyclopedia*. Vol. 4. Jerusalem: Talmudic Encyclopedia Institute, 1984.

---------*Talmudic Encyclopedia*. fifth ed., Vol. 2. ed. J. Hutner. Jerusalem: Talmudic Encyclopedia Foundation, 1979.

Ziegler, I. *Die Königsgleichnisse des Midrasch beleuchtet durch die römische Kaiserzeit*. Breslau: Schlesische Verlags, 1903.

Zimmermann, F., ed. *The Book of Tobit*. Dropsie College Edition: Jewish Apocryphal Literature. New York: Harper & Brothers for Dropsie College, Philadelphia, 1958.

Zulay, Menahem, ed. *Piyyute yannai*. Vol. 3:2. Publications of the Research Institute for Hebrew Poetry. Berlin: Schocken, 1938.

Zunz, L. *Die gottesdienstlichen Vorträge der Juden historisch Entwickelt (Hadderashot beyisrael)*. Translated by Ch. Albeck. Jerusalem: Mosad Bialik, 1974.

Zuri, J. S. *Rabbi yose bar ḥanina mikkisrin*. Jerusalem: 1926.

Index

Sources

Hebrew Bible

Note that references to material contained in the footnotes are to the numbers of the pages on which the references appear in the main text, even in cases where the notes extend over two or more pages.

Targums and Ancient Versions

New Testament

Mishnah

Tosefta

Tannaitic (Halakhic) Midrash

Palestinian Talmud

---

[1] According to page numbers in Epstein–Melamed edition.

[2] According to page numbers in Hoffmann's edition.

Babylonian Talmud

Aggadic Midrash[3]

3 Listed alphabetically by title.

4 According to page numbers in S. Buber's edition.

5 According to page numbers in S. Buber's edition.

---

6 According to page numbers in S. Buber's edition.

7 According to page numbers in S. Buber's edition.

Apocrypha

Medieval Aggadic Anthologies

Medieval Aggadic Anthologies

Talmudic Rabbis

[8] According to page numbers in S. Buber's edition.

[9] According to page numbers in S. Buber's edition.

Language and Terminology

Biblical Figures

Authors and Titles

Subjects

Brown Judaic Studies

140001	*Approaches to Ancient Judaism I*	William S. Green
140002	*The Traditions of Eleazar Ben Azariah*	Tzvee Zahavy
140003	*Persons and Institutions in Early Rabbinic Judaism*	William S. Green
140004	*Claude Goldsmid Montefiore on the Ancient Rabbis*	Joshua B. Stein
140005	*The Ecumenical Perspective and the Modernization of Jewish Religion*	S. Daniel Breslauer
140006	*The Sabbath-Law of Rabbi Meir*	Robert Goldenberg
140007	*Rabbi Tarfon*	Joel Gereboff
140008	*Rabban Gamaliel II*	Shamai Kanter
140009	*Approaches to Ancient Judaism II*	William S. Green
140010	*Method and Meaning in Ancient Judaism I*	Jacob Neusner
140011	*Approaches to Ancient Judaism III*	William S. Green
140012	*Turning Point: Zionism and Reform Judaism*	Howard R. Greenstein
140013	*Buber on God and the Perfect Man*	Pamela Vermes
140014	*Scholastic Rabbinism*	Anthony J. Saldarini
140015	*Method and Meaning in Ancient Judaism II*	Jacob Neusner
140016	*Method and Meaning in Ancient Judaism III*	Jacob Neusner
140017	*Post Mishnaic Judaism in Transition*	Baruch M. Bokser
140018	*A History of the Mishnaic Law of Agriculture: Tractate Maaser Sheni*	Peter J. Haas
140019	*Mishnah's Theology of Tithing*	Martin S. Jaffee
140020	*The Priestly Gift in Mishnah: A Study of Tractate Terumot*	Alan. J. Peck
140021	*History of Judaism: The Next Ten Years*	Baruch M. Bokser
140022	*Ancient Synagogues*	Joseph Gutmann
140023	*Warrant for Genocide*	Norman Cohn
140024	*The Creation of the World According to Gersonides*	Jacob J. Staub
140025	*Two Treatises of Philo of Alexandria: A Commentary on* De Gigantibus *and* Quod Deus Sit Immutabilis	Winston/Dillon
140026	*A History of the Mishnaic Law of Agriculture: Kilayim*	Irving Mandelbaum
140027	*Approaches to Ancient Judaism IV*	William S. Green
140028	*Judaism in the American Humanities I*	Jacob Neusner
140029	*Handbook of Synagogue Architecture*	Marilyn Chiat
140030	*The Book of Mirrors*	Daniel C. Matt
140031	*Ideas in Fiction: The Works of Hayim Hazaz*	Warren Bargad
140032	*Approaches to Ancient Judaism V*	William S. Green
140033	*Sectarian Law in the Dead Sea Scrolls: Courts, Testimony and the Penal Code*	Lawrence H. Schiffman
140034	*A History of the United Jewish Appeal: 1939-1982*	Marc L. Raphael
140035	*The Academic Study of Judaism*	Jacob Neusner
140036	*Woman Leaders in the Ancient Synagogue*	Bernadette Brooten
140037	*Formative Judaism I: Religious, Historical, and Literary Studies*	Jacob Neusner
140038	*Ben Sira's View of Women: A Literary Analysis*	Warren C. Trenchard
140039	*Barukh Kurzweil and Modern Hebrew Literature*	James S. Diamond
140040	*Israeli Childhood Stories of the Sixties: Yizhar, Aloni, Shahar, Kahana-Carmon*	Gideon Telpaz
140041	*Formative Judaism II: Religious, Historical, and Literary Studies*	Jacob Neusner
140042	*Judaism in the American Humanities II: Jewish Learning and the New Humanities*	Jacob Neusner

140043	*Support for the Poor in the Mishnaic Law of Agriculture: Tractate Peah*	Roger Brooks
140044	*The Sanctity of the Seventh Year: A Study of Mishnah Tractate Shebiit*	Louis E. Newman
140045	*Character and Context: Studies in the Fiction of Abramovitsh, Brenner, and Agnon*	Jeffrey Fleck
140046	*Formative Judaism III: Religious, Historical, and Literary Studies*	Jacob Neusner
140047	*Pharaoh's Counsellors: Job, Jethro, and Balaam in Rabbinic and Patristic Tradition*	Judith Baskin
140048	*The Scrolls and Christian Origins: Studies in the Jewish Background of the New Testament*	Matthew Black
140049	*Approaches to Modern Judaism I*	Marc Lee Raphael
140050	*Mysterious Encounters at Mamre and Jabbok*	William T. Miller
140051	*The Mishnah Before 70*	Jacob Neusner
140052	*Sparda by the Bitter Sea: Imperial Interaction in Western Anatolia*	Jack Martin Balcer
140053	*Hermann Cohen: The Challenge of a Religion of Reason*	William Kluback
140054	*Approaches to Judaism in Medieval Times I*	David R. Blumenthal
140055	*In the Margins of the Yerushalmi: Glosses on the English Translation*	Jacob Neusner
140056	*Approaches to Modern Judaism II*	Marc Lee Raphael
140057	*Approaches to Judaism in Medieval Times II*	David R. Blumenthal
140058	*Midrash as Literature: The Primacy of Documentary Discourse*	Jacob Neusner
140059	*The Commerce of the Sacred: Mediation of the Divine Among Jews in the Graeco-Roman Diaspora*	Jack N. Lightstone
140060	*Major Trends in Formative Judaism I: Society and Symbol in Political Crisis*	Jacob Neusner
140061	*Major Trends in Formative Judaism II: Texts, Contents, and Contexts*	Jacob Neusner
140062	*A History of the Jews in Babylonia I: The Parthian Period*	Jacob Neusner
140063	*The Talmud of Babylonia: An American Translation XXXII: Tractate Arakhin*	Jacob Neusner
140064	*Ancient Judaism: Debates and Disputes*	Jacob Neusner
140065	*Prayers Alleged to Be Jewish: An Examination of the Constitutiones Apostolorum*	David Fiensy
140066	*The Legal Methodology of Hai Gaon*	Tsvi Groner
140067	*From Mishnah to Scripture: The Problem of the Unattributed Saying*	Jacob Neusner
140068	*Halakhah in a Theological Dimension*	David Novak
140069	*From Philo to Origen: Middle Platonism in Transition*	Robert M. Berchman
140070	*In Search of Talmudic Biography: The Problem of the Attributed Saying*	Jacob Neusner
140071	*The Death of the Old and the Birth of the New: The Framework of the Book of Numbers and the Pentateuch*	Dennis T. Olson
140072	*The Talmud of Babylonia: An American Translation XVII: Tractate Sotah*	Jacob Neusner
140073	*Understanding Seeking Faith: Essays on the Case of Judaism II: Literature, Religion and the Social Study of Judiasm*	Jacob Neusner
140074	*The Talmud of Babylonia: An American Translation VI: Tractate Sukkah*	Jacob Neusner
140075	*Fear Not Warrior: A Study of 'al tira' Pericopes in the Hebrew Scriptures*	Edgar W. Conrad

140076	*Formative Judaism IV: Religious, Historical, and Literary Studies*	Jacob Neusner
140077	*Biblical Patterns in Modern Literature*	Hirsch/Aschkenasy
140078	*The Talmud of Babylonia: An American Translation I: Tractate Berakhot*	Jacob Neusner
140079	*Mishnah's Division of Agriculture: A History and Theology of Seder Zeraim*	Alan J. Avery-Peck
140080	*From Tradition to Imitation: The Plan and Program of Pesiqta Rabbati and Pesiqta deRab Kahana*	Jacob Neusner
140081	*The Talmud of Babylonia: An American Translation XXIII.A: Tractate Sanhedrin, Chapters 1-3*	Jacob Neusner
140082	*Jewish Presence in T. S. Eliot and Franz Kafka*	Melvin Wilk
140083	*School, Court, Public Administration: Judaism and its Institutions in Talmudic Babylonia*	Jacob Neusner
140084	*The Talmud of Babylonia: An American Translation XXIII.B: Tractate Sanhedrin, Chapters 4-8*	Jacob Neusner
140085	*The Bavli and Its Sources: The Question of Tradition in the Case of Tractate Sukkah*	Jacob Neusner
140086	*From Description to Conviction: Essays on the History and Theology of Judaism*	Jacob Neusner
140087	*The Talmud of Babylonia: An American Translation XXIII.C: Tractate Sanhedrin, Chapters 9-11*	Jacob Neusner
140088	*Mishnaic Law of Blessings and Prayers: Tractate Berakhot*	Tzvee Zahavy
140089	*The Peripatetic Saying: The Problem of the Thrice-Told Tale in Talmudic Literature*	Jacob Neusner
140090	*The Talmud of Babylonia: An American Translation XXVI: Tractate Horayot*	Martin S. Jaffee
140091	*Formative Judaism V: Religious, Historical, and Literary Studies*	Jacob Neusner
140092	*Essays on Biblical Method and Translation*	Edward Greenstein
140093	*The Integrity of Leviticus Rabbah*	Jacob Neusner
140094	*Behind the Essenes: History and Ideology of the Dead Sea Scrolls*	Philip R. Davies
140095	*Approaches to Judaism in Medieval Times III*	David R. Blumenthal
140096	*The Memorized Torah: The Mnemonic System of the Mishnah*	Jacob Neusner
140097	*Knowledge and Illumination*	Hossein Ziai
140098	*Sifre to Deuteronomy: An Analytical Translation I: Pisqaot 1-143. Debarim,Waethanan, Eqeb*	Jacob Neusner
140099	*Major Trends in Formative Judaism III: The Three Stages in the Formation of Judaism*	Jacob Neusner
140101	*Sifre to Deuteronomy: An Analytical Translation II: Pisqaot 144-357. Shofetim, Ki Tese, Ki Tabo, Nesabim, Ha'azinu, Zot Habberakhah*	Jacob Neusner
140102	*Sifra: The Rabbinic Commentary on Leviticus*	Neusner/Brooks
140103	*The Human Will in Judaism*	Howard Eilberg-Schwartz
140104	*Genesis Rabbah I: Genesis 1:1 to 8:14*	Jacob Neusner
140105	*Genesis Rabbah II: Genesis 8:15 to 28:9*	Jacob Neusner
140106	*Genesis Rabbah III: Genesis 28:10 to 50:26*	Jacob Neusner
140107	*First Principles of Systemic Analysis*	Jacob Neusner
140108	*Genesis and Judaism*	Jacob Neusner
140109	*The Talmud of Babylonia: An American Translation XXXV: Tractates Meilah and Tamid*	Peter J. Haas
140110	*Studies in Islamic and Judaic Traditions I*	Brinner/Ricks

140111	*Comparative Midrash: The Plan and Program of Genesis Rabbah and Leviticus Rabbah*	Jacob Neusner
140112	*The Tosefta: Its Structure and its Sources*	Jacob Neusner
140113	*Reading and Believing*	Jacob Neusner
140114	*The Fathers According to Rabbi Nathan*	Jacob Neusner
140115	*Etymology in Early Jewish Interpretation: The Hebrew Names in Philo*	Lester L. Grabbe
140116	*Understanding Seeking Faith: Essays on the Case of Judaism I: Debates on Method, Reports of Results*	Jacob Neusner
140117	*The Talmud of Babylonia: An American Translation VII: Tractate Besah*	Alan J. Avery-Peck
140118	*Sifre to Numbers: An American Translation and Explanation I: Sifre to Numbers 1-58*	Jacob Neusner
140119	*Sifre to Numbers: An American Translation and Explanation II: Sifre to Numbers 59-115*	Jacob Neusner
140120	*Cohen and Troeltsch: Ethical Monotheistic Religion and Theory of Culture*	Wendell S. Dietrich
140121	*Goodenough on the History of Religion and on Judaism*	Neusner/Frerichs
140122	*Pesiqta deRab Kahana I: Pisqaot 1-14*	Jacob Neusner
140123	*Pesiqta deRab Kahana II: Pisqaot 15-28 and Introduction to Pesiqta deRab Kahana*	Jacob Neusner
140124	*Sifre to Deuteronomy: Introduction*	Jacob Neusner
140126	*A Conceptual Commentary on Midrash Leviticus Rabbah: Value Concepts in Jewish Thought*	Max Kadushin
140127	*The Other Judaisms of Late Antiquity*	Alan F. Segal
140128	*Josephus as a Historical Source in Patristic Literature through Eusebius*	Michael Hardwick
140129	*Judaism: The Evidence of the Mishnah*	Jacob Neusner
140131	*Philo, John and Paul: New Perspectives on Judaism and Early Christianity*	Peder Borgen
140132	*Babylonian Witchcraft Literature*	Tzvi Abusch
140133	*The Making of the Mind of Judaism: The Formative Age*	Jacob Neusner
140135	*Why No Gospels in Talmudic Judaism?*	Jacob Neusner
140136	*Torah: From Scroll to Symbol Part III: Doctrine*	Jacob Neusner
140137	*The Systemic Analysis of Judaism*	Jacob Neusner
140138	*Sifra: An Analytical Translation I*	Jacob Neusner
140139	*Sifra: An Analytical Translation II*	Jacob Neusner
140140	*Sifra: An Analytical Translation III*	Jacob Neusner
140141	*Midrash in Context: Exegesis in Formative Judaism*	Jacob Neusner
140142	*Sifra: An Analytical Translation IV*	Jacob Neusner
140143	*Oxen, Women or Citizens? Slaves in the System of Mishnah*	Paul V. Flesher
140144	*The Book of the Pomegranate*	Elliot R. Wolfson
140145	*Wrong Ways and Right Ways in the Study of Formative Judaism*	Jacob Neusner
140146	*Sifra in Perspective: The Documentary Comparison of the Midrashim of Ancient Judaism*	Jacob Neusner
140147	*Uniting the Dual Torah: Sifra and the Problem of the Mishnah*	Jacob Neusner
140148	*Mekhilta According to Rabbi Ishmael: An Analytical Translation I*	Jacob Neusner
140149	*The Doctrine of the Divine Name: An Introduction to Classical Kabbalistic Theology*	Stephen G. Wald
140150	*Water into Wine and the Beheading of John the Baptist*	Roger Aus
140151	*The Formation of the Jewish Intellect*	Jacob Neusner
140152	*Mekhilta According to Rabbi Ishmael: An Introduction to Judaism's First Scriptural Encyclopaedia*	Jacob Neusner

140153	*Understanding Seeking Faith: Essays on the Case of Judaism III: Society, History, and Political and Philosophical Uses of Judaism*	Jacob Neusner
140154	*Mekhilta According to Rabbi Ishmael: An Analytical Translation II*	Jacob Neusner
140155	*Goyim: Gentiles and Israelites in Mishnah-Tosefta*	Gary P. Porton
140156	*A Religion of Pots and Pans?*	Jacob Neusner
140157	*Claude Montefiore and Christianity*	Maurice Gerald Bowler
140158	*The Philosophical Mishnah III: The Tractates' Agenda: From Nazir to Zebahim*	Jacob Neusner
140159	*From Ancient Israel to Modern Judaism I: Intellect in Quest of Understanding*	Neusner/Frerichs/Sarna
140160	*The Social Study of Judaism I*	Jacob Neusner
140161	*Philo's Jewish Identity*	Alan Mendelson
140162	*The Social Study of Judaism II*	Jacob Neusner
140163	*The Philosophical Mishnah I: The Initial Probe*	Jacob Neusner
140164	*The Philosophical Mishnah II: The Tractates' Agenda: From Abodah Zarah Through Moed Qatan*	Jacob Neusner
140166	*Women's Earliest Records*	Barbara S. Lesko
140167	*The Legacy of Hermann Cohen*	William Kluback
140168	*Method and Meaning in Ancient Judaism*	Jacob Neusner
140169	*The Role of the Messenger and Message in the Ancient Near East*	John T. Greene
140171	*Abraham Heschel's Idea of Revelation*	Lawerence Perlman
140172	*The Philosophical Mishnah IV: The Repertoire*	Jacob Neusner
140173	*From Ancient Israel to Modern Judaism II: Intellect in Quest of Understanding*	Neusner/Frerichs/Sarna
140174	*From Ancient Israel to Modern Judaism III: Intellect in Quest of Understanding*	Neusner/Frerichs/Sarna
140175	*From Ancient Israel to Modern Judaism IV: Intellect in Quest of Understanding*	Neusner/Frerichs/Sarna
140176	*Translating the Classics of Judaism: In Theory and In Practice*	Jacob Neusner
140177	*Profiles of a Rabbi: Synoptic Opportunities in Reading About Jesus*	Bruce Chilton
140178	*Studies in Islamic and Judaic Traditions II*	Brinner/Ricks
140179	*Medium and Message in Judaism: First Series*	Jacob Neusner
140180	*Making the Classics of Judaism: The Three Stages of Literary Formation*	Jacob Neusner
140181	*The Law of Jealousy: Anthropology of Sotah*	Adriana Destro
140182	*Esther Rabbah I: An Analytical Translation*	Jacob Neusner
140183	*Ruth Rabbah: An Analytical Translation*	Jacob Neusner
140184	*Formative Judaism: Religious, Historical and Literary Studies*	Jacob Neusner
140185	*The Studia Philonica Annual 1989*	David T. Runia
140186	*The Setting of the Sermon on the Mount*	W.D. Davies
140187	*The Midrash Compilations of the Sixth and Seventh Centuries I*	Jacob Neusner
140188	*The Midrash Compilations of the Sixth and Seventh Centuries II*	Jacob Neusner
140189	*The Midrash Compilations of the Sixth and Seventh Centuries III*	Jacob Neusner
140190	*The Midrash Compilations of the Sixth and Seventh Centuries IV*	Jacob Neusner
140191	*The Religious World of Contemporary Judaism: Observations and Convictions*	Jacob Neusner
140192	*Approaches to Ancient Judaism VI*	Neusner/Frerichs
140193	*Lamentations Rabbah: An Analytical Translation*	Jacob Neusner
140194	*Early Christian Texts on Jews and Judaism*	Robert S. MacLennan
140196	*Torah and the Chronicler's History Work*	Judson R. Shaver

140197	*Song of Songs Rabbah: An Analytical Translation I*	Jacob Neusner
140198	*Song of Songs Rabbah: An Analytical Translation II*	Jacob Neusner
140199	*From Literature to Theology in Formative Judaism*	Jacob Neusner
140202	*Maimonides on Perfection*	Menachem Kellner
140203	*The Martyr's Conviction*	Eugene Weiner/Anita Weiner
140204	*Judaism, Christianity, and Zoroastrianism in Talmudic Babylonia*	Jacob Neusner
140205	*Tzedakah: Can Jewish Philanthropy Buy Jewish Survival?*	Jacob Neusner
140206	*New Perspectives on Ancient Judaism I*	Neusner/Borgen/Frerichs/Horsley
140207	*Scriptures of the Oral Torah*	Jacob Neusner
140208	*Christian Faith and the Bible of Judaism*	Jacob Neusner
140209	*Philo's Perception of Women*	Dorothy Sly
140210	*Case Citation in the Babylonian Talmud: The Evidence Tractate Neziqin*	Eliezer Segal
140211	*The Biblical Herem: A Window on Israel's Religious Experience*	Philip D. Stern
140212	*Goodenough on the Beginnings of Christianity*	A.T. Kraabel
140213	*The Talmud of Babylonia: An American Translation XXI.A: Tractate Bava Mesia Chapters 1-2*	Jacob Neusner
140214	*The Talmud of Babylonia: An American Translation XXI.B: Tractate Bava Mesia Chapters 3-4*	Jacob Neusner
140215	*The Talmud of Babylonia: An American Translation XXI.C: Tractate Bava Mesia Chapters 5-6*	Jacob Neusner
140216	*The Talmud of Babylonia: An American Translation XXI.D: Tractate Bava Mesia Chapters 7-10*	Jacob Neusner
140217	*Semites, Iranians, Greeks and Romans: Studies in their Interactions*	Jonathan A. Goldstein
140218	*The Talmud of Babylonia: An American Translation XXXIII: Temurah*	Jacob Neusner
140219	*The Talmud of Babylonia: An American Translation XXXI.A: Tractate Bekhorot Chapters 1-4*	Jacob Neusner
140220	*The Talmud of Babylonia: An American Translation XXXI.B: Tractate Bekhorot Chapters 5-9*	Jacob Neusner
140221	*The Talmud of Babylonia: An American Translation XXXVI.A: Tractate Niddah Chapters 1-3*	Jacob Neusner
140222	*The Talmud of Babylonia: An American Translation XXXVI.B: Tractate Niddah Chapters 4-10*	Jacob Neusner
140223	*The Talmud of Babylonia: An American Translation XXXIV: Tractate Keritot*	Jacob Neusner
140224	*Paul, the Temple, and the Presence of God*	David A. Renwick
140225	*The Book of the People*	William W. Hallo
140226	*The Studia Philonica Annual 1990*	David Runia
140227	*The Talmud of Babylonia: An American Translation XXV.A: Tractate Abodah Zarah Chapters 1-2*	Jacob Neusner
140228	*The Talmud of Babylonia: An American Translation XXV.B: Tractate Abodah Zarah Chapters 3-5*	Jacob Neusner
140230	*The Studia Philonica Annual 1991*	David Runia
140231	*The Talmud of Babylonia: An American Translation XXVIII.A: Tractate Zebahim Chapters 1-3*	Jacob Neusner
140232	*Both Literal and Allegorical: Studies in Philo of Alexandria's Questions and Answers on Genesis and Exodus*	David M. Hay
140233	*The Talmud of Babylonia: An American Translation XXVIII.B: Tractate Zebahim Chapters 4-8*	Jacob Neusner

140234	*The Talmud of Babylonia: An American Translation XXVIII.C: Tractate Zebahim Chapters 9-14*	Jacob Neusner
140235	*The Talmud of Babylonia: An American Translation XXIX.A: Tractate Menahot Chapters 1-3*	Jacob Neusner
140236	*The Talmud of Babylonia: An American Translation XXIX.B: Tractate Menahot Chapters 4-7*	Jacob Neusner
140237	*The Talmud of Babylonia: An American Translation XXIX.C: Tractate Menahot Chapters 8-13*	Jacob Neusner
140238	*The Talmud of Babylonia: An American Translation XXIX: Tractate Makkot*	Jacob Neusner
140239	*The Talmud of Babylonia: An American Translation XXII.A: Tractate Baba Batra Chapters 1 and 2*	Jacob Neusner
140240	*The Talmud of Babylonia: An American Translation XXII.B: Tractate Baba Batra Chapter 3*	Jacob Neusner
140241	*The Talmud of Babylonia: An American Translation XXII.C: Tractate Baba Batra Chapters 4-6*	Jacob Neusner
140242	*The Talmud of Babylonia: An American Translation XXVII.A: Tractate Shebuot Chapters 1-3*	Jacob Neusner
140243	*The Talmud of Babylonia: An American Translation XXVII.B: Tractate Shebuot Chapters 4-8*	Jacob Neusner
140244	*Balaam and His Interpreters: A Hermeneutical History of the Balaam Traditions*	John T. Greene
140245	*Courageous Universality: The Work of Schmuel Hugo Bergman*	William Kluback
140246	*The Mechanics of Change: Essays in the Social History of German Jewry*	Steven M. Lowenstein
140247	*The Talmud of Babylonia: An American Translation XX.A: Tractate Baba Qamma Chapters 1-3*	Jacob Neusner
140248	*The Talmud of Babylonia: An American Translation XX.B: Tractate Baba Qamma Chapters 4-7*	Jacob Neusner
140249	*The Talmud of Babylonia: An American Translation XX.C: Tractate Baba Qamma Chapters 8-10*	Jacob Neusner
140250	*The Talmud of Babylonia: An American Translation XIII.A: Tractate Yebamot Chapters 1-3*	Jacob Neusner
140251	*The Talmud of Babylonia: An American Translation XIII.B: Tractate Yebamot Chapters 4-6*	Jacob Neusner
140252	*The Talmud of Babylonia: An American Translation XI: Tractate Moed Qatan*	Jacob Neusner
140253	*The Talmud of Babylonia: An American Translation XXX.A: Tractate Hullin Chapters 1 and 2*	Tzvee Zahavy
140254	*The Talmud of Babylonia: An American Translation XXX.B: Tractate Hullin Chapters 3-6*	Tzvee Zahavy
140255	*The Talmud of Babylonia: An American Translation XXX.C: Tractate Hullin Chapters 7-12*	Tzvee Zahavy
140256	*The Talmud of Babylonia: An American Translation XIII.C: Tractate Yebamot Chapters 7-9*	Jacob Neusner
140257	*The Talmud of Babylonia: An American Translation XIV.A: Tractate Ketubot Chapters 1-3*	Jacob Neusner
140258	*The Talmud of Babylonia: An American Translation XIV.B: Tractate Ketubot Chapters 4-7*	Jacob Neusner
140259	*Jewish Thought Adrift: Max Wiener (1882-1950)*	Robert S. Schine
140260	*The Talmud of Babylonia: An American Translation XIV.C: Tractate Ketubot Chapters 8-13*	Jacob Neusner

140261	*The Talmud of Babylonia: An American Translation XIII.D: Tractate Yebamot Chapters 10-16*	Jacob Neusner
140262	*The Talmud of Babylonia: An American Translation XV. A: Tractate Nedarim Chapters 1-4*	Jacob Neusner
140263	*The Talmud of Babylonia: An American Translation XV.B: Tractate Nedarim Chapters 5-11*	Jacob Neusner
140264	*Studia Philonica Annual 1992*	David T. Runia
140265	*The Talmud of Babylonia: An American Translation XVIII.A: Tractate Gittin Chapters 1-3*	Jacob Neusner
140266	*The Talmud of Babylonia: An American Translation XVIII.B: Tractate Gittin Chapters 4 and 5*	Jacob Neusner
140267	*The Talmud of Babylonia: An American Translation XIX.A: Tractate Qiddushin Chapter 1*	Jacob Neusner
140268	*The Talmud of Babylonia: An American Translation XIX.B: Tractate Qiddushin Chapters 2-4*	Jacob Neusner
140269	*The Talmud of Babylonia: An American Translation XVIII.C: Tractate Gittin Chapters 6-9*	Jacob Neusner
140270	*The Talmud of Babylonia: An American Translation II.A: Tractate Shabbat Chapters 1 and 2*	Jacob Neusner
140271	*The Theology of Nahmanides Systematically Presented*	David Novak
140272	*The Talmud of Babylonia: An American Translation II.B: Tractate Shabbat Chapters 3-6*	Jacob Neusner
140273	*The Talmud of Babylonia: An American Translation II.C: Tractate Shabbat Chapters 7-10*	Jacob Neusner
140274	*The Talmud of Babylonia: An American Translation II.D: Tractate Shabbat Chapters 11-17*	Jacob Neusner
140275	*The Talmud of Babylonia: An American Translation II.E: Tractate Shabbat Chapters 18-24*	Jacob Neusner
140276	*The Talmud of Babylonia: An American Translation III.A: Tractate Erubin Chapters 1 and 2*	Jacob Neusner
140277	*The Talmud of Babylonia: An American Translation III.B: Tractate Erubin Chapters 3 and 4*	Jacob Neusner
140278	*The Talmud of Babylonia: An American Translation III.C: Tractate Erubin Chapters 5 and 6*	Jacob Neusner
140279	*The Talmud of Babylonia: An American Translation III.D: Tractate Erubin Chapters 7-10*	Jacob Neusner
140280	*The Talmud of Babylonia: An American Translation XII: Tractate Hagigah*	Jacob Neusner
140281	*The Talmud of Babylonia: An American Translation IV.A: Tractate Pesahim Chapter I*	Jacob Neusner
140282	*The Talmud of Babylonia: An American Translation IV.B: Tractate Pesahim Chapters 2 and 3*	Jacob Neusner
140283	*The Talmud of Babylonia: An American Translation IV.C: Tractate Pesahim Chapters 4-6*	Jacob Neusner
140284	*The Talmud of Babylonia: An American Translation IV.D: Tractate Pesahim Chapters 7 and 8*	Jacob Neusner
140285	*The Talmud of Babylonia: An American Translation IV.E: Tractate Pesahim Chapters 9 and 10*	Jacob Neusner
140286	*From Christianity to Gnosis and From Gnosis to Christianity*	Jean Magne
140287	*Studia Philonica Annual 1993*	David T. Runia
140288	*Diasporas in Antiquity*	Shaye J. D. Cohen, Ernest S. Frerichs
140289	*The Jewish Family in Antiquity*	Shaye J. D. Cohen
140290	*The Place of Judaism in Philo's Thought*	Ellen Birnbaum

140291	*The Babylonian Esther Midrash, Vol. 1*	Eliezer Segal
140292	*The Babylonian Esther Midrash, Vol. 2*	Eliezer Segal
140293	*The Babylonian Esther Midrash, Vol. 3*	Eliezer Segal

Brown Studies on Jews and Their Societies

145001	*American Jewish Fertility*	Calvin Goldscheider
145002	*The Impact of Religious Schooling: The Effects of Jewish Education Upon Religious Involvement*	Harold S. Himmelfarb
145003	*The American Jewish Community*	Calvin Goldscheider
145004	*The Naturalized Jews of the Grand Duchy of Posen in 1834 and 1835*	Edward David Luft
145005	*Suburban Communities: The Jewishness of American Reform Jews*	Gerald L. Showstack
145007	*Ethnic Survival in America*	David Schoem
145008	*American Jews in the 21st Century: A Leadership Challenge*	Earl Raab

Brown Studies in Religion

147001	*Religious Writings and Religious Systems I*	Jacob Neusner, et al
147002	*Religious Writings and Religious Systems II*	Jacob Neusner, et al
147003	*Religion and the Social Sciences*	Robert Segal